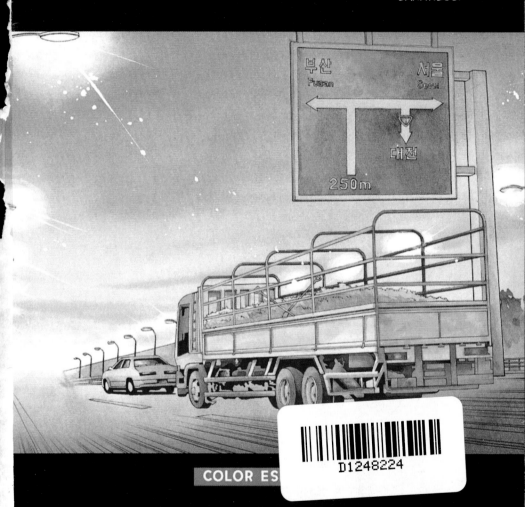

WHERE SHOULD WE GO?

ANYWHERE. AS LONG AS IT'S FAR FROM THE DARKNESS.

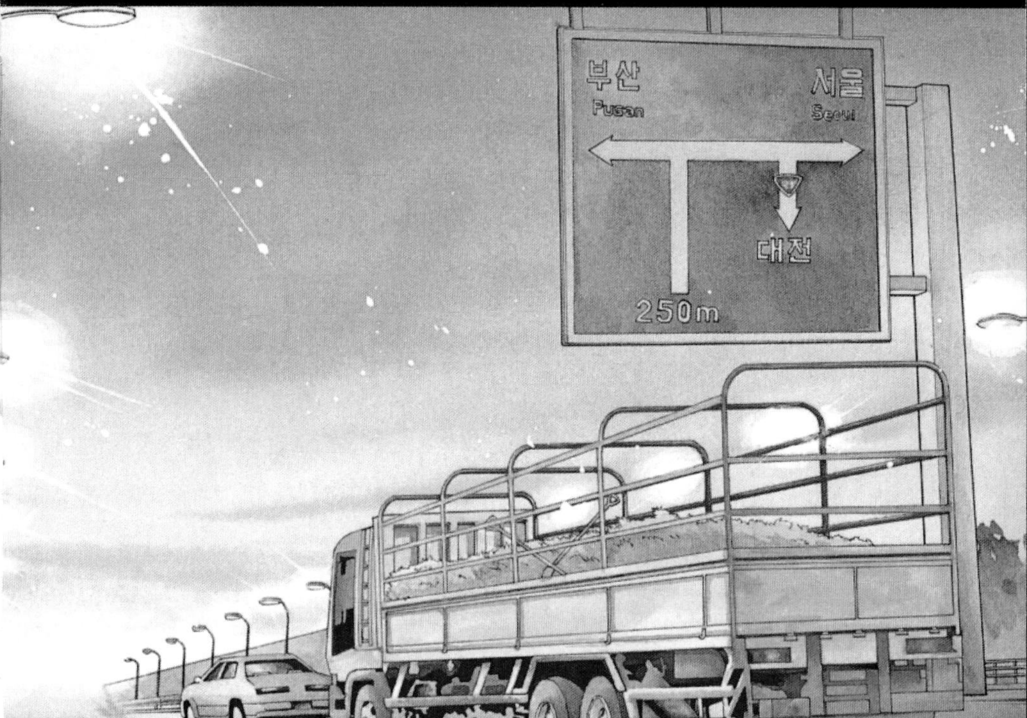

부산
Pusan
서울
Seoul
대전
250m

COLOR ES

HITCHHIKE

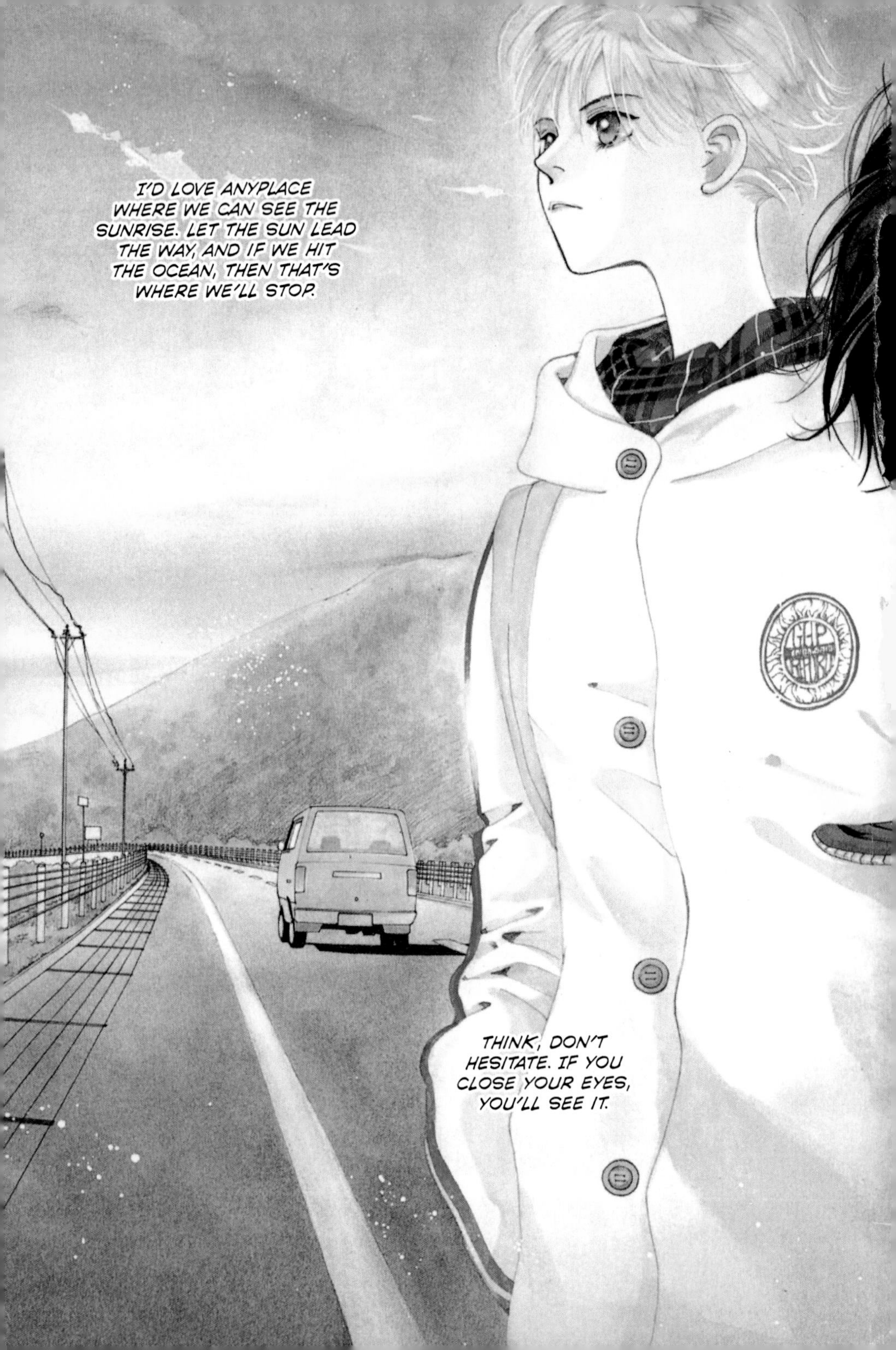
I'D LOVE ANYPLACE WHERE WE CAN SEE THE SUNRISE. LET THE SUN LEAD THE WAY, AND IF WE HIT THE OCEAN, THEN THAT'S WHERE WE'LL STOP.
THINK, DON'T HESITATE. IF YOU CLOSE YOUR EYES, YOU'LL SEE IT.

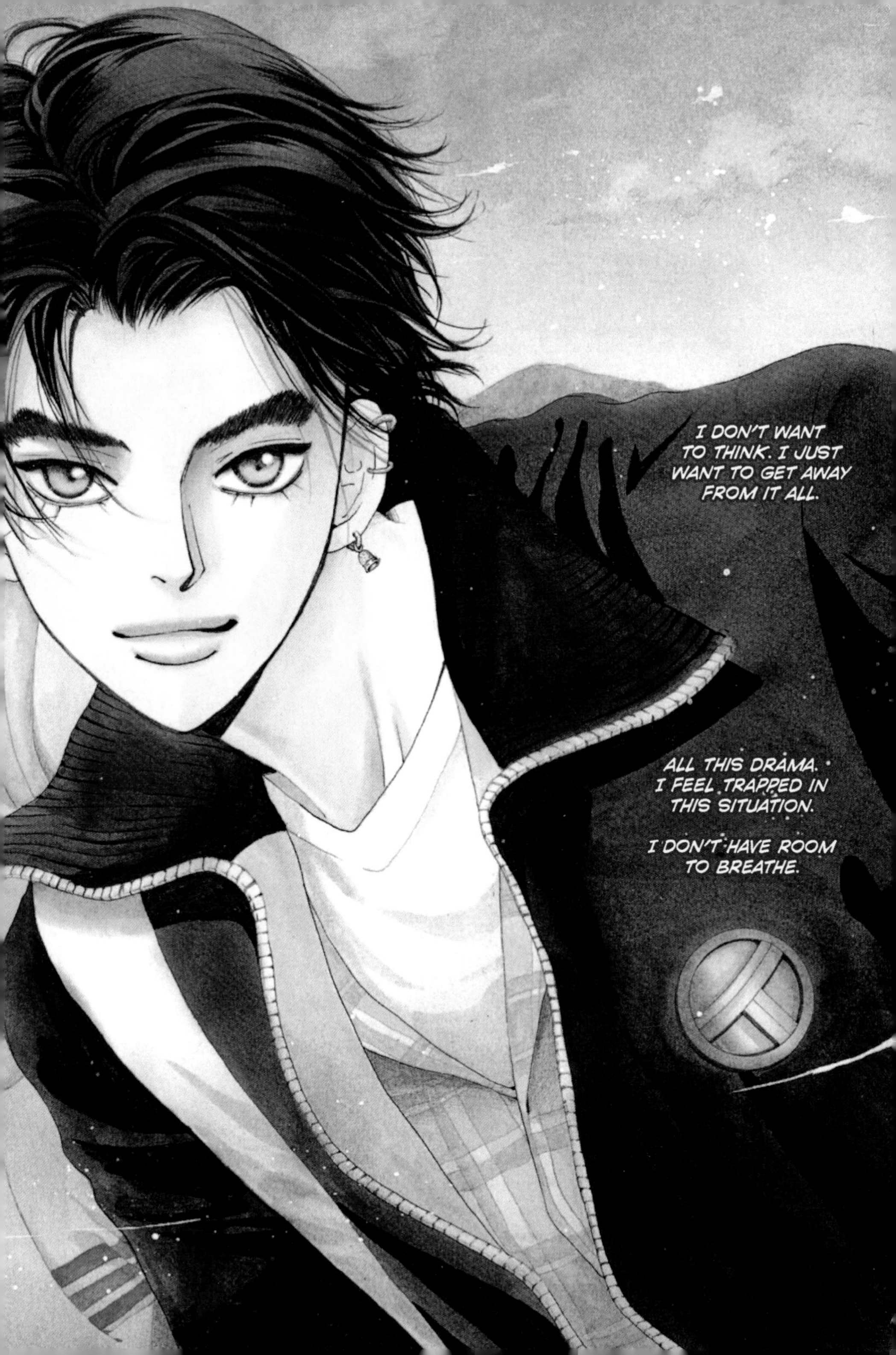
I DON'T WANT TO THINK. I JUST WANT TO GET AWAY FROM IT ALL.
ALL THIS DRAMA. I FEEL TRAPPED IN THIS SITUATION.
I DON'T HAVE ROOM TO BREATHE.

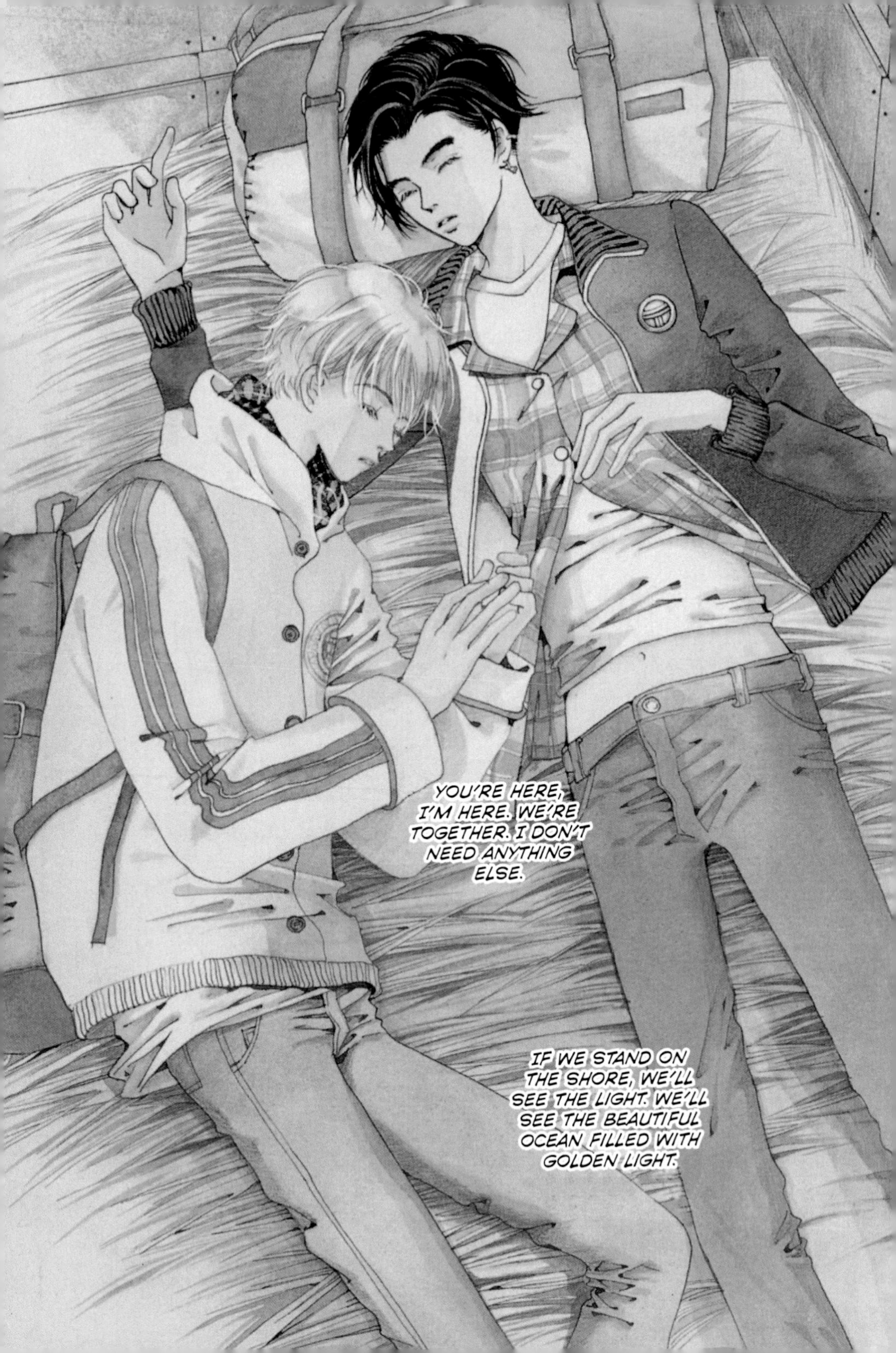
YOU'RE HERE, I'M HERE. WE'RE TOGETHER. I DON'T NEED ANYTHING ELSE.
IF WE STAND ON THE SHORE, WE'LL SEE THE LIGHT. WE'LL SEE THE BEAUTIFUL OCEAN FILLED WITH GOLDEN LIGHT.

COMIC

vol. 7

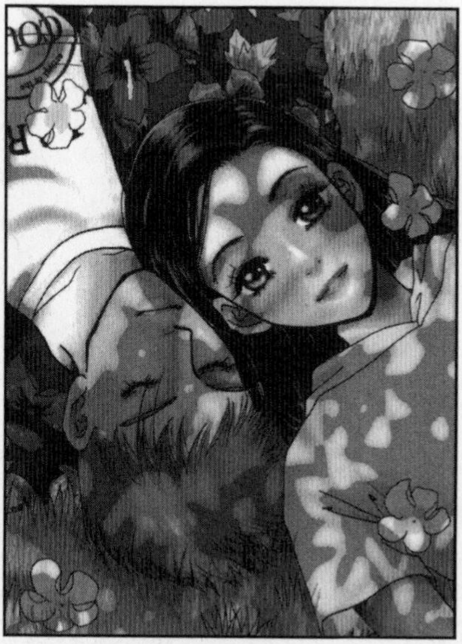

Ha SiHyun

Yen Press

CONTENTS

COLOR ESPRIT
HITCHHIKE
· 3 ·

Chapter 19
HEARTBREAK
· 9 ·

Chapter 20
NIGHT OF THE FESTIVAL
· 74 ·

COMIC'S WORLD
· 166 ·

MAJESTIC COMIC TALK
· 179 ·

CHAPTER 19 - HEARTBREAK

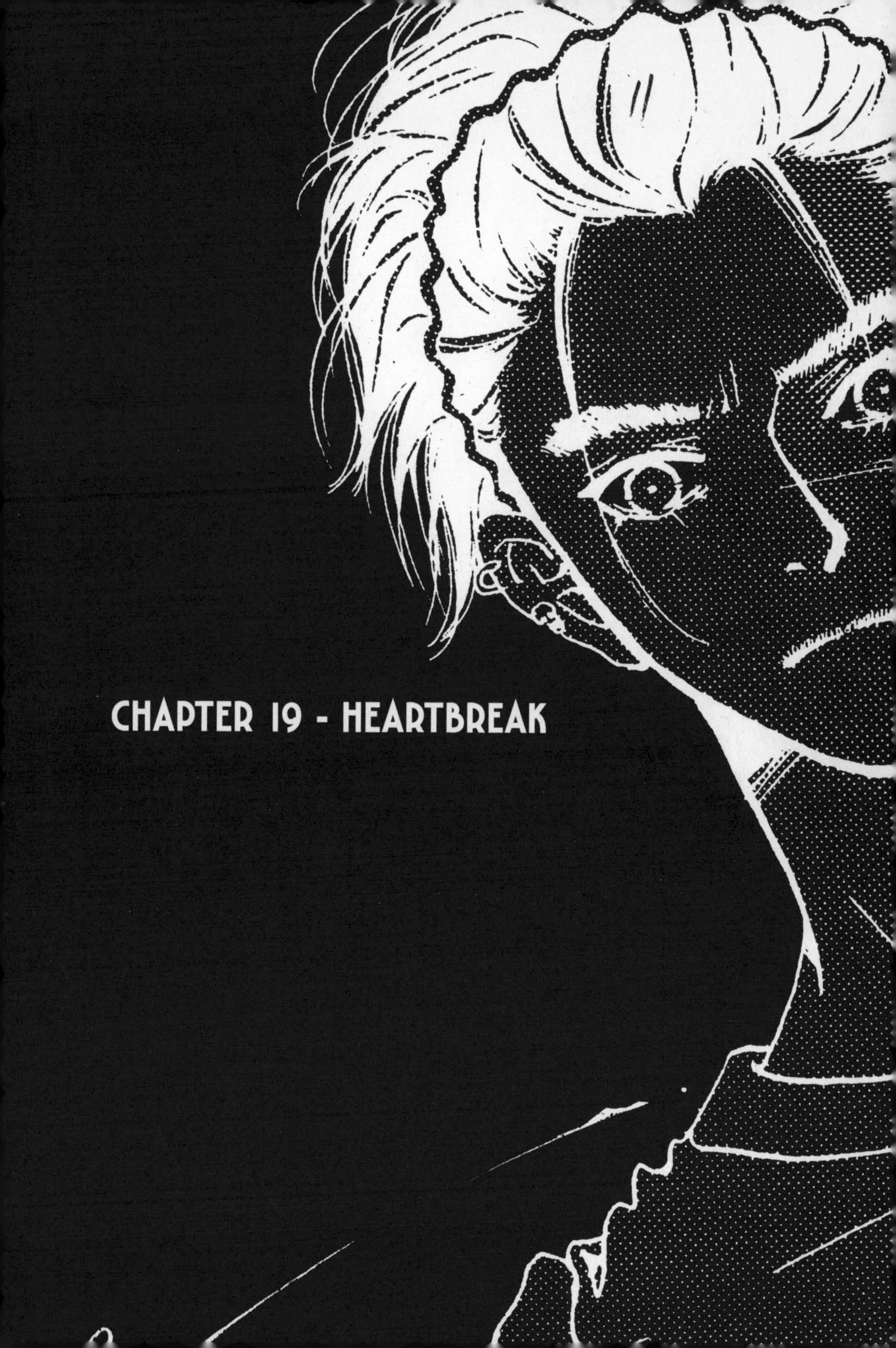

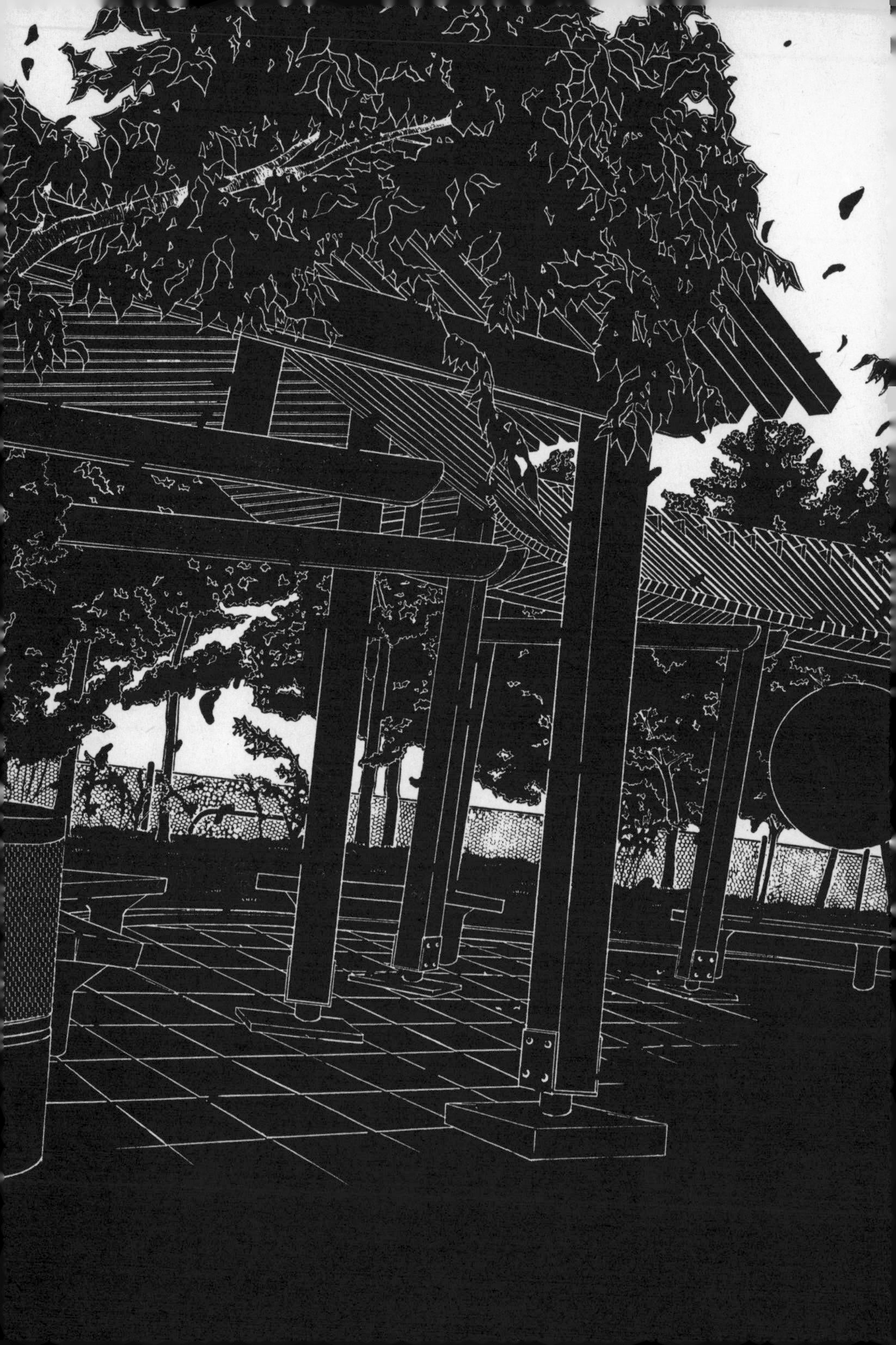

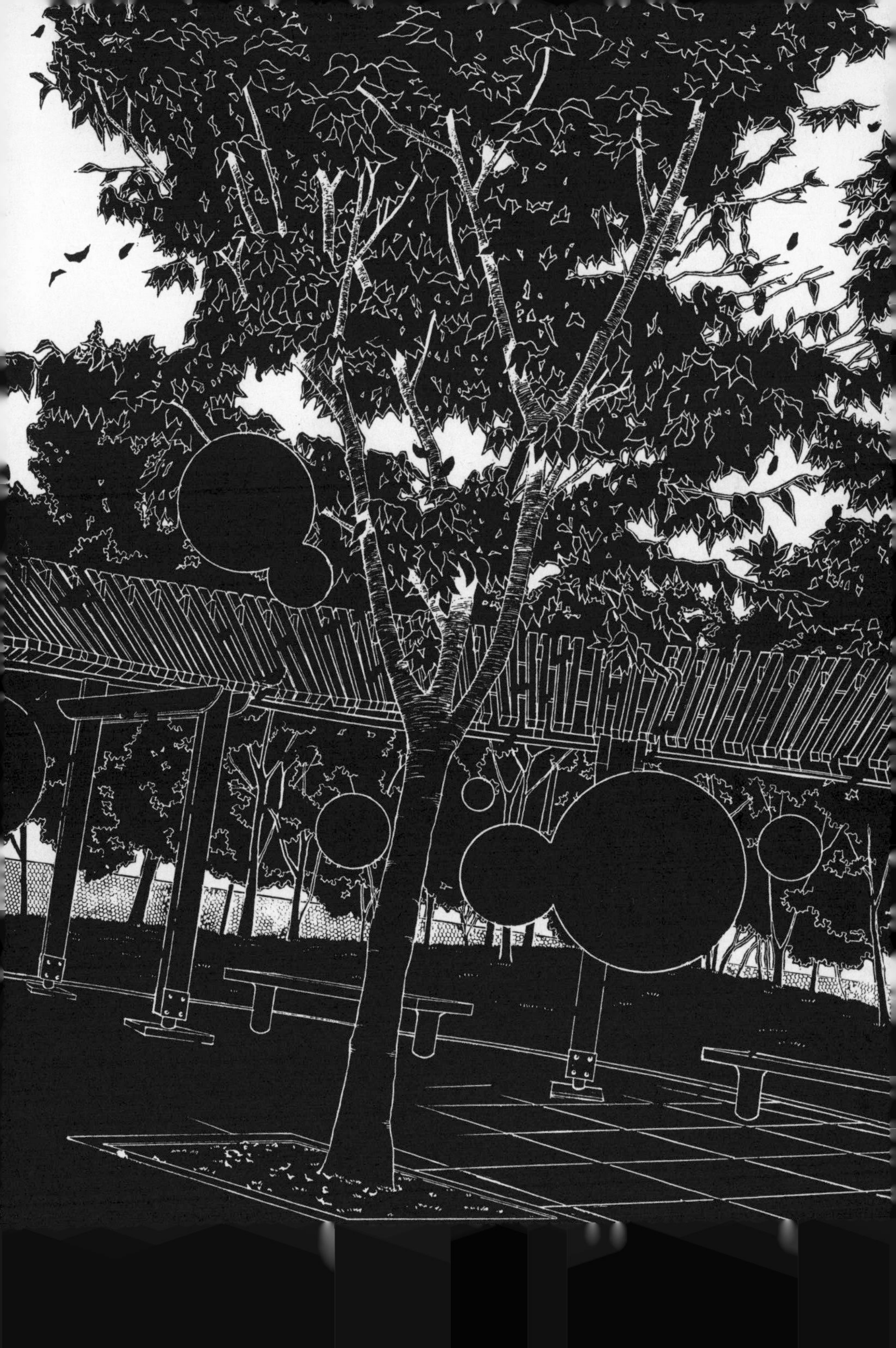

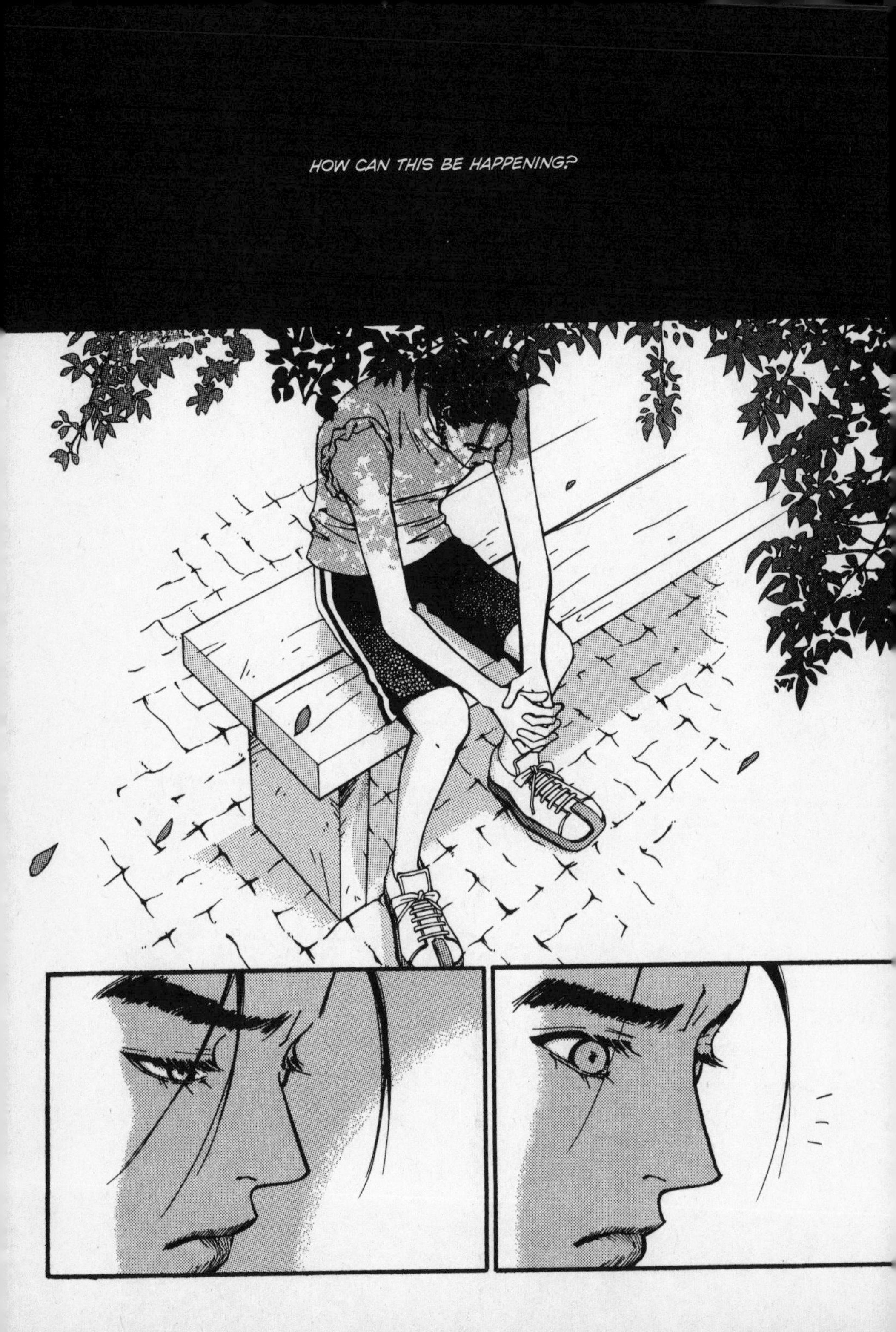
HOW CAN THIS BE HAPPENING?

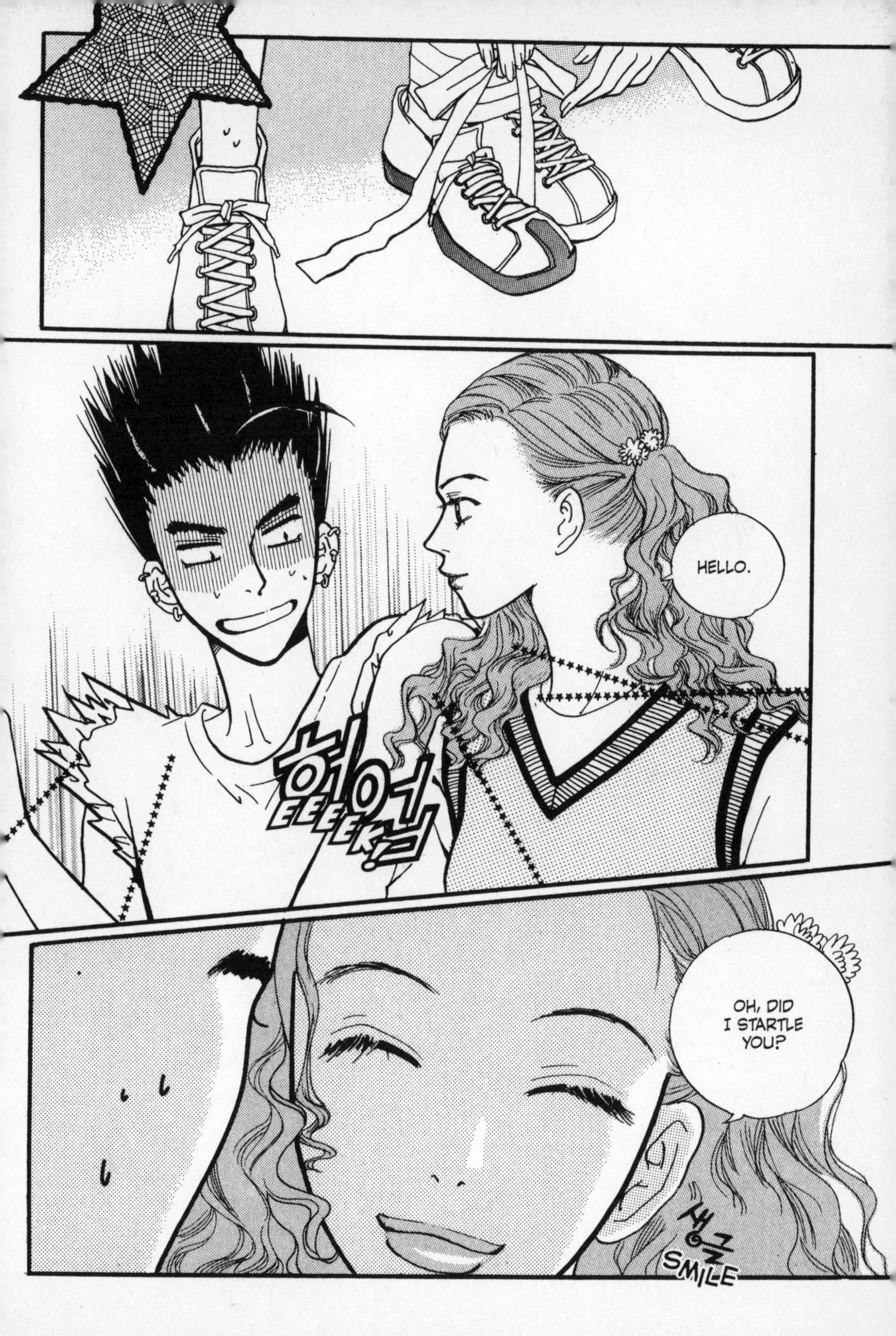

EEEEK!
HELLO.
OH, DID I STARTLE YOU?
SMILE

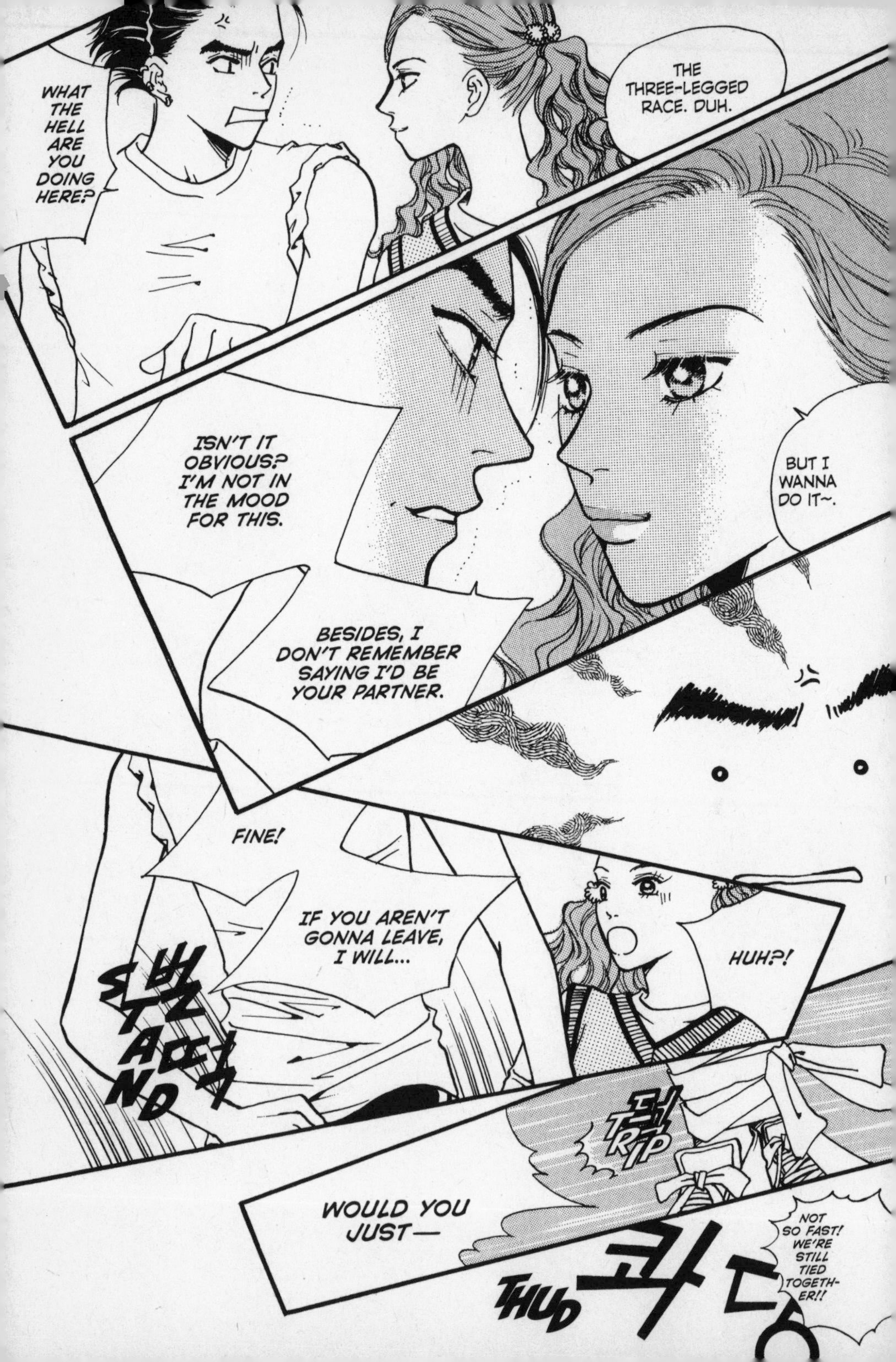
WHAT THE HELL ARE YOU DOING HERE?
THE THREE-LEGGED RACE. DUH.
ISN'T IT OBVIOUS? I'M NOT IN THE MOOD FOR THIS.
BUT I WANNA DO IT~.
BESIDES, I DON'T REMEMBER SAYING I'D BE YOUR PARTNER.
FINE!
IF YOU AREN'T GONNA LEAVE, I WILL...
STAND
HUH?!
TRIP
WOULD YOU JUST—
THUD
NOT SO FAST! WE'RE STILL TIED TOGETHER!!

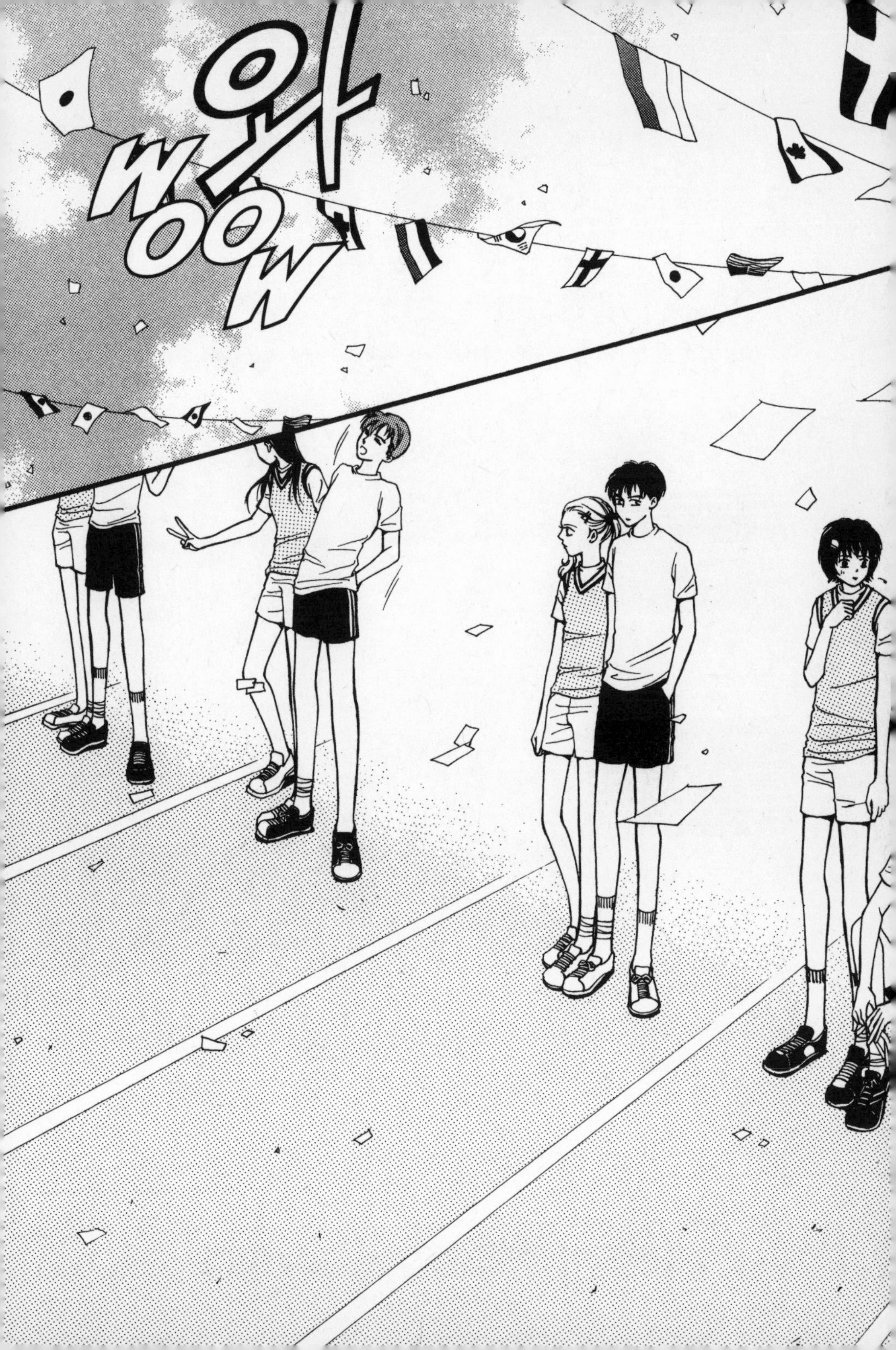
와
WOOOW

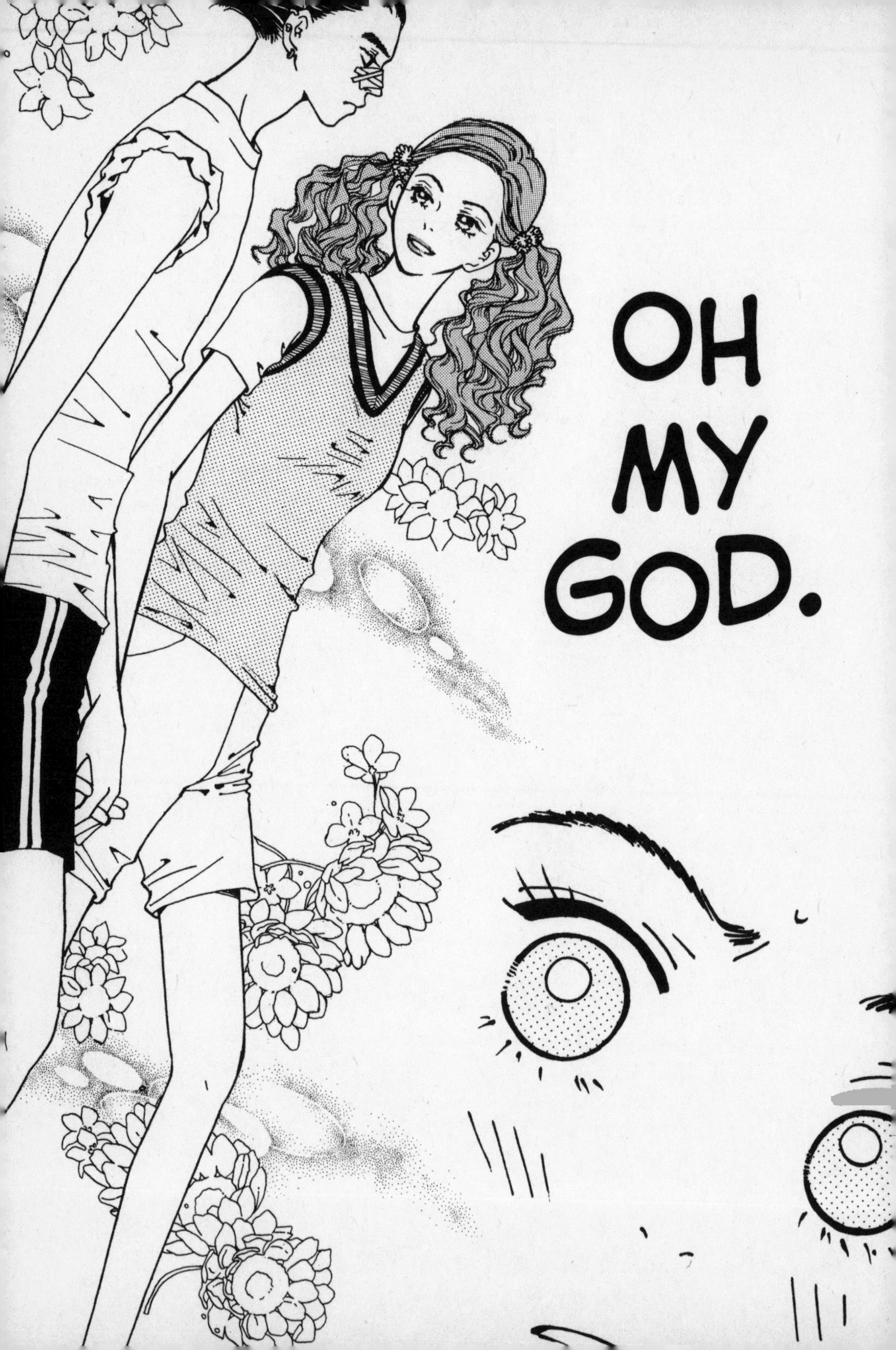
OH MY GOD.

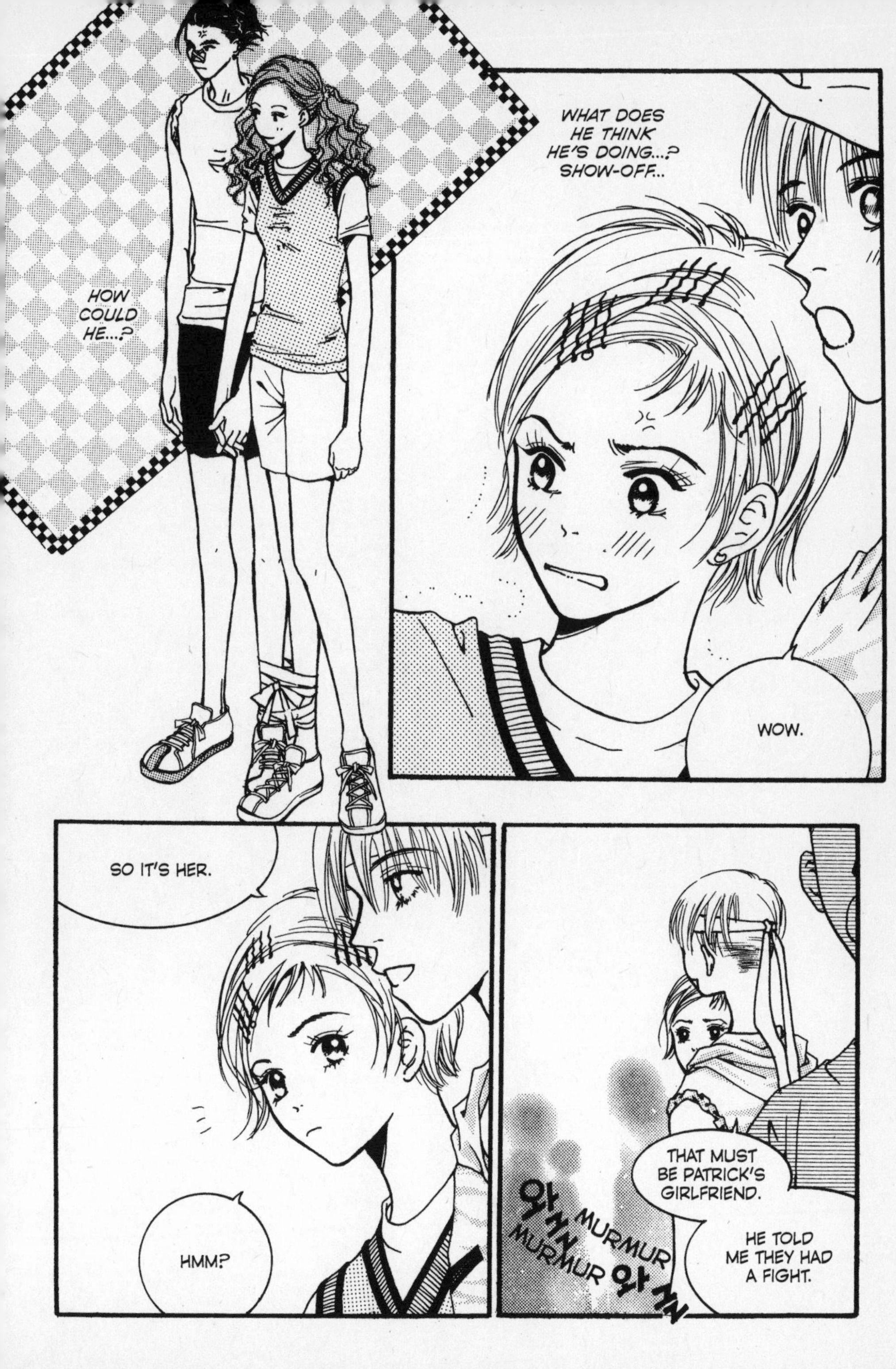
HOW COULD HE...?
WHAT DOES HE THINK HE'S DOING...? SHOW-OFF...
WOW.
SO IT'S HER.
HMM?
MURMUR MURMUR
THAT MUST BE PATRICK'S GIRLFRIEND.
HE TOLD ME THEY HAD A FIGHT.

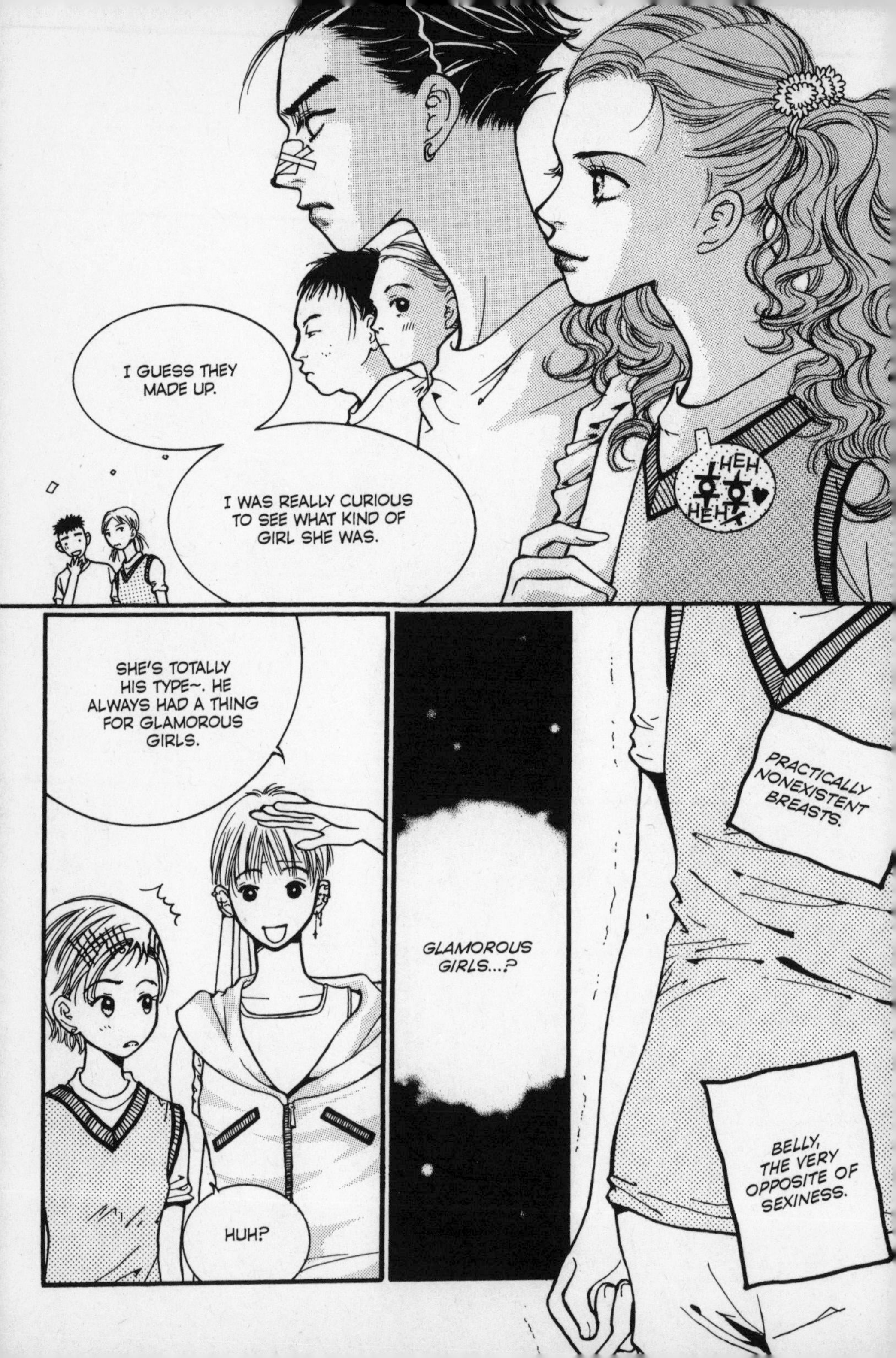

I GUESS THEY MADE UP.
I WAS REALLY CURIOUS TO SEE WHAT KIND OF GIRL SHE WAS.
HEH HEH
SHE'S TOTALLY HIS TYPE~. HE ALWAYS HAD A THING FOR GLAMOROUS GIRLS.
HUH?
GLAMOROUS GIRLS...?
PRACTICALLY NONEXISTENT BREASTS.
BELLY, THE VERY OPPOSITE OF SEXINESS.

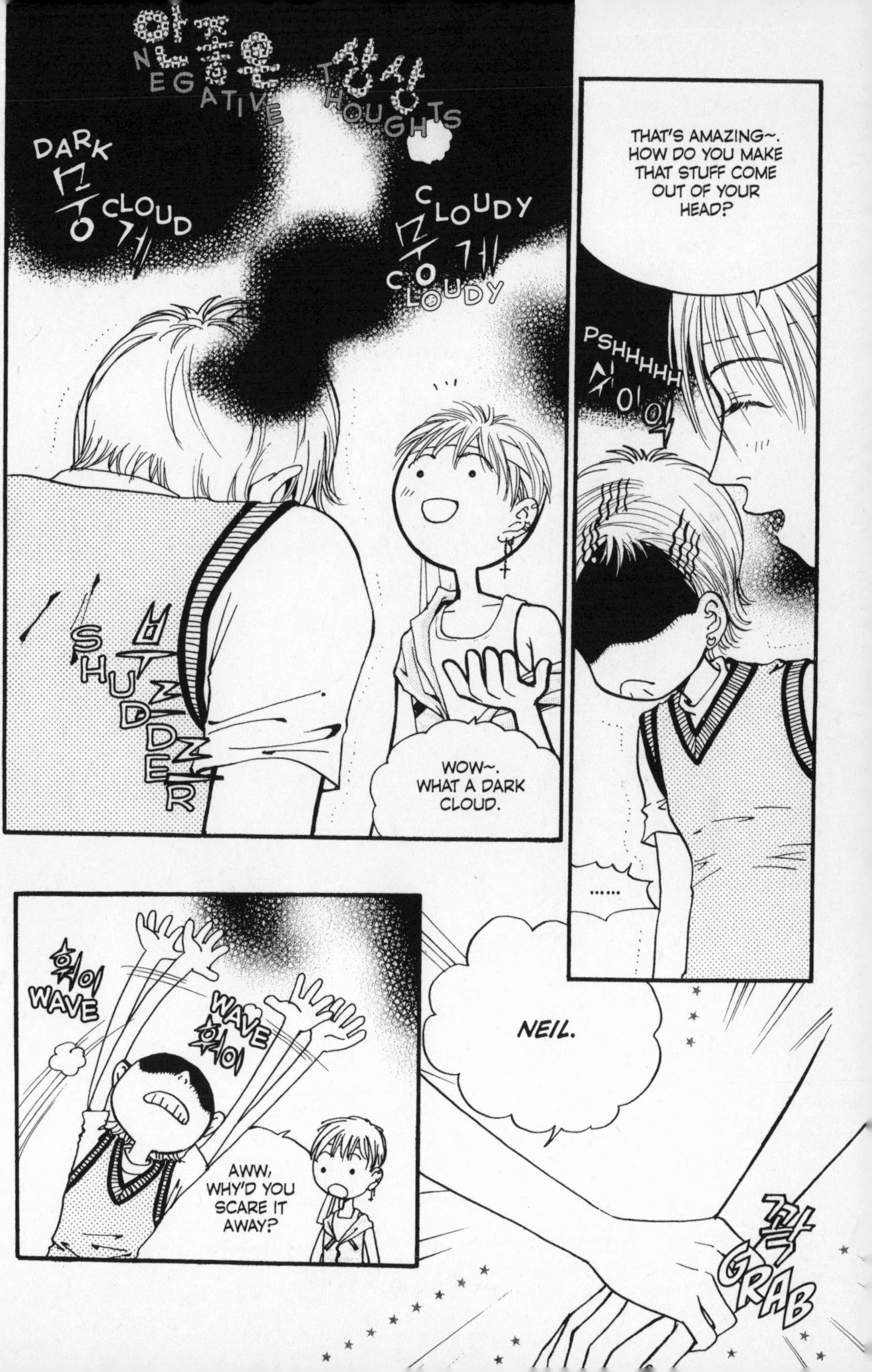
NEGATIVE THOUGHTS
DARK CLOUD
CLOUDY CLOUDY
SHUDDER
WOW~. WHAT A DARK CLOUD.
THAT'S AMAZING~. HOW DO YOU MAKE THAT STUFF COME OUT OF YOUR HEAD?
PSHHHHH
......
WAVE
WAVE
AWW, WHY'D YOU SCARE IT AWAY?
NEIL.
GRAB

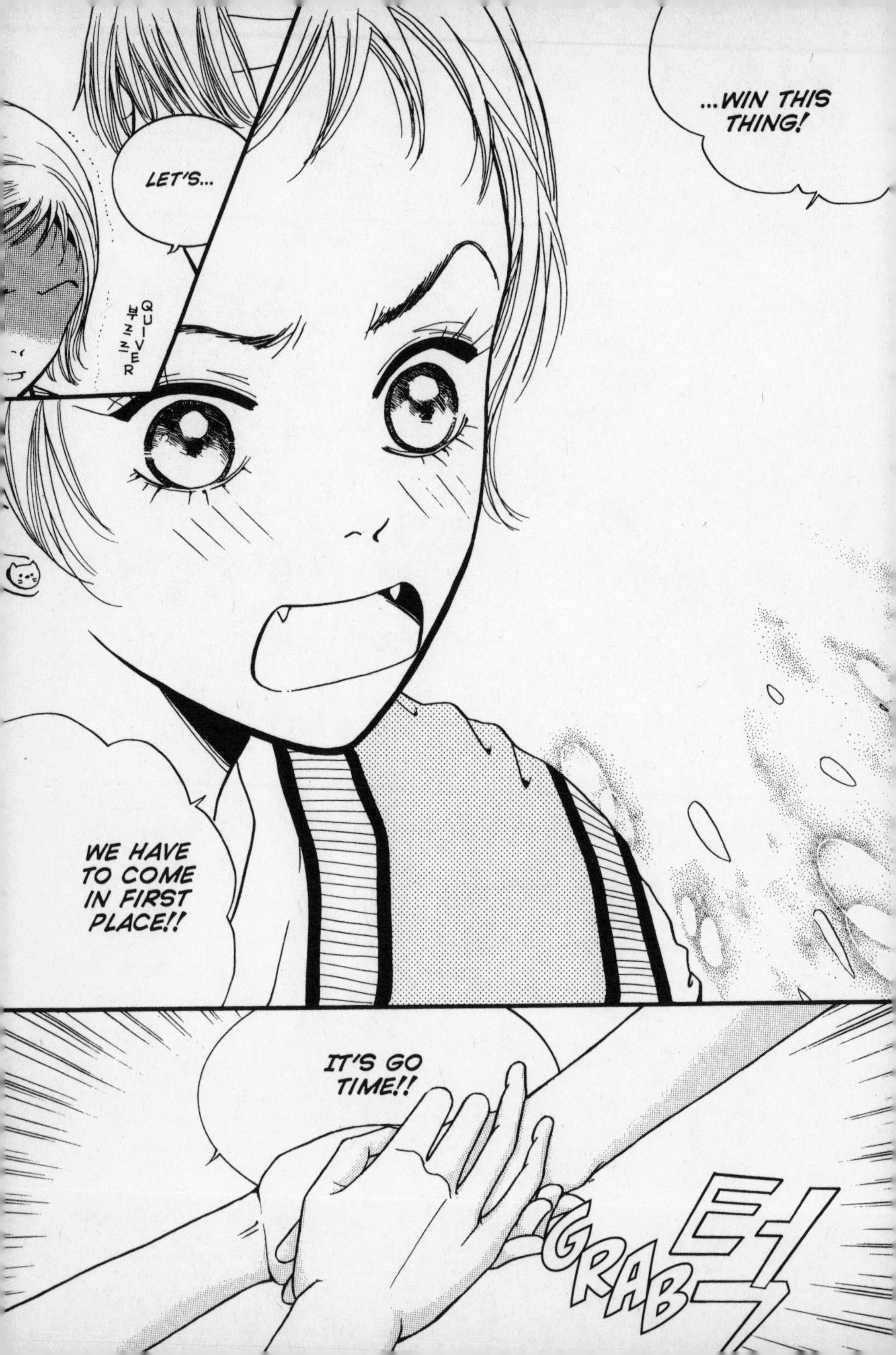
LET'S...
QUIVER
...WIN THIS THING!
WE HAVE TO COME IN FIRST PLACE!!
IT'S GO TIME!!
GRAB

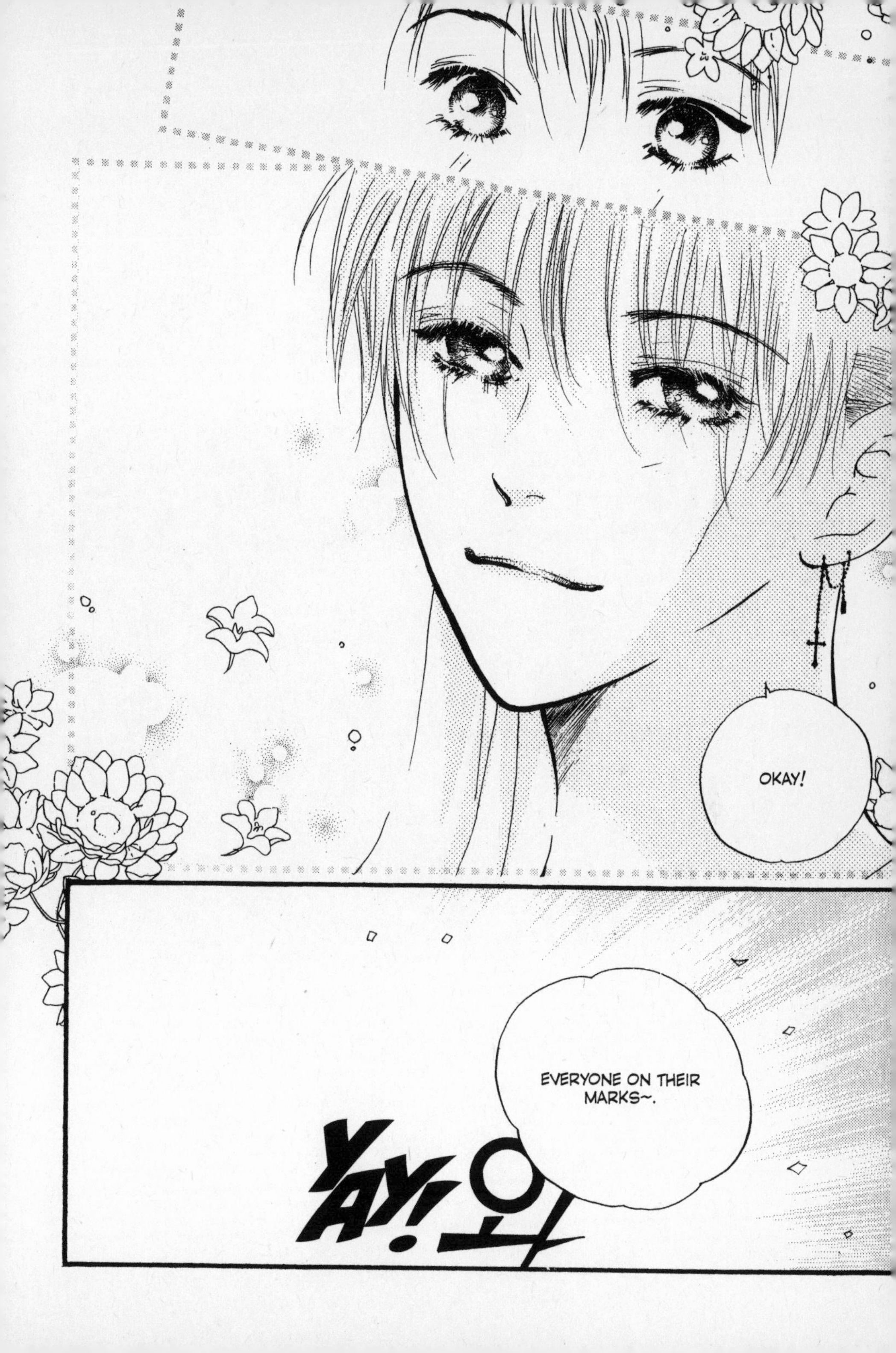
OKAY!
EVERYONE ON THEIR MARKS~.
YAY!

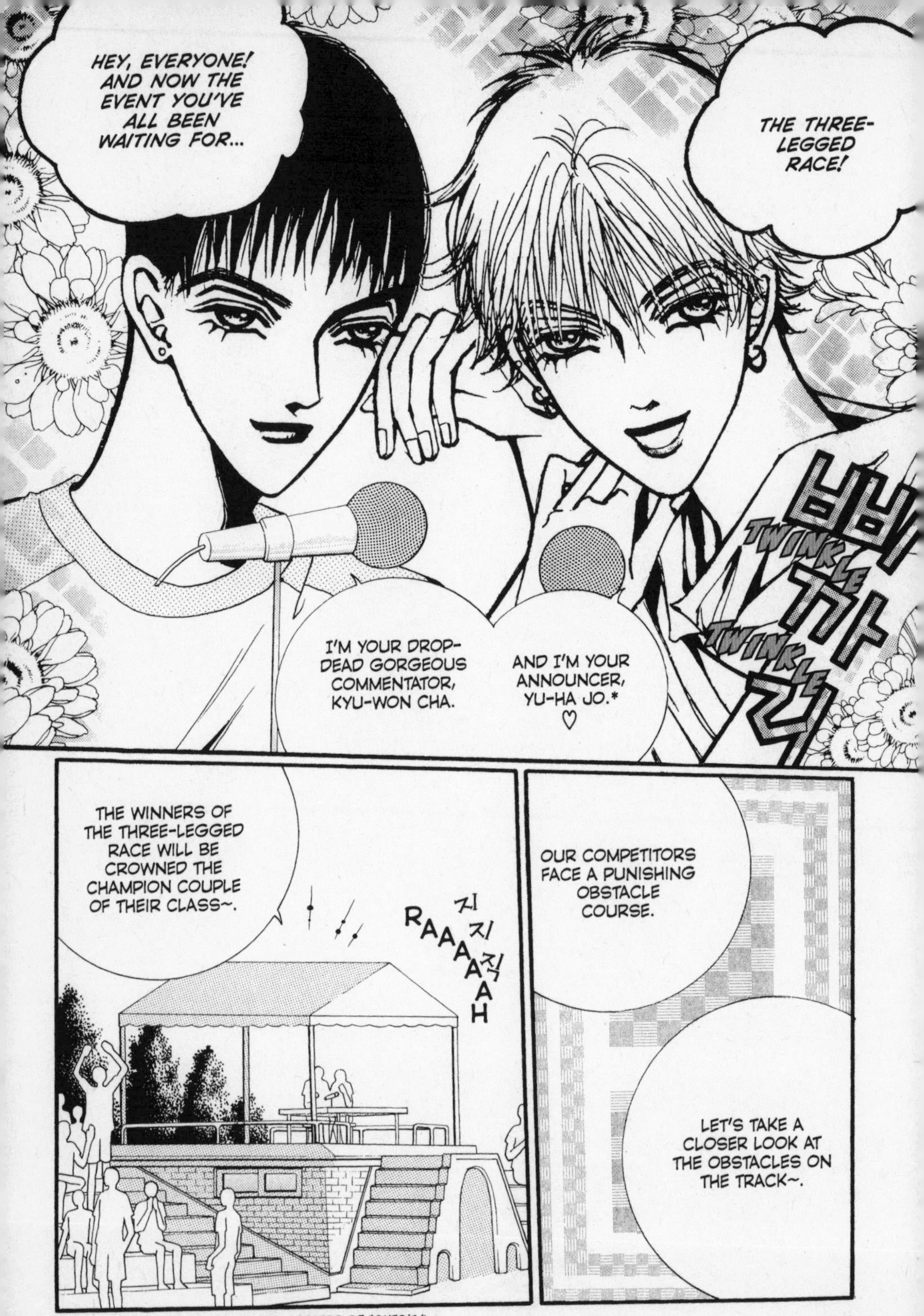
HEY, EVERYONE! AND NOW THE EVENT YOU'VE ALL BEEN WAITING FOR...
THE THREE-LEGGED RACE!
I'M YOUR DROP-DEAD GORGEOUS COMMENTATOR, KYU-WON CHA.
AND I'M YOUR ANNOUNCER, YU-HA JO.* ♡
TWINKLE
TWINKLE
THE WINNERS OF THE THREE-LEGGED RACE WILL BE CROWNED THE CHAMPION COUPLE OF THEIR CLASS~.
지지직
RAAAAAAH
OUR COMPETITORS FACE A PUNISHING OBSTACLE COURSE.
LET'S TAKE A CLOSER LOOK AT THE OBSTACLES ON THE TRACK~.

*SPECIAL THANKS TO SO-YOUNG LEE, CREATOR OF "CHECK."

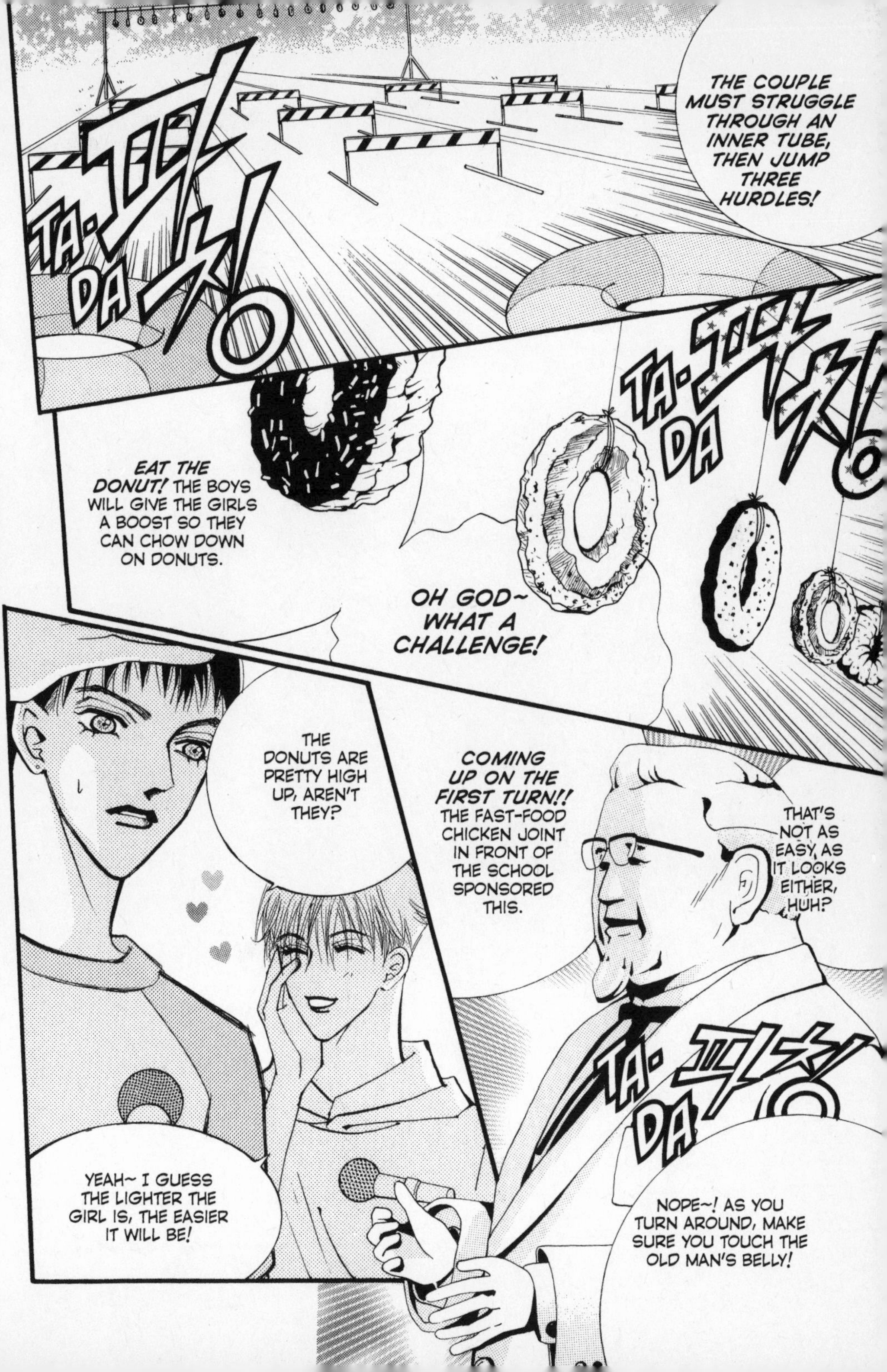

TA-DA!
THE COUPLE MUST STRUGGLE THROUGH AN INNER TUBE, THEN JUMP THREE HURDLES!
EAT THE DONUT! THE BOYS WILL GIVE THE GIRLS A BOOST SO THEY CAN CHOW DOWN ON DONUTS.
TA-DA!
OH GOD~ WHAT A CHALLENGE!
THE DONUTS ARE PRETTY HIGH UP, AREN'T THEY?
YEAH~ I GUESS THE LIGHTER THE GIRL IS, THE EASIER IT WILL BE!
COMING UP ON THE FIRST TURN!! THE FAST-FOOD CHICKEN JOINT IN FRONT OF THE SCHOOL SPONSORED THIS.
THAT'S NOT AS EASY AS IT LOOKS EITHER, HUH?
TA-DA!
NOPE~! AS YOU TURN AROUND, MAKE SURE YOU TOUCH THE OLD MAN'S BELLY!

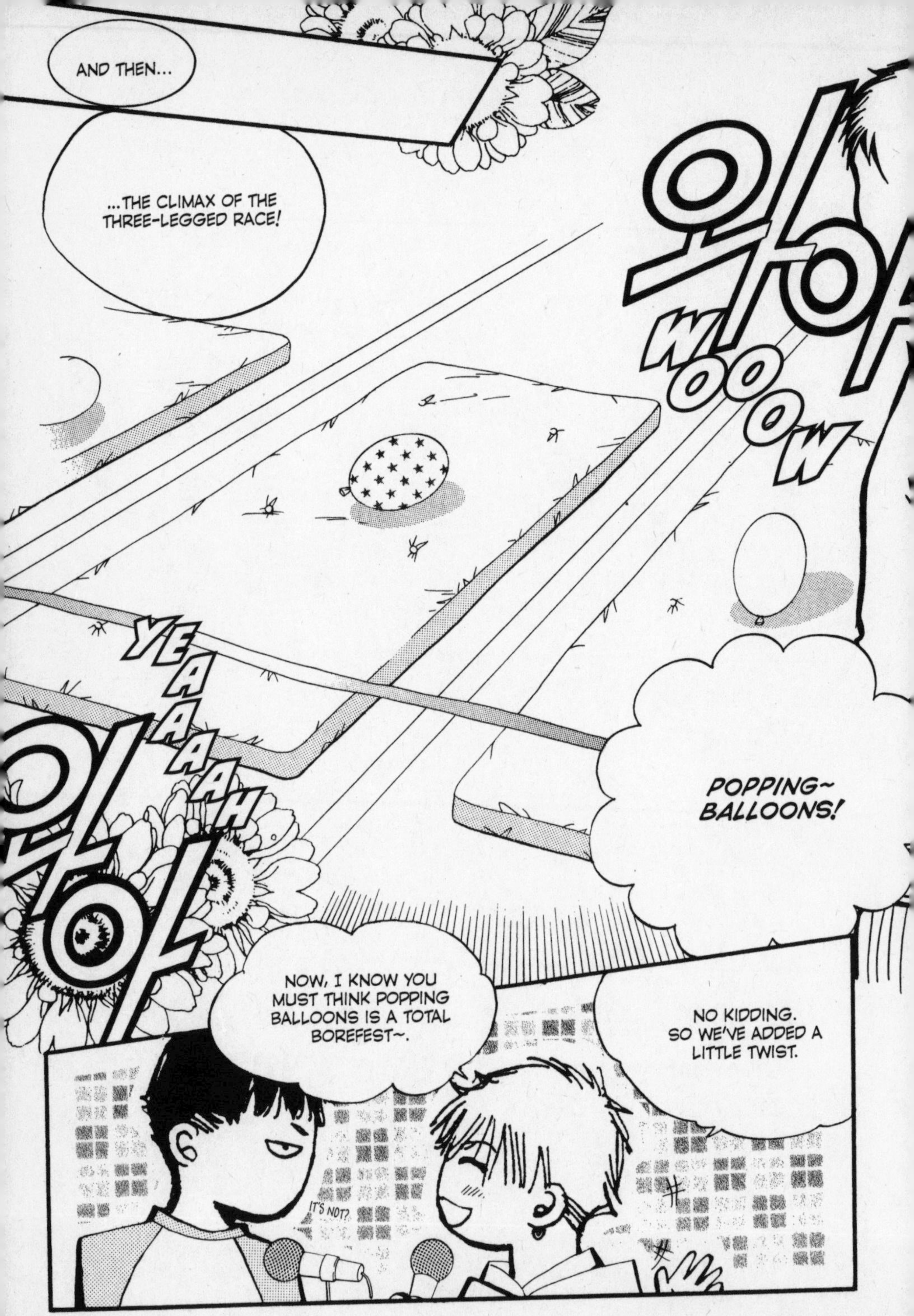
AND THEN...
...THE CLIMAX OF THE THREE-LEGGED RACE!
와아
WOOOOW
YEAAAAAH
와아
POPPING~ BALLOONS!
NOW, I KNOW YOU MUST THINK POPPING BALLOONS IS A TOTAL BOREFEST~.
IT'S NOT?
NO KIDDING. SO WE'VE ADDED A LITTLE TWIST.

TO POP THE BALLOON, THE BOYS AND GIRLS MUST *ROLL* DOWN THE MAT!!

POP!

OH MY—!!

HEH HEH

WHAT WACKY OBSTACLES! FULL BODY CONTACT, LIKE THE GAMES YOU'D PLAY ON YOUR HONEYMOON!!

CHAMPION

CHAMPION-SHIP BELT

THAT'S JUST WRONG.

HOW COULD WE?

IT'S A DEATH-DEFYING SURVIVAL COURSE!!

WELL, IT'S IMPORTANT FOR US TO DO OUR BEST—

YEAH, YEAH—

WHICH COUPLE WILL BEAT OUT THE COMPETITION FOR THIS GLORIOUS CHAMPIONSHIP BELT?!

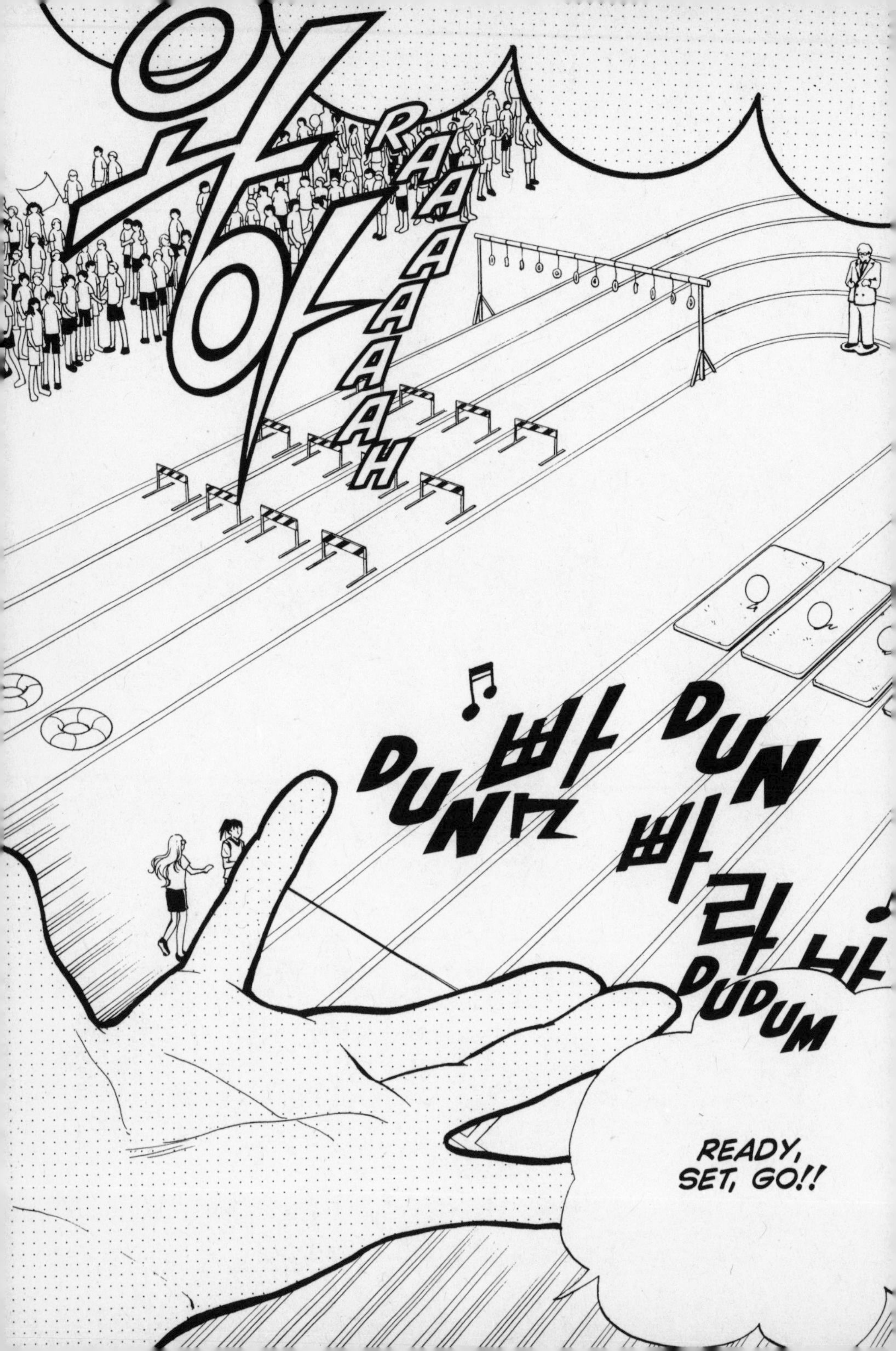

와아아
RAAAAAAAAAH
빠 DUN DUN
빠라바 DUDUM
READY, SET, GO!!

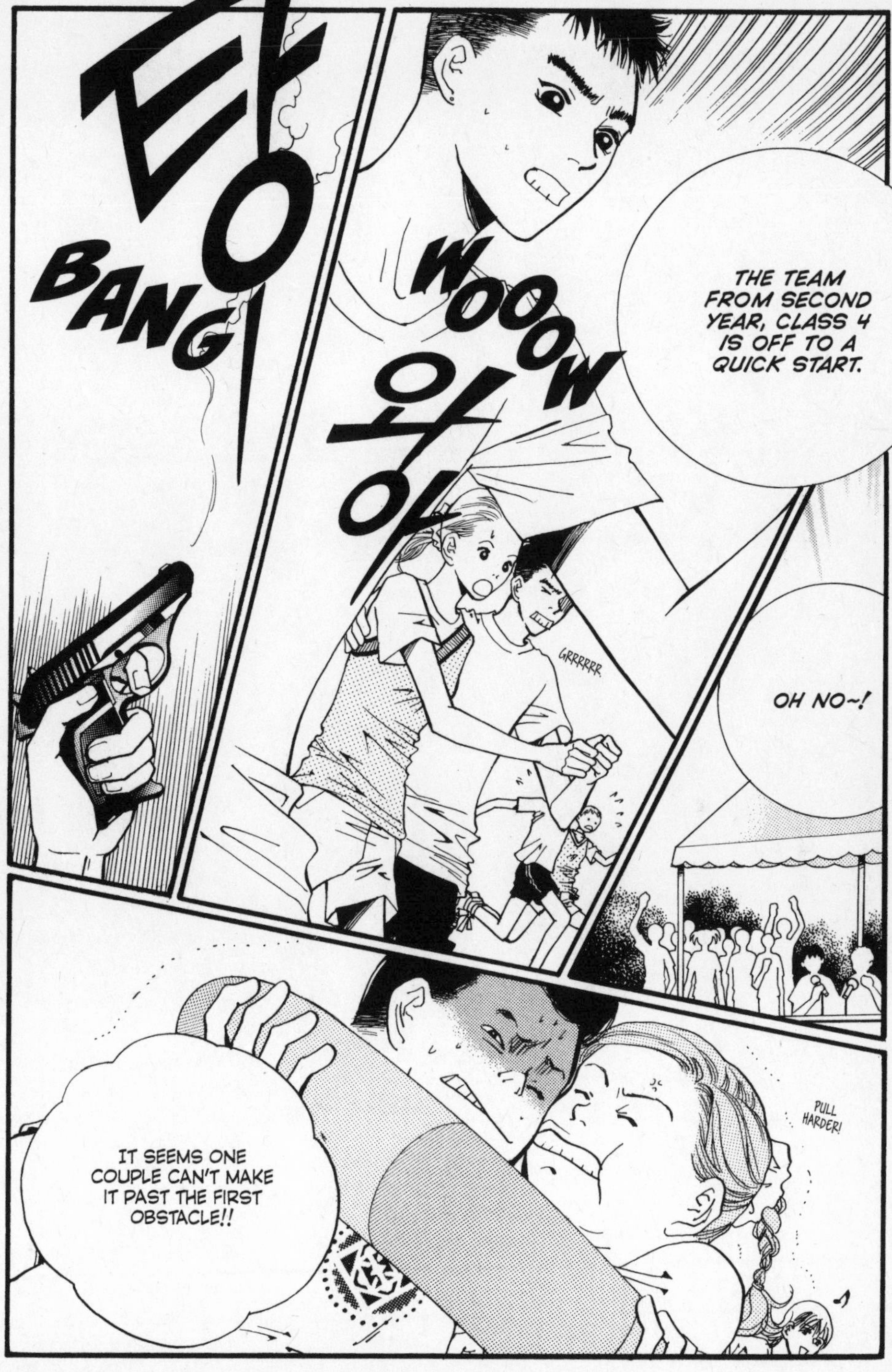
탕
BANG
WOOOW
와아
GRRRRRR
THE TEAM FROM SECOND YEAR, CLASS 4 IS OFF TO A QUICK START.
OH NO~!
IT SEEMS ONE COUPLE CAN'T MAKE IT PAST THE FIRST OBSTACLE!!
PULL HARDER!

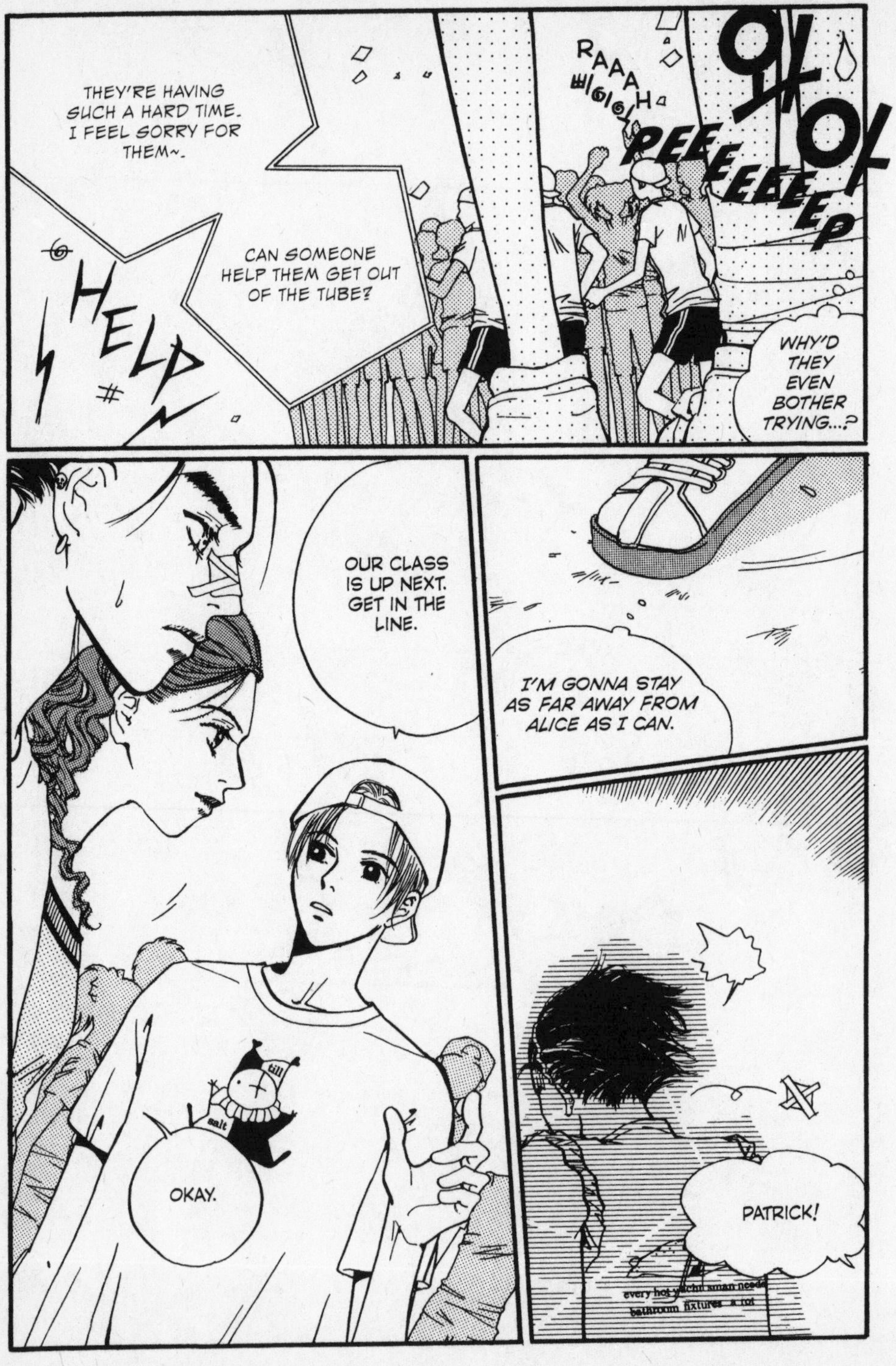
THEY'RE HAVING SUCH A HARD TIME. I FEEL SORRY FOR THEM~.
HELP
CAN SOMEONE HELP THEM GET OUT OF THE TUBE?
RAAAAH
PEEEEEEEEP
WHY'D THEY EVEN BOTHER TRYING...?
OUR CLASS IS UP NEXT. GET IN THE LINE.
OKAY.
I'M GONNA STAY AS FAR AWAY FROM ALICE AS I CAN.
PATRICK!

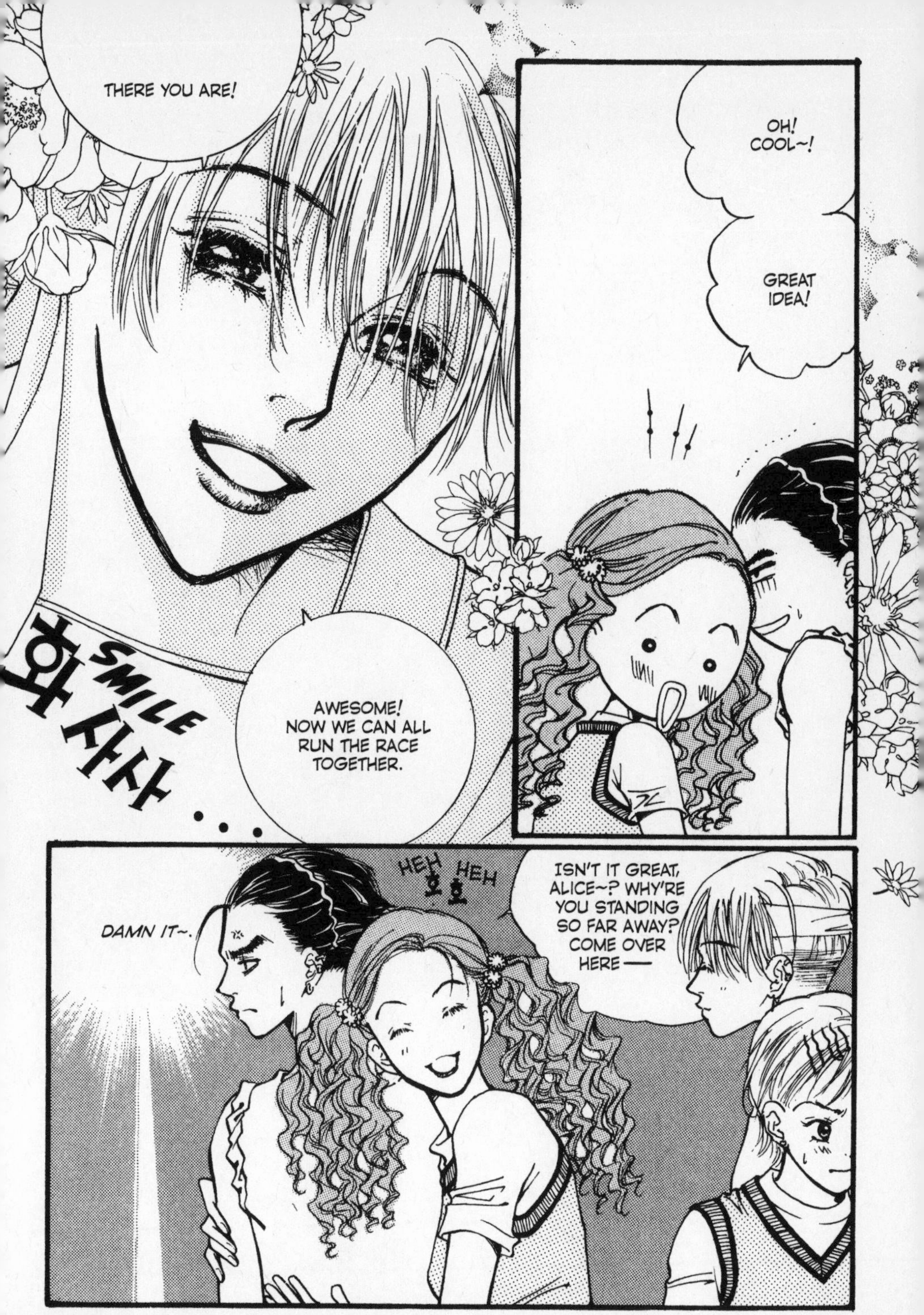
THERE YOU ARE!
SMILE
AWESOME! NOW WE CAN ALL RUN THE RACE TOGETHER.
OH! COOL~!
GREAT IDEA!
DAMN IT~.
HEH HEH
ISN'T IT GREAT, ALICE~? WHY'RE YOU STANDING SO FAR AWAY? COME OVER HERE —

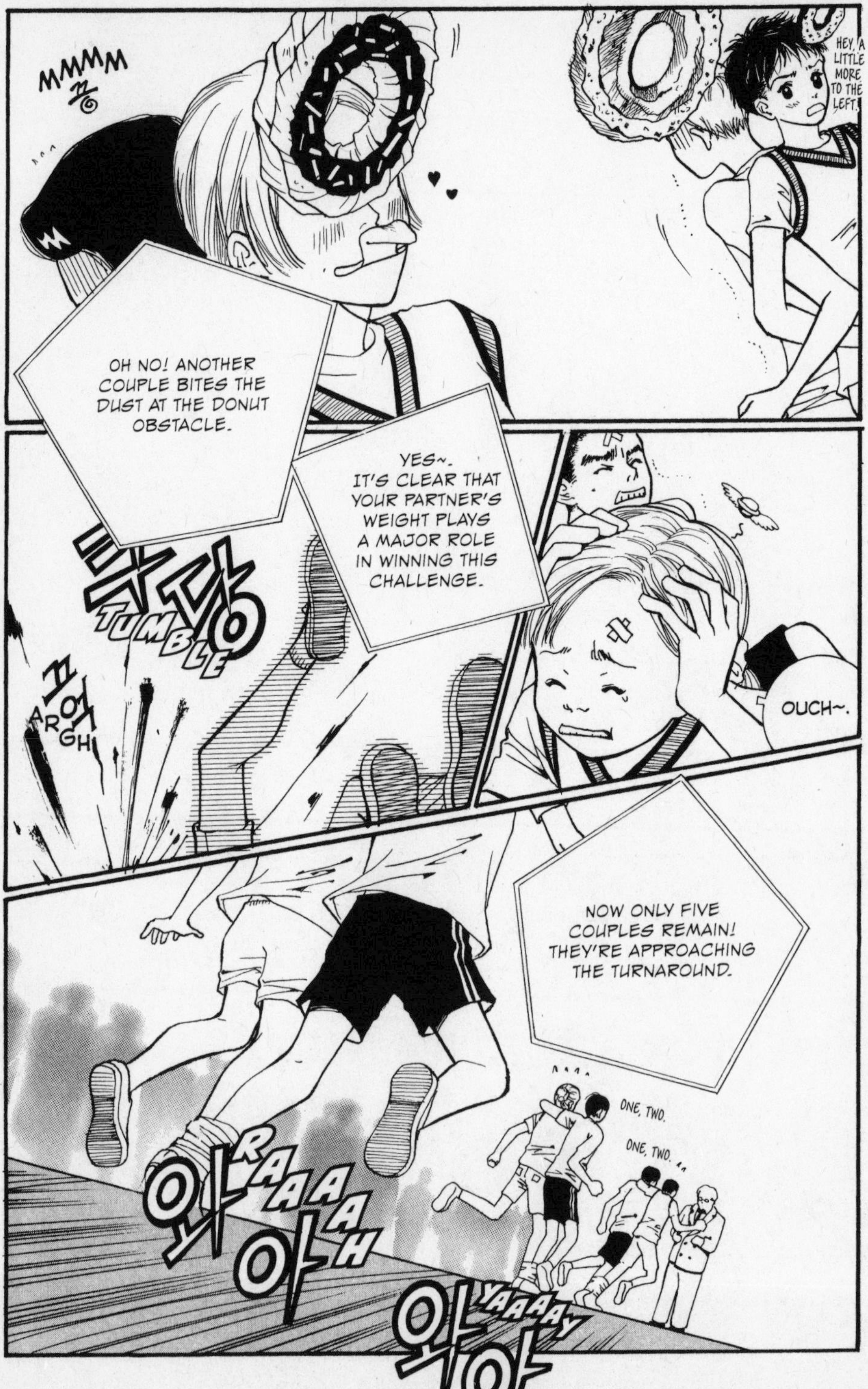
MMMM
HEY, A LITTLE MORE TO THE LEFT.
OH NO! ANOTHER COUPLE BITES THE DUST AT THE DONUT OBSTACLE.
YES~. IT'S CLEAR THAT YOUR PARTNER'S WEIGHT PLAYS A MAJOR ROLE IN WINNING THIS CHALLENGE.
TUMBLE
ARGH
OUCH~.
NOW ONLY FIVE COUPLES REMAIN! THEY'RE APPROACHING THE TURNAROUND.
RAAAAH
ONE, TWO.
ONE, TWO.
YAAAAY

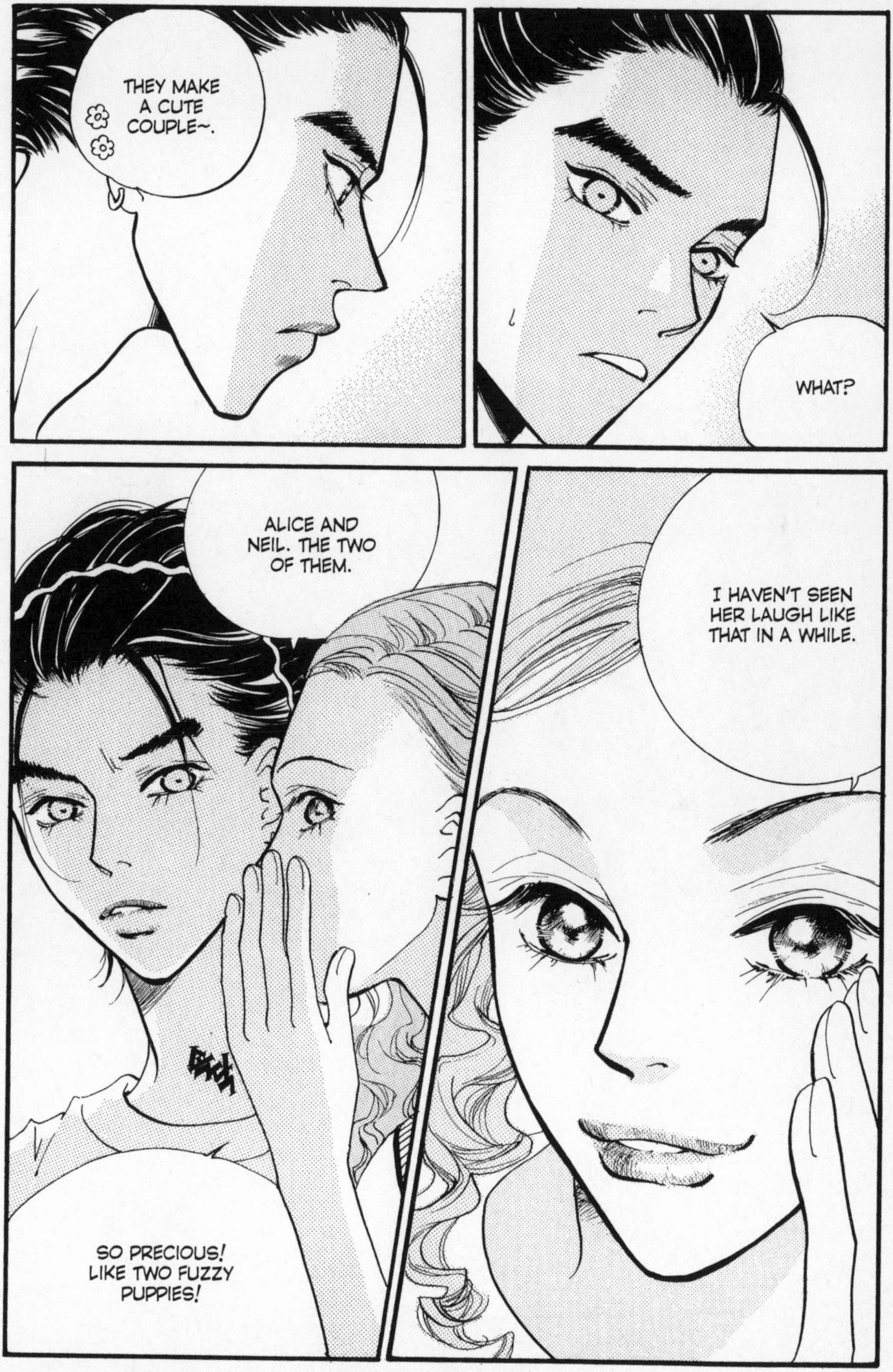
THEY MAKE A CUTE COUPLE~.
WHAT?
ALICE AND NEIL. THE TWO OF THEM.
SO PRECIOUS! LIKE TWO FUZZY PUPPIES!
I HAVEN'T SEEN HER LAUGH LIKE THAT IN A WHILE.

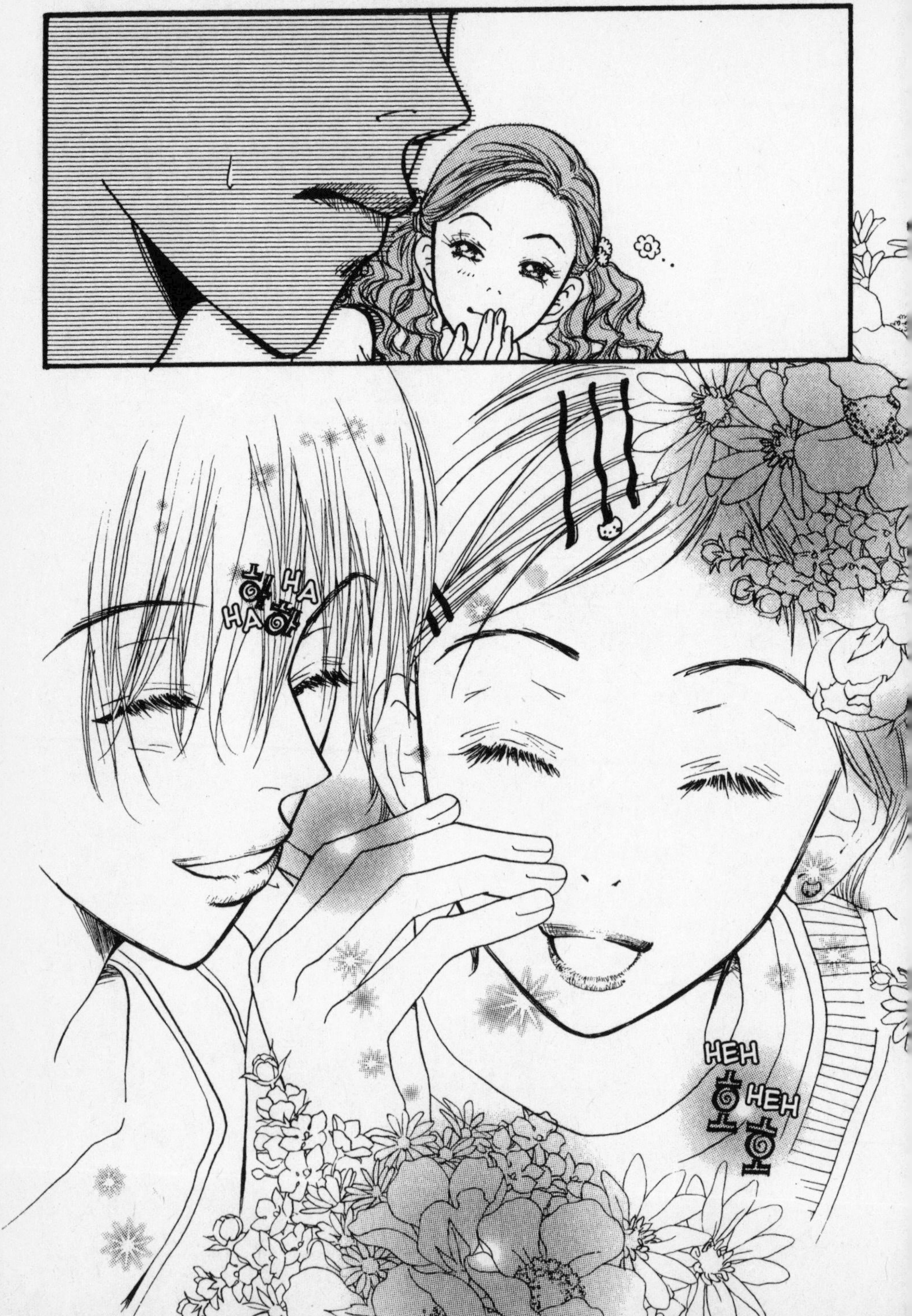
HA HA
HEH HEH

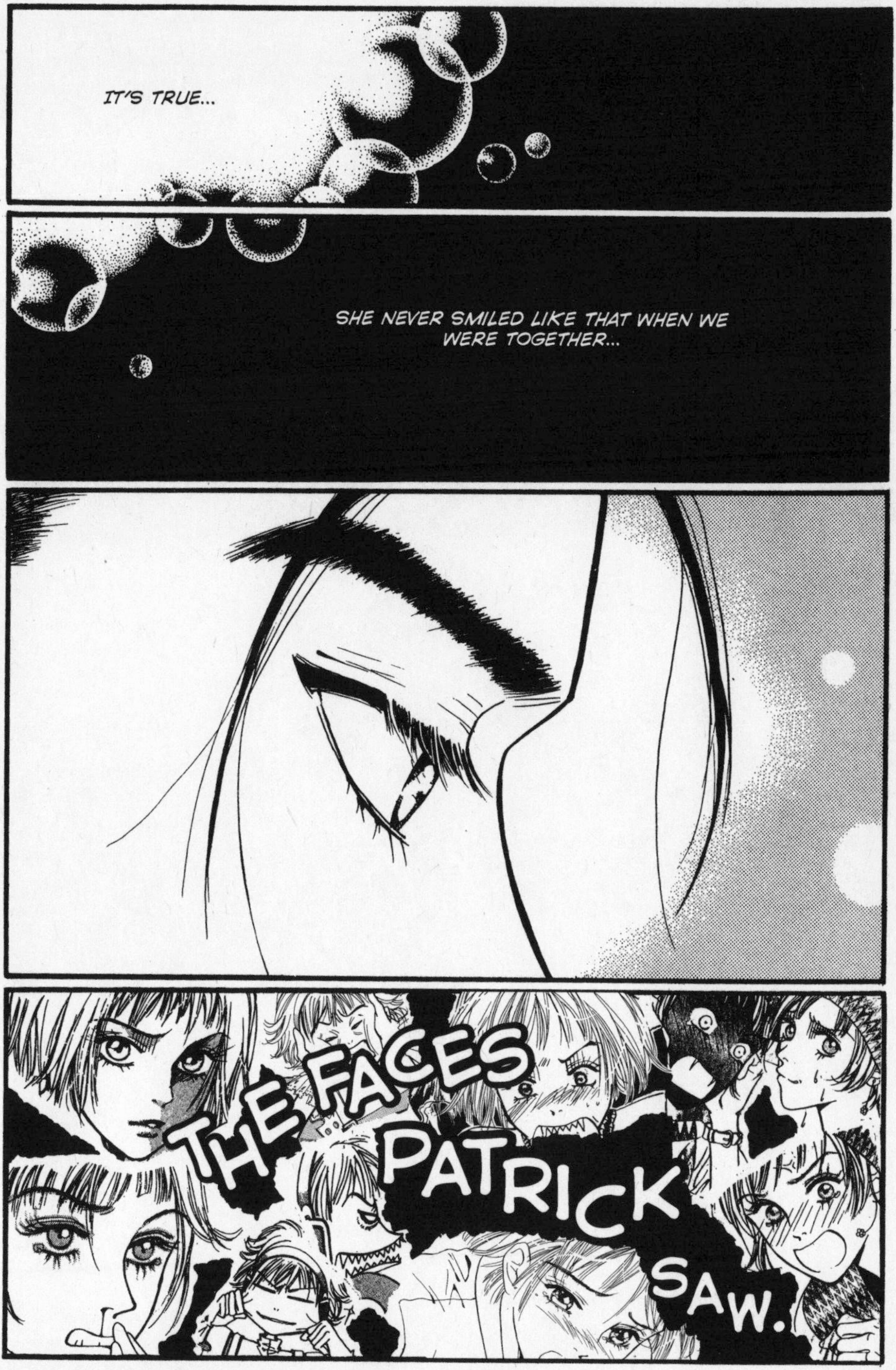
IT'S TRUE...
SHE NEVER SMILED LIKE THAT WHEN WE WERE TOGETHER...
THE FACES PATRICK SAW.

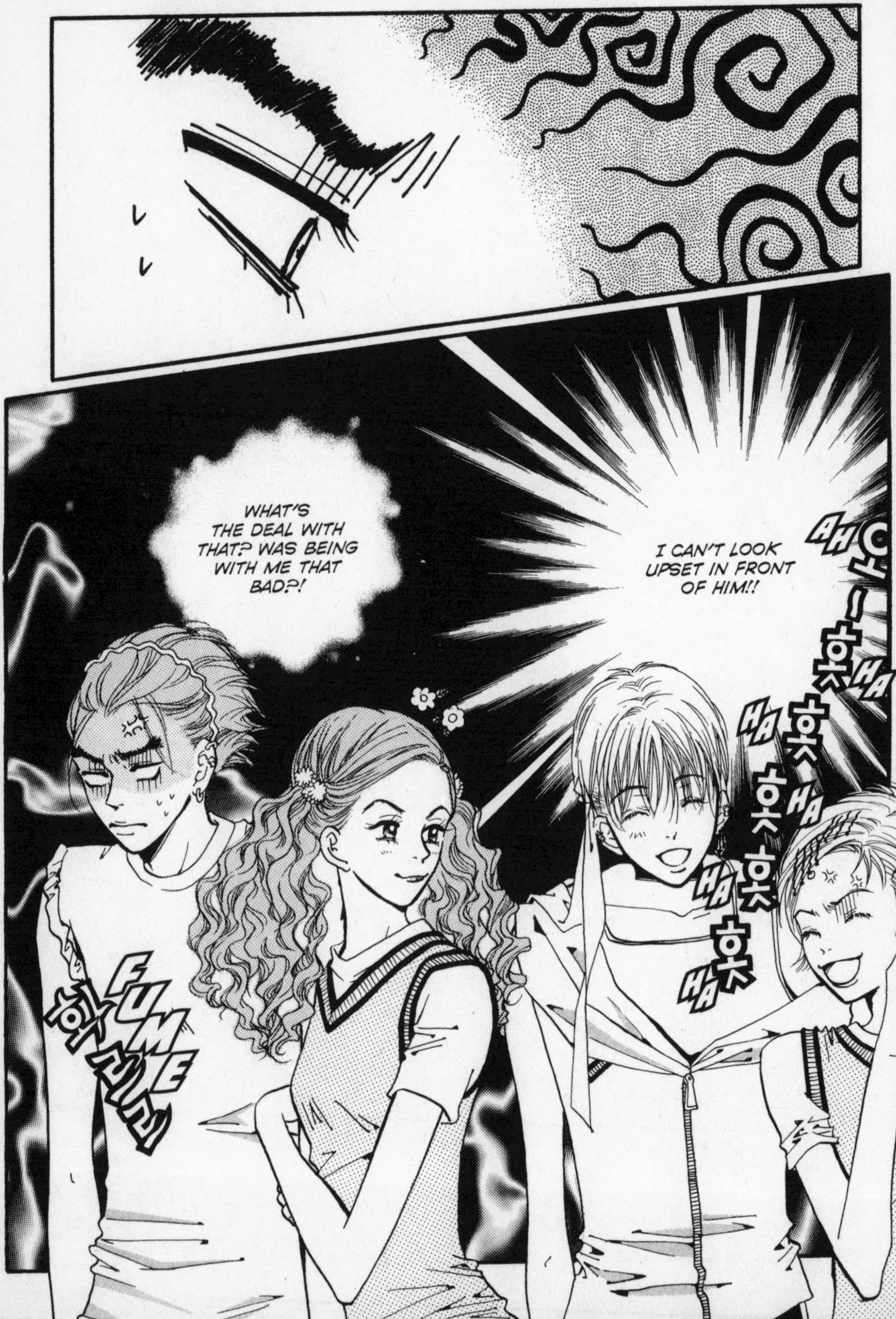
WHAT'S THE DEAL WITH THAT? WAS BEING WITH ME THAT BAD?!
FUME
I CAN'T LOOK UPSET IN FRONT OF HIM!!
AH
HA
HA
HA
HA
HA

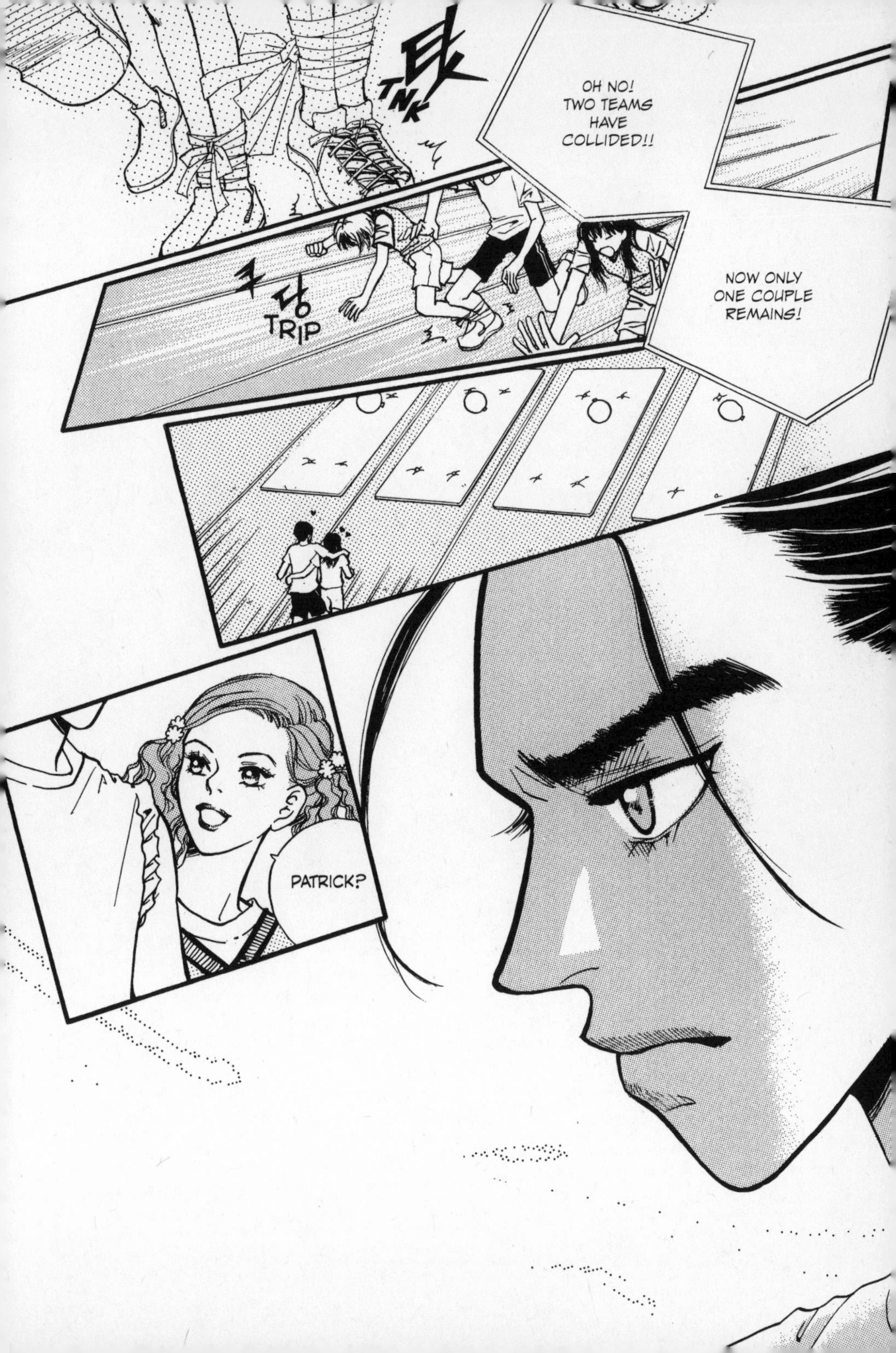

탁
TNK
OH NO! TWO TEAMS HAVE COLLIDED!!
쿠당
TRIP
NOW ONLY ONE COUPLE REMAINS!
PATRICK?

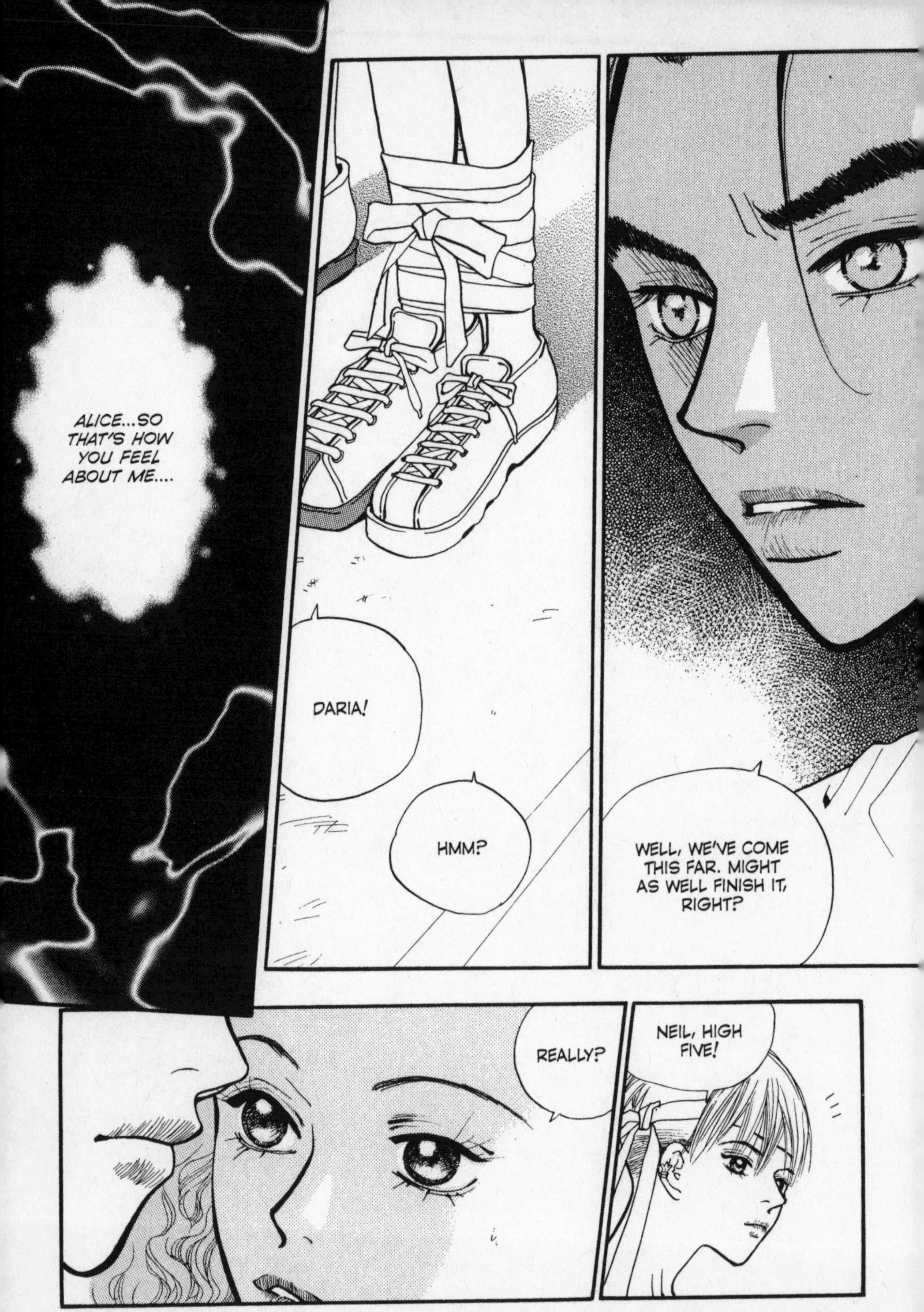
ALICE...SO THAT'S HOW YOU FEEL ABOUT ME....
DARIA!
HMM?
WELL, WE'VE COME THIS FAR. MIGHT AS WELL FINISH IT, RIGHT?
REALLY?
NEIL, HIGH FIVE!

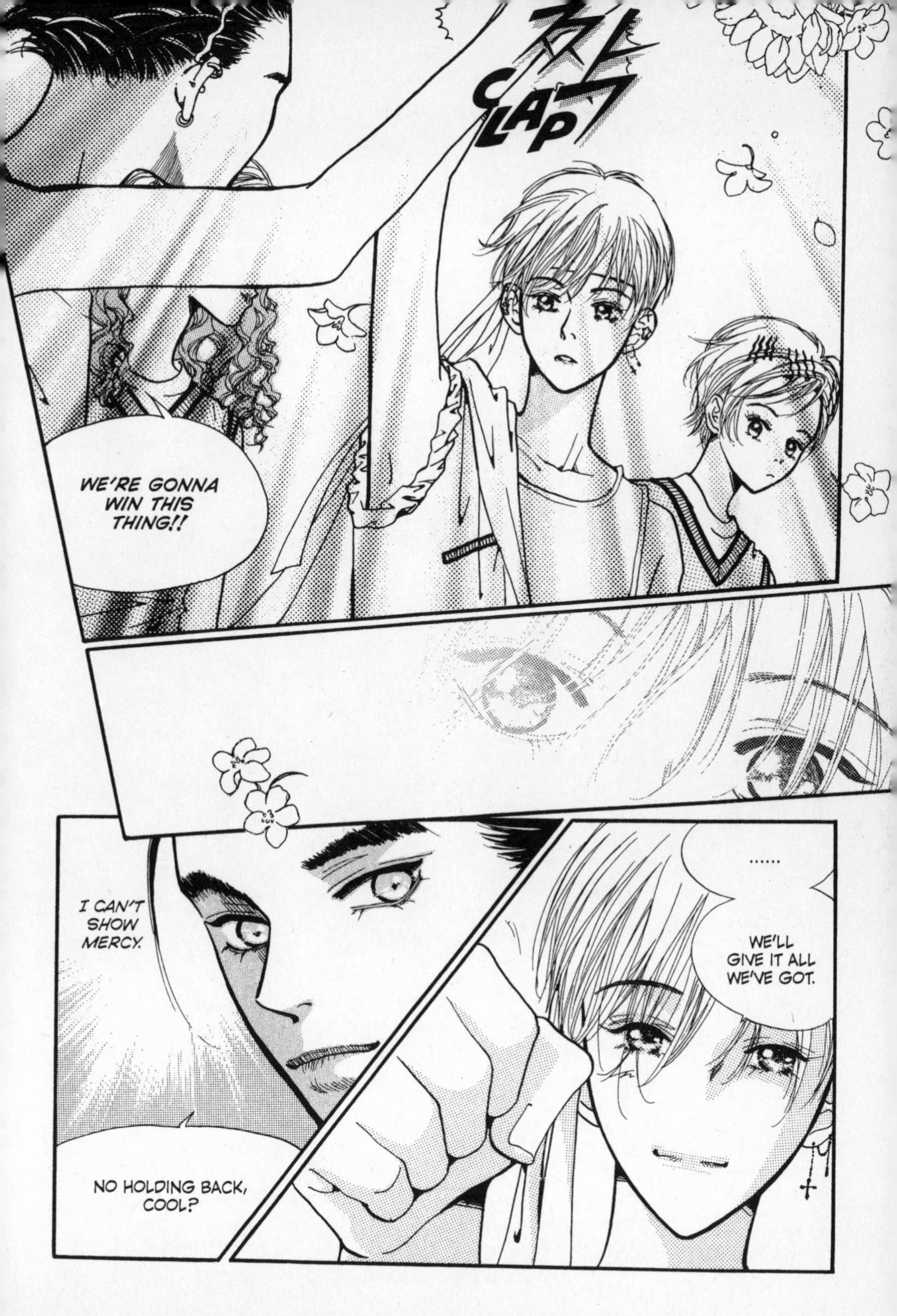

CLAP
WE'RE GONNA WIN THIS THING!!
I CAN'T SHOW MERCY.
NO HOLDING BACK, COOL?
......
WE'LL GIVE IT ALL WE'VE GOT.

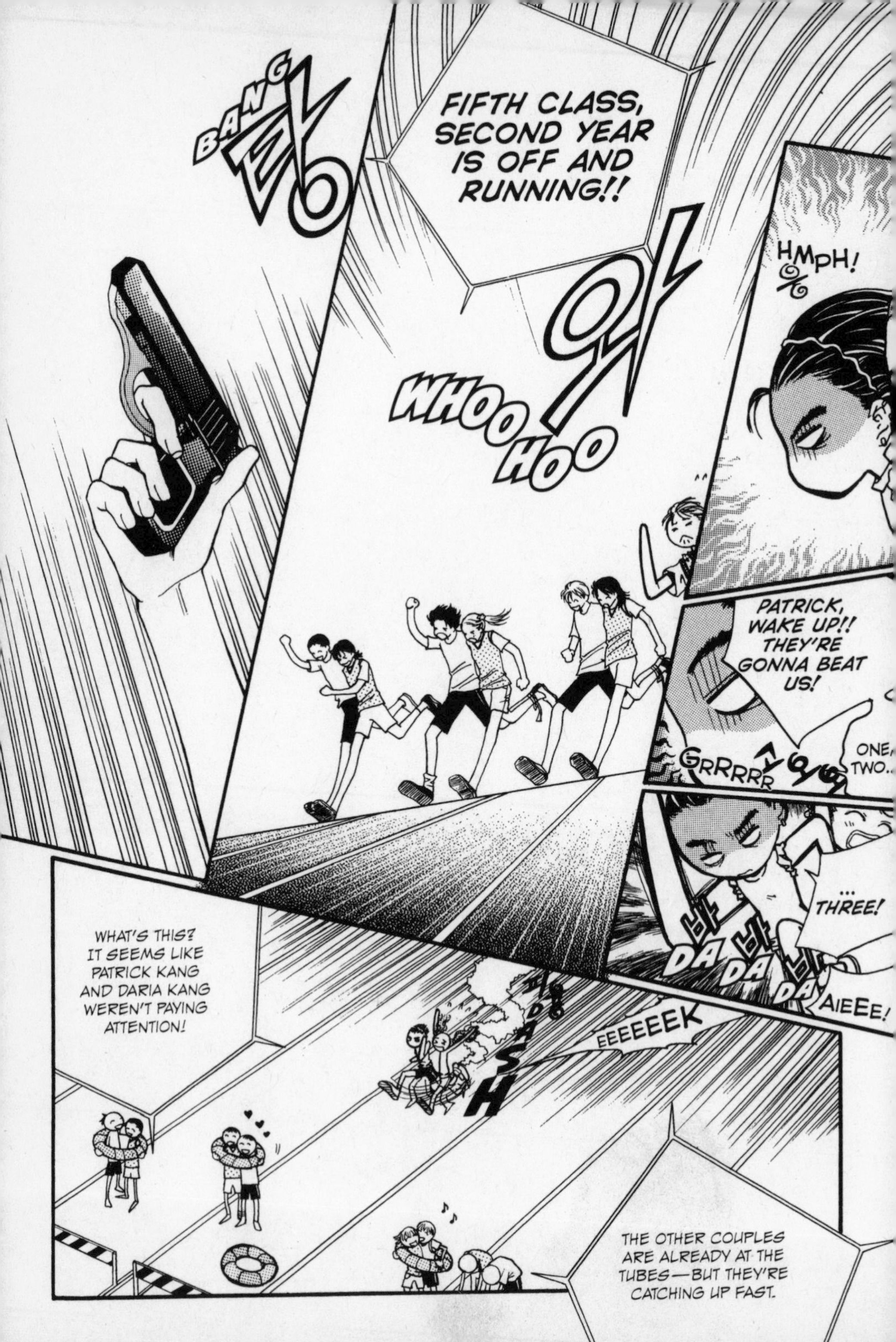
BANG
FIFTH CLASS, SECOND YEAR IS OFF AND RUNNING!!
WHOO HOO
HMPH!
PATRICK, WAKE UP!! THEY'RE GONNA BEAT US!
GRRRRR
ONE, TWO...
...THREE!
DA DA DA
AIEEE!
WHAT'S THIS? IT SEEMS LIKE PATRICK KANG AND DARIA KANG WEREN'T PAYING ATTENTION!
DASH
EEEEEEK
THE OTHER COUPLES ARE ALREADY AT THE TUBES—BUT THEY'RE CATCHING UP FAST.

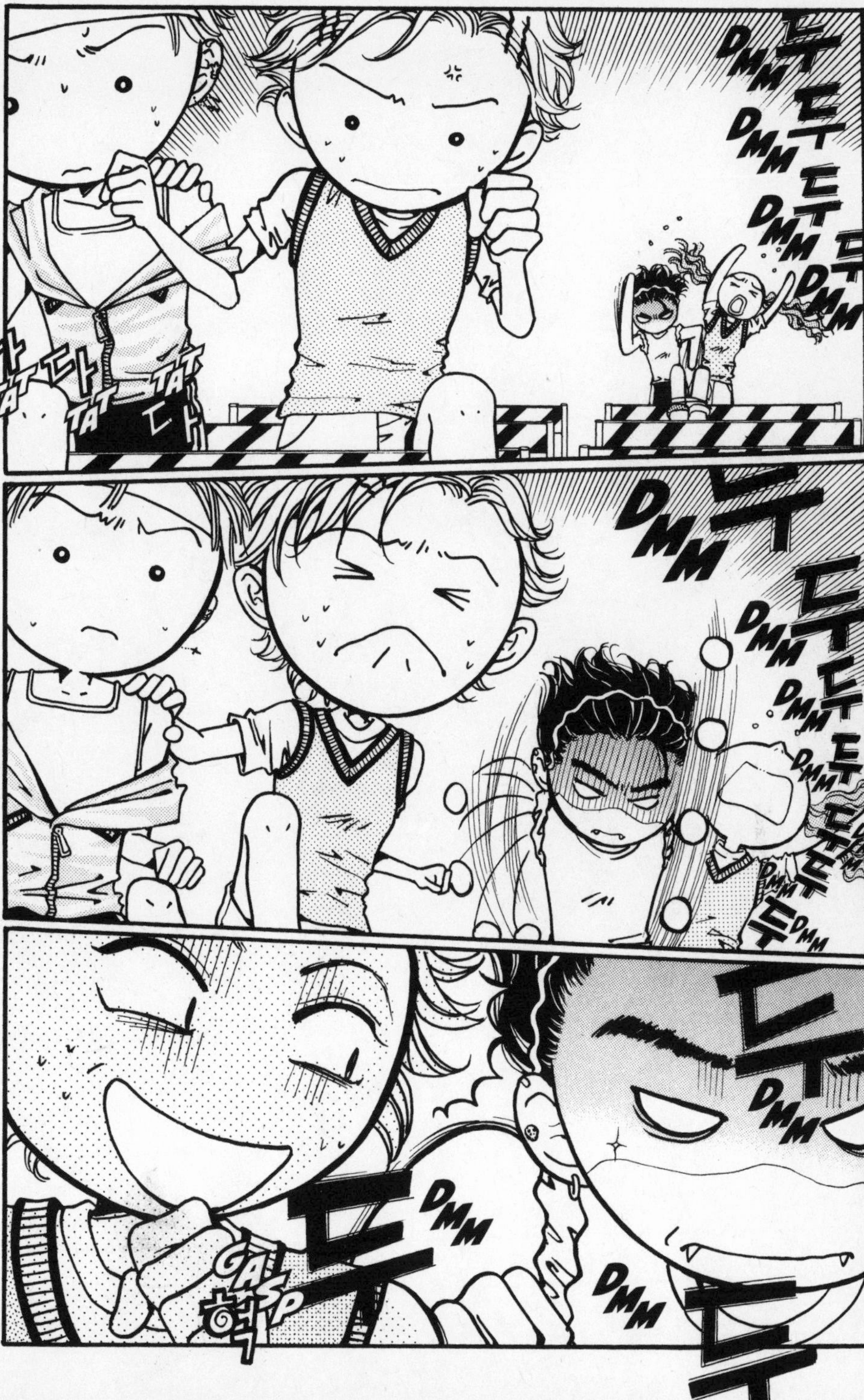

다 TAT 다 TAT 다 TAT
DMM DMM DMM DMM DMM
DMM DMM DMM DMM DMM DMM
GASP 헉
DMM DMM DMM

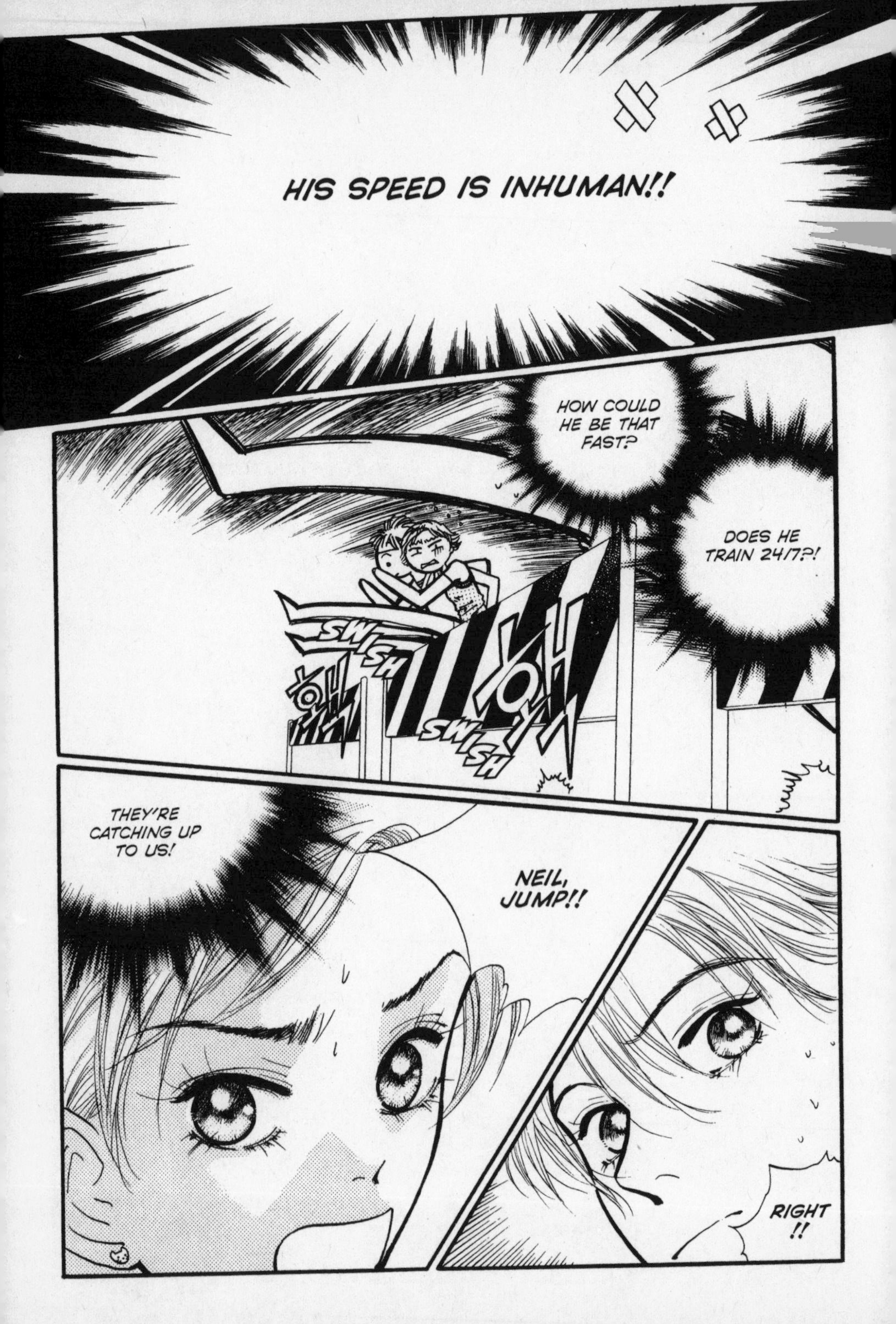
HIS SPEED IS INHUMAN!!
HOW COULD HE BE THAT FAST?
DOES HE TRAIN 24/7?!
SWISH
SWISH
THEY'RE CATCHING UP TO US!
NEIL, JUMP!!
RIGHT !!

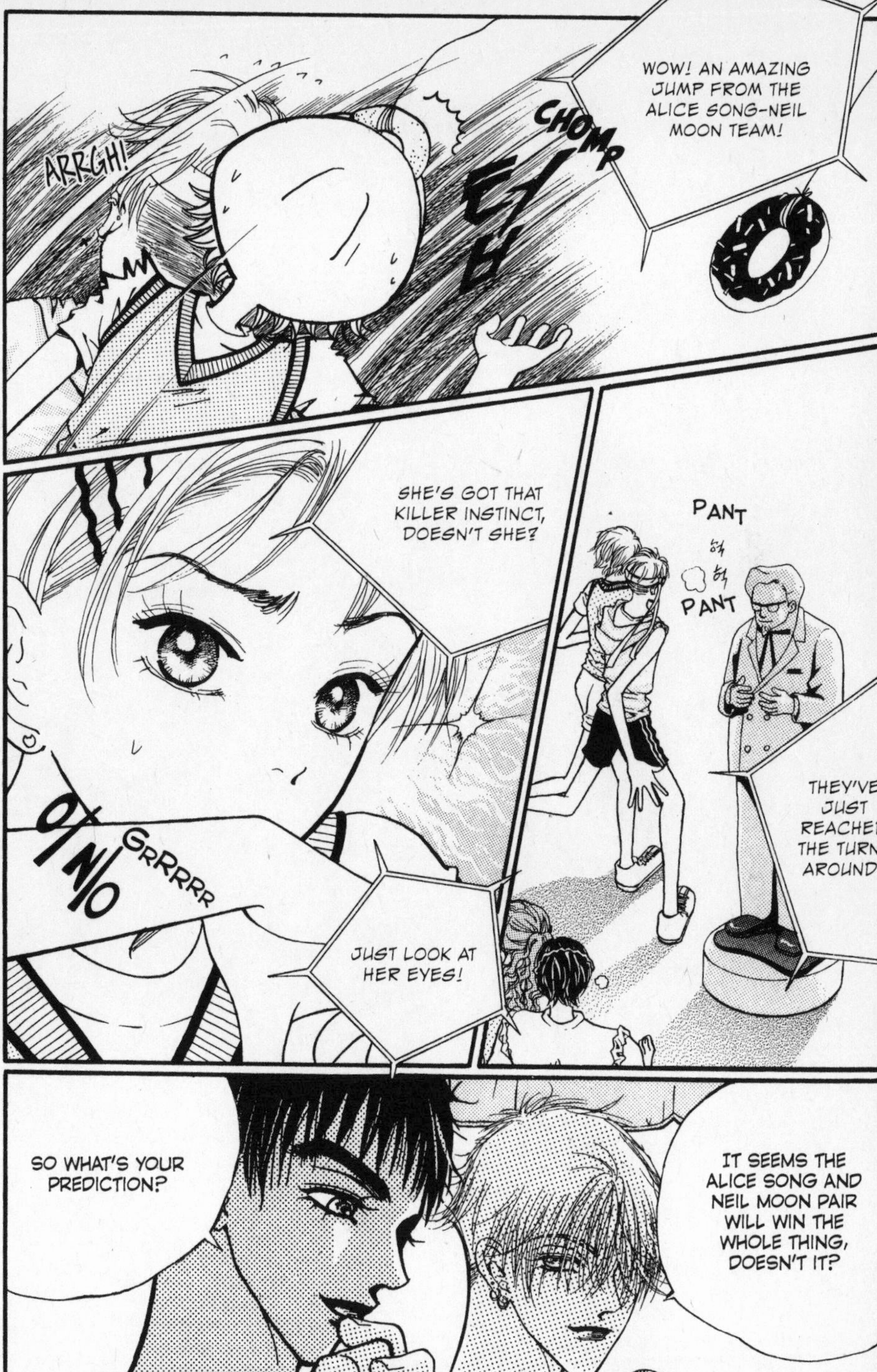
ARRGH!
CHOMP
WOW! AN AMAZING JUMP FROM THE ALICE SONG-NEIL MOON TEAM!
SHE'S GOT THAT KILLER INSTINCT, DOESN'T SHE?
GRRRRR
JUST LOOK AT HER EYES!
PANT
PANT
THEY'VE JUST REACHED THE TURN-AROUND!
SO WHAT'S YOUR PREDICTION?
IT SEEMS THE ALICE SONG AND NEIL MOON PAIR WILL WIN THE WHOLE THING, DOESN'T IT?

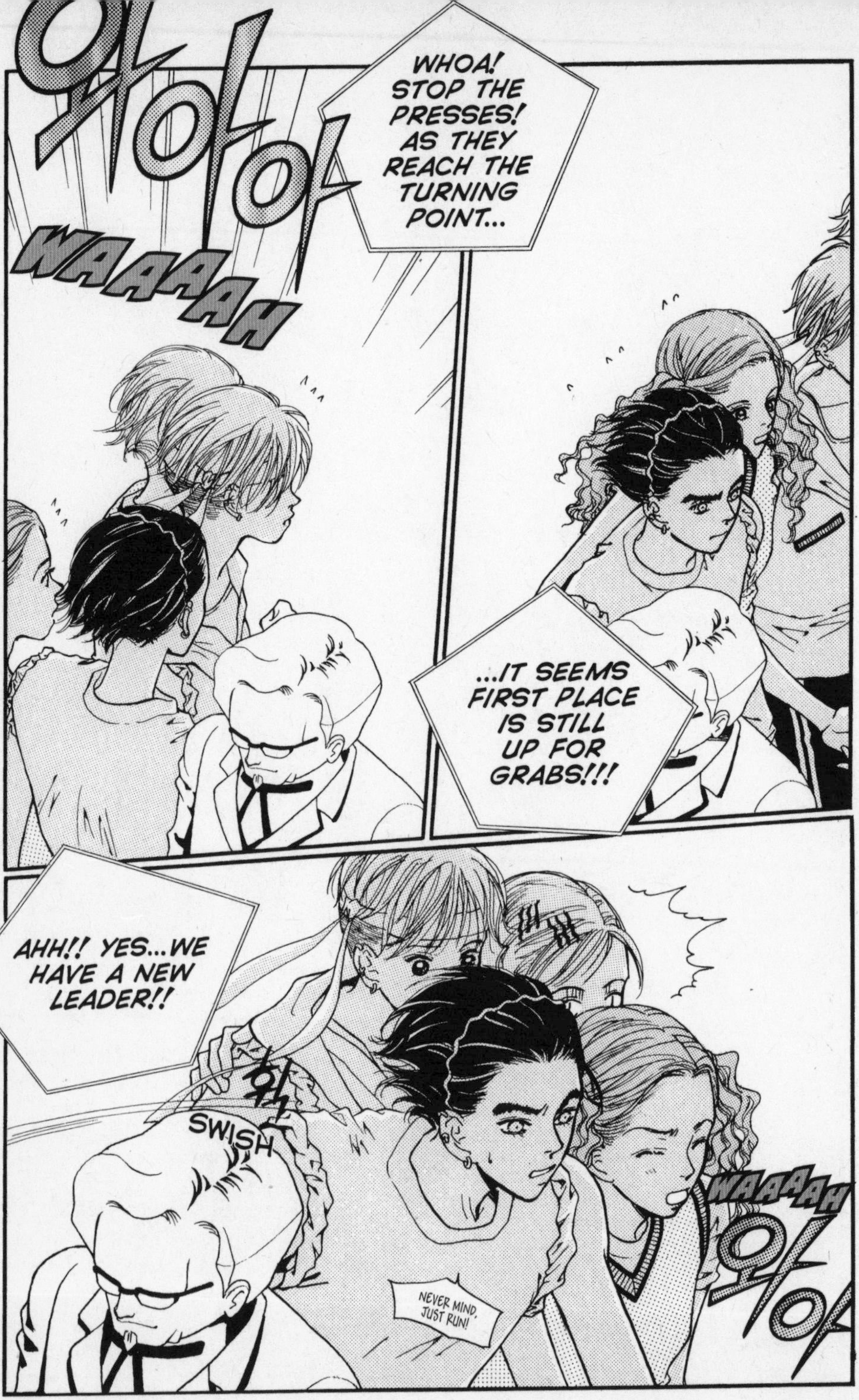
WAAAAH
WHOA! STOP THE PRESSES! AS THEY REACH THE TURNING POINT...
...IT SEEMS FIRST PLACE IS STILL UP FOR GRABS!!!
AHH!! YES...WE HAVE A NEW LEADER!!
SWISH
NEVER MIND, JUST RUN!
WAAAAH

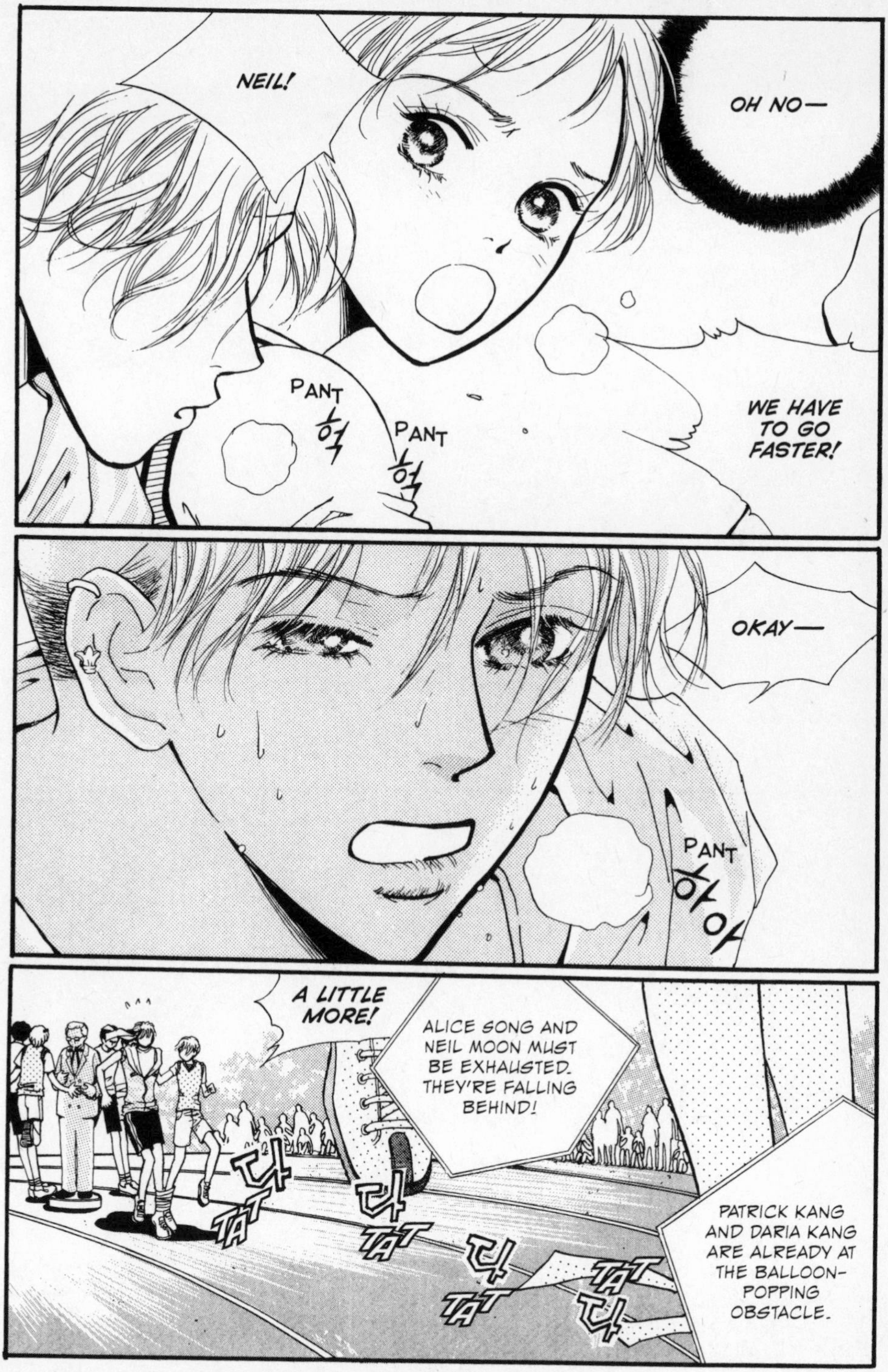
NEIL!
OH NO—
PANT
PANT
WE HAVE TO GO FASTER!
OKAY—
PANT
A LITTLE MORE!
ALICE SONG AND NEIL MOON MUST BE EXHAUSTED. THEY'RE FALLING BEHIND!
TAT
TAT
TAT
TAT
PATRICK KANG AND DARIA KANG ARE ALREADY AT THE BALLOON-POPPING OBSTACLE.

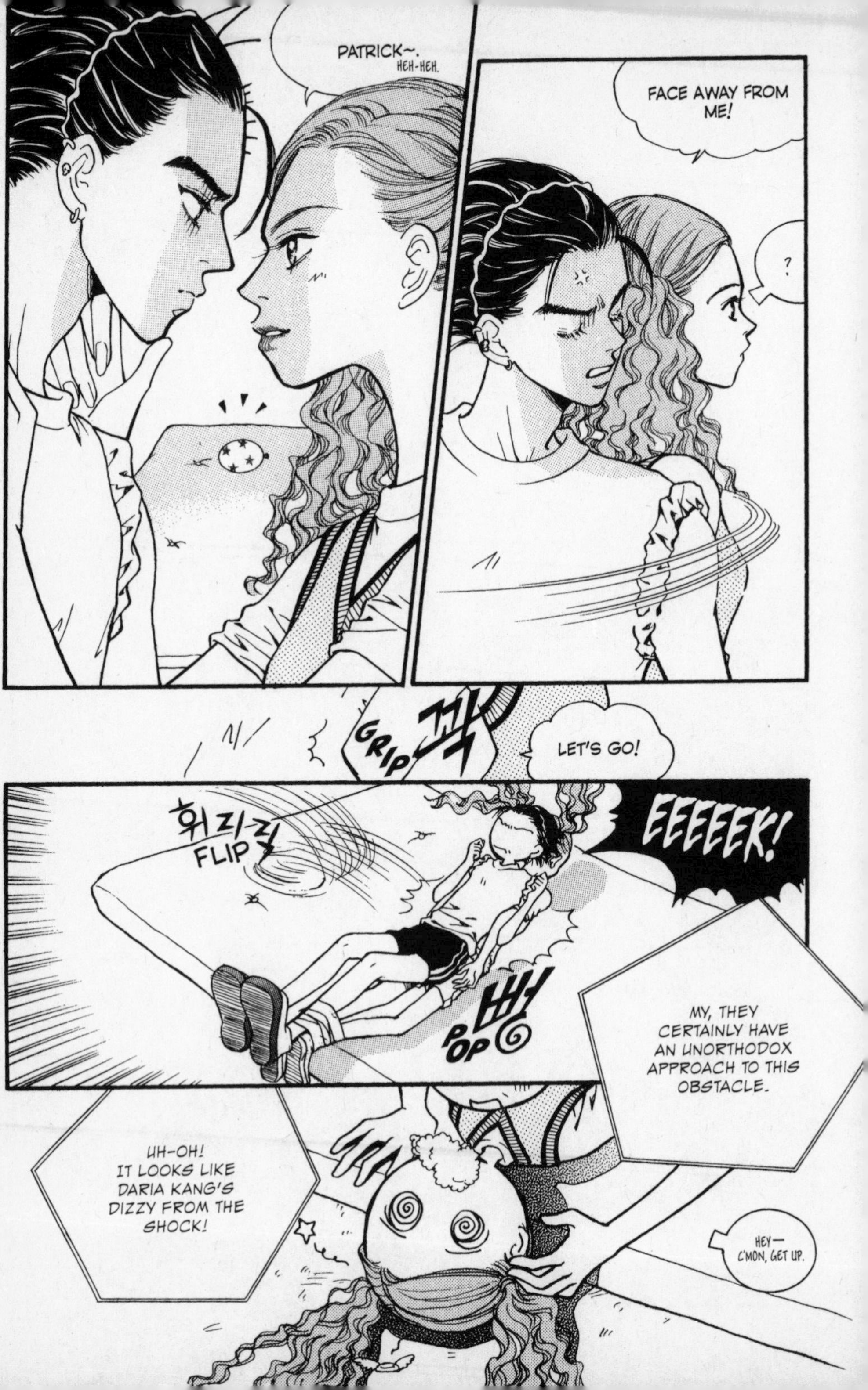
PATRICK~.
HEH-HEH.
FACE AWAY FROM ME!
?
GRIP
LET'S GO!
휘리릭
FLIP
EEEEEK!
POP
MY, THEY CERTAINLY HAVE AN UNORTHODOX APPROACH TO THIS OBSTACLE.
UH-OH! IT LOOKS LIKE DARIA KANG'S DIZZY FROM THE SHOCK!
HEY— C'MON, GET UP.

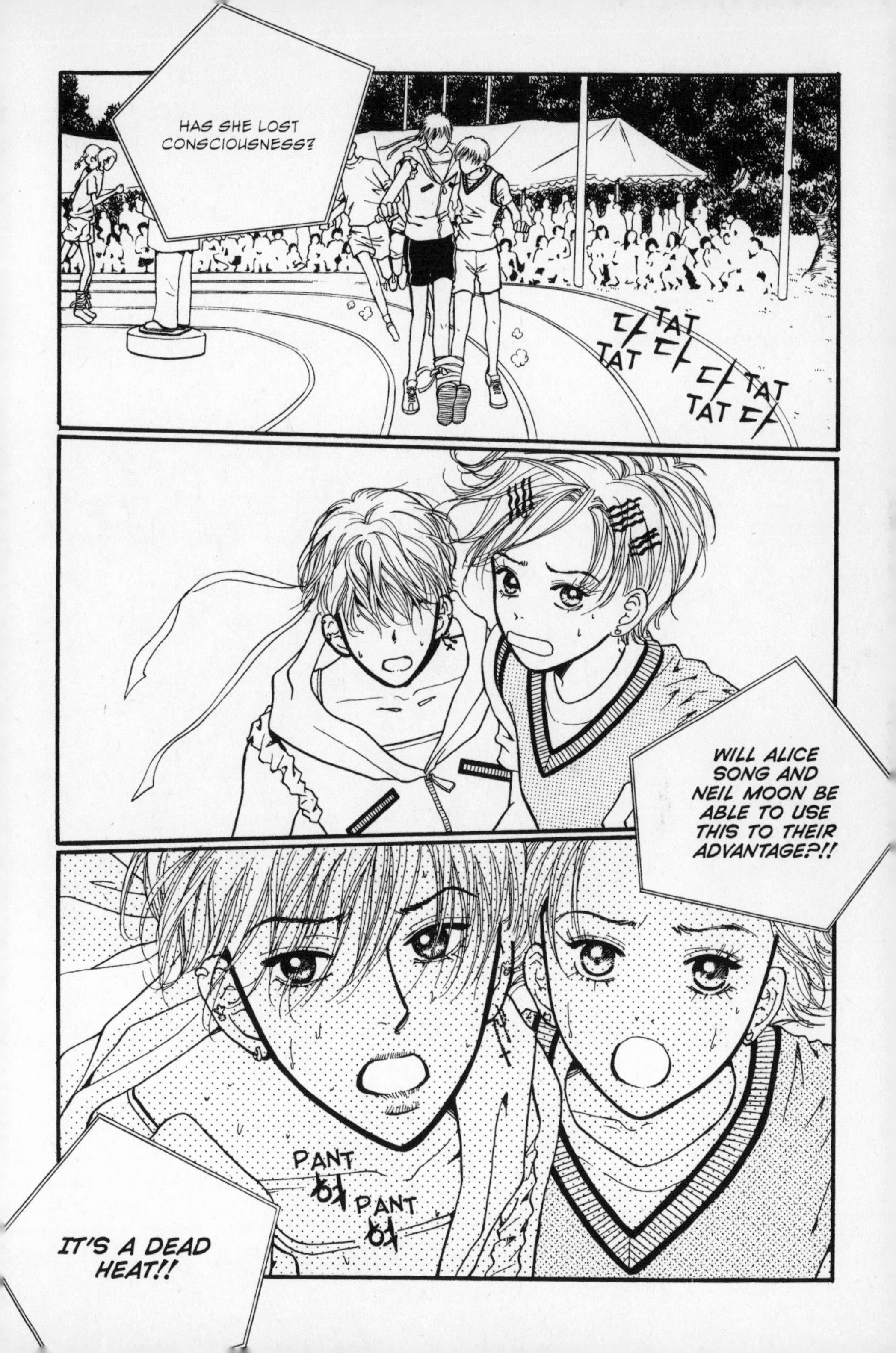

HAS SHE LOST CONSCIOUSNESS?
TAT TAT TAT TAT
WILL ALICE SONG AND NEIL MOON BE ABLE TO USE THIS TO THEIR ADVANTAGE?!!
IT'S A DEAD HEAT!!
PANT PANT

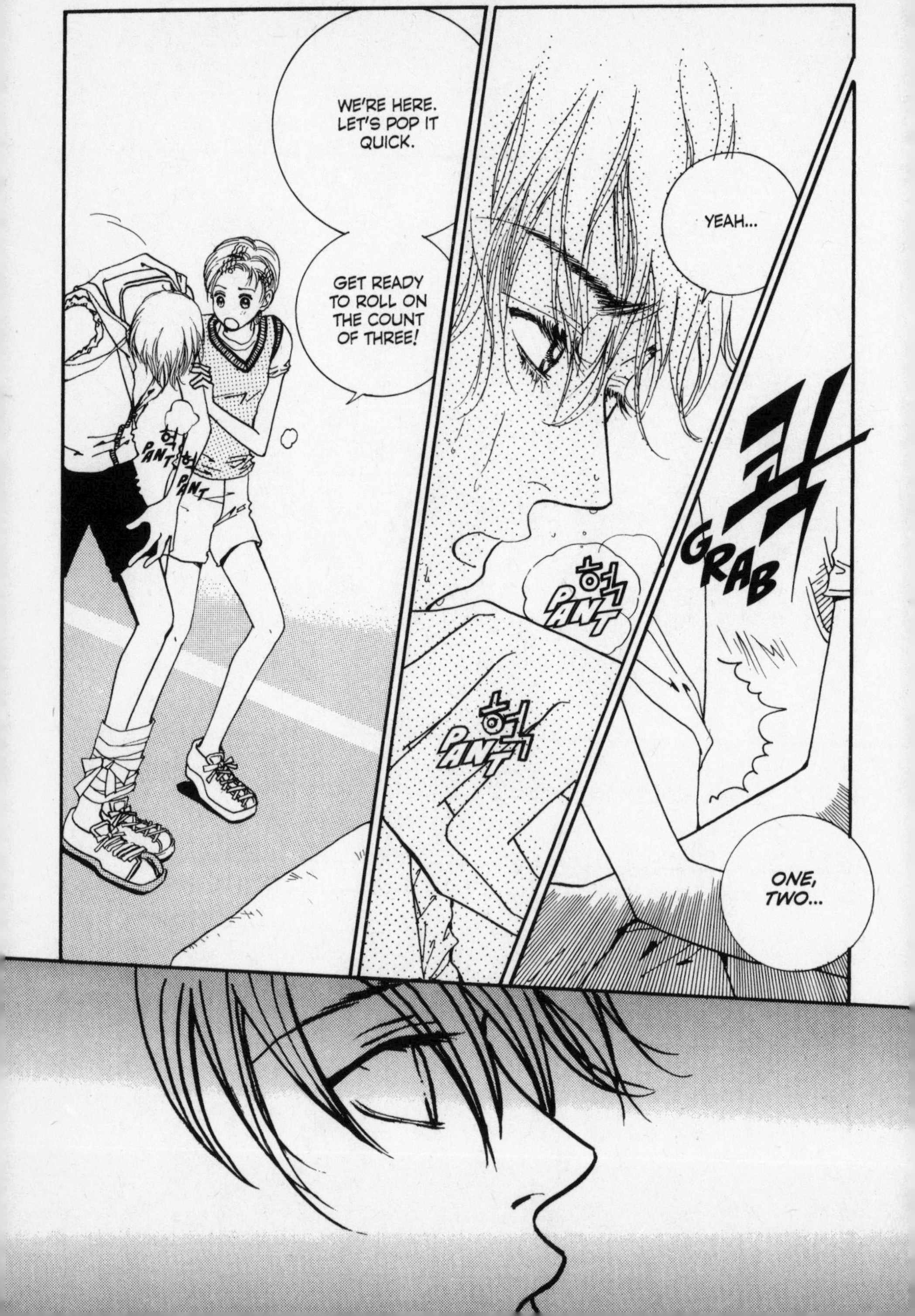

WE'RE HERE. LET'S POP IT QUICK.
GET READY TO ROLL ON THE COUNT OF THREE!
PANT PANT
YEAH...
PANT
PANT
GRAB
ONE, TWO...

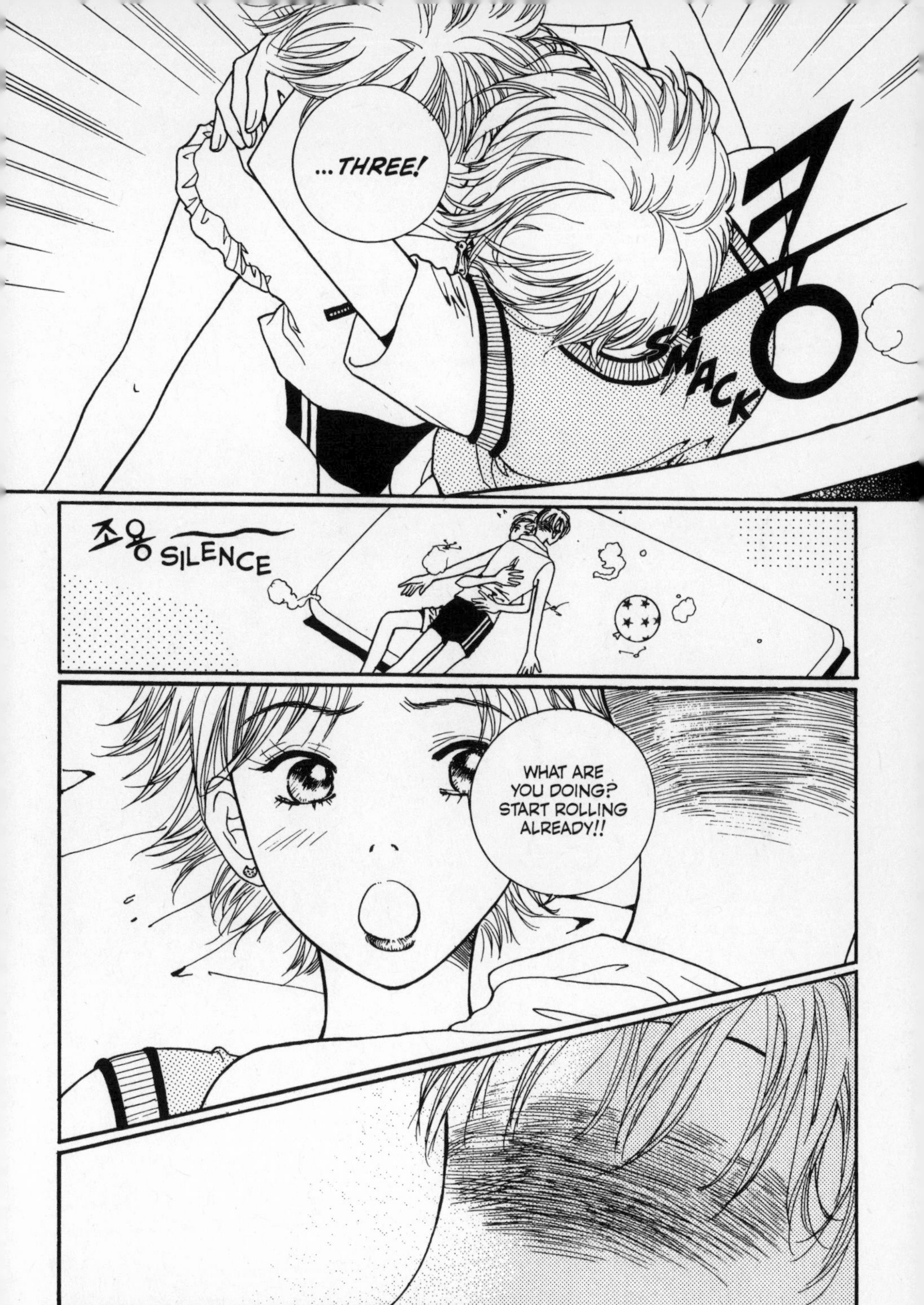
...THREE!
SMACK
조용 SILENCE
WHAT ARE YOU DOING? START ROLLING ALREADY!!

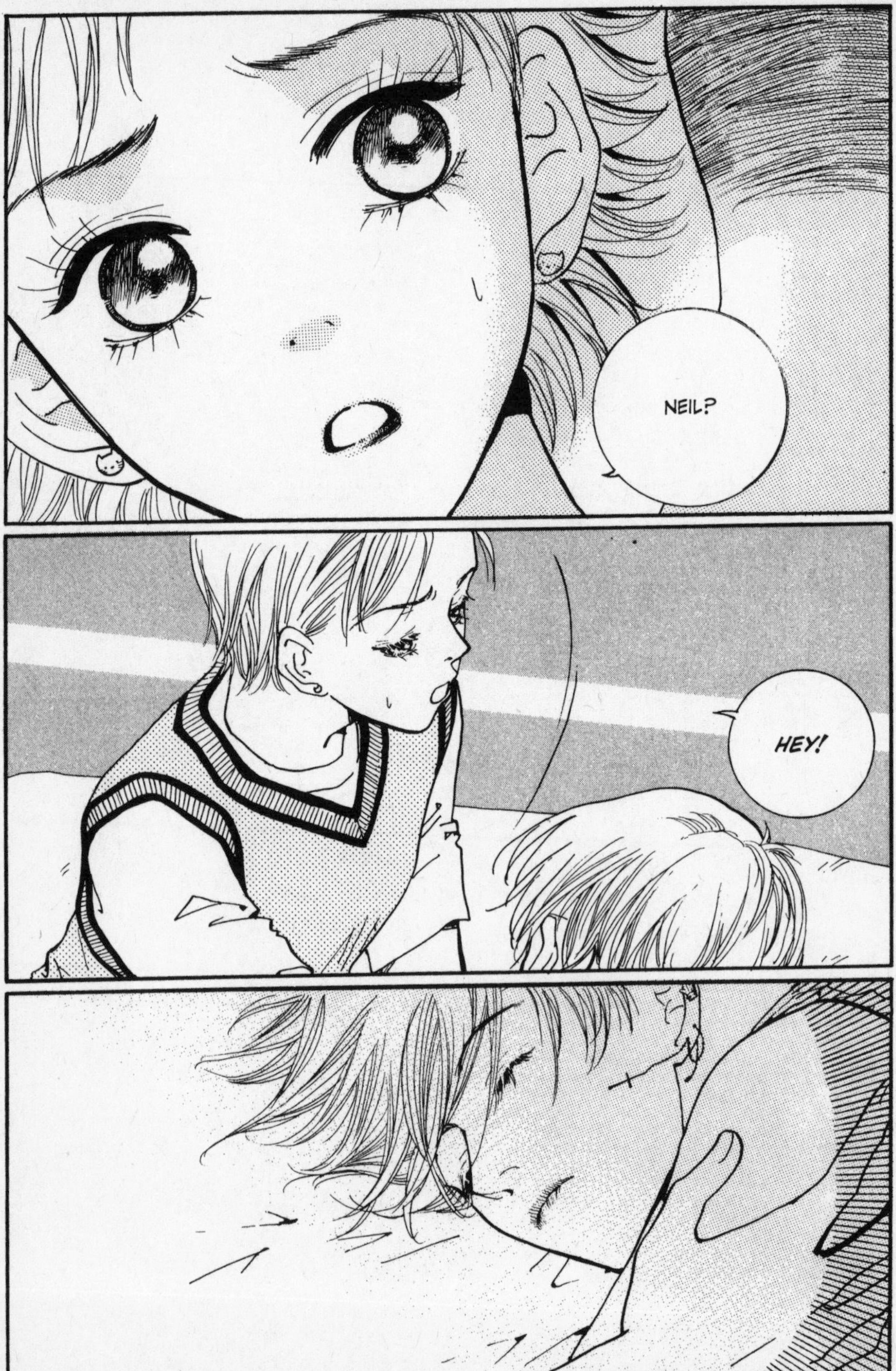
NEIL?
HEY!

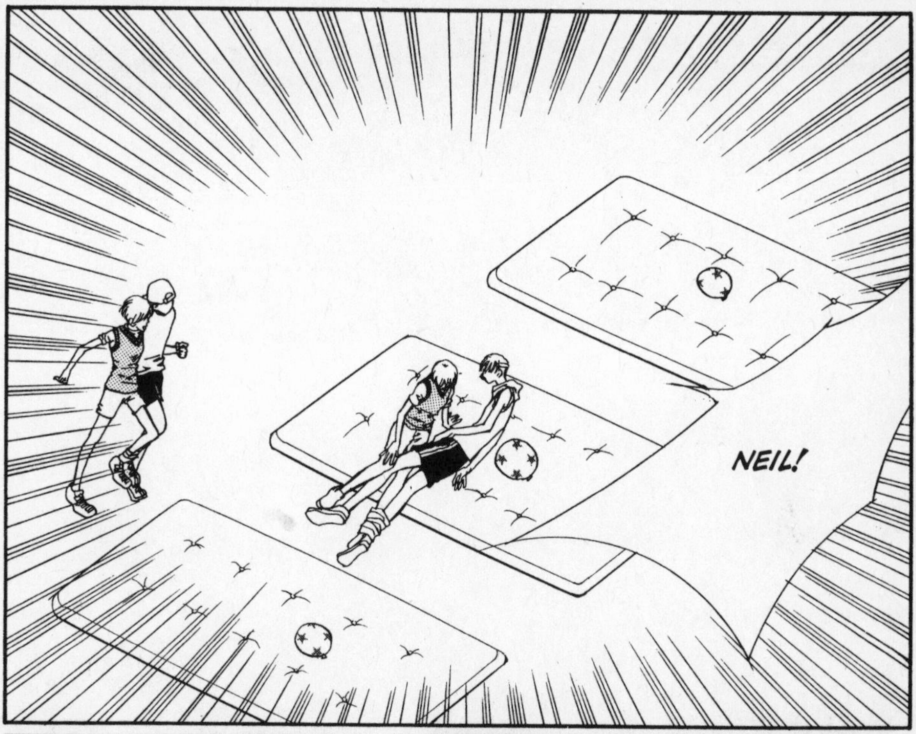
NEIL!
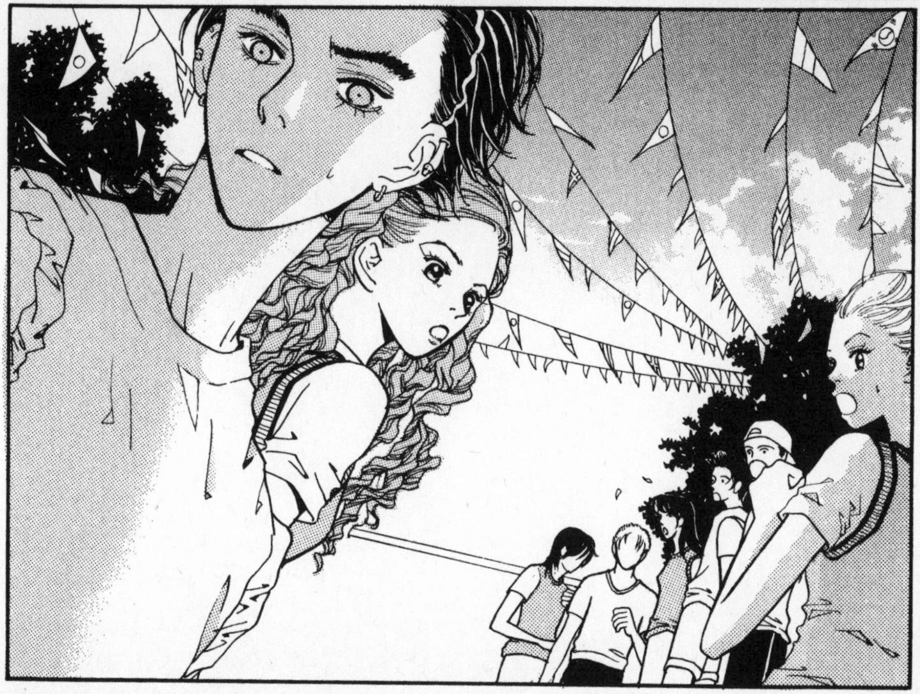

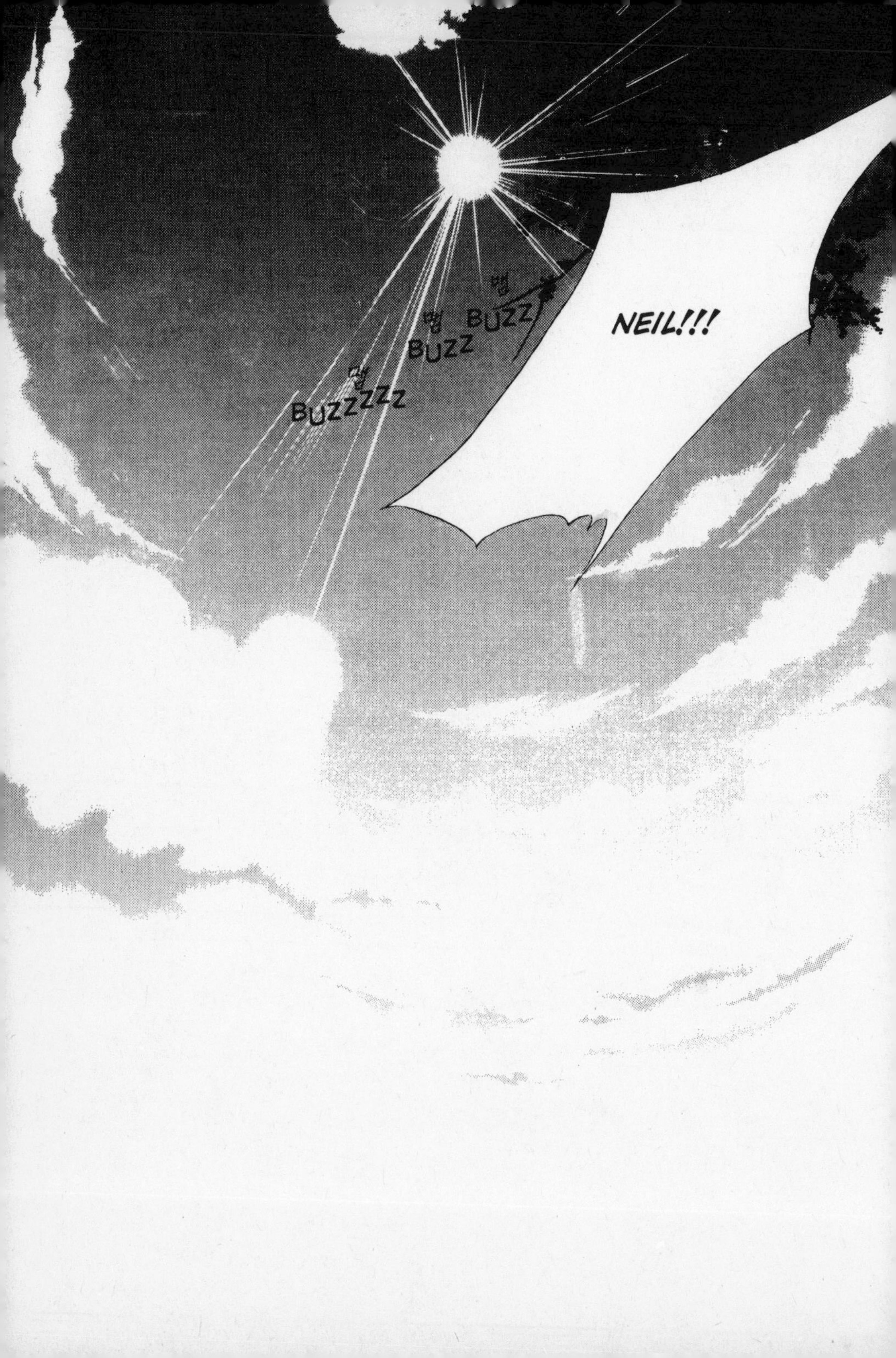
BUZZ
BUZZ
BUZZZZZ
NEIL!!!

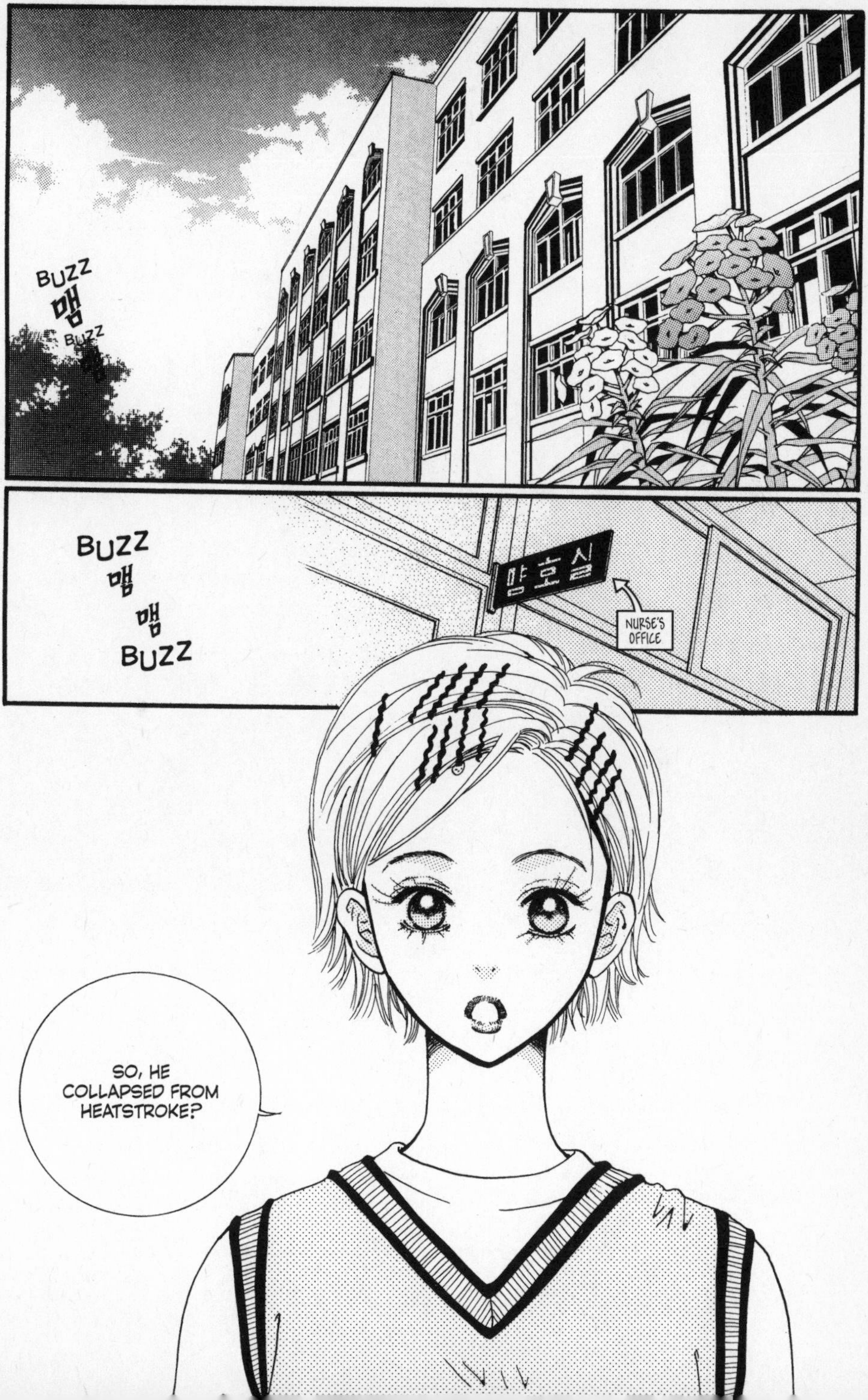
BUZZ
맴
BUZZ
맴
BUZZ
맴
맴
BUZZ
NURSE'S OFFICE
SO, HE COLLAPSED FROM HEATSTROKE?

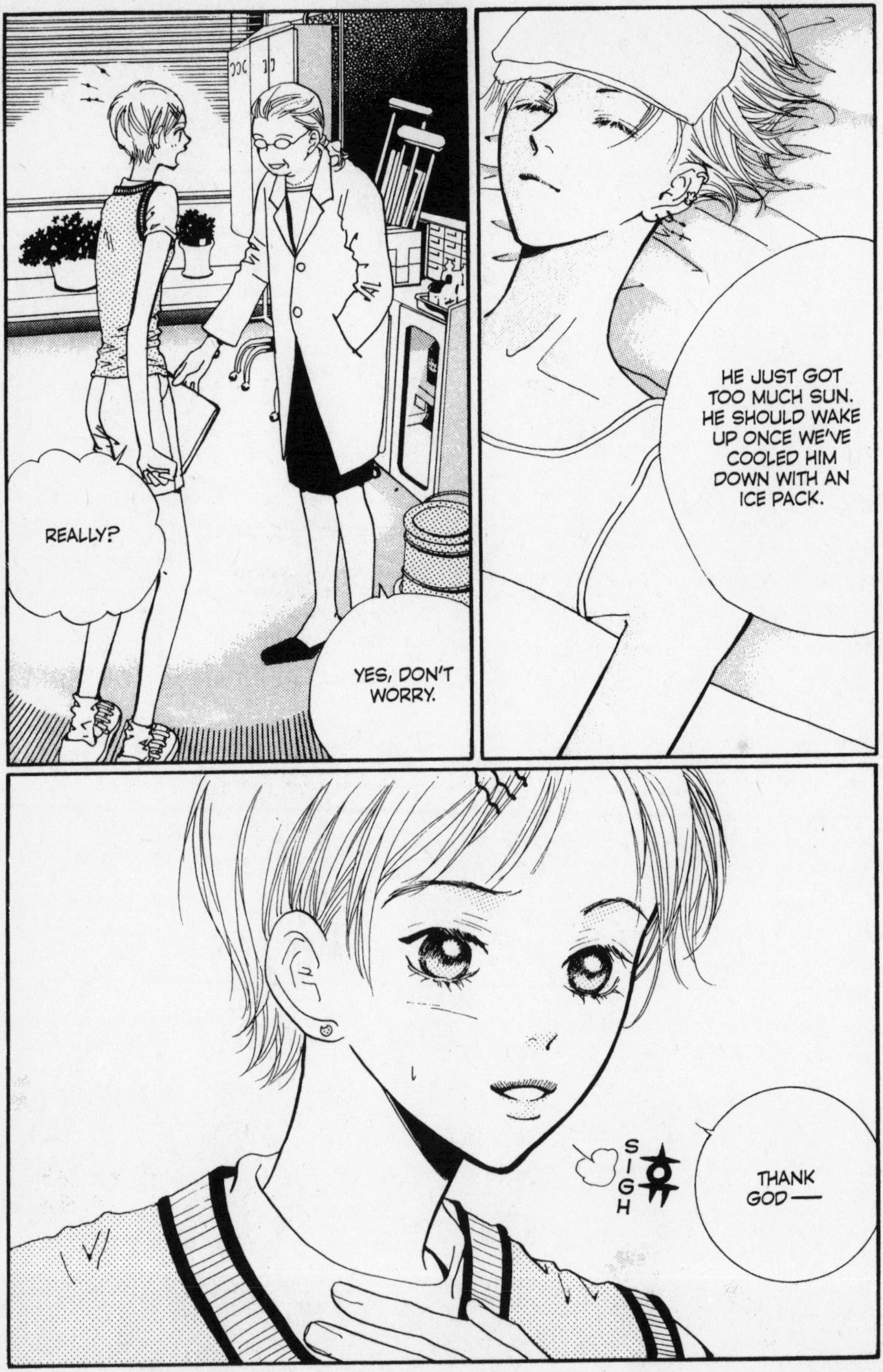
REALLY?
YES, DON'T WORRY.
HE JUST GOT TOO MUCH SUN. HE SHOULD WAKE UP ONCE WE'VE COOLED HIM DOWN WITH AN ICE PACK.
SIGH
THANK GOD—

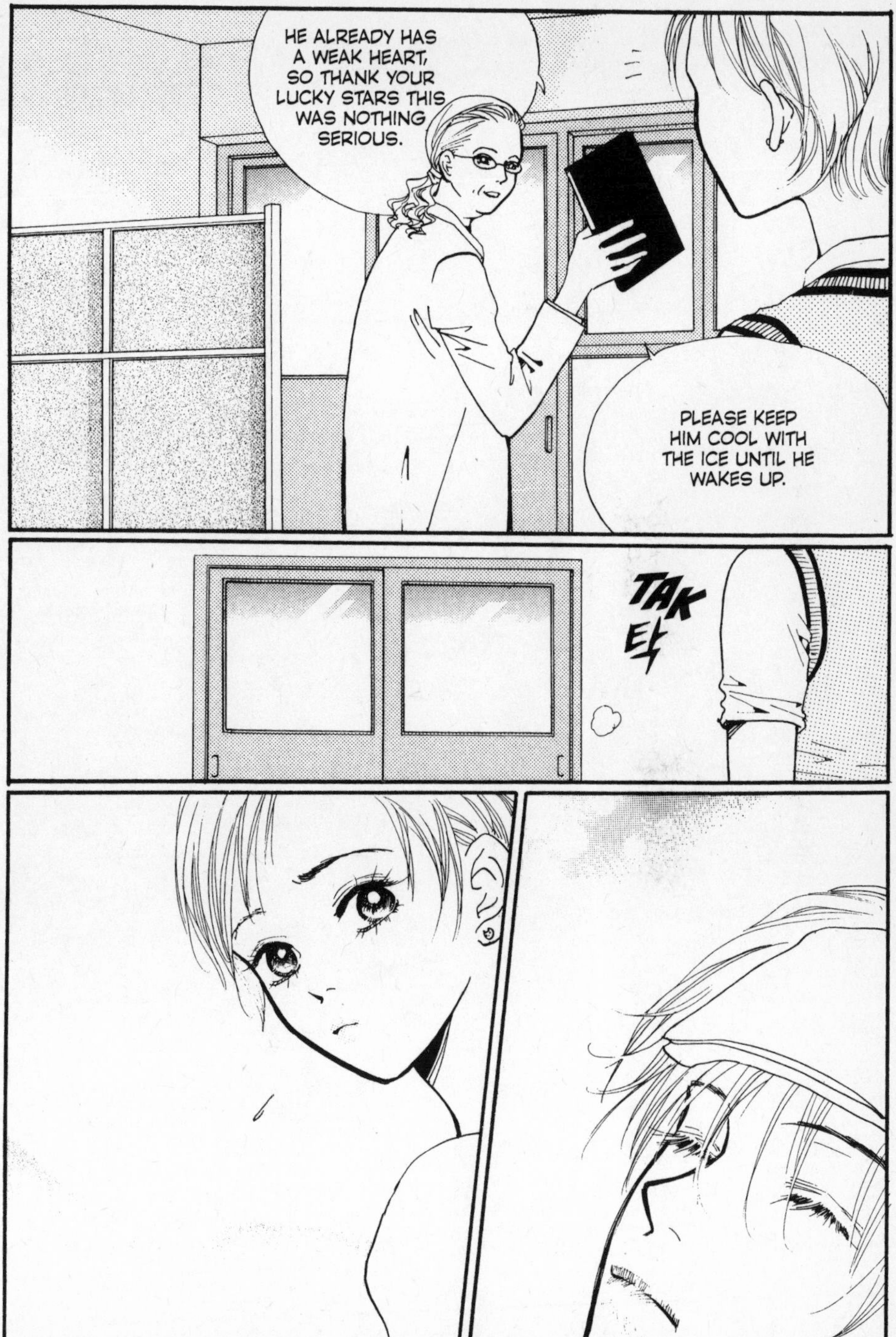
HE ALREADY HAS A WEAK HEART, SO THANK YOUR LUCKY STARS THIS WAS NOTHING SERIOUS.
PLEASE KEEP HIM COOL WITH THE ICE UNTIL HE WAKES UP.
TAK
탁

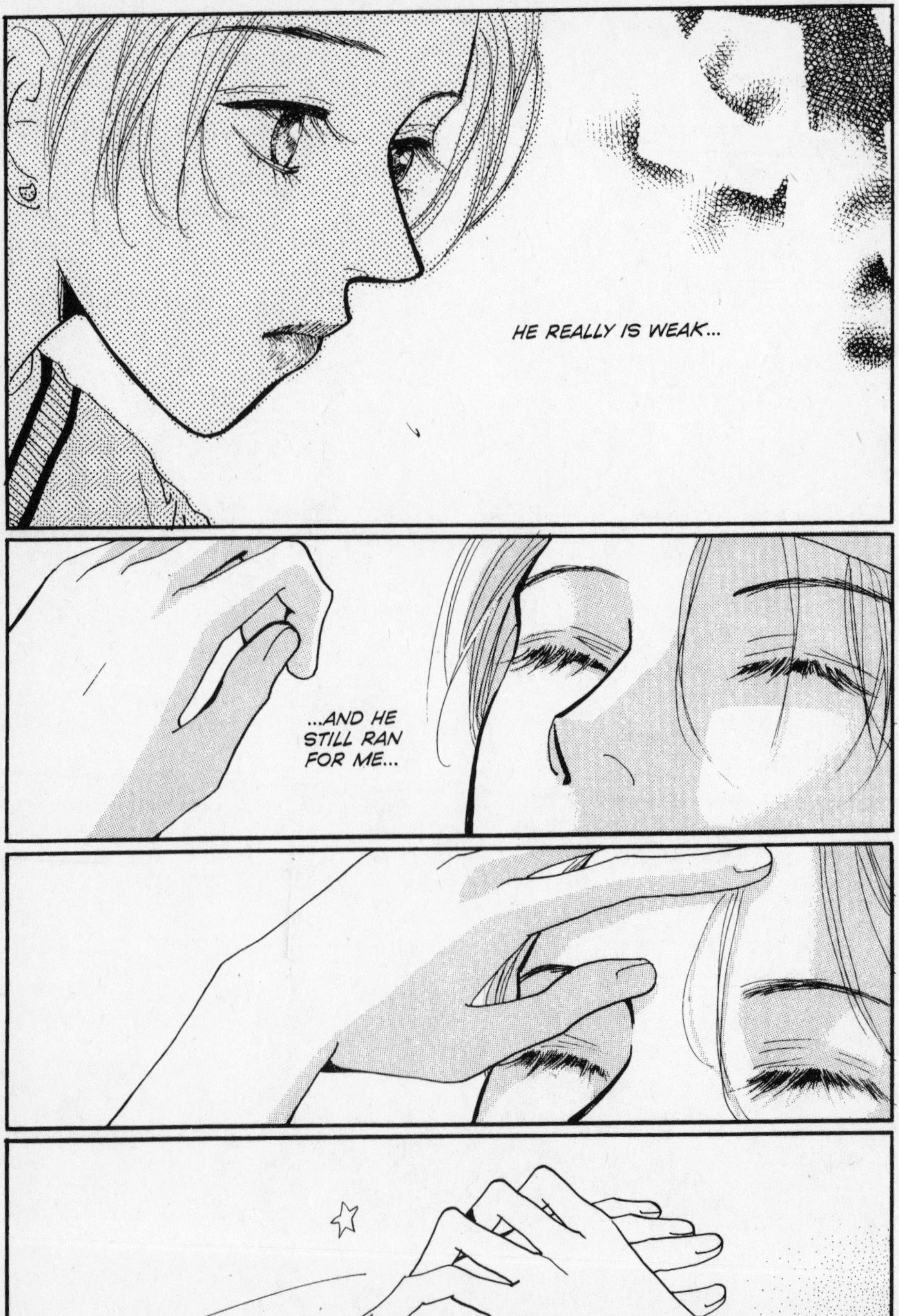
HE REALLY IS WEAK...
...AND HE STILL RAN FOR ME...

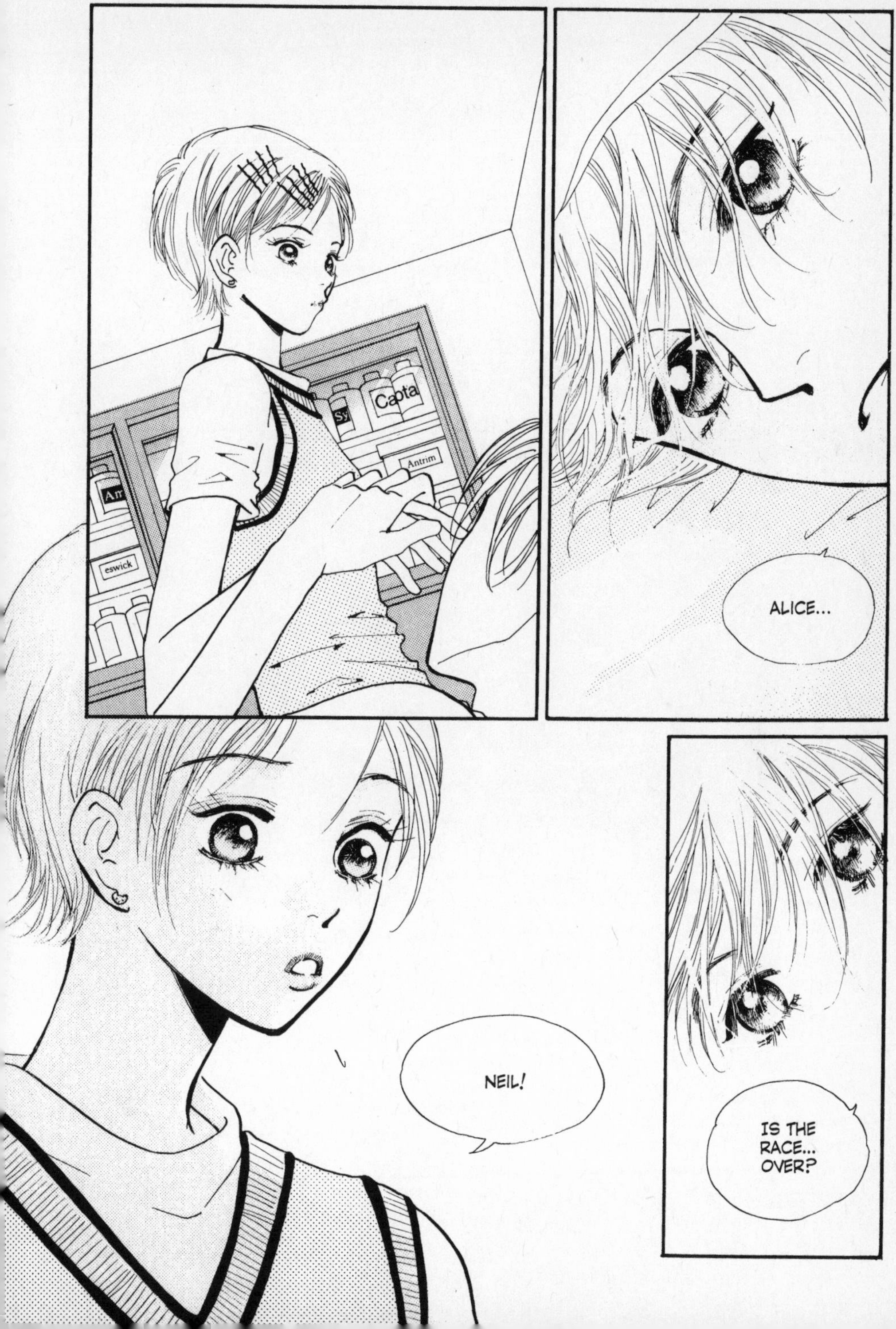
Capta
Antrim
eswick
ALICE...
NEIL!
IS THE RACE... OVER?

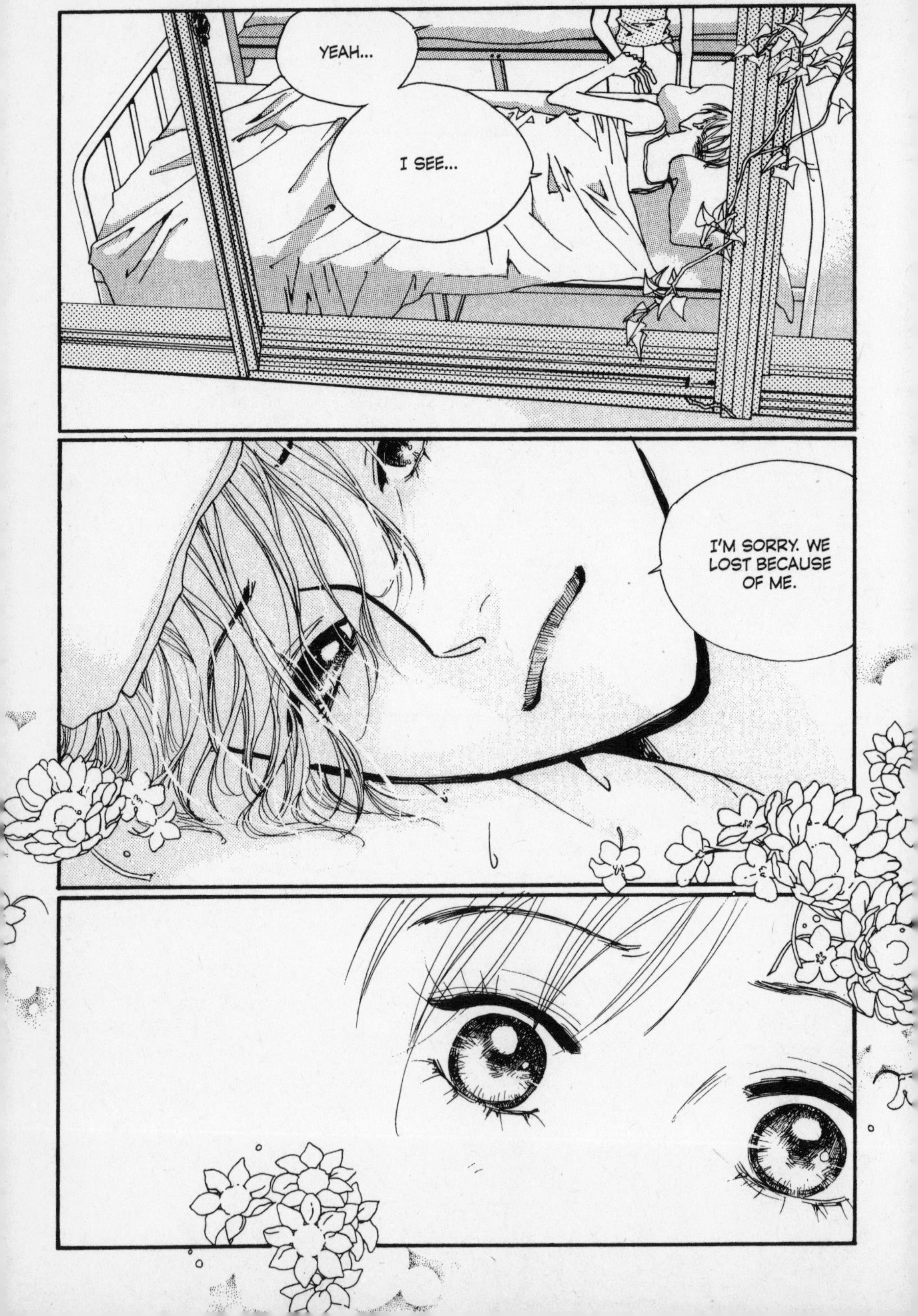
YEAH...
I SEE...
I'M SORRY. WE LOST BECAUSE OF ME.

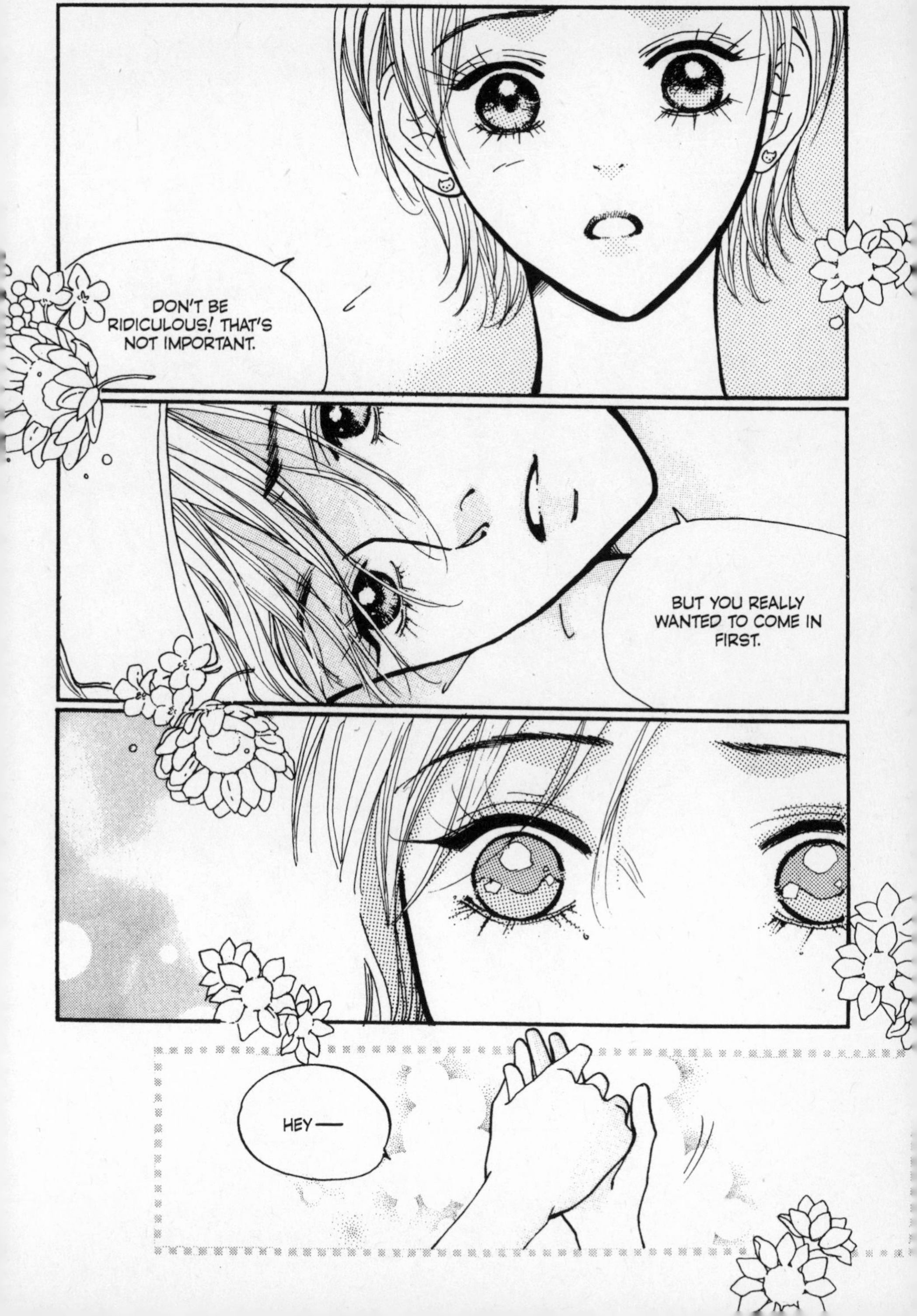
DON'T BE RIDICULOUS! THAT'S NOT IMPORTANT.
BUT YOU REALLY WANTED TO COME IN FIRST.
HEY—

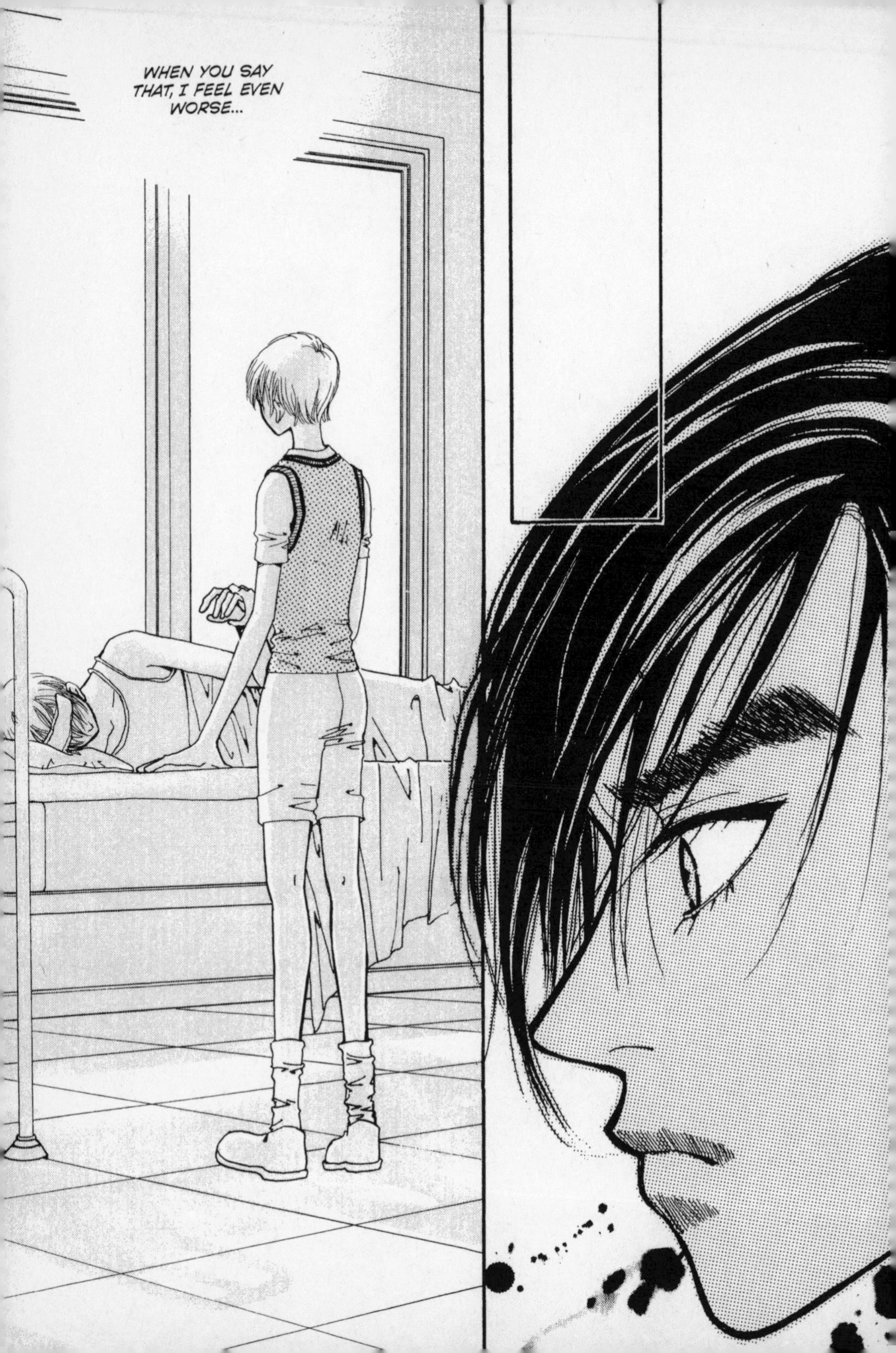
WHEN YOU SAY
THAT, I FEEL EVEN
WORSE...

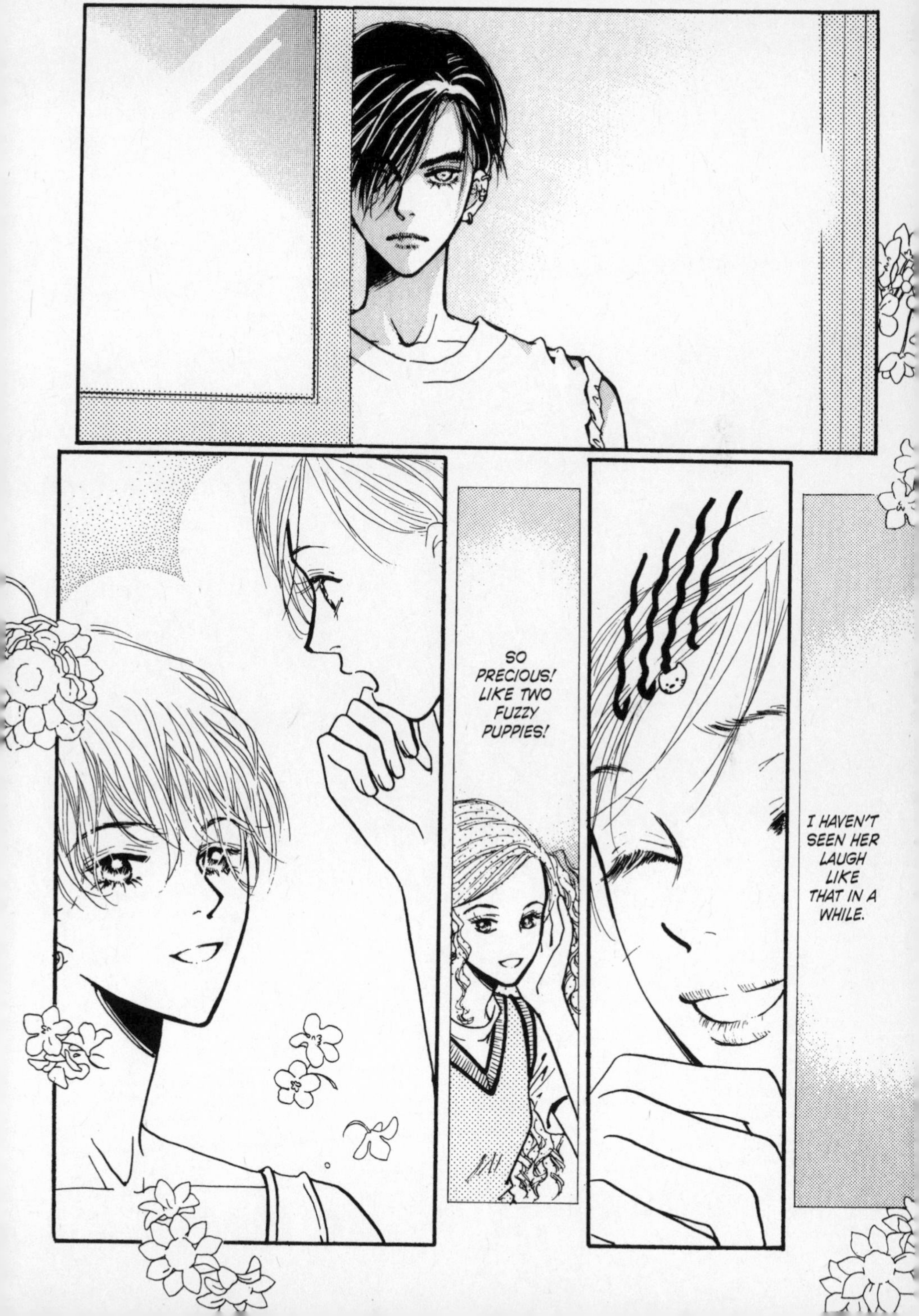
SO PRECIOUS! LIKE TWO FUZZY PUPPIES!
I HAVEN'T SEEN HER LAUGH LIKE THAT IN A WHILE.

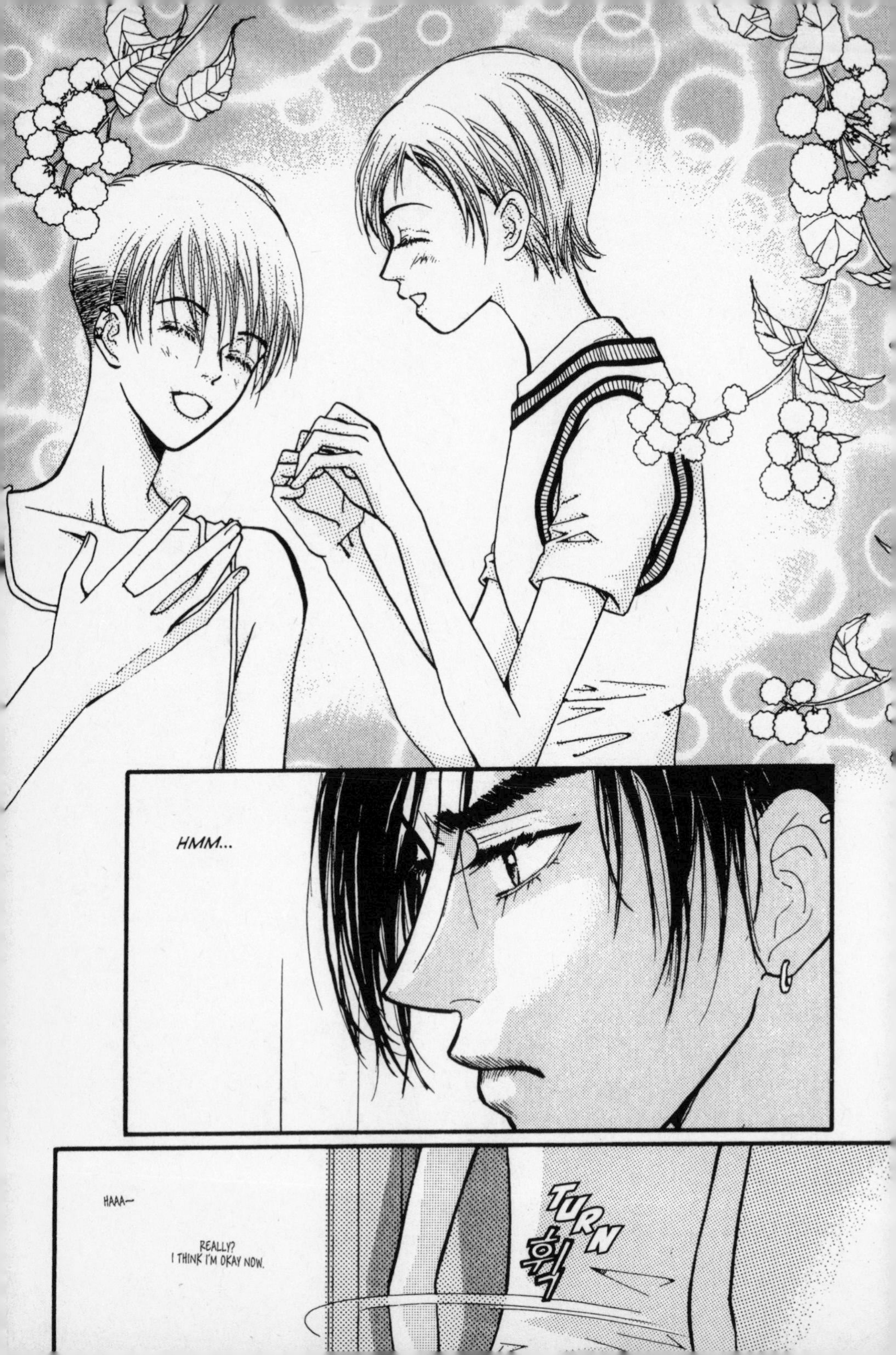
HMM...
HAAA—
REALLY?
I THINK I'M OKAY NOW.
TURN
휙

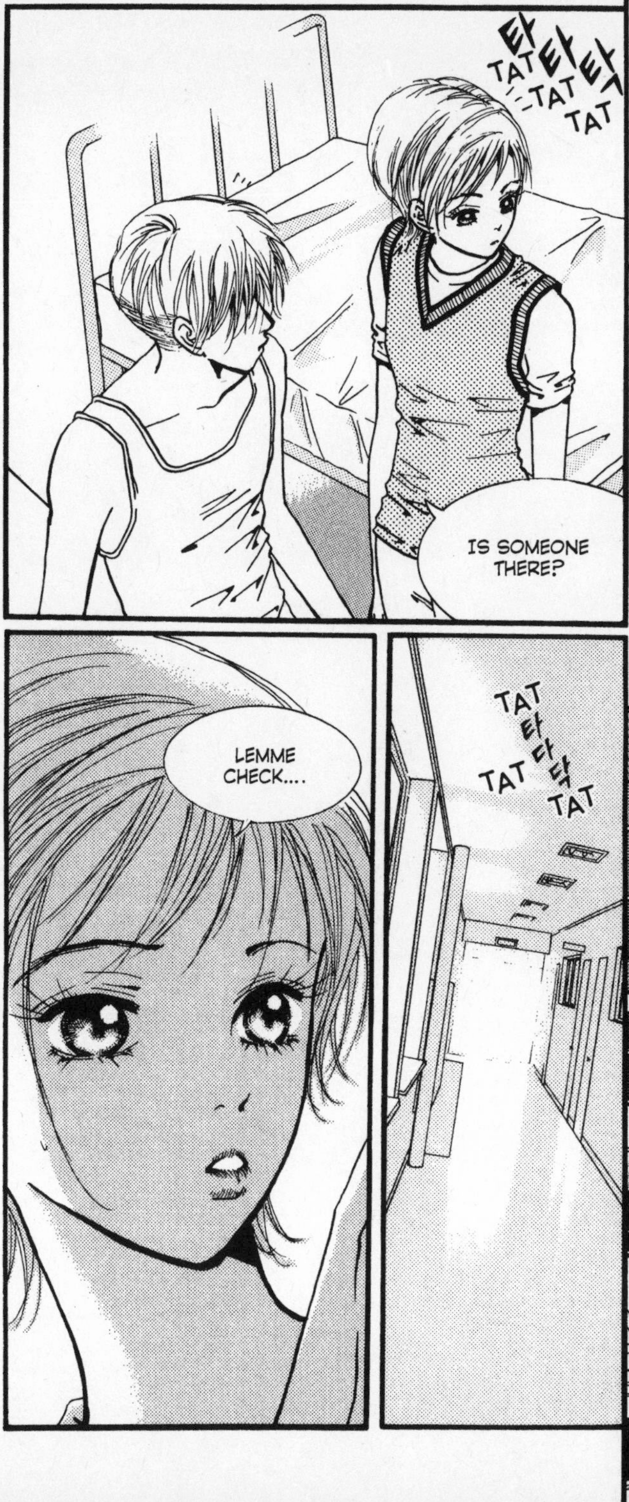
TAT TAT TAT
IS SOMEONE THERE?
LEMME CHECK....
TAT TAT TAT
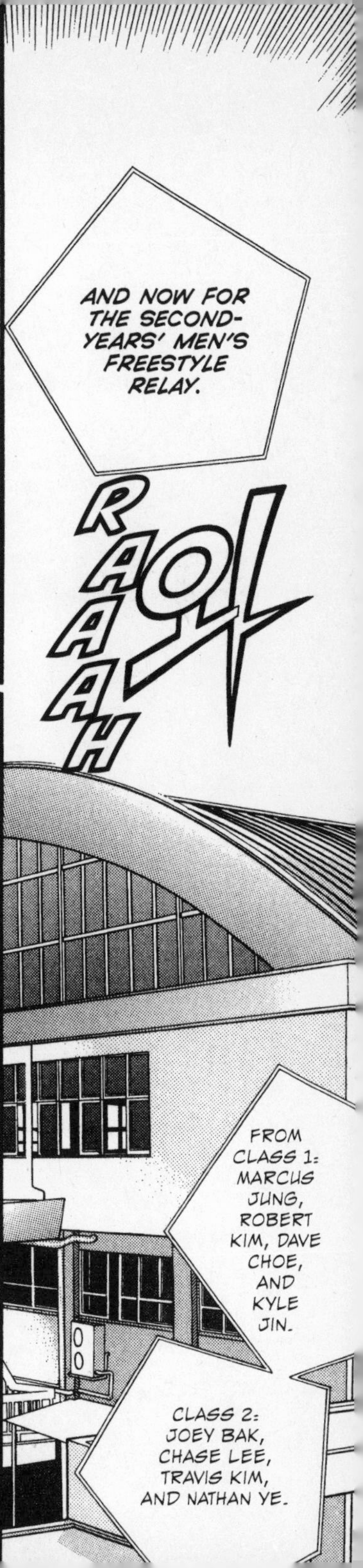
AND NOW FOR THE SECOND-YEARS' MEN'S FREESTYLE RELAY.
RAAAAH
FROM CLASS 1: MARCUS JUNG, ROBERT KIM, DAVE CHOE, AND KYLE JIN.
CLASS 2: JOEY BAK, CHASE LEE, TRAVIS KIM, AND NATHAN YE.

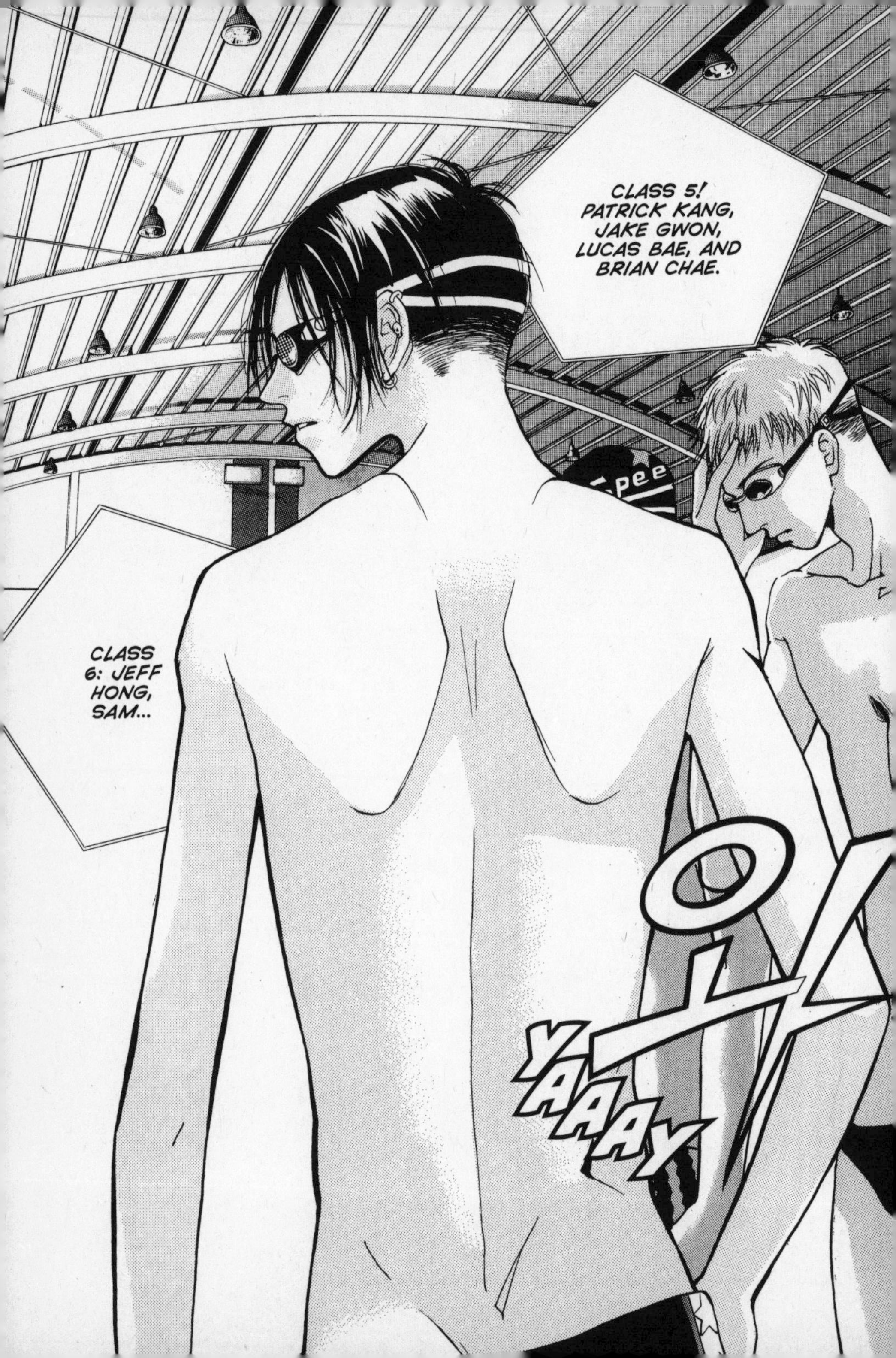

CLASS 6: JEFF HONG, SAM...
CLASS 5! PATRICK KANG, JAKE GWON, LUCAS BAE, AND BRIAN CHAE.
YAAAY

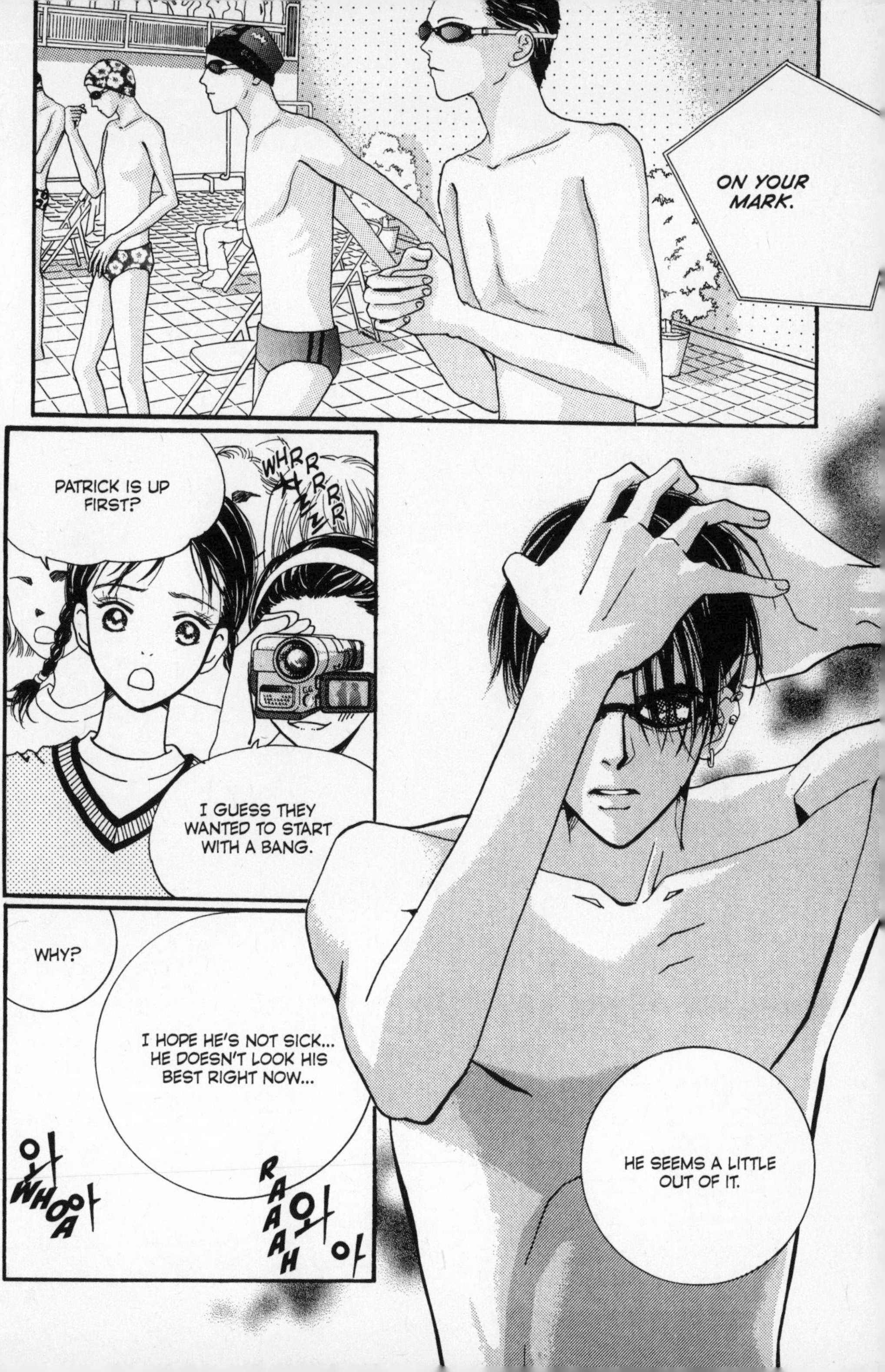

ON YOUR MARK.
PATRICK IS UP FIRST?
WHRRRRR
I GUESS THEY WANTED TO START WITH A BANG.
WHY?
I HOPE HE'S NOT SICK... HE DOESN'T LOOK HIS BEST RIGHT NOW...
WHOA
RAAAH
HE SEEMS A LITTLE OUT OF IT.

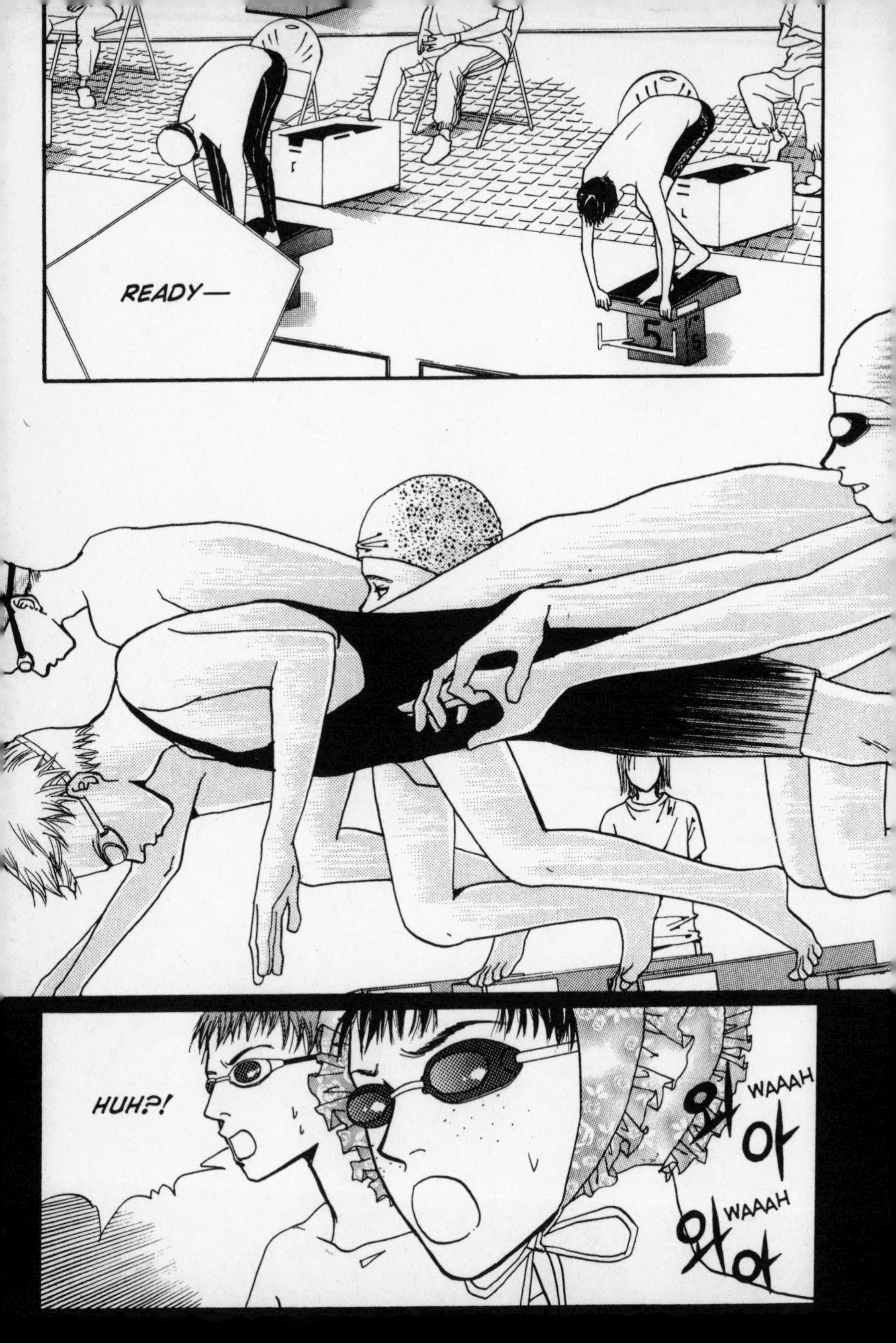
READY—
HUH?!
와아
WAAAH
와아
WAAAH

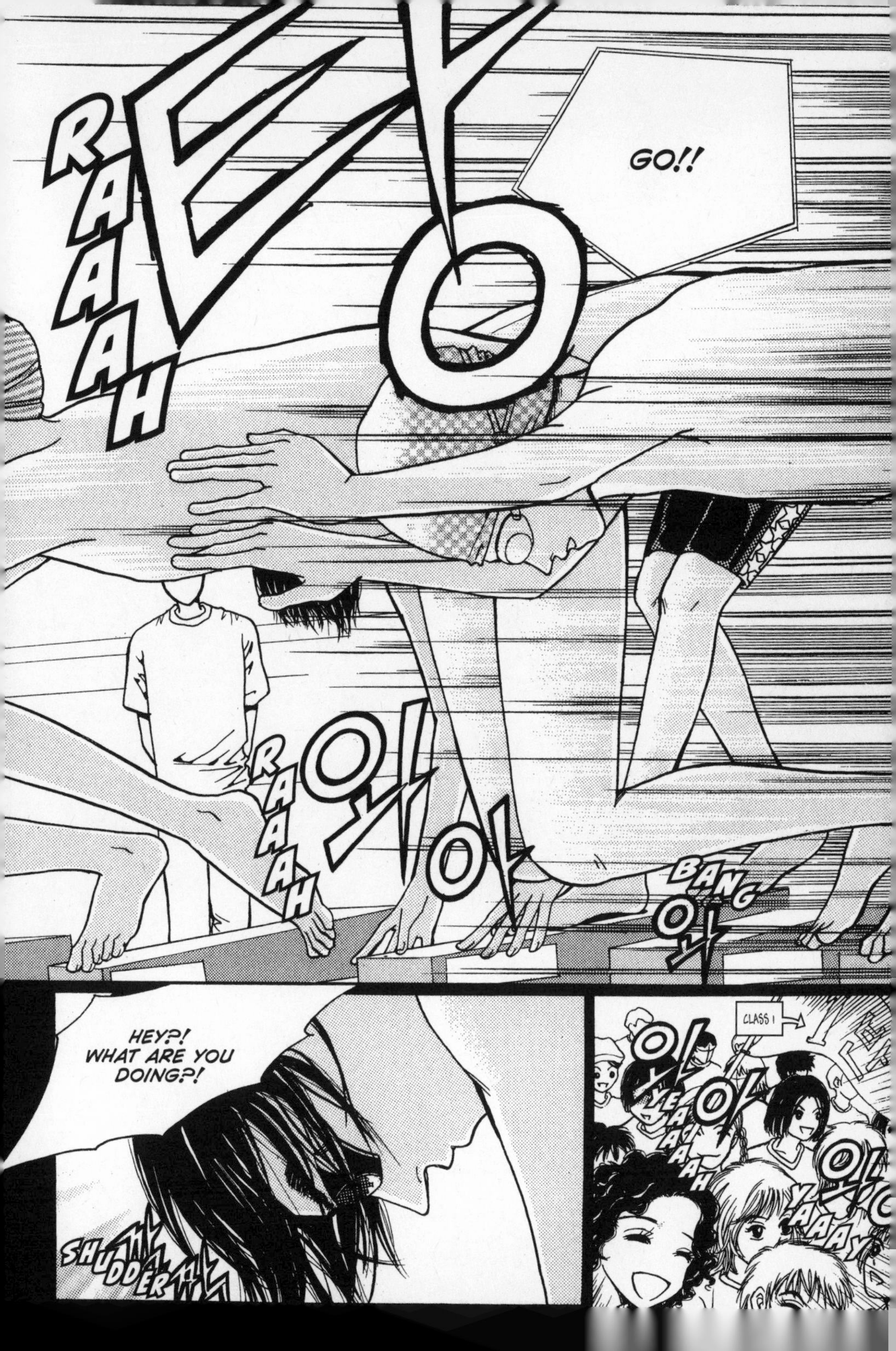
RAAAAH
GO!!
REEYO
RAAAAH
OOYOO
BANG
OOY
HEY?! WHAT ARE YOU DOING?!
SHUDDERRR
CLASS 1
OOYOO
YEAAAAAH
OOYOO
YAAAAY

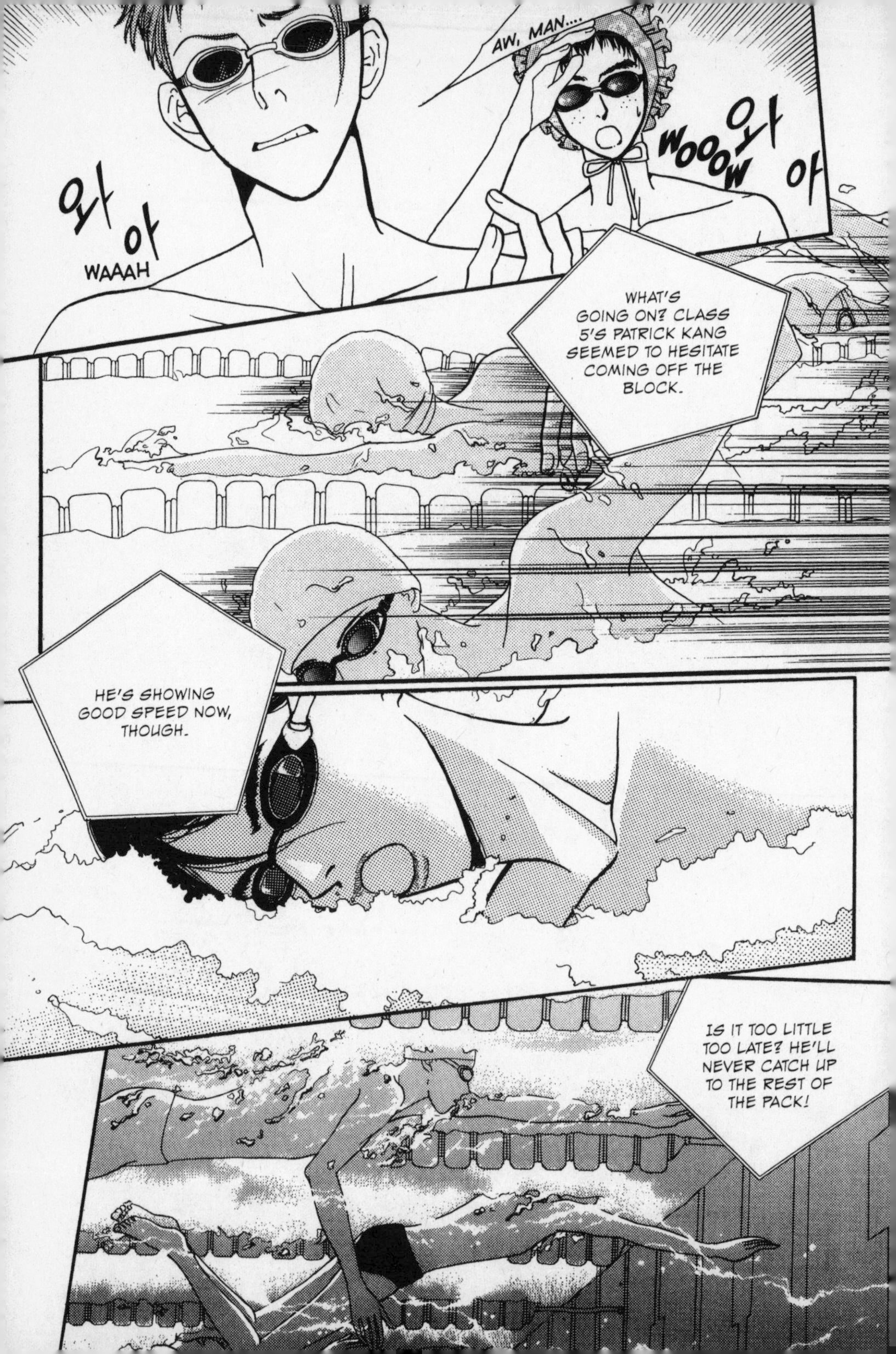

와 아
WAAAH
AW, MAN....
와 아
WOOOW
WHAT'S GOING ON? CLASS 5'S PATRICK KANG SEEMED TO HESITATE COMING OFF THE BLOCK.
HE'S SHOWING GOOD SPEED NOW, THOUGH.
IS IT TOO LITTLE TOO LATE? HE'LL NEVER CATCH UP TO THE REST OF THE PACK!

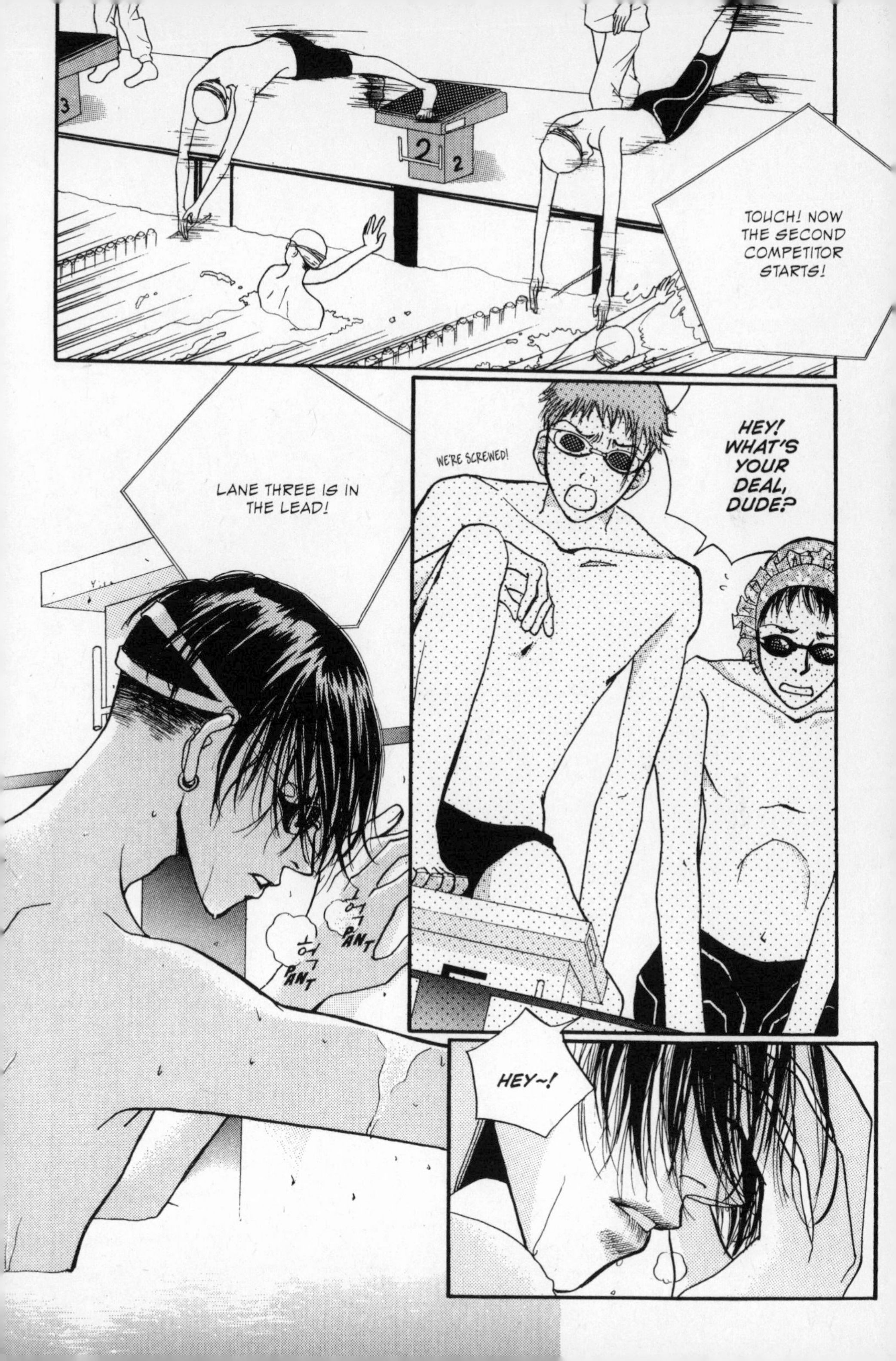
TOUCH! NOW THE SECOND COMPETITOR STARTS!
LANE THREE IS IN THE LEAD!
PANT
PANT
WE'RE SCREWED!
HEY! WHAT'S YOUR DEAL, DUDE?
HEY~!

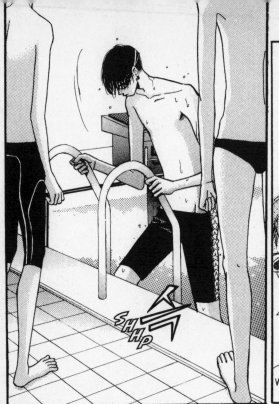

GEEZ, WHAT'S WITH HIM...?

SPOOSH

SPOOSH

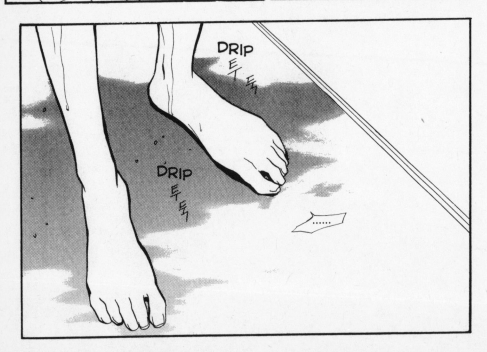

DRIP

DRIP

......

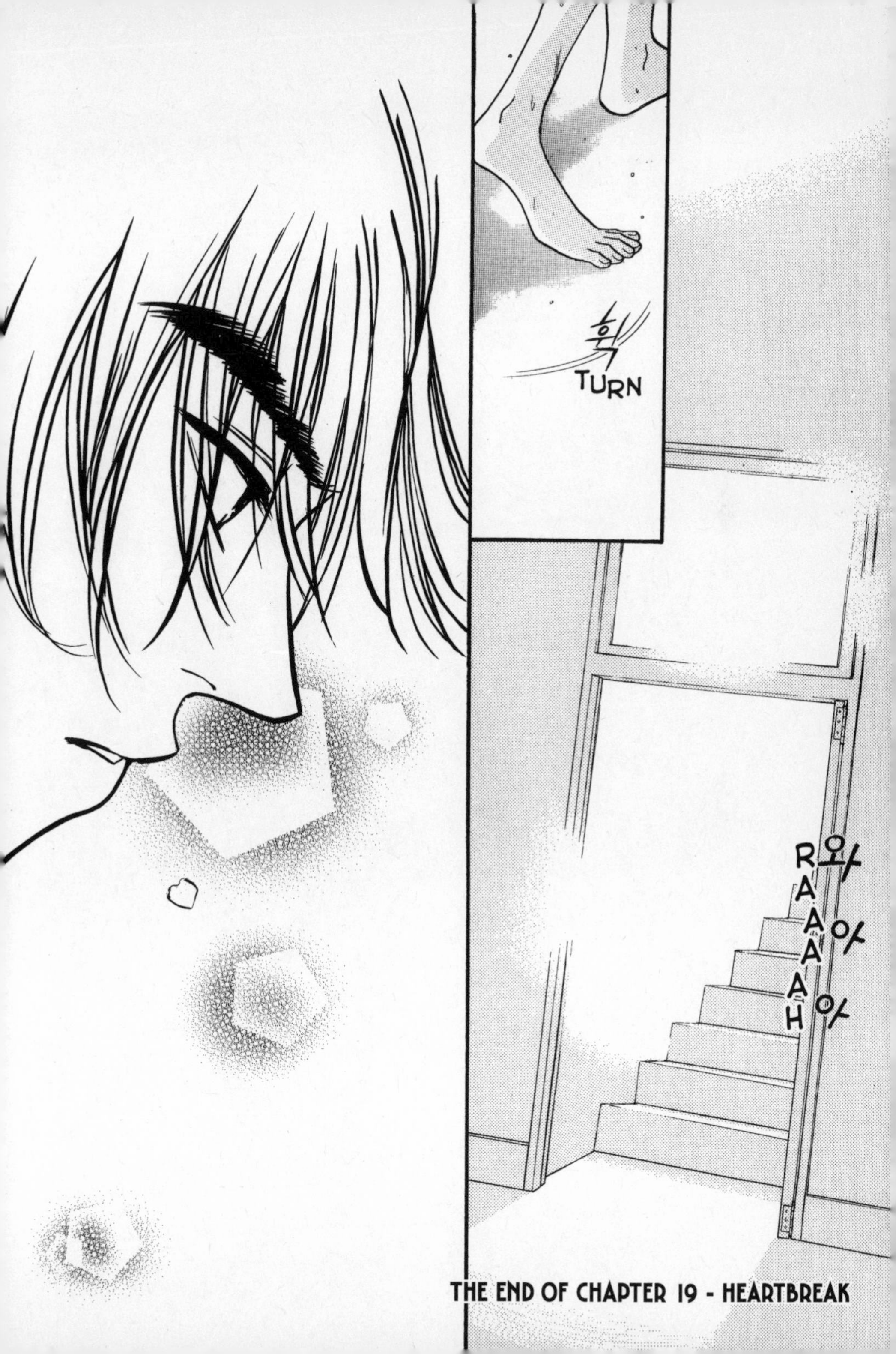
휙
TURN
와아아
RAAAAH
THE END OF CHAPTER 19 - HEARTBREAK

CHAPTER 20 - NIGHT OF THE FESTIVAL

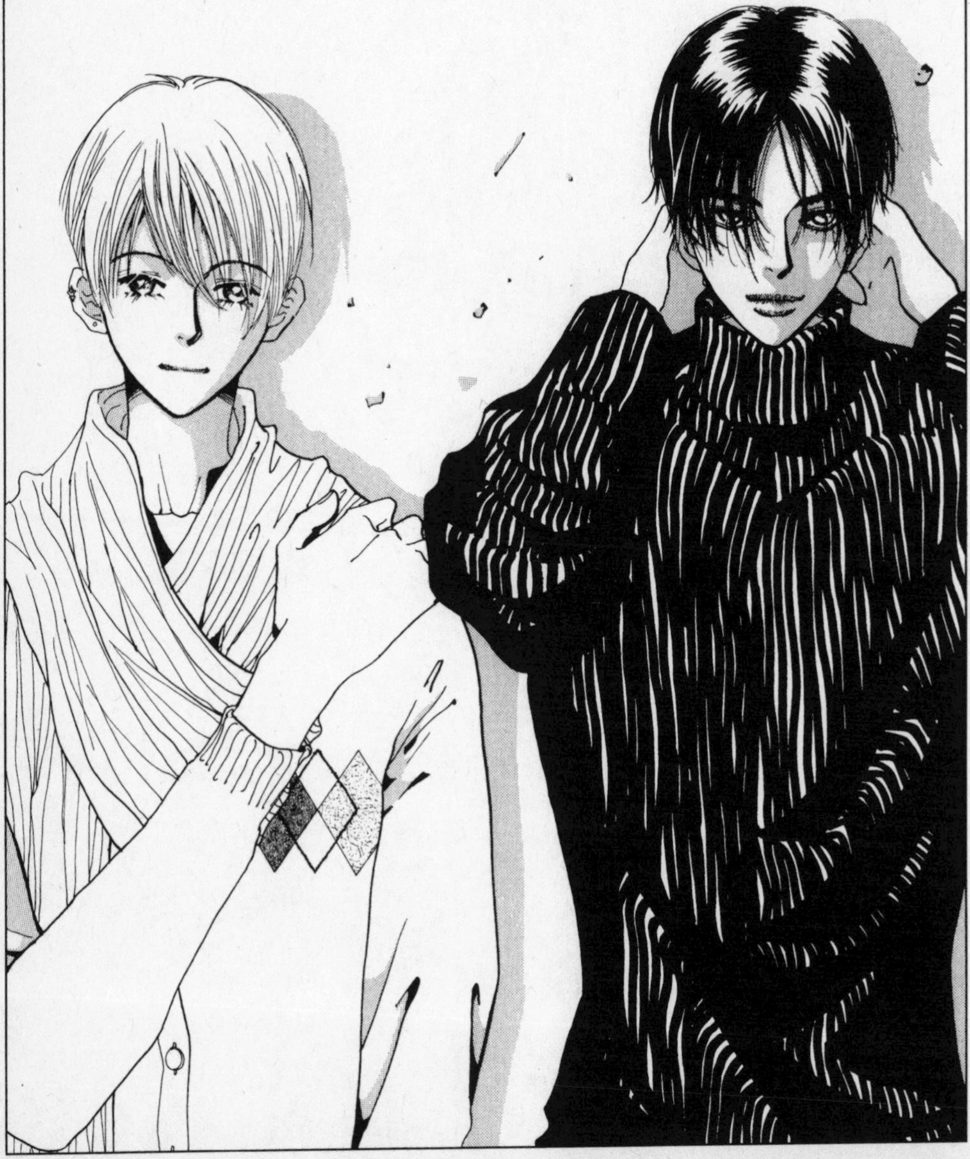

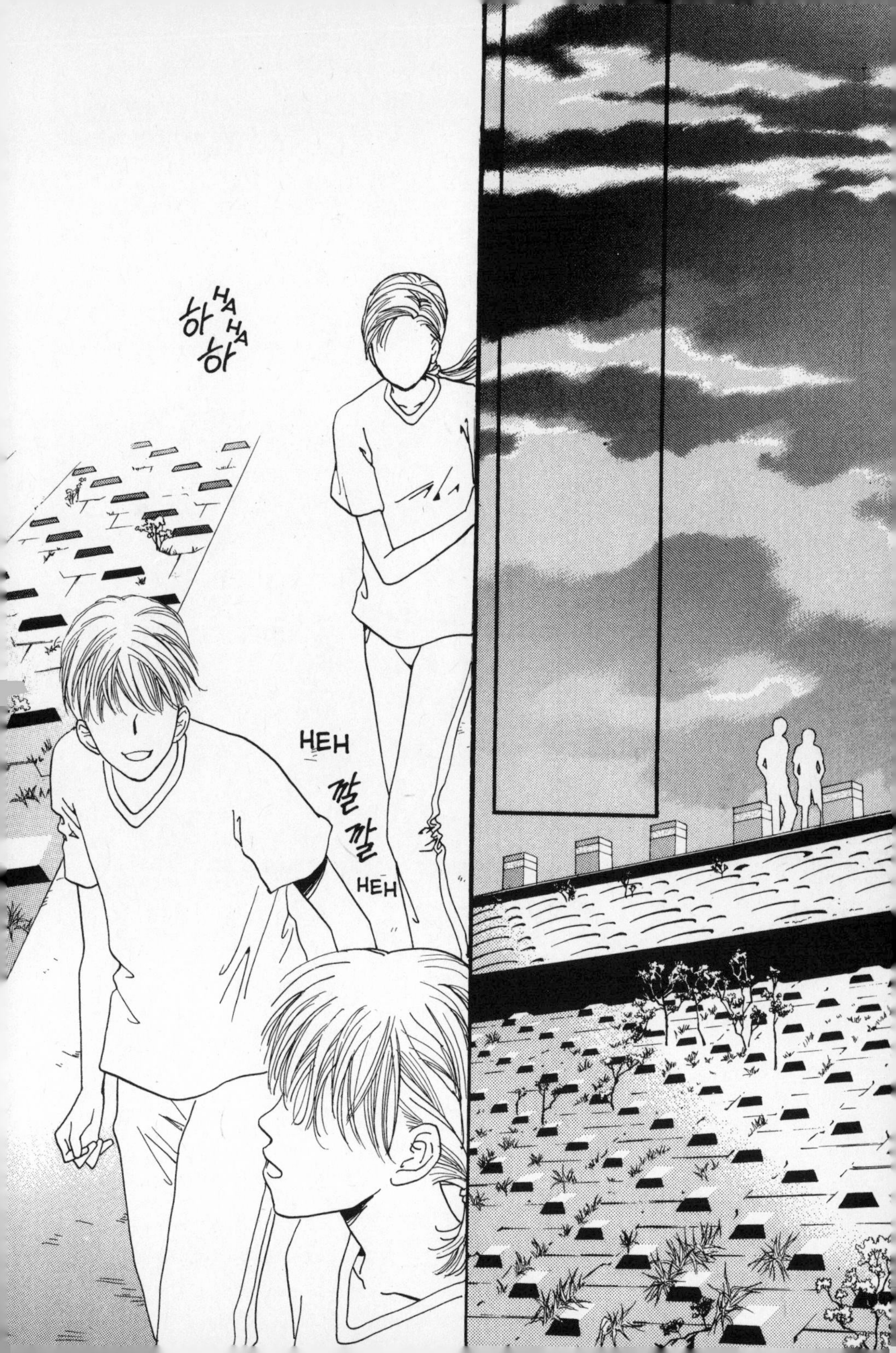
하 HA
하 HA
HEH
깔
깔
HEH

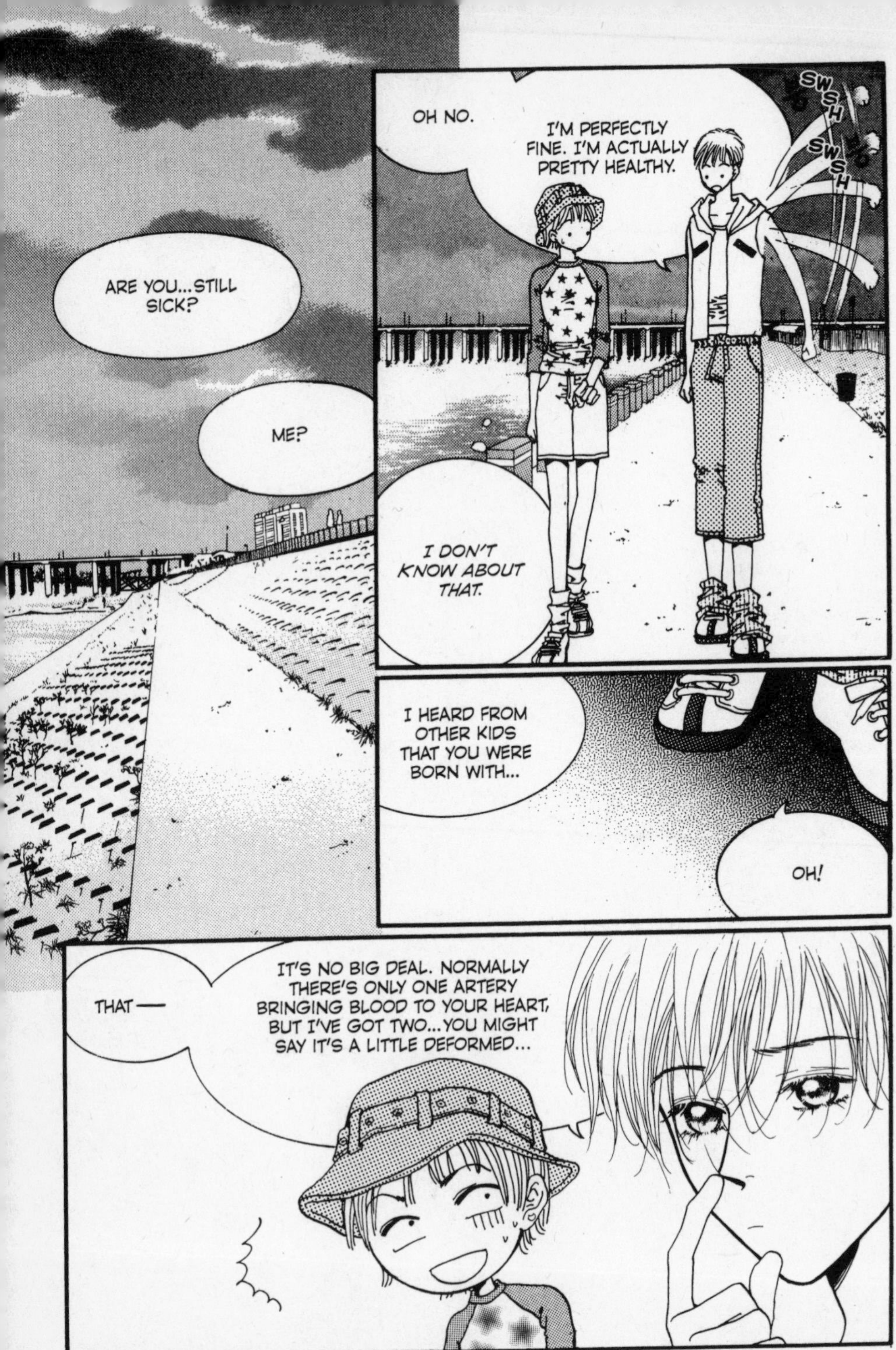
ARE YOU...STILL SICK?
ME?
OH NO.
I'M PERFECTLY FINE. I'M ACTUALLY PRETTY HEALTHY.
SWSH SWSH
I DON'T KNOW ABOUT THAT.
I HEARD FROM OTHER KIDS THAT YOU WERE BORN WITH...
OH!
THAT —
IT'S NO BIG DEAL. NORMALLY THERE'S ONLY ONE ARTERY BRINGING BLOOD TO YOUR HEART, BUT I'VE GOT TWO...YOU MIGHT SAY IT'S A LITTLE DEFORMED...

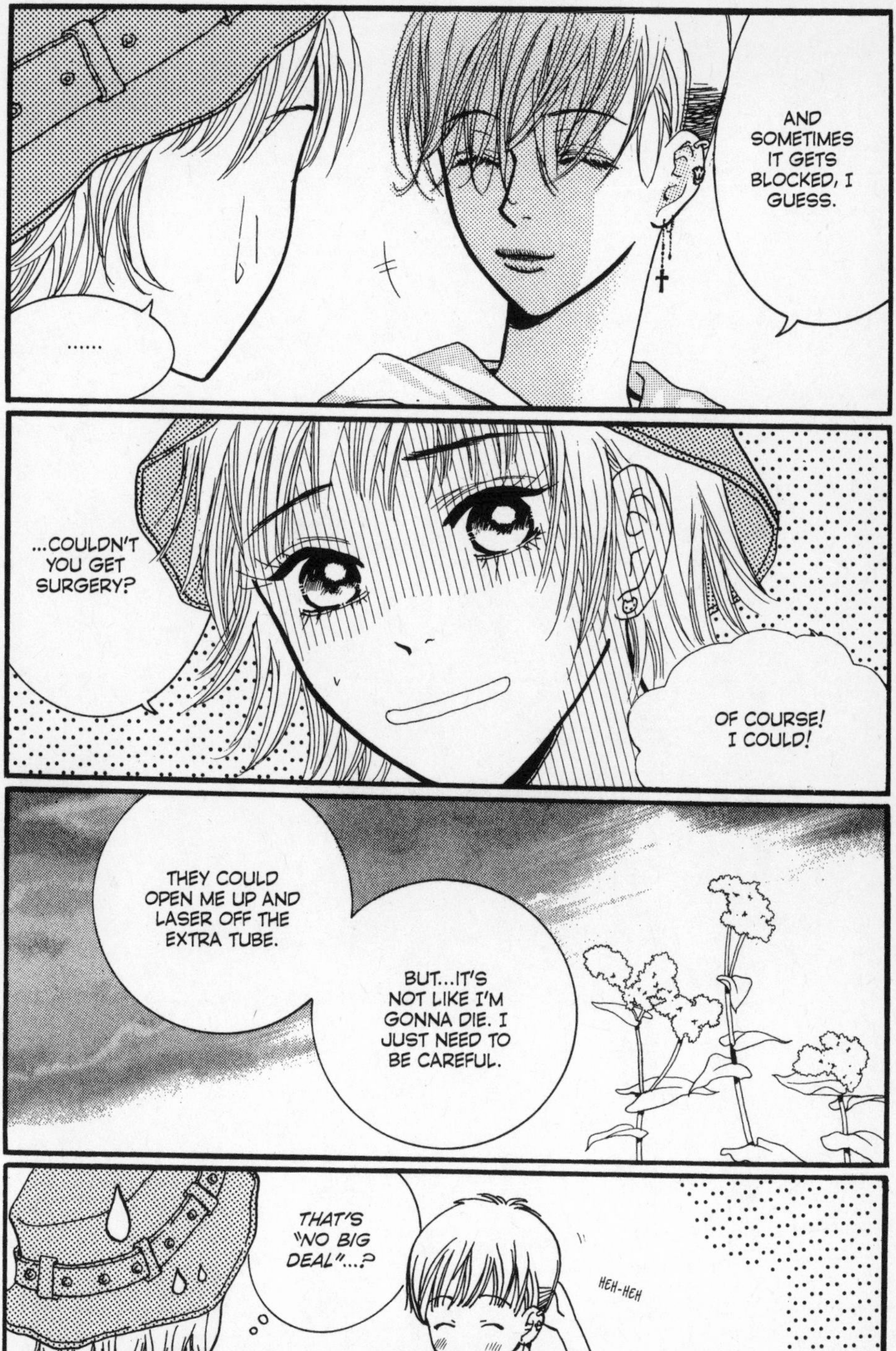
......
AND SOMETIMES IT GETS BLOCKED, I GUESS.
...COULDN'T YOU GET SURGERY?
OF COURSE! I COULD!
THEY COULD OPEN ME UP AND LASER OFF THE EXTRA TUBE.
BUT...IT'S NOT LIKE I'M GONNA DIE. I JUST NEED TO BE CAREFUL.
THAT'S "NO BIG DEAL"...?
HEH-HEH

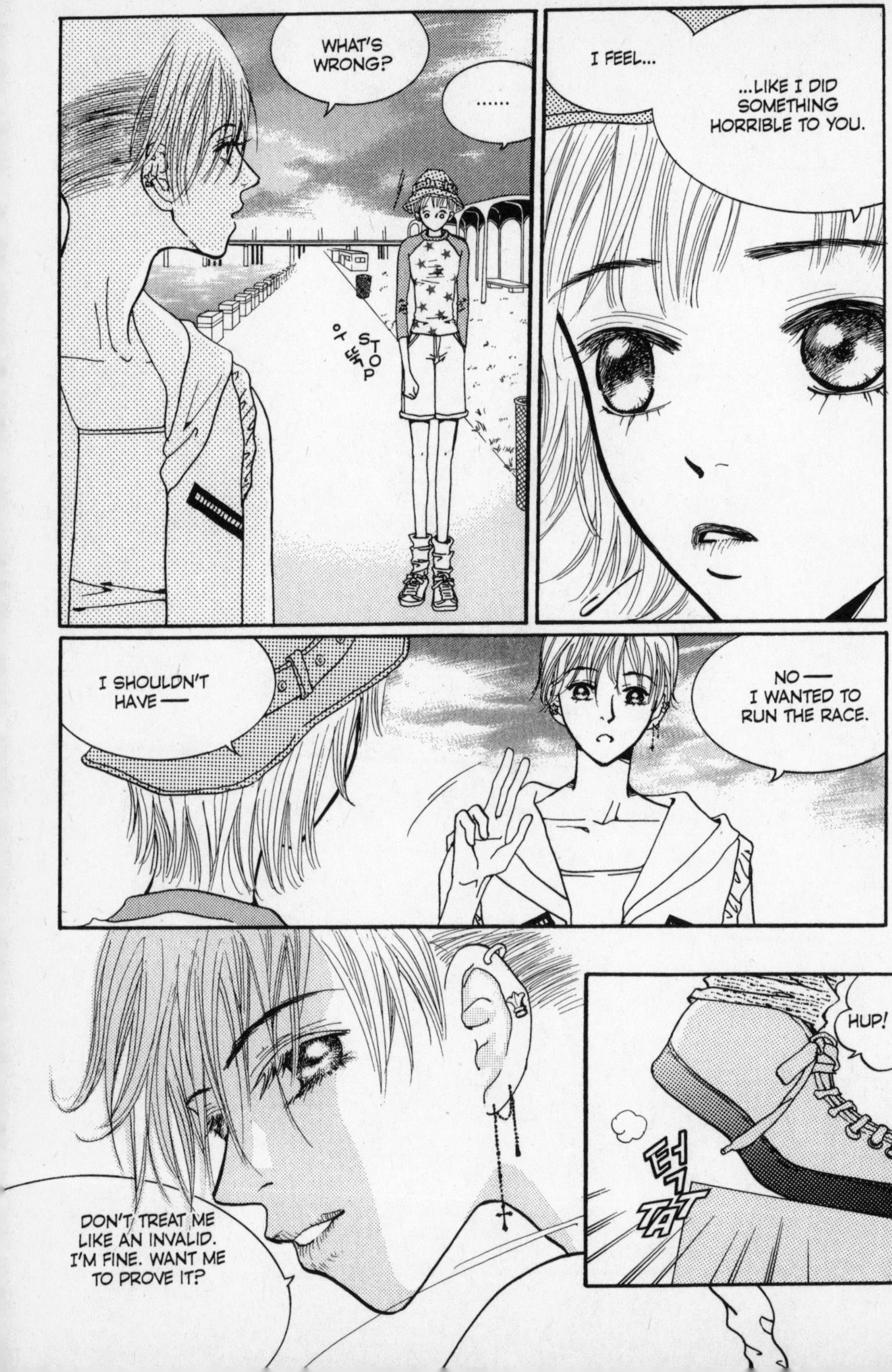
WHAT'S WRONG?
......
STOP
I FEEL...
...LIKE I DID SOMETHING HORRIBLE TO YOU.
I SHOULDN'T HAVE—
NO— I WANTED TO RUN THE RACE.
DON'T TREAT ME LIKE AN INVALID. I'M FINE. WANT ME TO PROVE IT?
HUP!
TAT

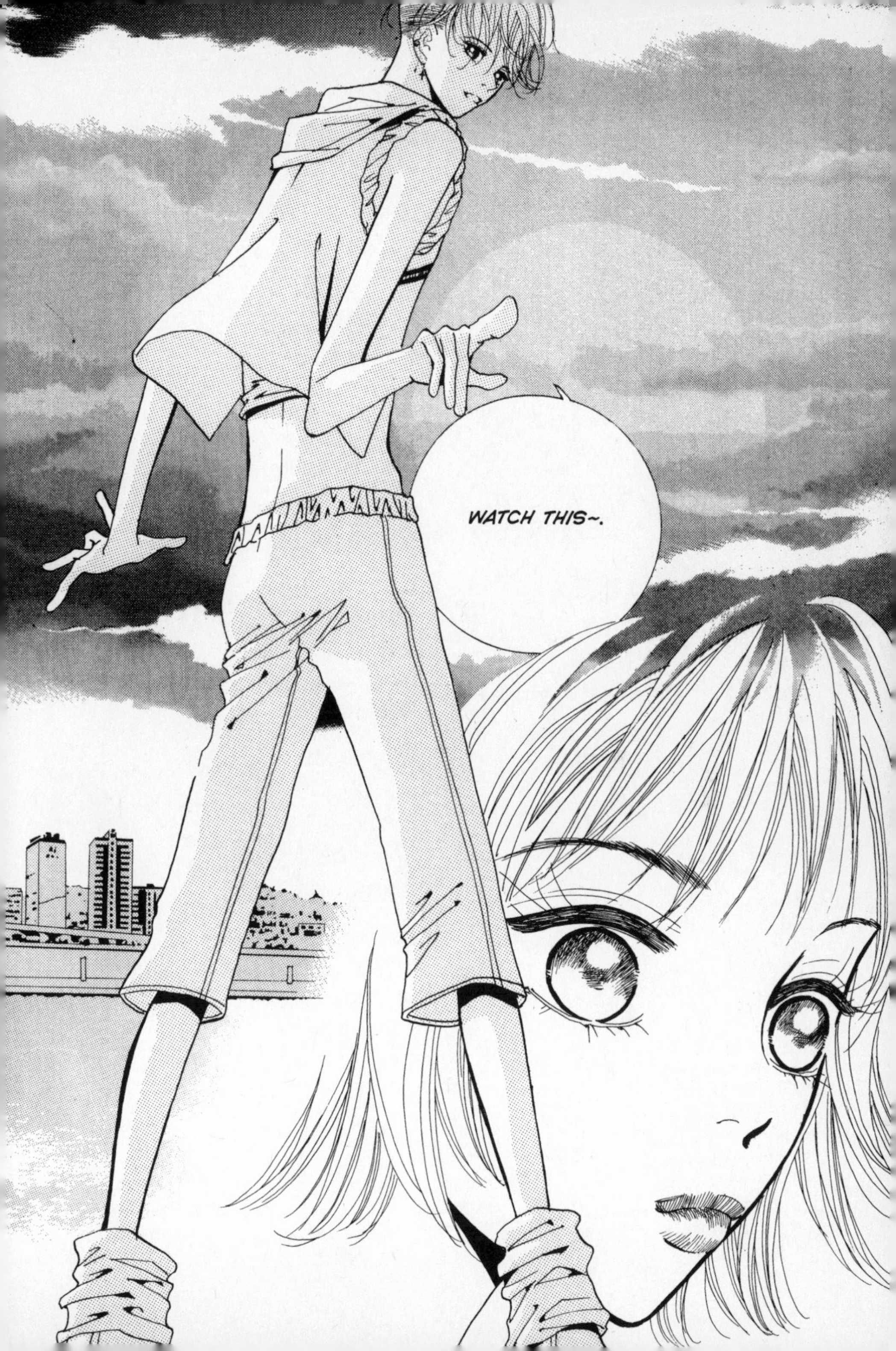
WATCH THIS~.

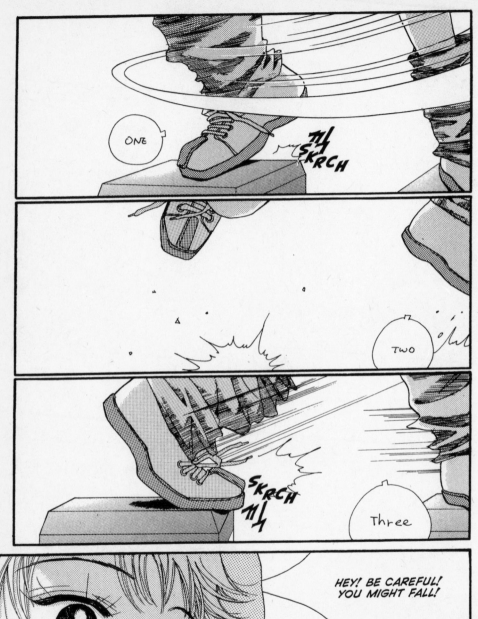

ONE

SKRCH

TWO

SKRCH

Three

HEY! BE CAREFUL!
YOU MIGHT FALL!

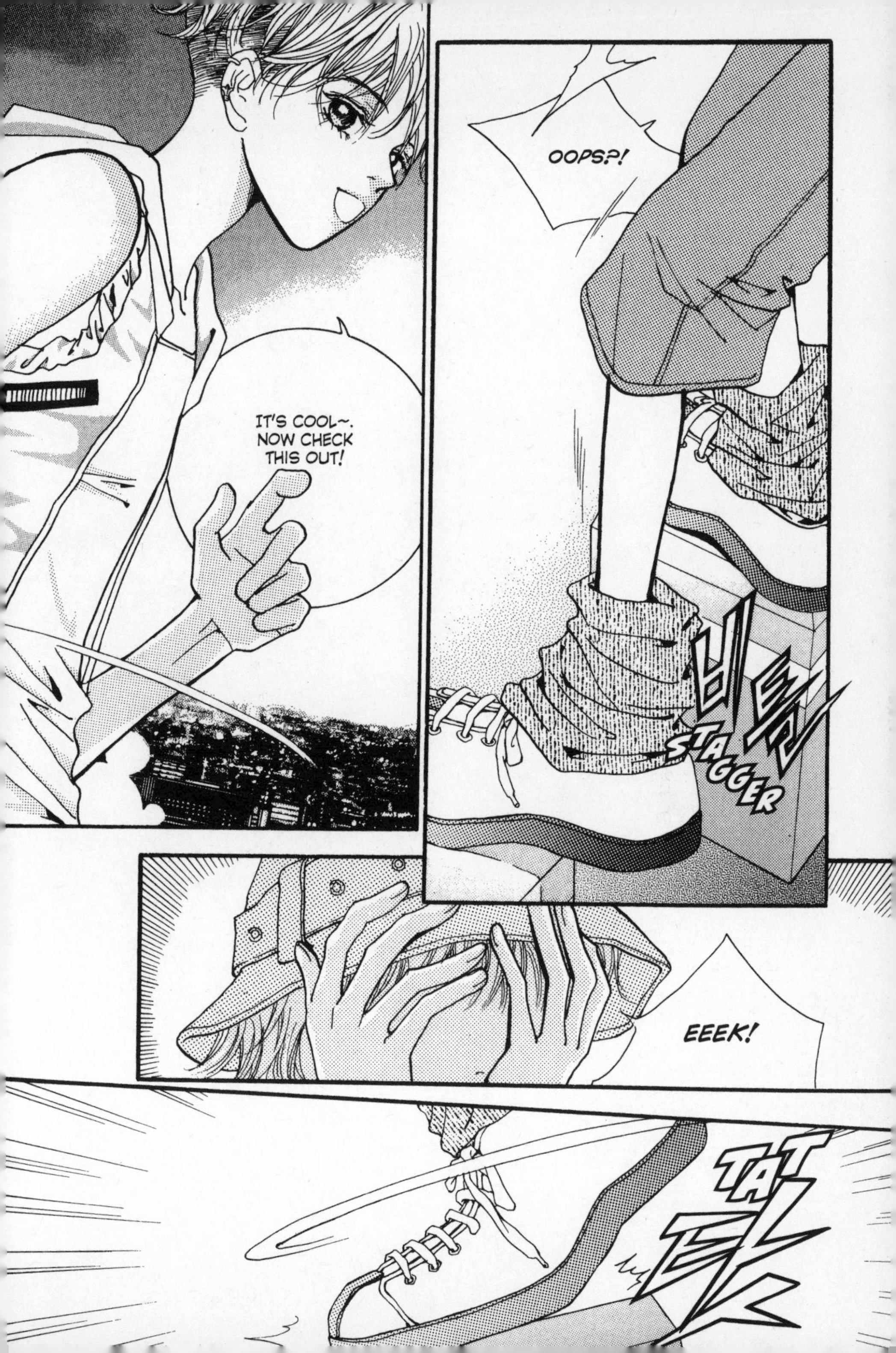
IT'S COOL~.
NOW CHECK
THIS OUT!
OOPS?!
STAGGER
EEEK!
TAT

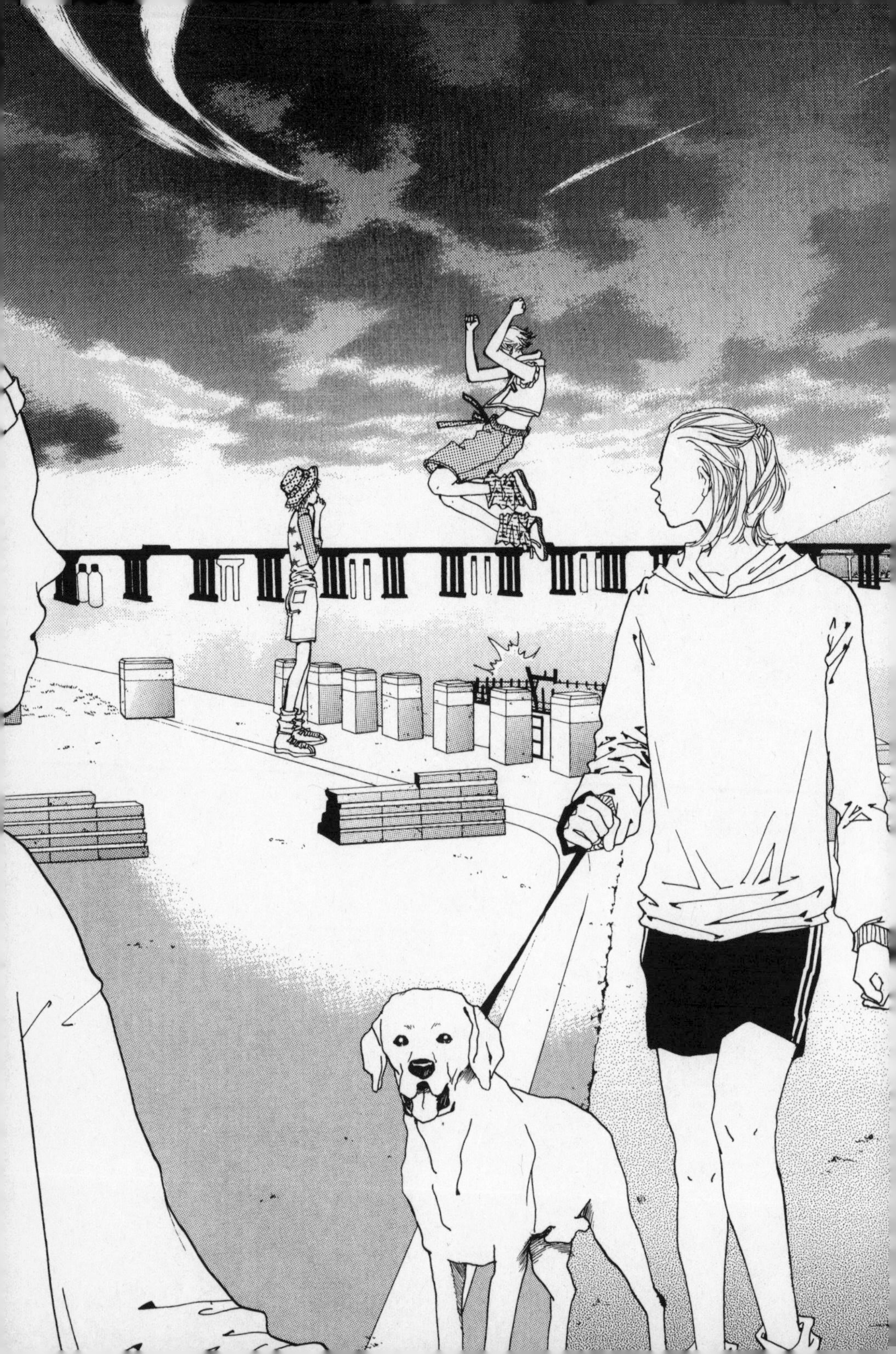

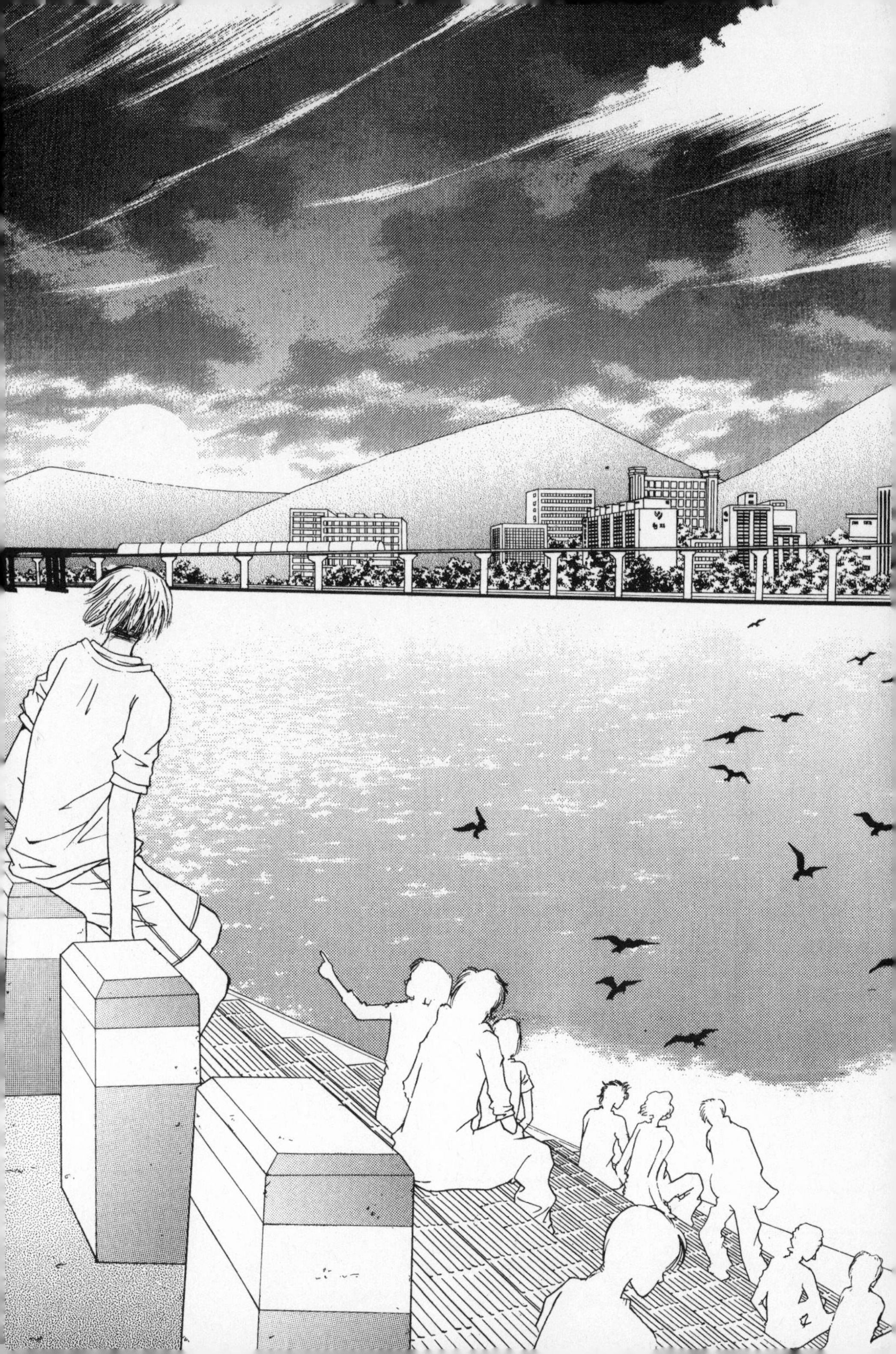

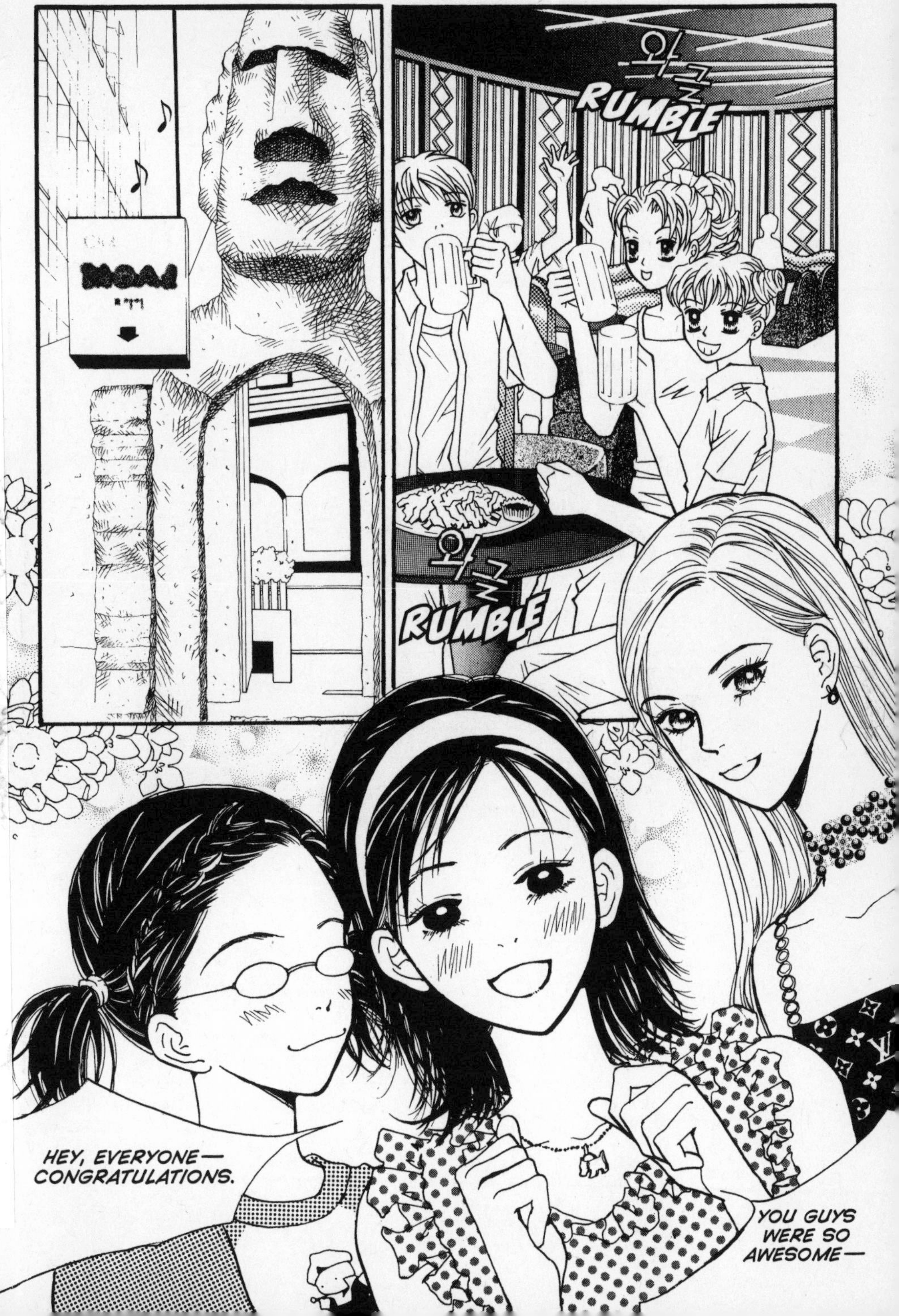
와글
RUMBLE
와글
RUMBLE
HEY, EVERYONE—
CONGRATULATIONS.
YOU GUYS
WERE SO
AWESOME—

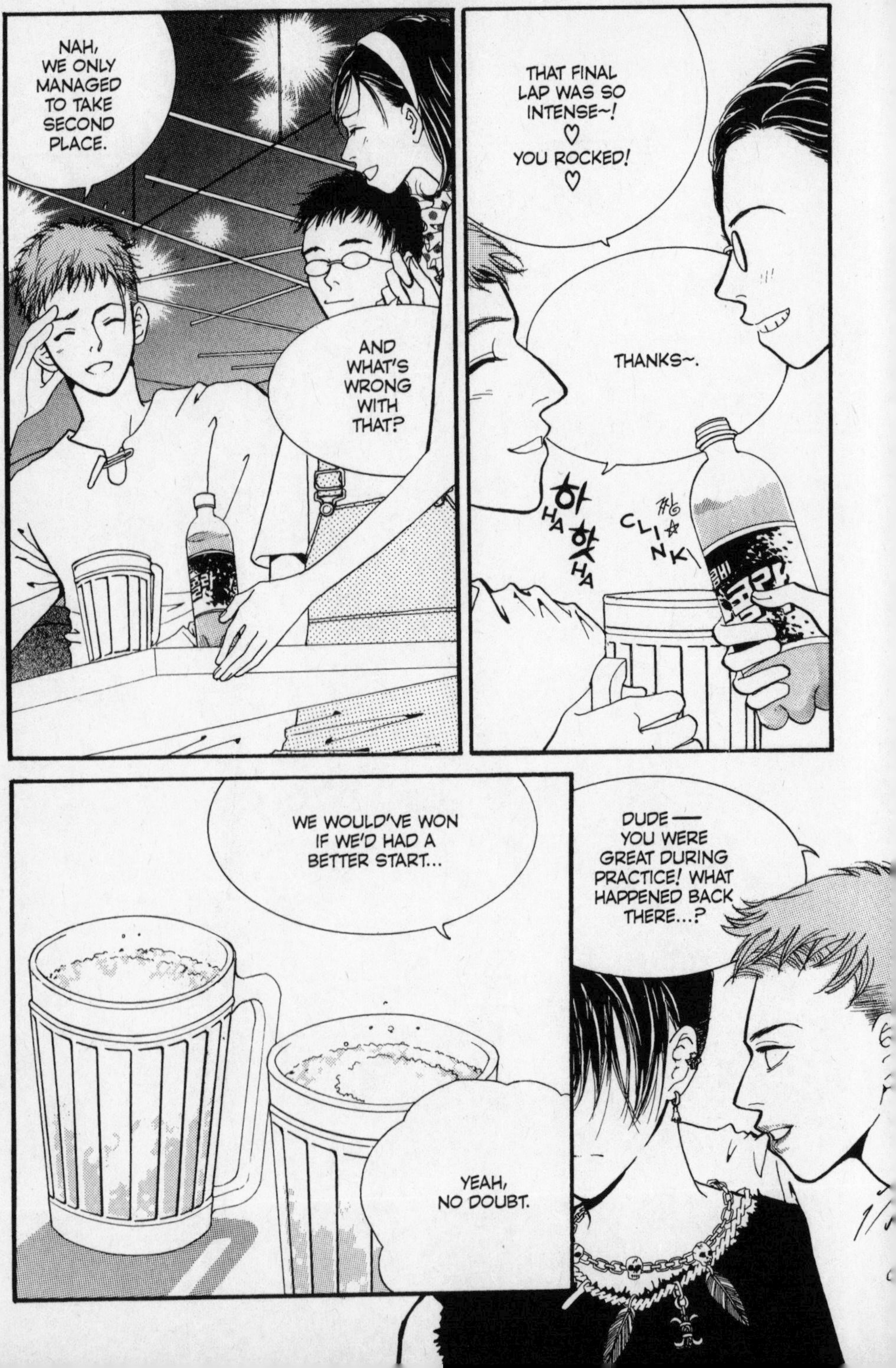
NAH, WE ONLY MANAGED TO TAKE SECOND PLACE.
AND WHAT'S WRONG WITH THAT?
THAT FINAL LAP WAS SO INTENSE~! ♡ YOU ROCKED! ♡
THANKS~.
하 HA 핫 HA
CLINK
WE WOULD'VE WON IF WE'D HAD A BETTER START...
DUDE— YOU WERE GREAT DURING PRACTICE! WHAT HAPPENED BACK THERE...?
YEAH, NO DOUBT.

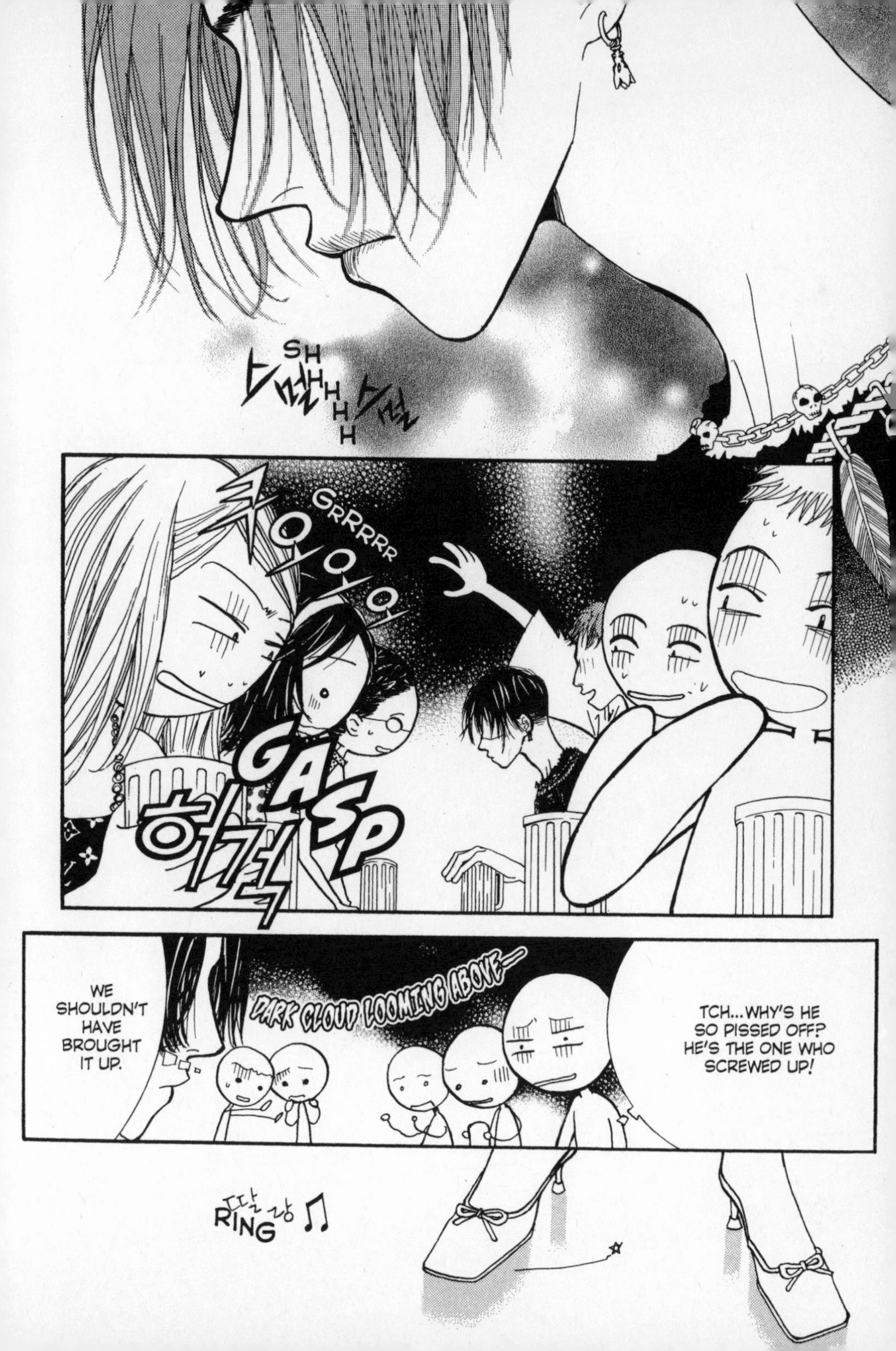
SHHHHHH
GRRRRR
GASP
WE SHOULDN'T HAVE BROUGHT IT UP.
DARK CLOUD LOOMING ABOVE—
TCH...WHY'S HE SO PISSED OFF? HE'S THE ONE WHO SCREWED UP!
RING

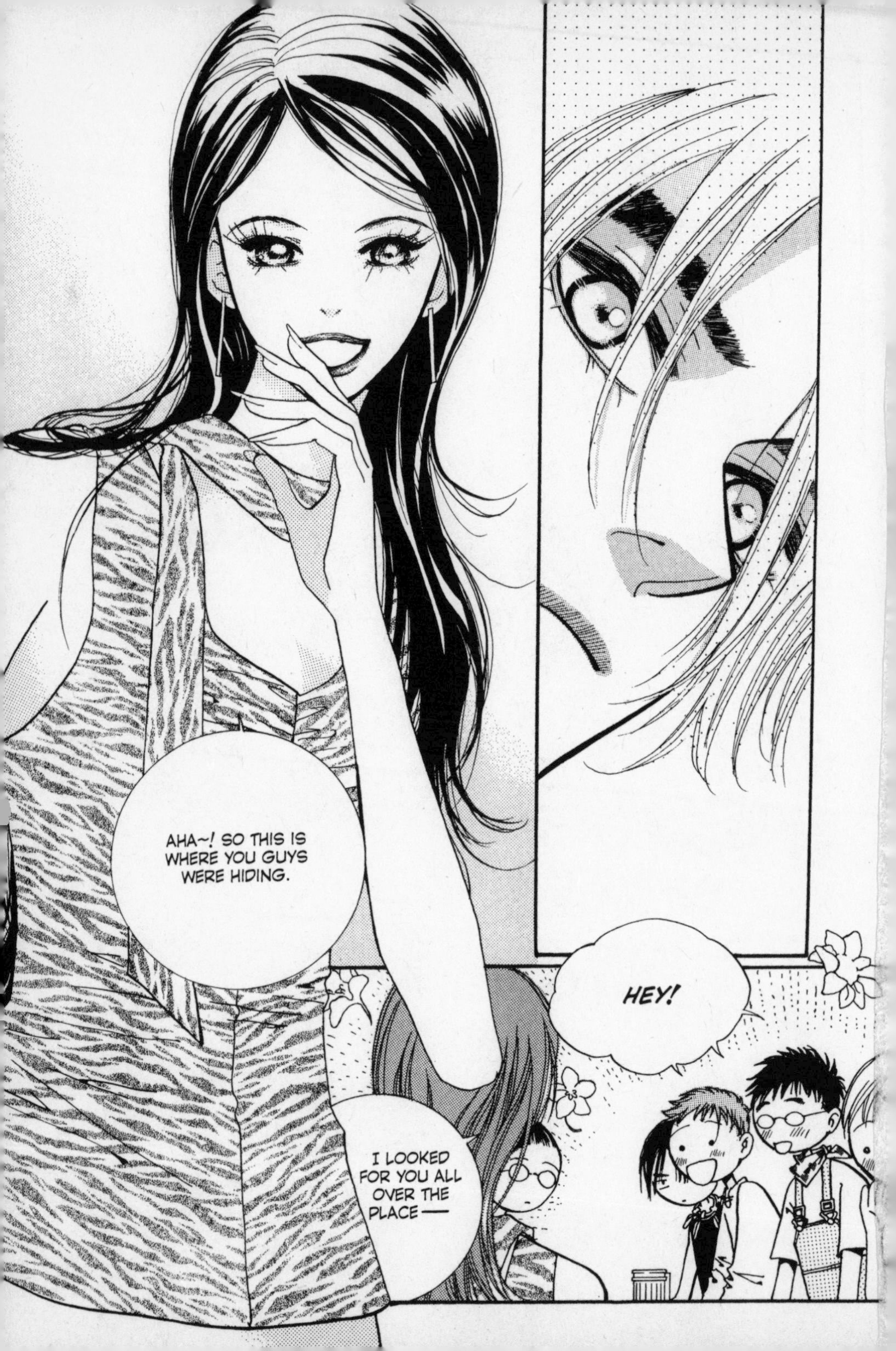
AHA~! SO THIS IS WHERE YOU GUYS WERE HIDING.
HEY!
I LOOKED FOR YOU ALL OVER THE PLACE—

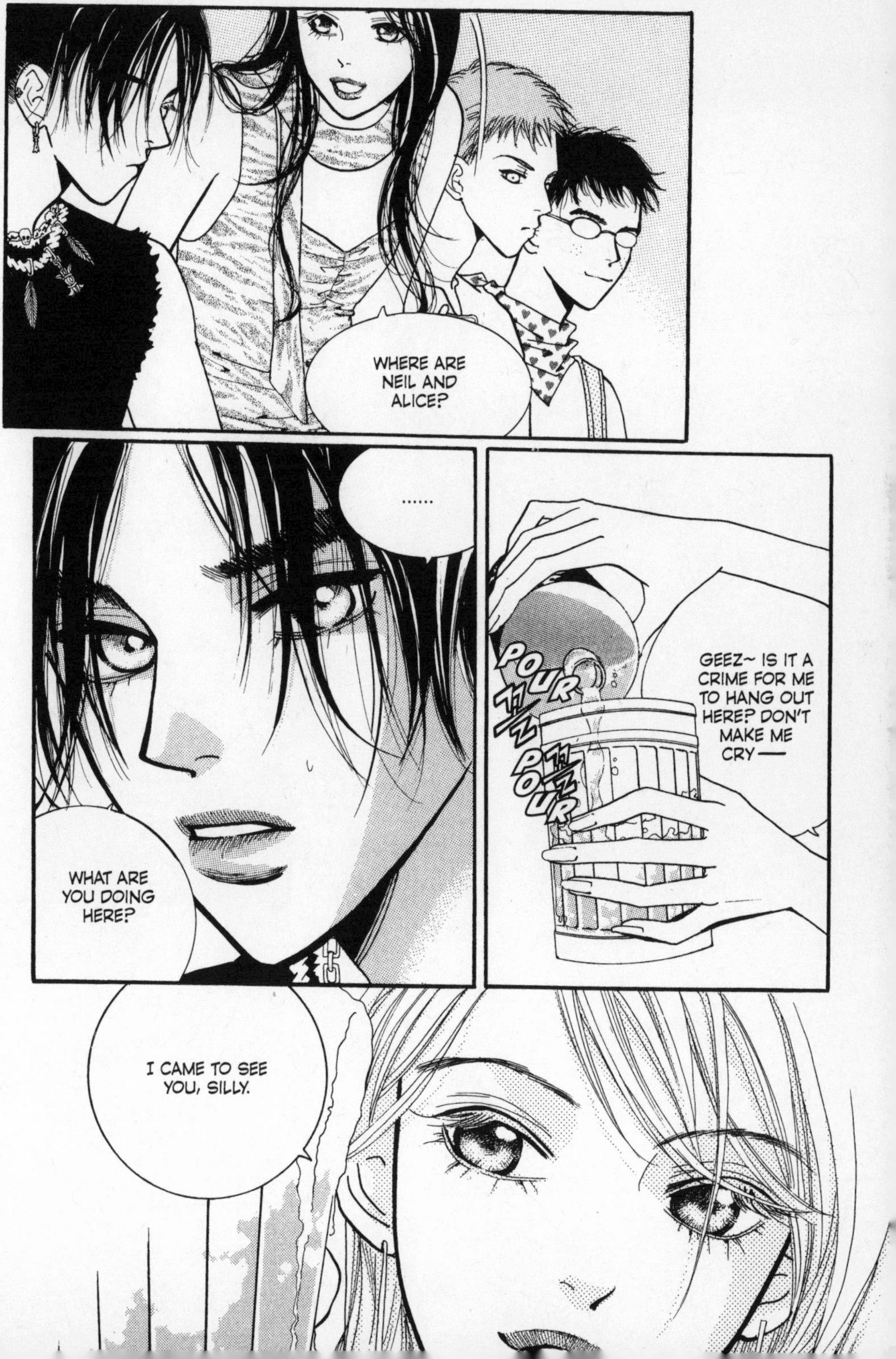
WHERE ARE NEIL AND ALICE?
......
WHAT ARE YOU DOING HERE?
POUR
POUR
POUR
GEEZ~ IS IT A CRIME FOR ME TO HANG OUT HERE? DON'T MAKE ME CRY—
I CAME TO SEE YOU, SILLY.

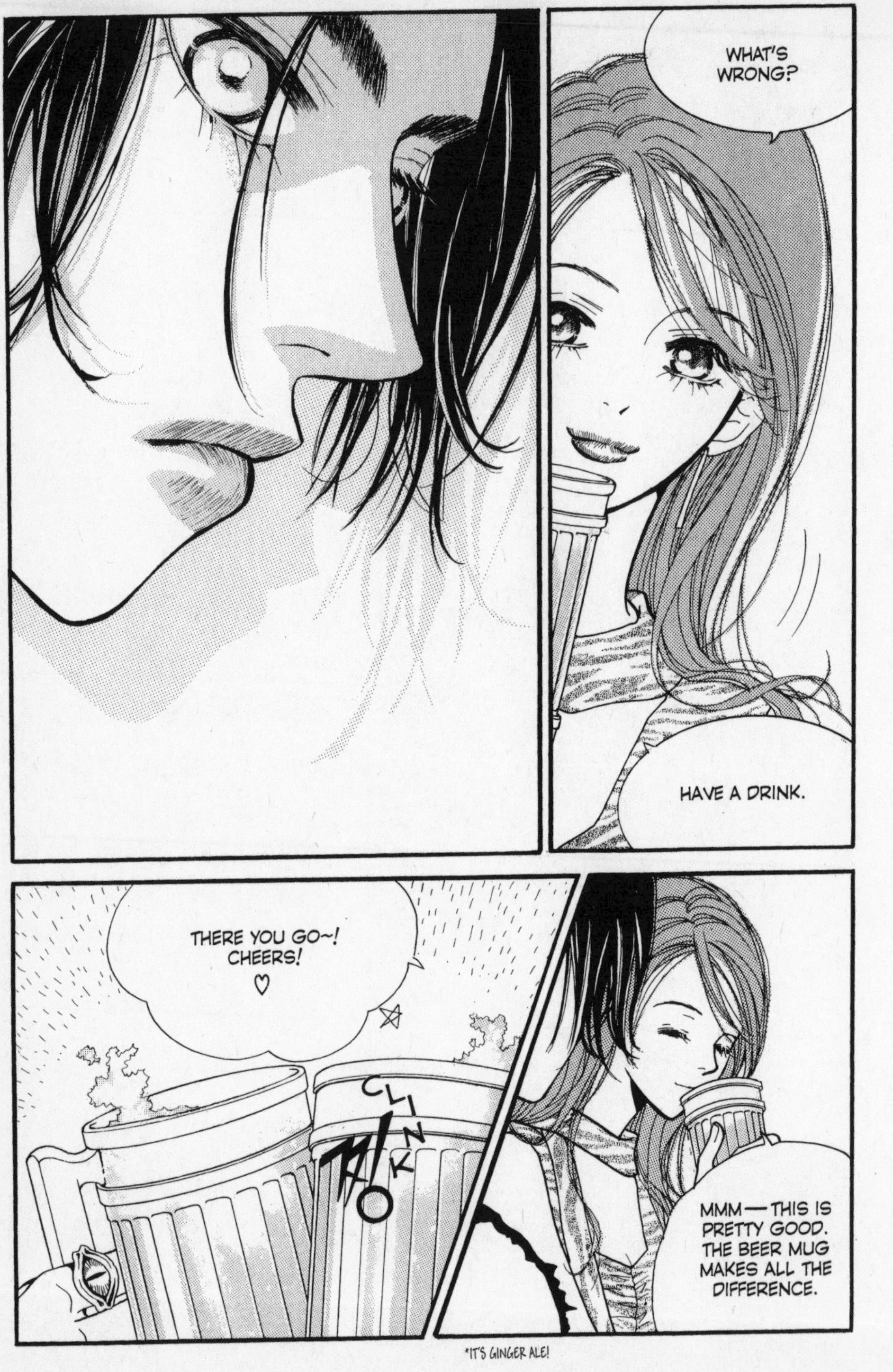
WHAT'S WRONG?
HAVE A DRINK.
THERE YOU GO~! CHEERS! ♡
CLINK
MMM—THIS IS PRETTY GOOD. THE BEER MUG MAKES ALL THE DIFFERENCE.

*IT'S GINGER ALE!

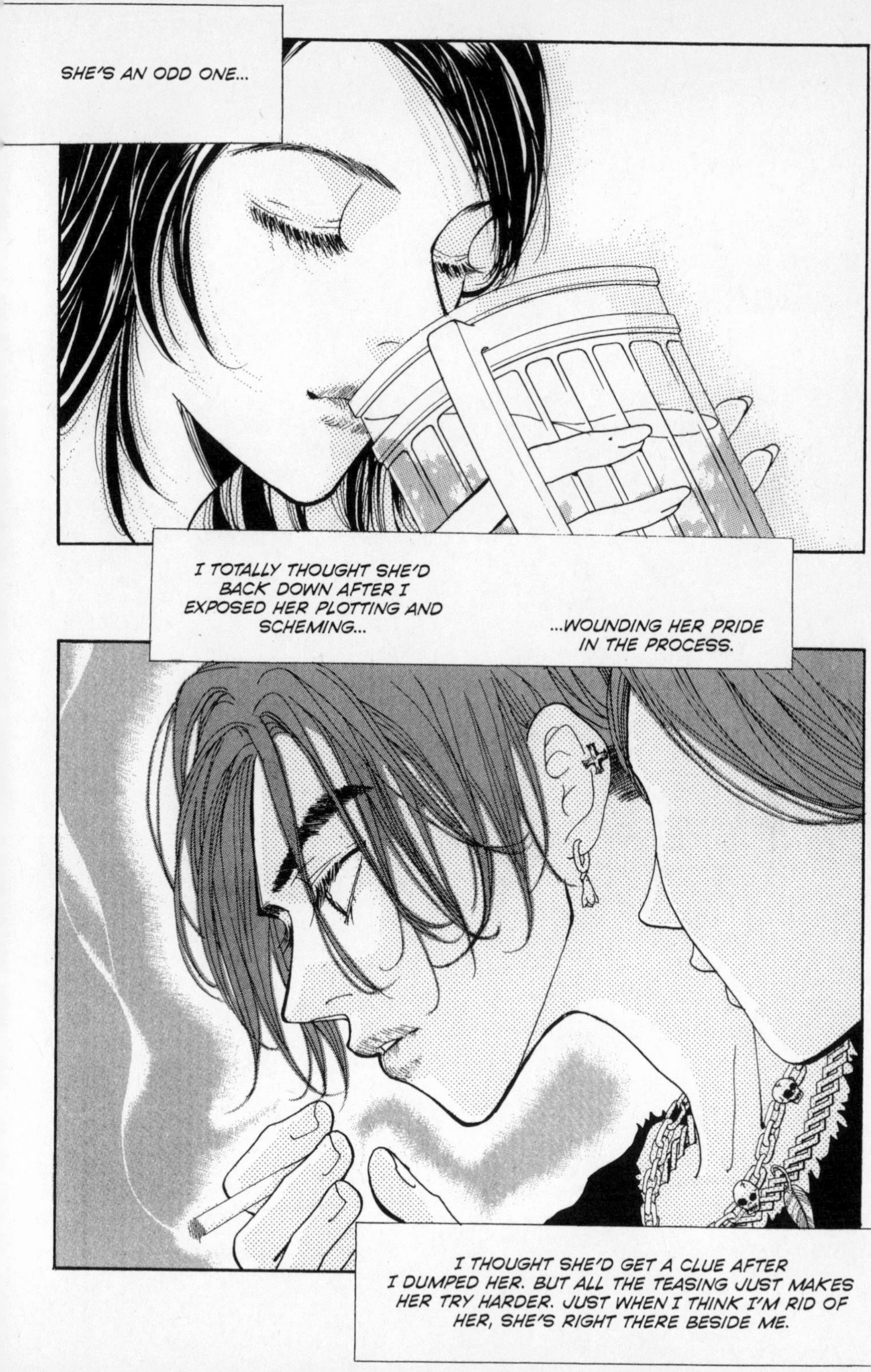
SHE'S AN ODD ONE...
I TOTALLY THOUGHT SHE'D BACK DOWN AFTER I EXPOSED HER PLOTTING AND SCHEMING...
...WOUNDING HER PRIDE IN THE PROCESS.
I THOUGHT SHE'D GET A CLUE AFTER I DUMPED HER. BUT ALL THE TEASING JUST MAKES HER TRY HARDER. JUST WHEN I THINK I'M RID OF HER, SHE'S RIGHT THERE BESIDE ME.

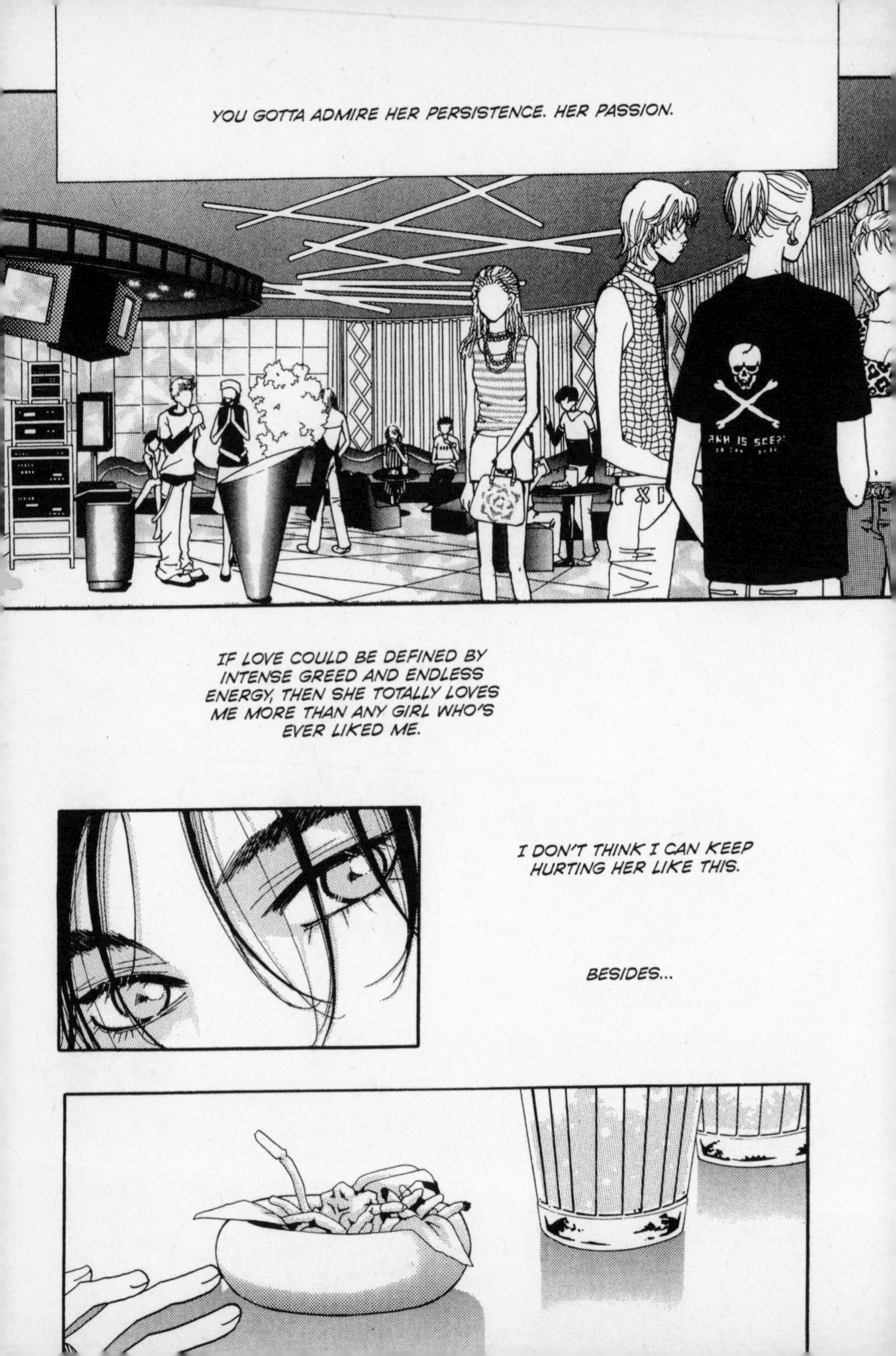
YOU GOTTA ADMIRE HER PERSISTENCE. HER PASSION.
IF LOVE COULD BE DEFINED BY INTENSE GREED AND ENDLESS ENERGY, THEN SHE TOTALLY LOVES ME MORE THAN ANY GIRL WHO'S EVER LIKED ME.
I DON'T THINK I CAN KEEP HURTING HER LIKE THIS.
BESIDES...

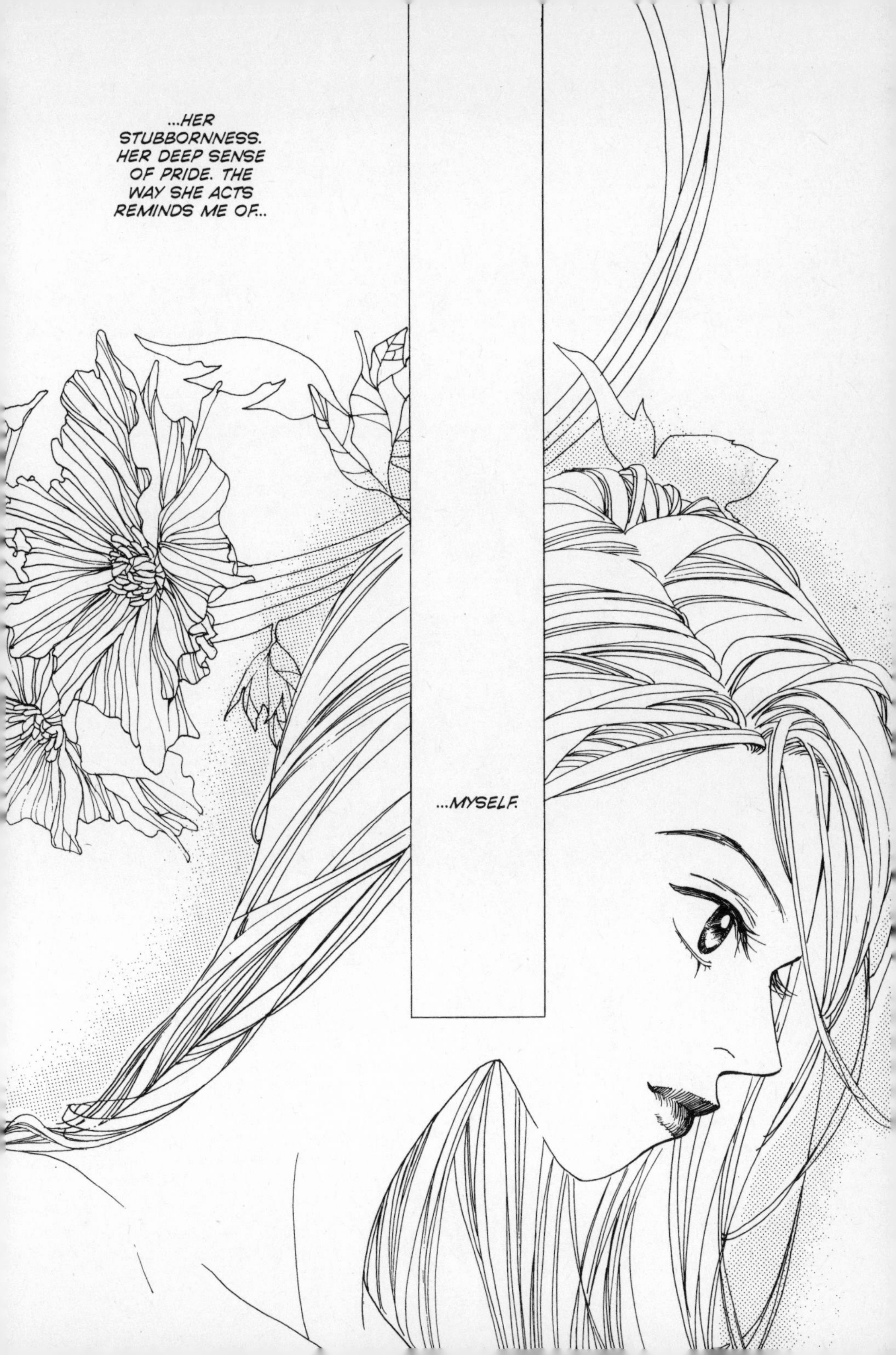
...HER STUBBORNNESS. HER DEEP SENSE OF PRIDE. THE WAY SHE ACTS REMINDS ME OF...
...MYSELF.

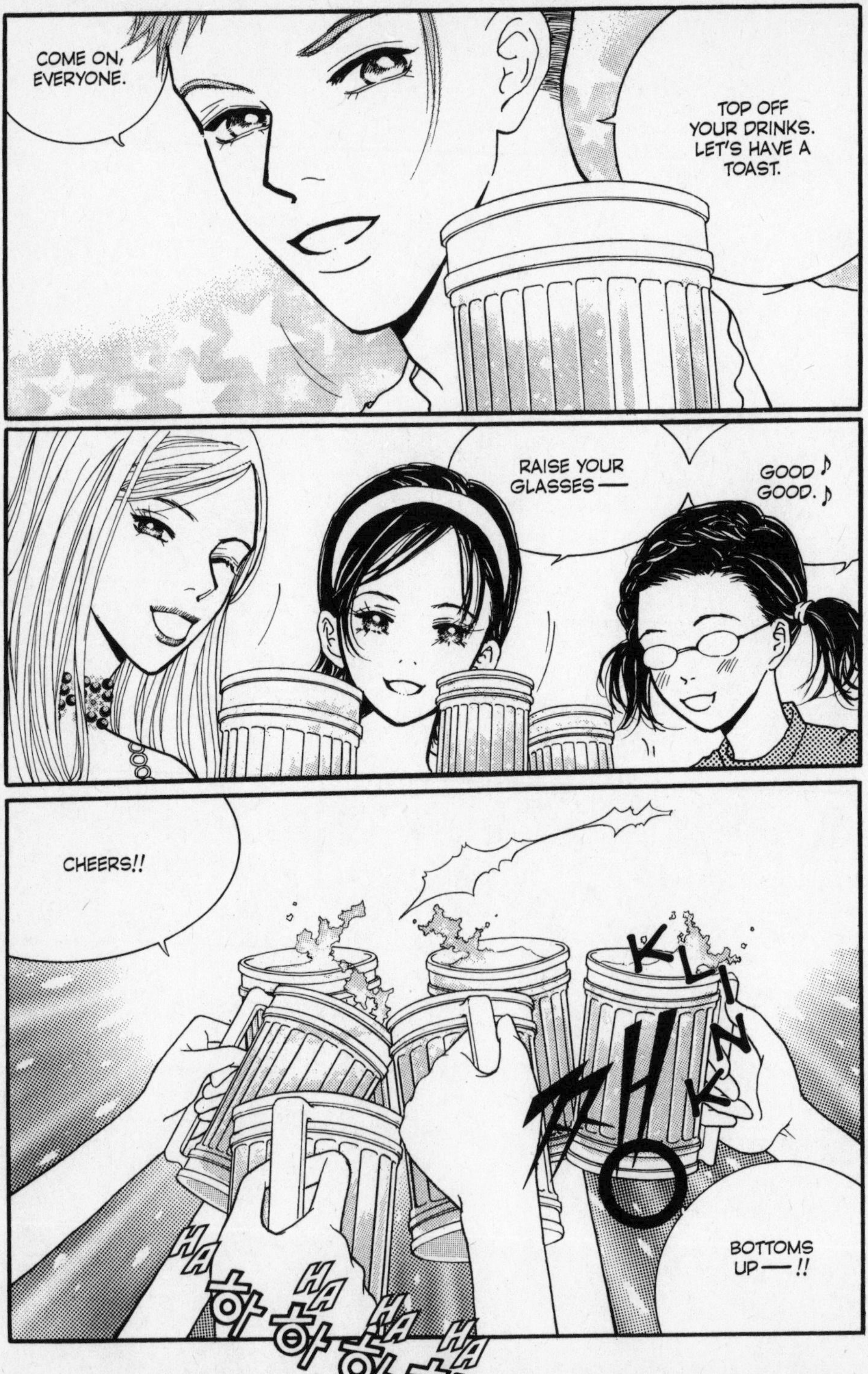
COME ON, EVERYONE.
TOP OFF YOUR DRINKS. LET'S HAVE A TOAST.
RAISE YOUR GLASSES—
GOOD ♪ GOOD. ♪
CHEERS!!
KLINK
BOTTOMS UP—!!
HA HA HA HA

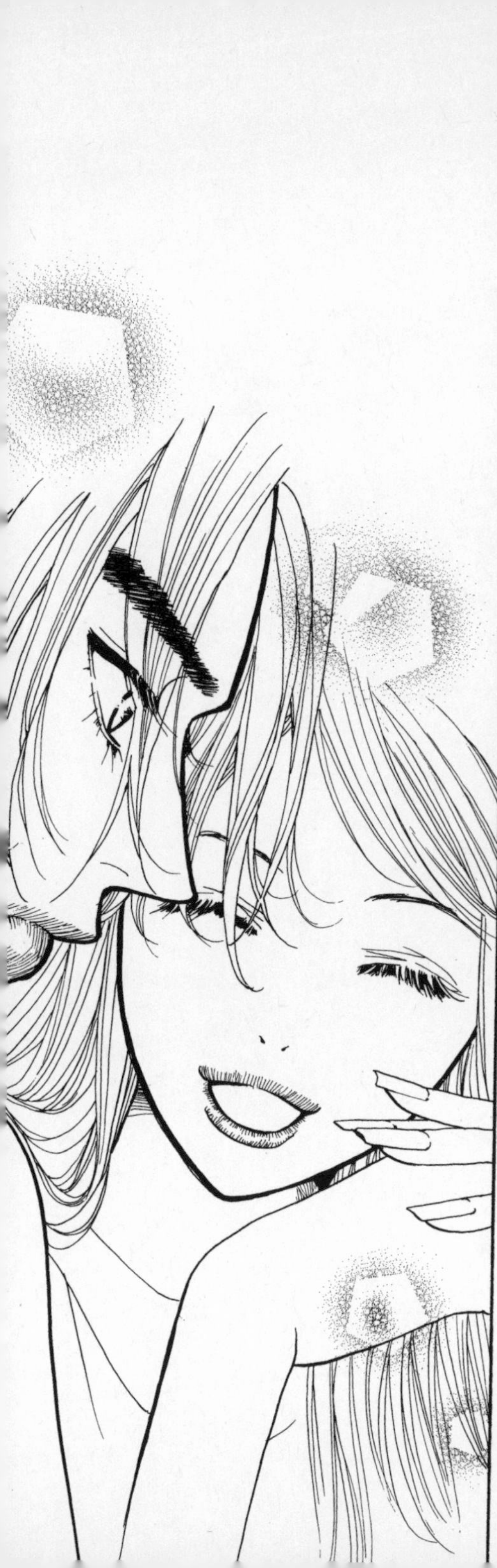

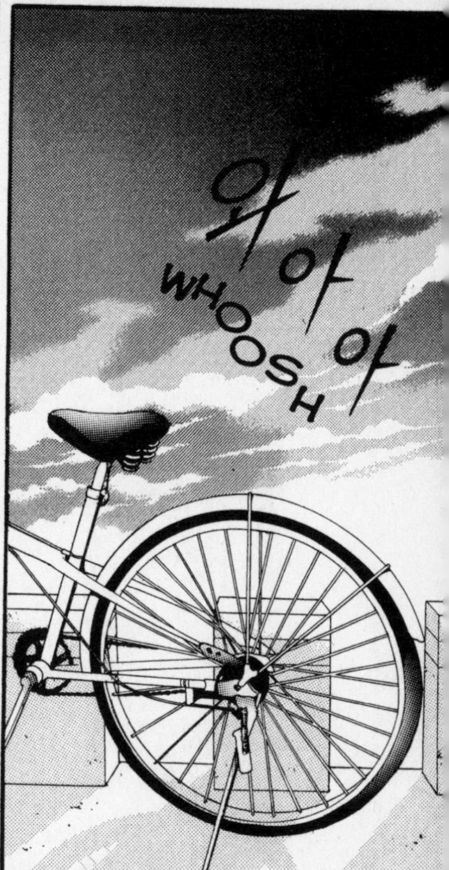
와아아
WHOOSH

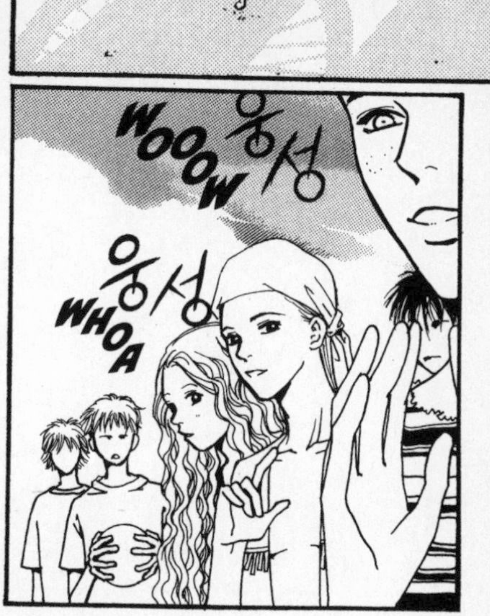
웅성
WOOOW
웅성
WHOA

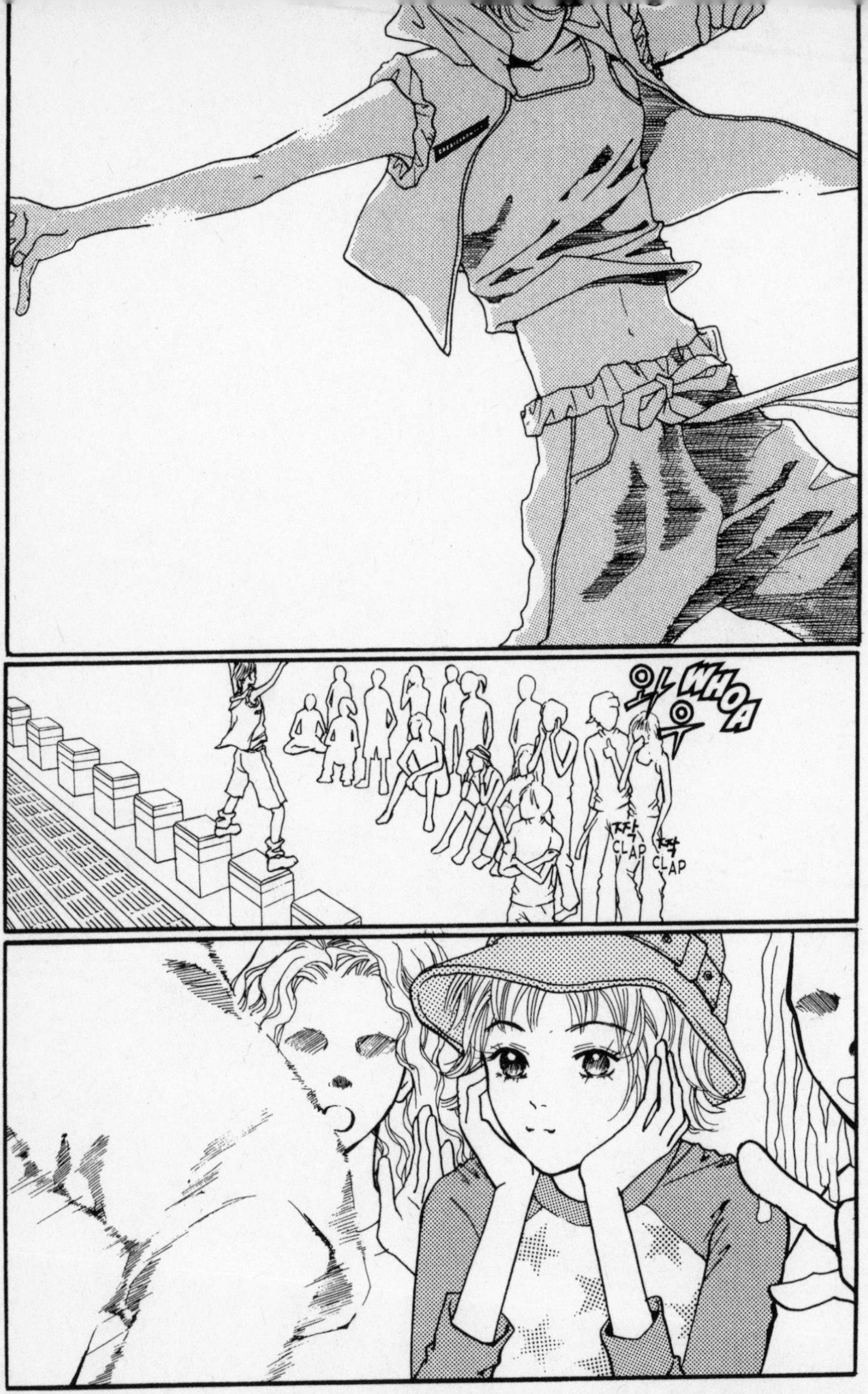
와우
WHOA
짝짝
CLAP
짝
CLAP

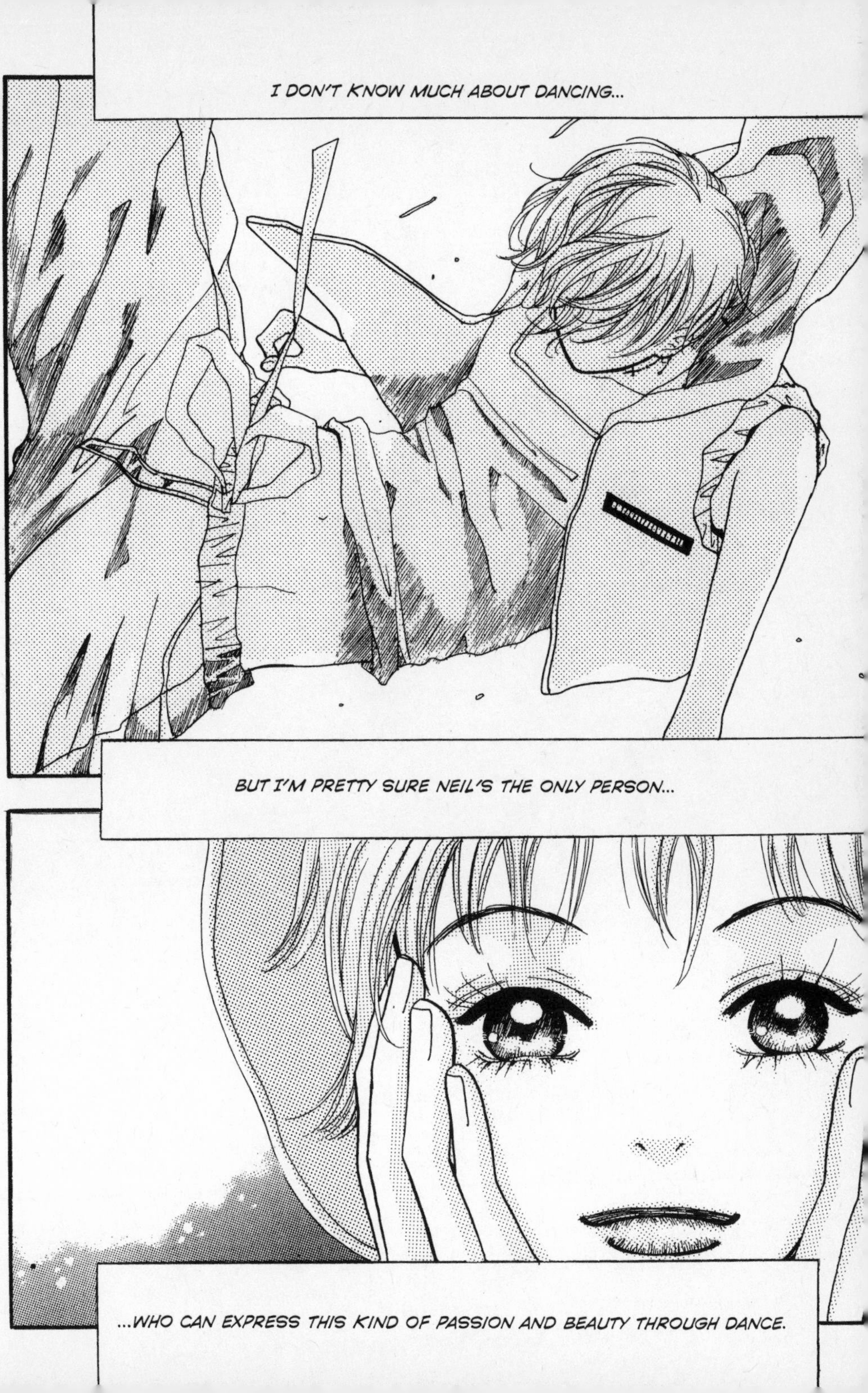
I DON'T KNOW MUCH ABOUT DANCING...
BUT I'M PRETTY SURE NEIL'S THE ONLY PERSON...
...WHO CAN EXPRESS THIS KIND OF PASSION AND BEAUTY THROUGH DANCE.

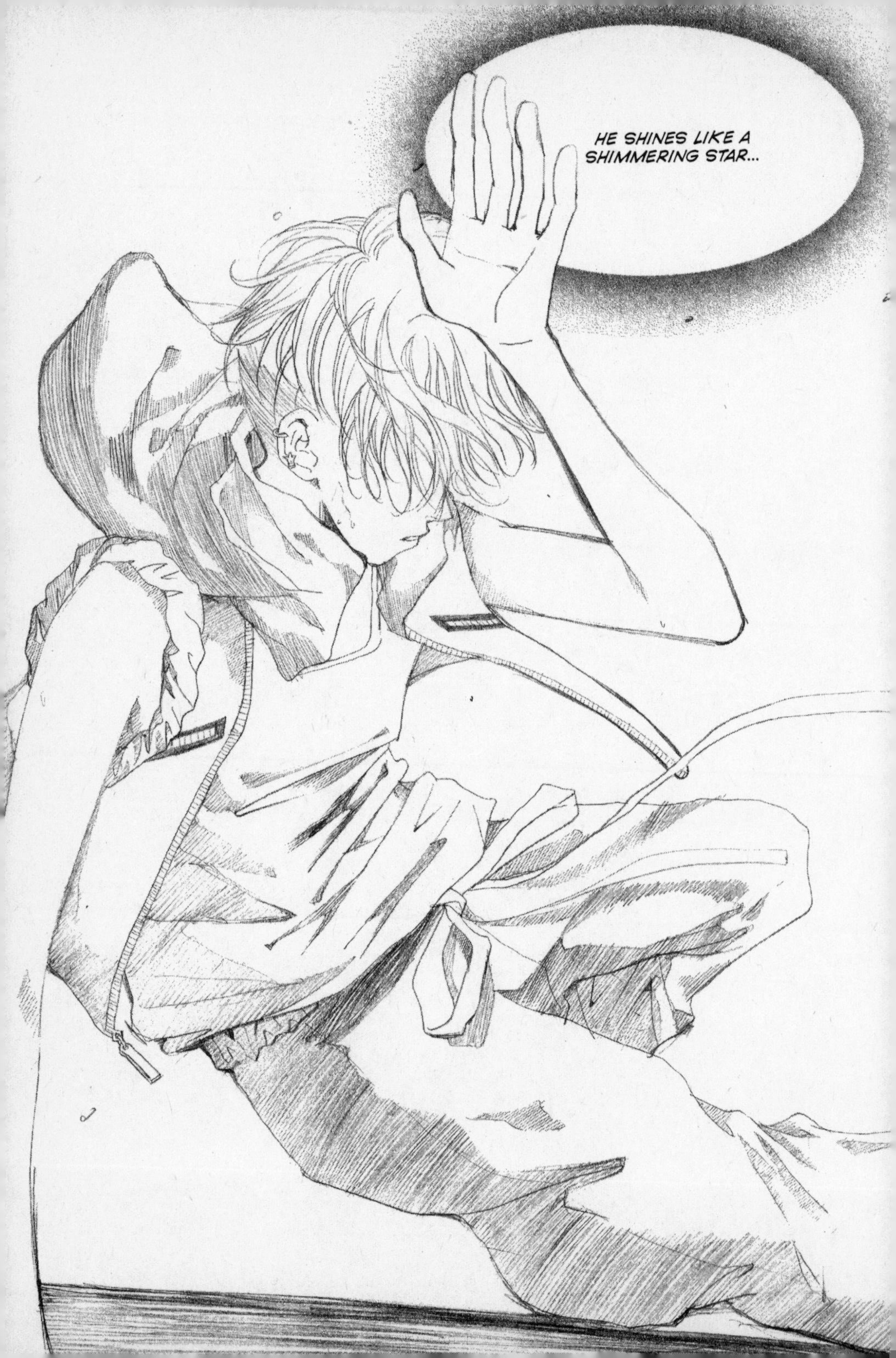
HE SHINES LIKE A SHIMMERING STAR...

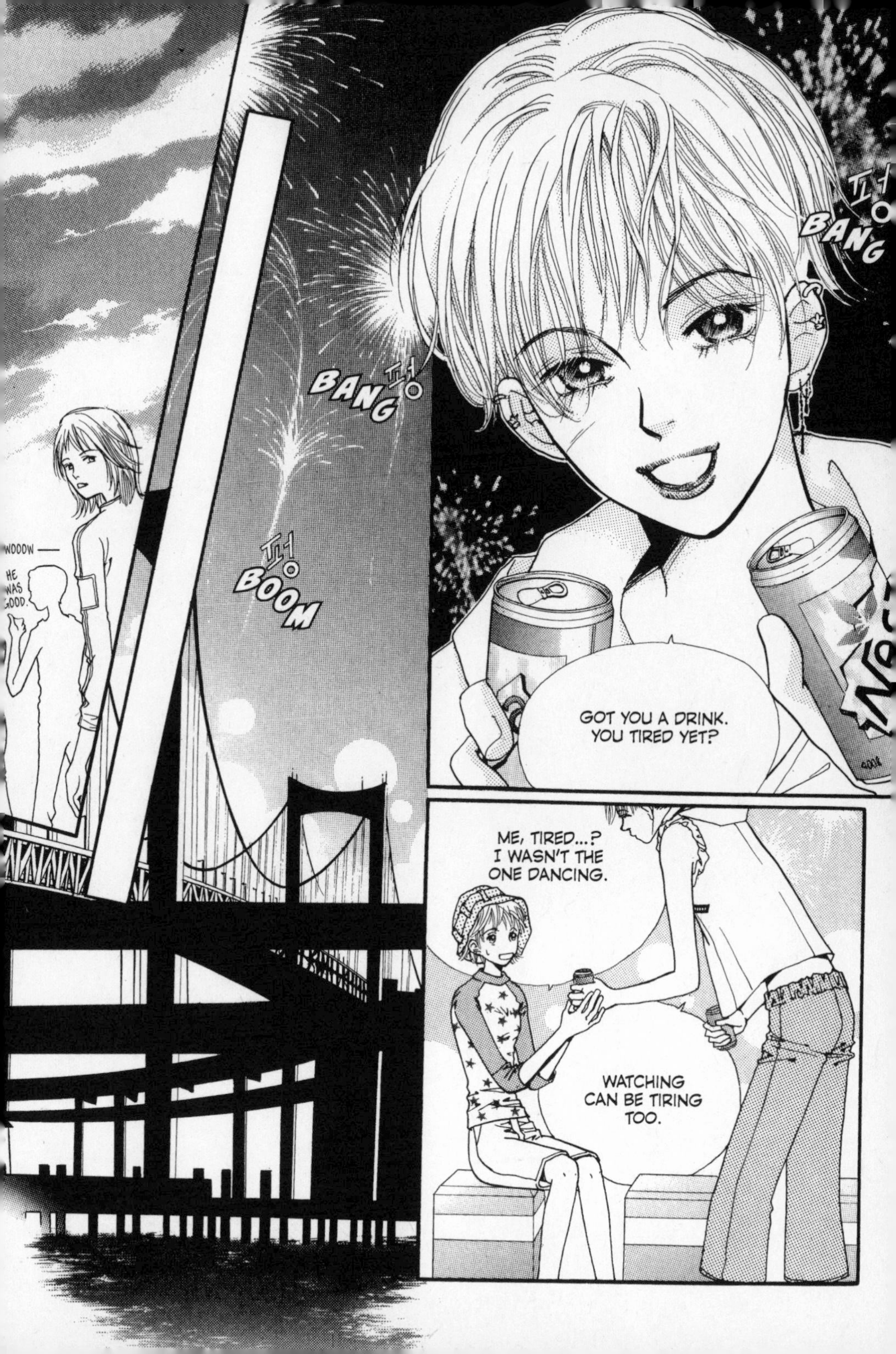

WOOOW —
HE WAS GOOD.
BANG
BOOM
BANG
GOT YOU A DRINK. YOU TIRED YET?
ME, TIRED...? I WASN'T THE ONE DANCING.
WATCHING CAN BE TIRING TOO.

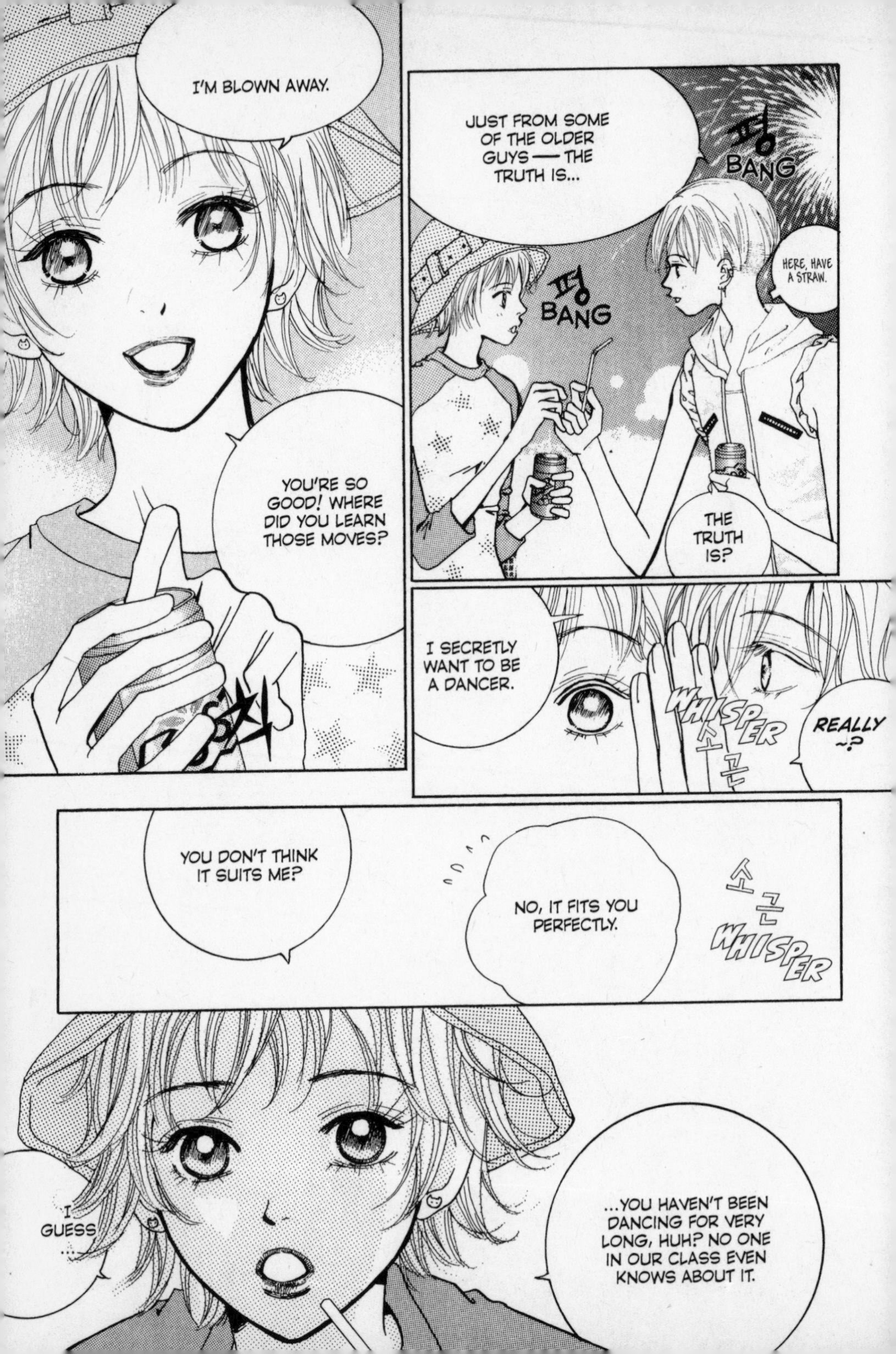

I'M BLOWN AWAY.
YOU'RE SO GOOD! WHERE DID YOU LEARN THOSE MOVES?
JUST FROM SOME OF THE OLDER GUYS — THE TRUTH IS...
펑
BANG
펑
BANG
HERE, HAVE A STRAW.
THE TRUTH IS?
I SECRETLY WANT TO BE A DANCER.
WHISPER
소곤
REALLY ~?
YOU DON'T THINK IT SUITS ME?
NO, IT FITS YOU PERFECTLY.
소곤
WHISPER
I GUESS...
...YOU HAVEN'T BEEN DANCING FOR VERY LONG, HUH? NO ONE IN OUR CLASS EVEN KNOWS ABOUT IT.

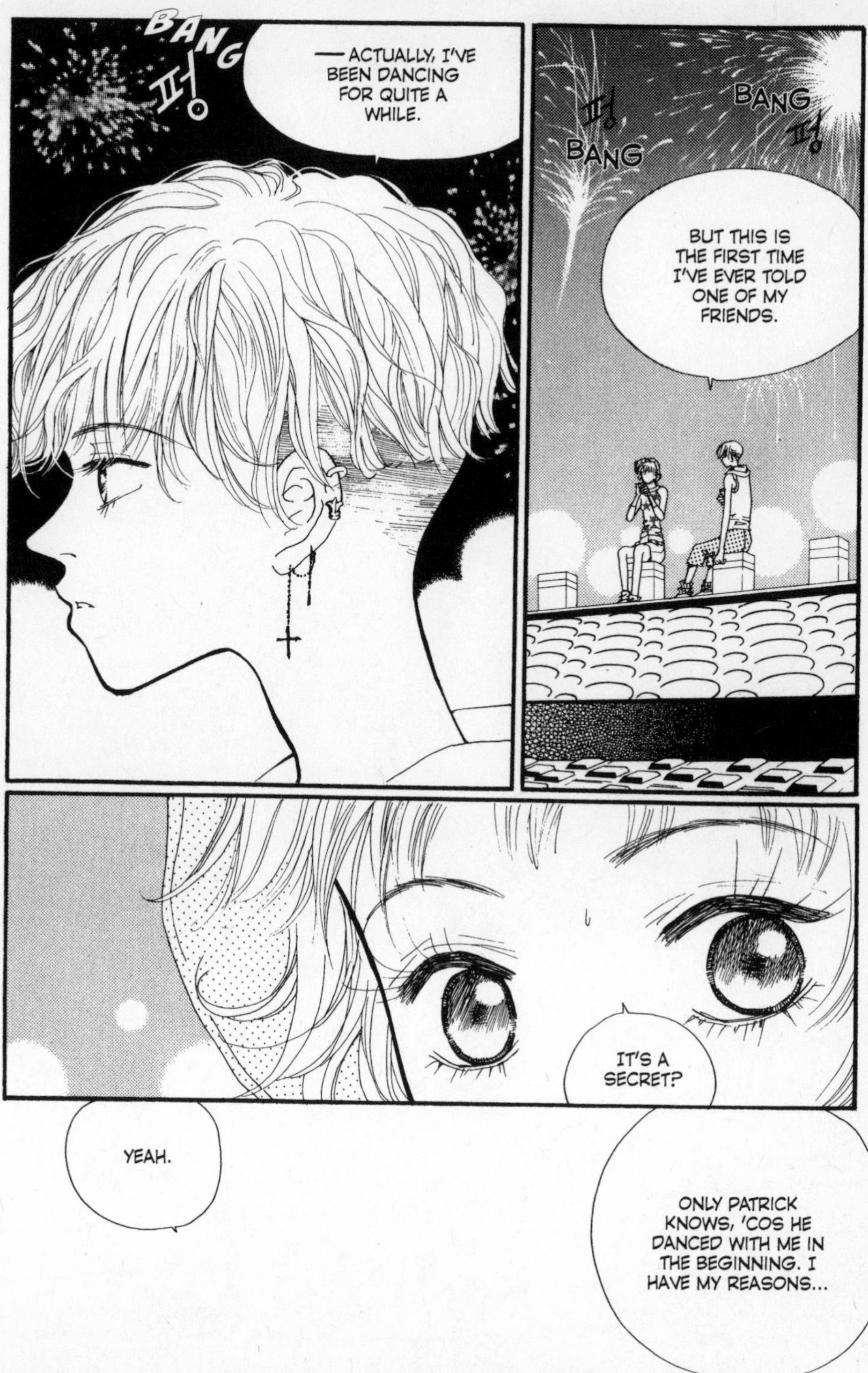
BANG
펑
—ACTUALLY, I'VE BEEN DANCING FOR QUITE A WHILE.
펑
BANG
BANG
펑
BUT THIS IS THE FIRST TIME I'VE EVER TOLD ONE OF MY FRIENDS.
IT'S A SECRET?
YEAH.
ONLY PATRICK KNOWS, 'COS HE DANCED WITH ME IN THE BEGINNING. I HAVE MY REASONS...

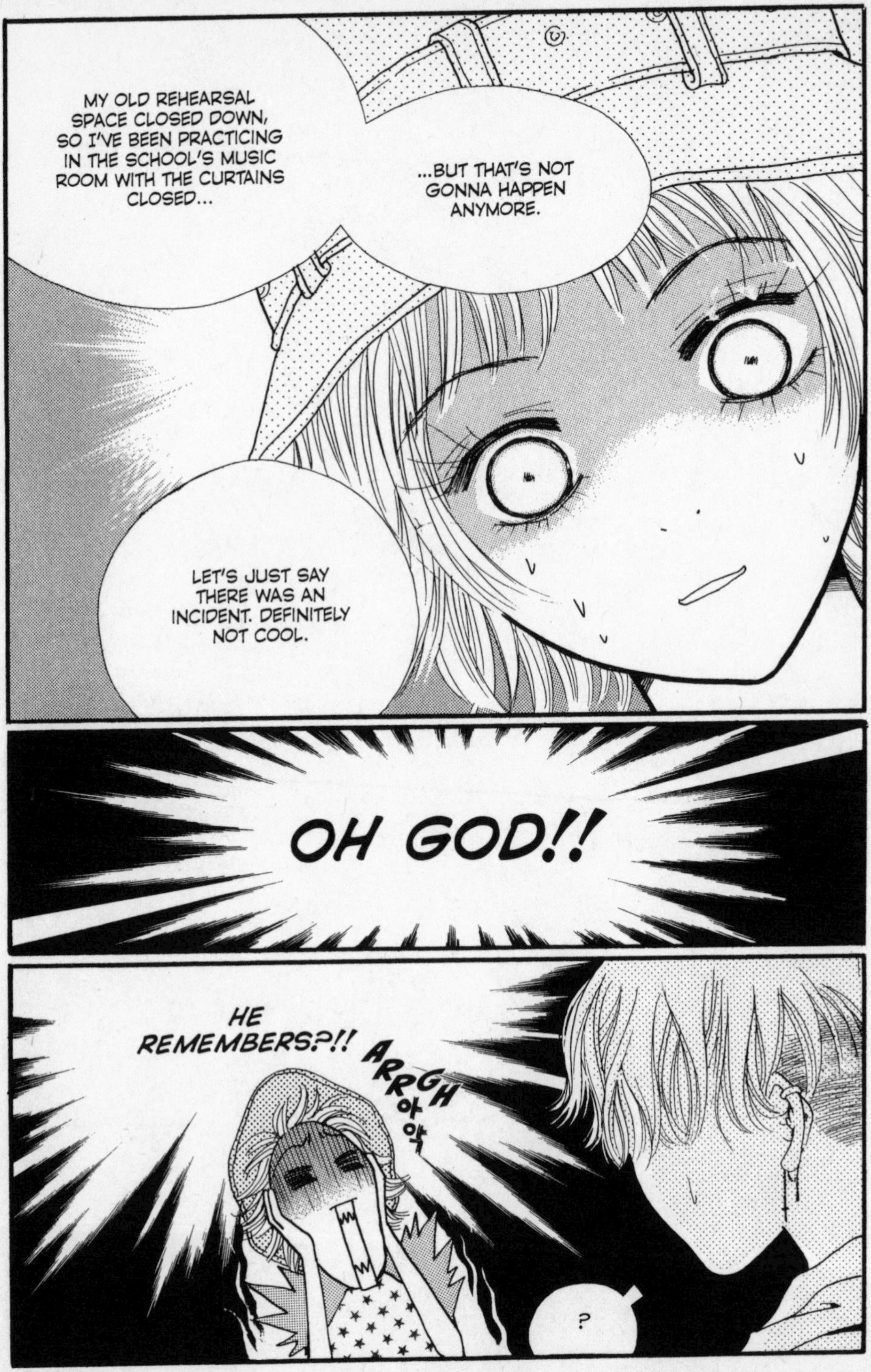
MY OLD REHEARSAL SPACE CLOSED DOWN, SO I'VE BEEN PRACTICING IN THE SCHOOL'S MUSIC ROOM WITH THE CURTAINS CLOSED...
...BUT THAT'S NOT GONNA HAPPEN ANYMORE.
LET'S JUST SAY THERE WAS AN INCIDENT. DEFINITELY NOT COOL.
OH GOD!!
HE REMEMBERS?!!
ARRGH
아악
?

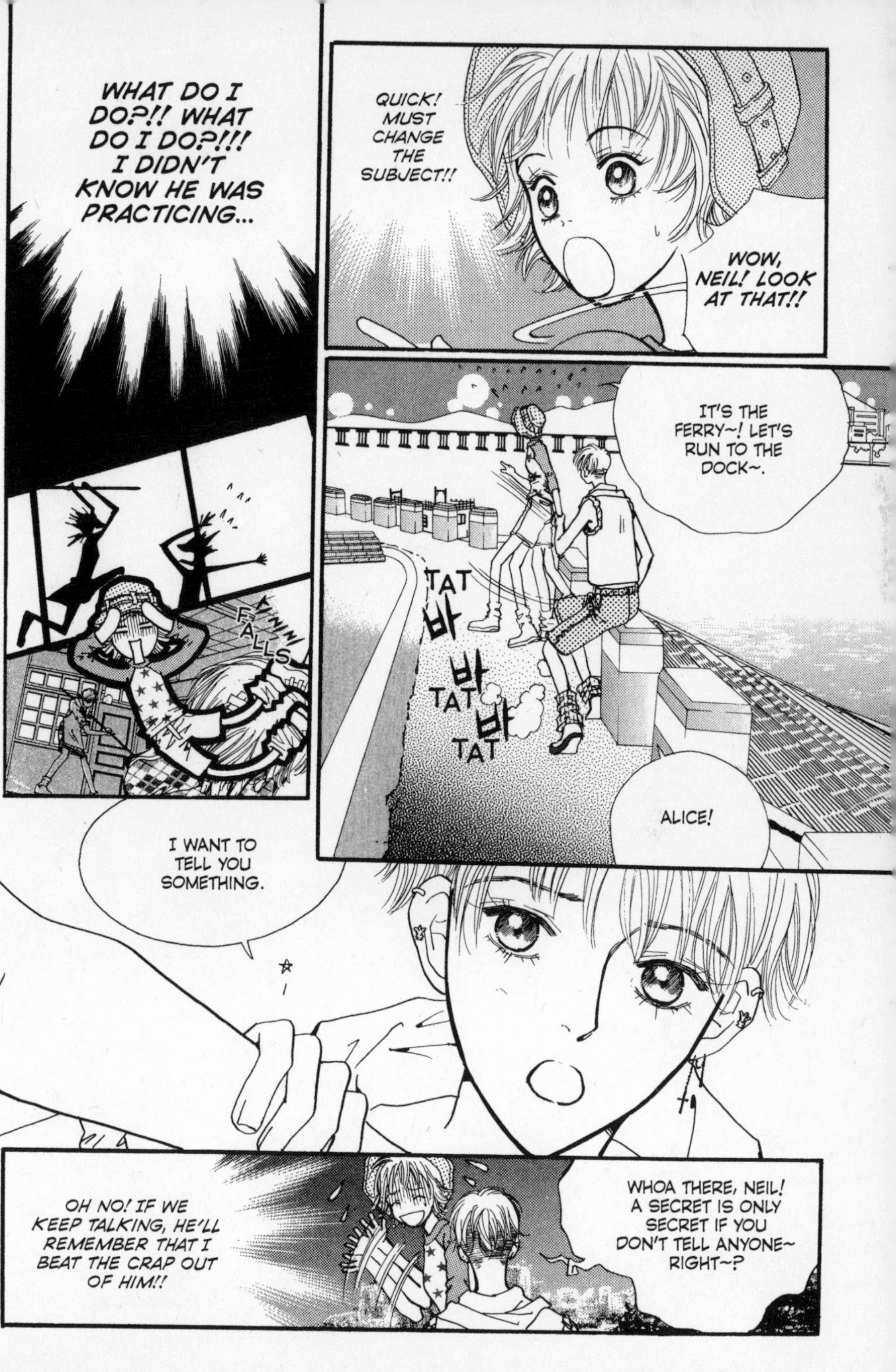

WHAT DO I DO?!! WHAT DO I DO?!!! I DIDN'T KNOW HE WAS PRACTICING...
FALLS
QUICK! MUST CHANGE THE SUBJECT!!
WOW, NEIL! LOOK AT THAT!!
IT'S THE FERRY~! LET'S RUN TO THE DOCK~.
TAT
바
바
TAT
바
TAT
ALICE!
I WANT TO TELL YOU SOMETHING.
OH NO! IF WE KEEP TALKING, HE'LL REMEMBER THAT I BEAT THE CRAP OUT OF HIM!!
WHOA THERE, NEIL! A SECRET IS ONLY SECRET IF YOU DON'T TELL ANYONE~ RIGHT~?

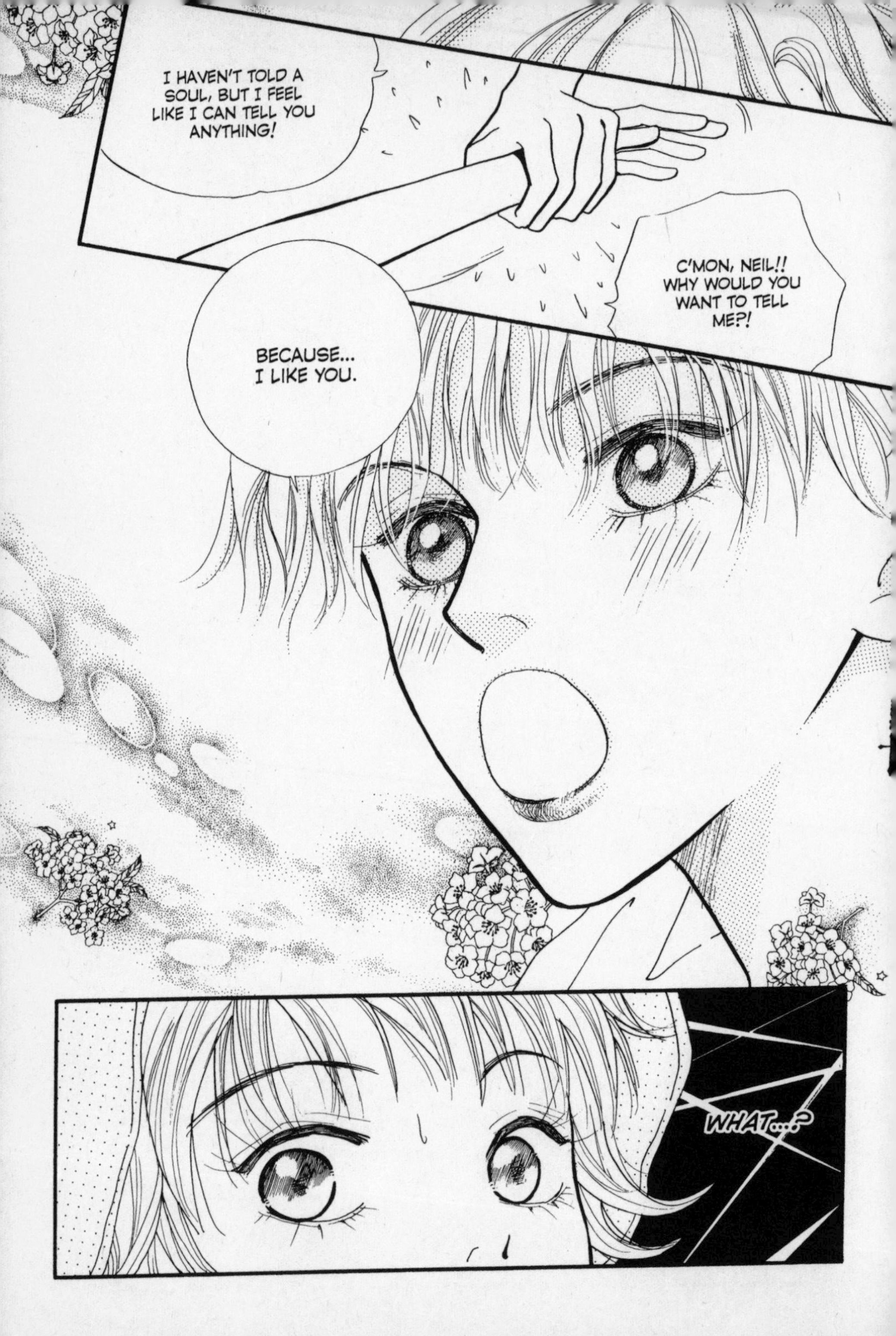
I HAVEN'T TOLD A SOUL, BUT I FEEL LIKE I CAN TELL YOU ANYTHING!
C'MON, NEIL!! WHY WOULD YOU WANT TO TELL ME?!
BECAUSE... I LIKE YOU.
WHAT...?

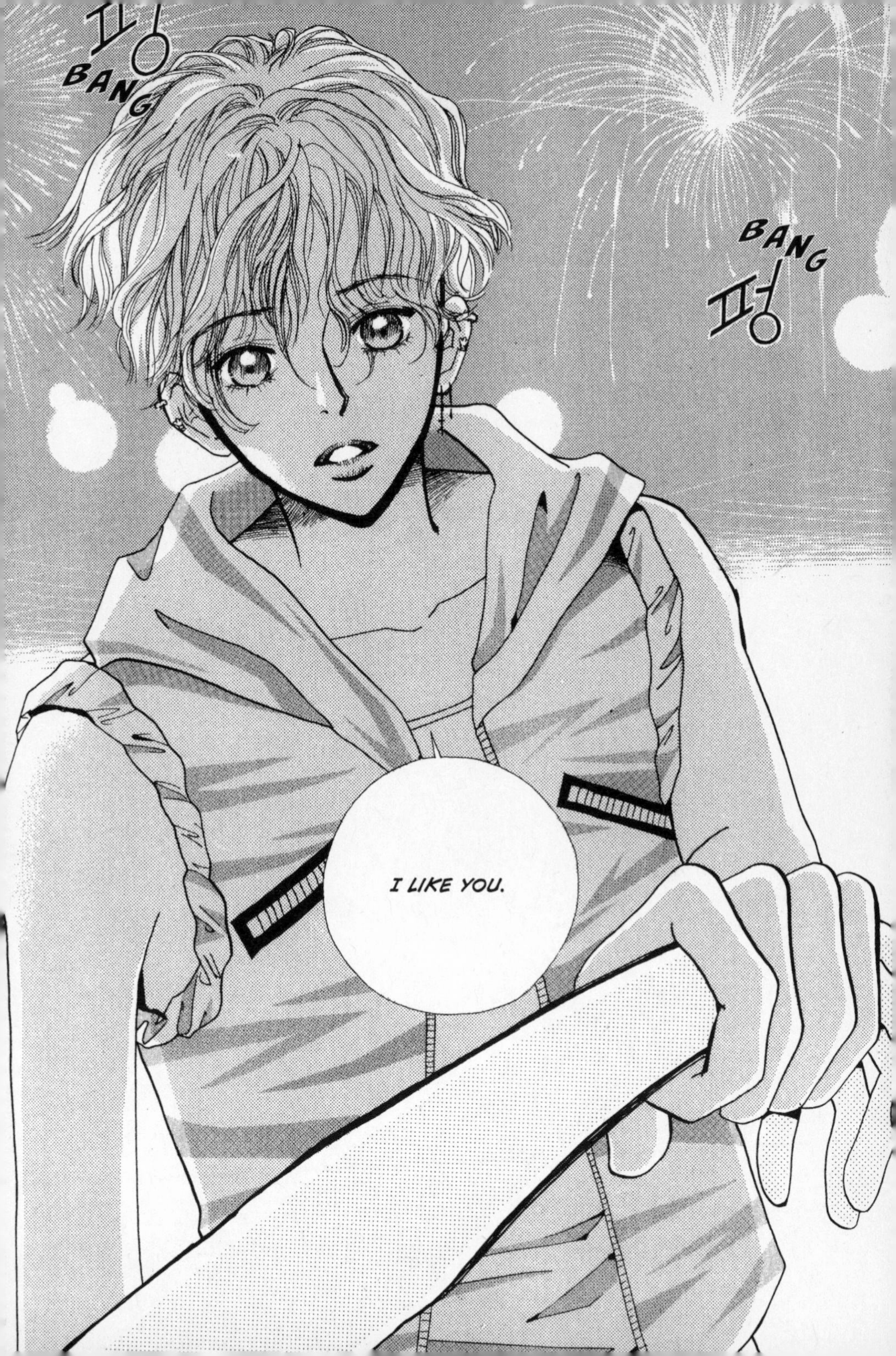
펑
BANG
BANG
펑
I LIKE YOU.

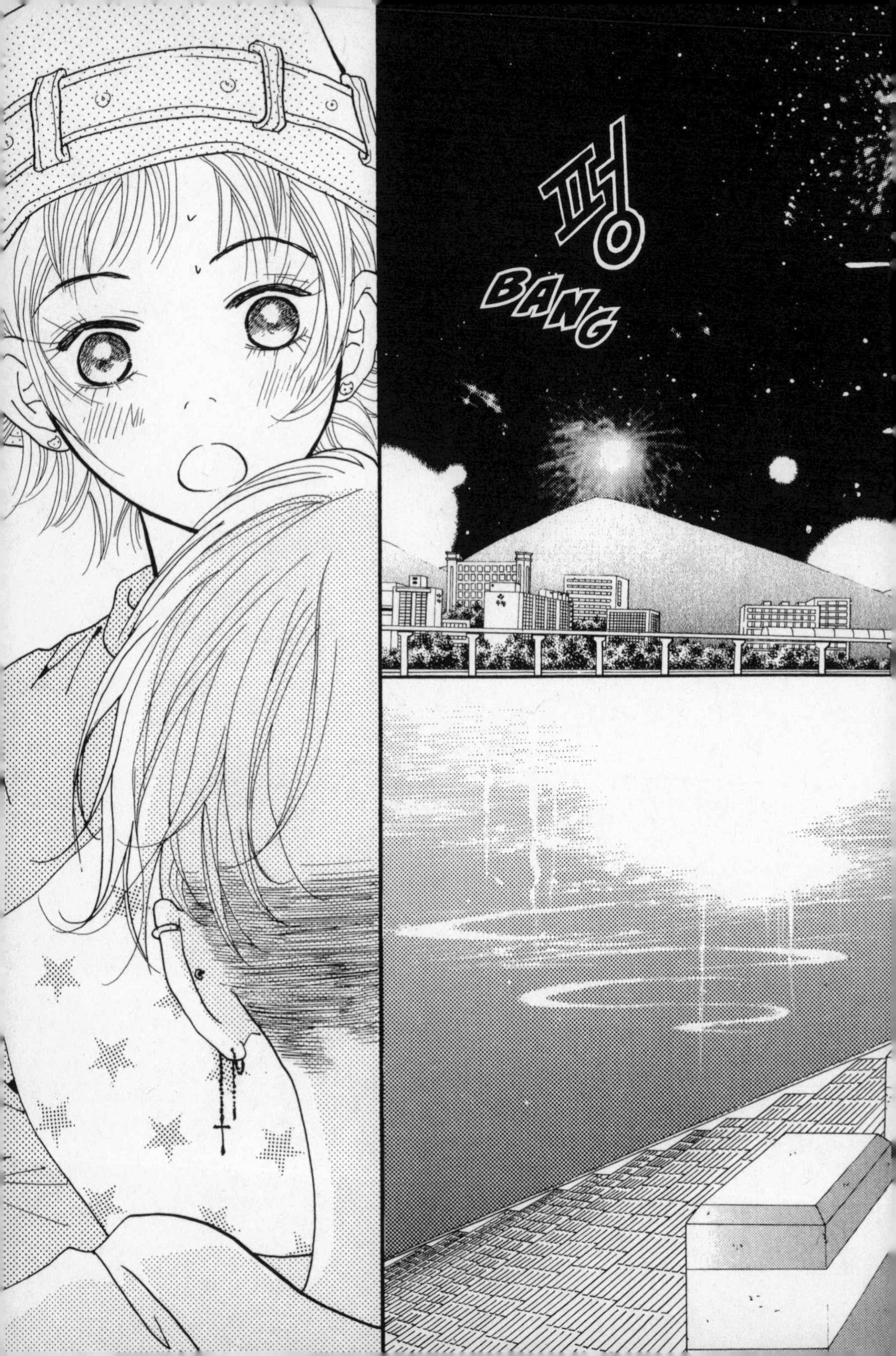
펑
BANG

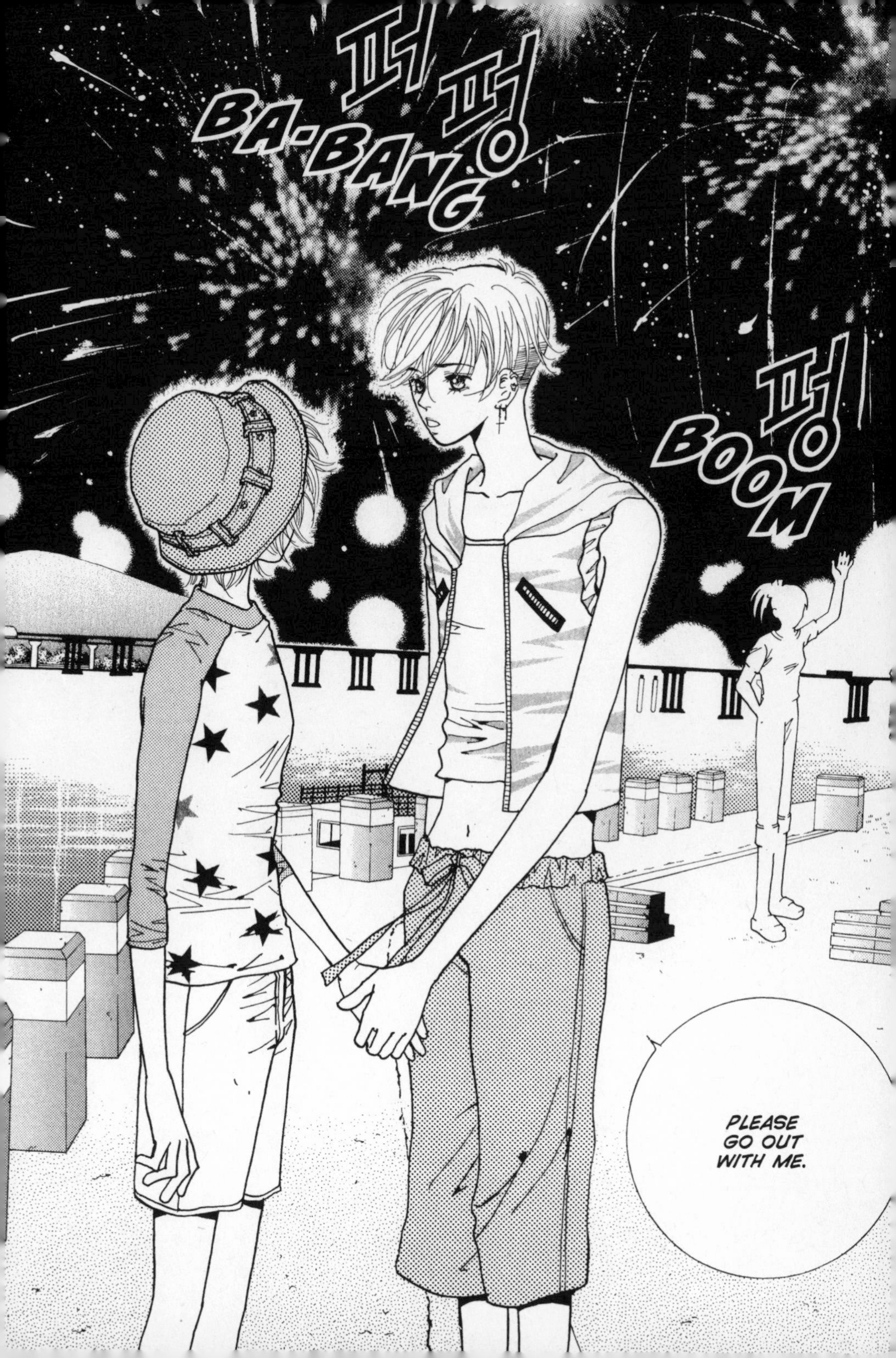
퍼펑
BA-BANG
펑
BOOM
PLEASE GO OUT WITH ME.

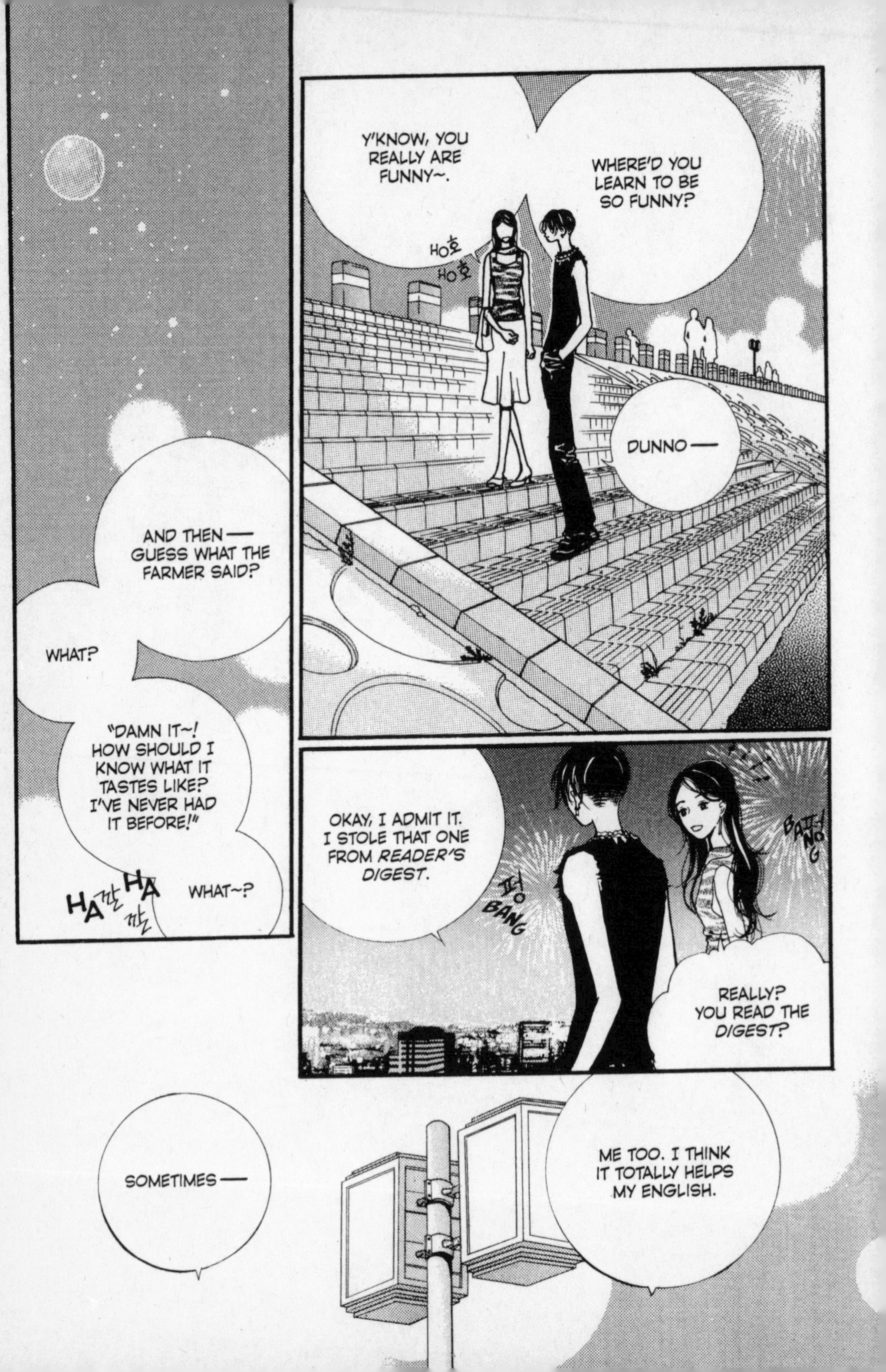

AND THEN — GUESS WHAT THE FARMER SAID?
WHAT?
"DAMN IT~! HOW SHOULD I KNOW WHAT IT TASTES LIKE? I'VE NEVER HAD IT BEFORE!"
HA 깔 HA 깔
WHAT~?
Y'KNOW, YOU REALLY ARE FUNNY~.
WHERE'D YOU LEARN TO BE SO FUNNY?
HO호 HO호
DUNNO —
OKAY, I ADMIT IT. I STOLE THAT ONE FROM *READER'S DIGEST*.
펑 BANG
REALLY? YOU READ THE *DIGEST*?
SOMETIMES —
ME TOO. I THINK IT TOTALLY HELPS MY ENGLISH.

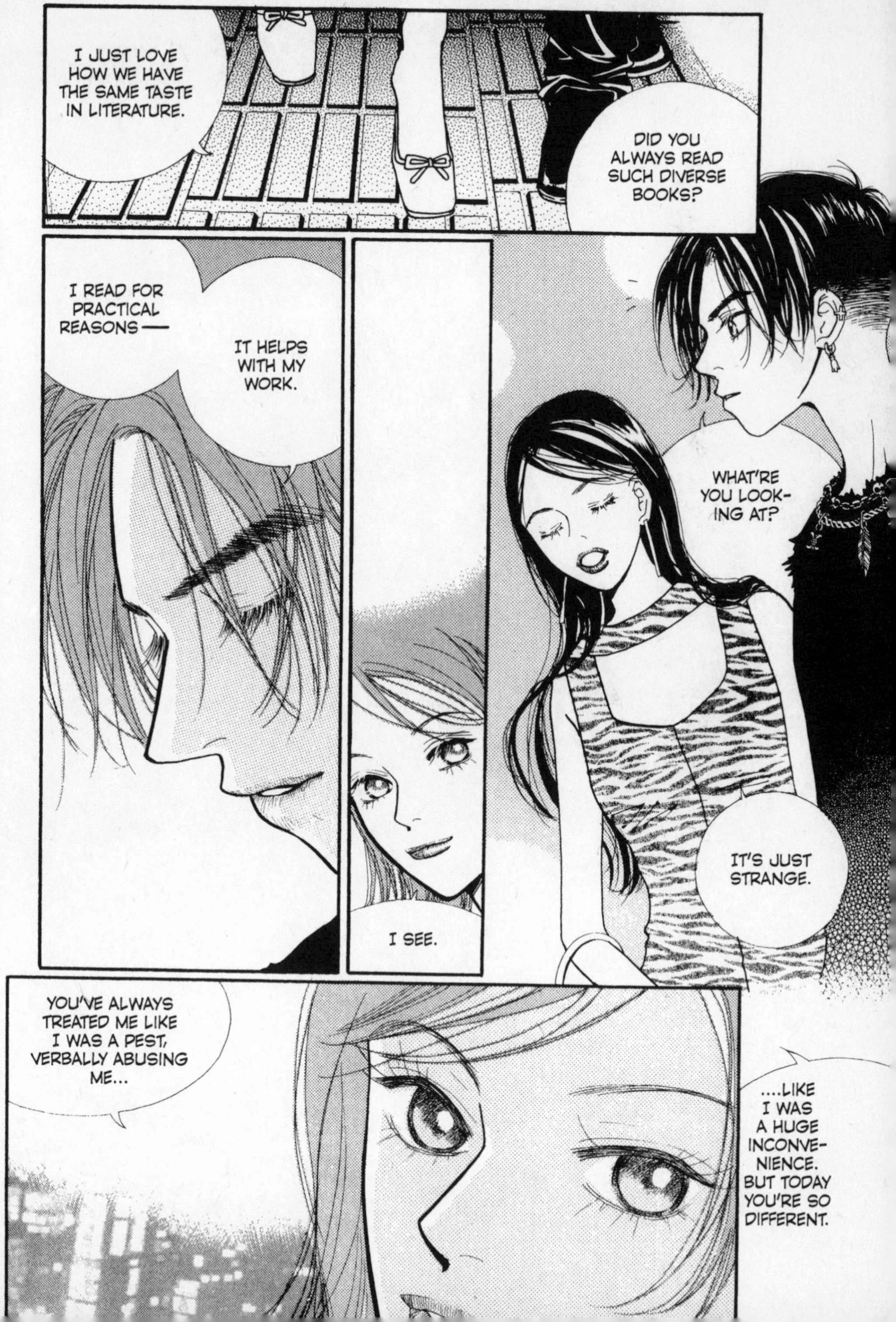
I JUST LOVE HOW WE HAVE THE SAME TASTE IN LITERATURE.
DID YOU ALWAYS READ SUCH DIVERSE BOOKS?
I READ FOR PRACTICAL REASONS—
IT HELPS WITH MY WORK.
I SEE.
WHAT'RE YOU LOOKING AT?
IT'S JUST STRANGE.
YOU'VE ALWAYS TREATED ME LIKE I WAS A PEST, VERBALLY ABUSING ME...
....LIKE I WAS A HUGE INCONVENIENCE. BUT TODAY YOU'RE SO DIFFERENT.

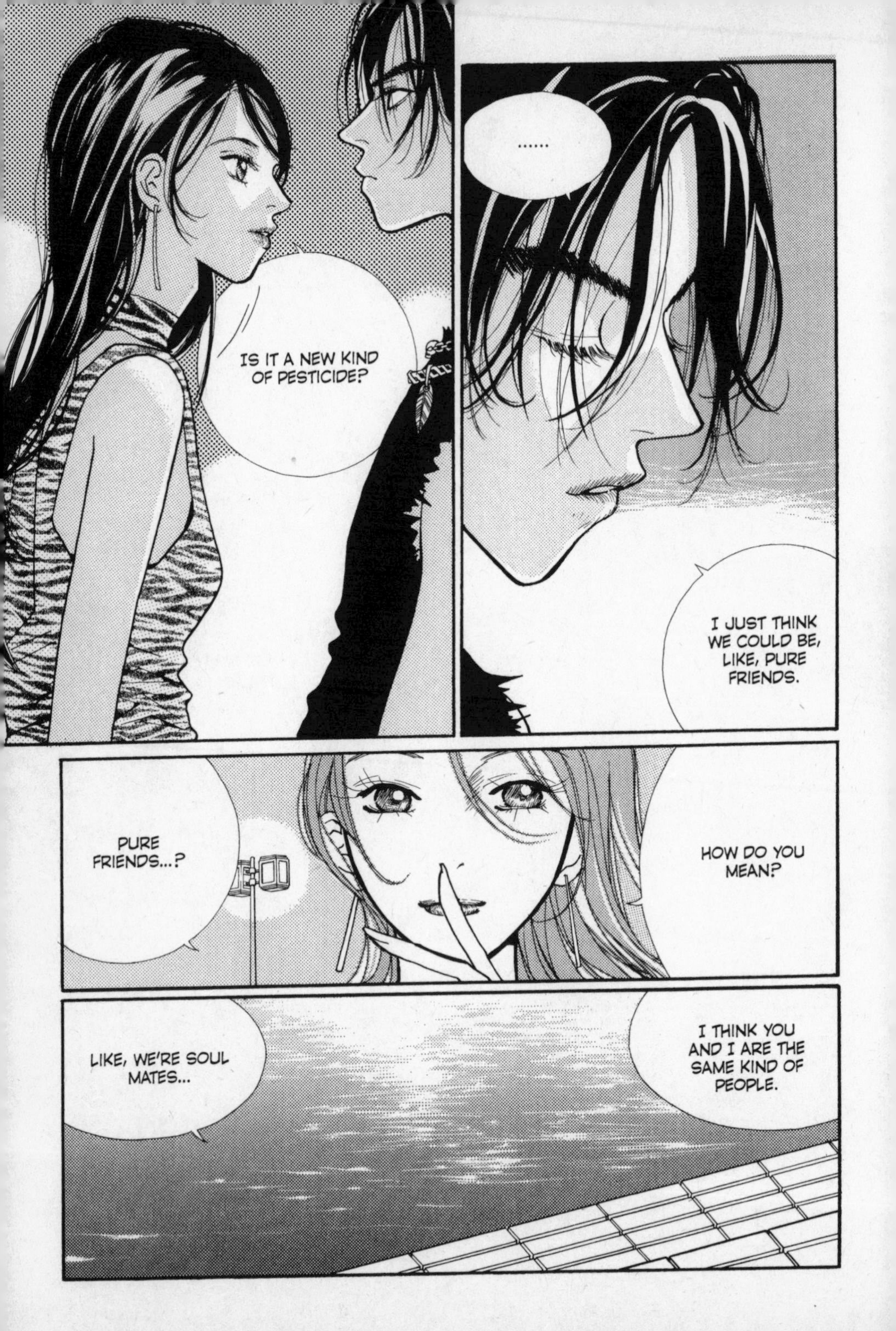
IS IT A NEW KIND OF PESTICIDE?
......
I JUST THINK WE COULD BE, LIKE, PURE FRIENDS.
PURE FRIENDS...?
HOW DO YOU MEAN?
LIKE, WE'RE SOUL MATES...
I THINK YOU AND I ARE THE SAME KIND OF PEOPLE.

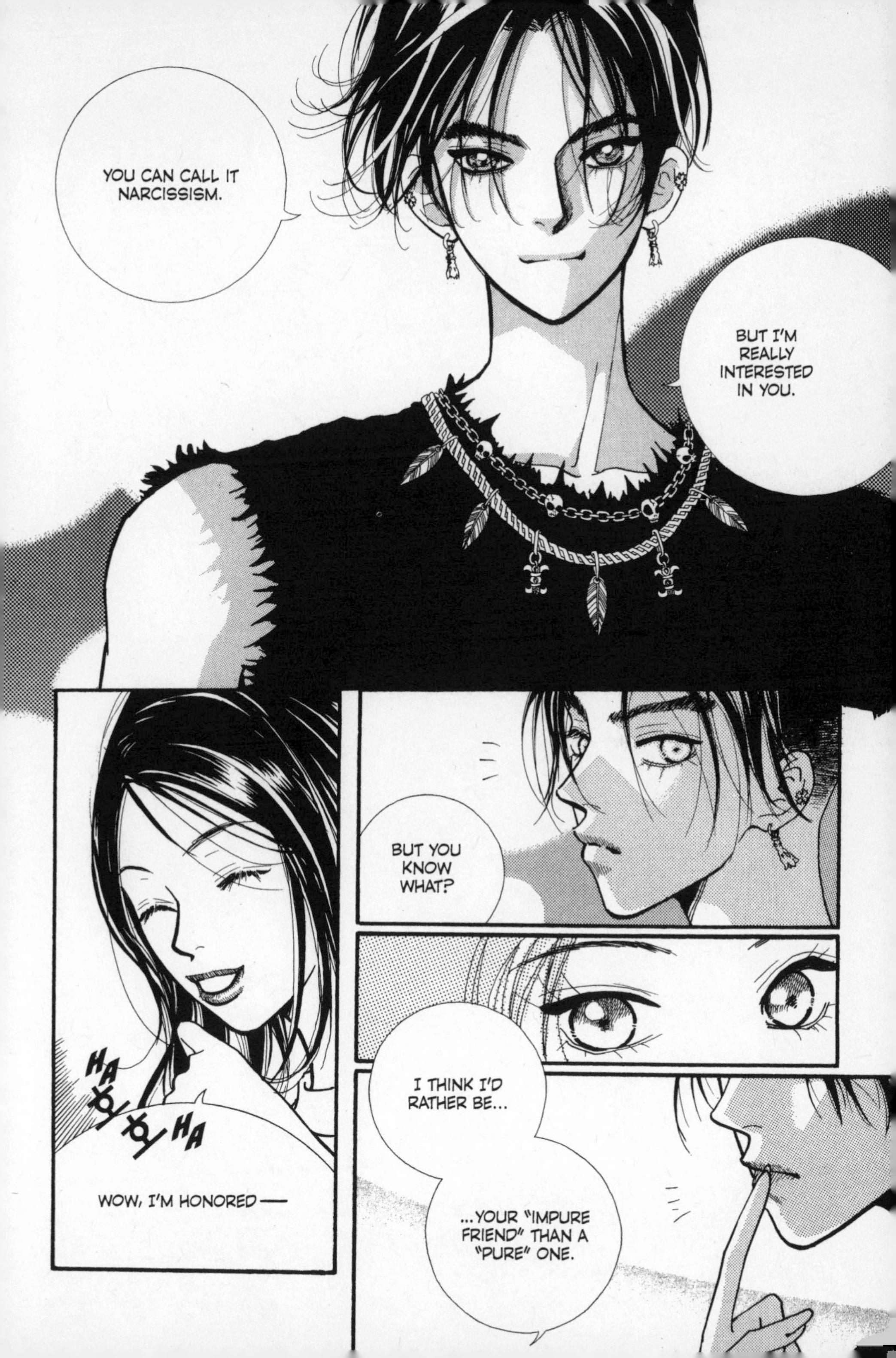
YOU CAN CALL IT NARCISSISM.
BUT I'M REALLY INTERESTED IN YOU.
HA 하 하 HA
WOW, I'M HONORED—
BUT YOU KNOW WHAT?
I THINK I'D RATHER BE...
...YOUR "IMPURE FRIEND" THAN A "PURE" ONE.

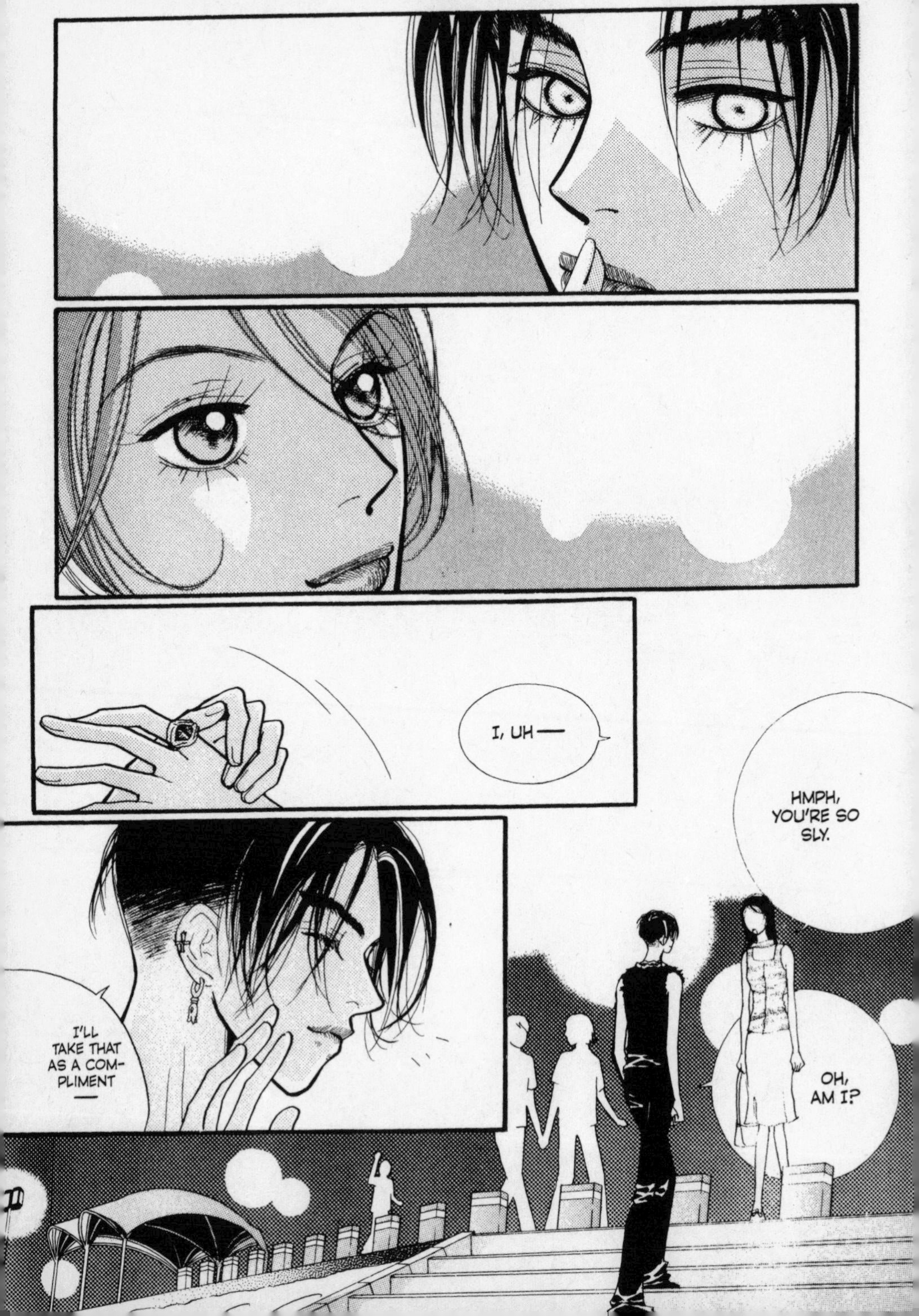
I, UH —
I'LL TAKE THAT AS A COMPLIMENT —
HMPH, YOU'RE SO SLY.
OH, AM I?

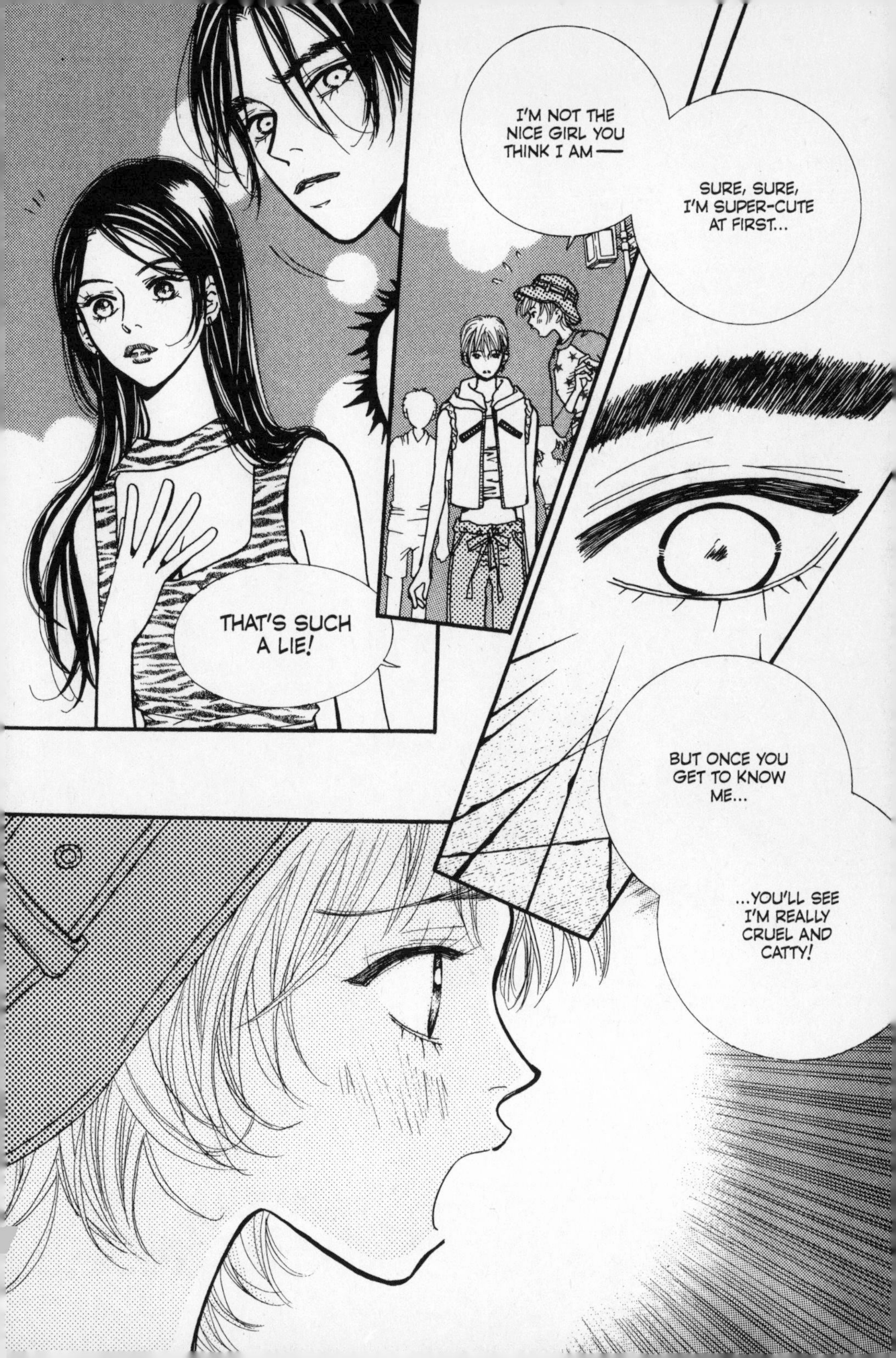
THAT'S SUCH A LIE!
I'M NOT THE NICE GIRL YOU THINK I AM—
SURE, SURE, I'M SUPER-CUTE AT FIRST...
BUT ONCE YOU GET TO KNOW ME...
...YOU'LL SEE I'M REALLY CRUEL AND CATTY!

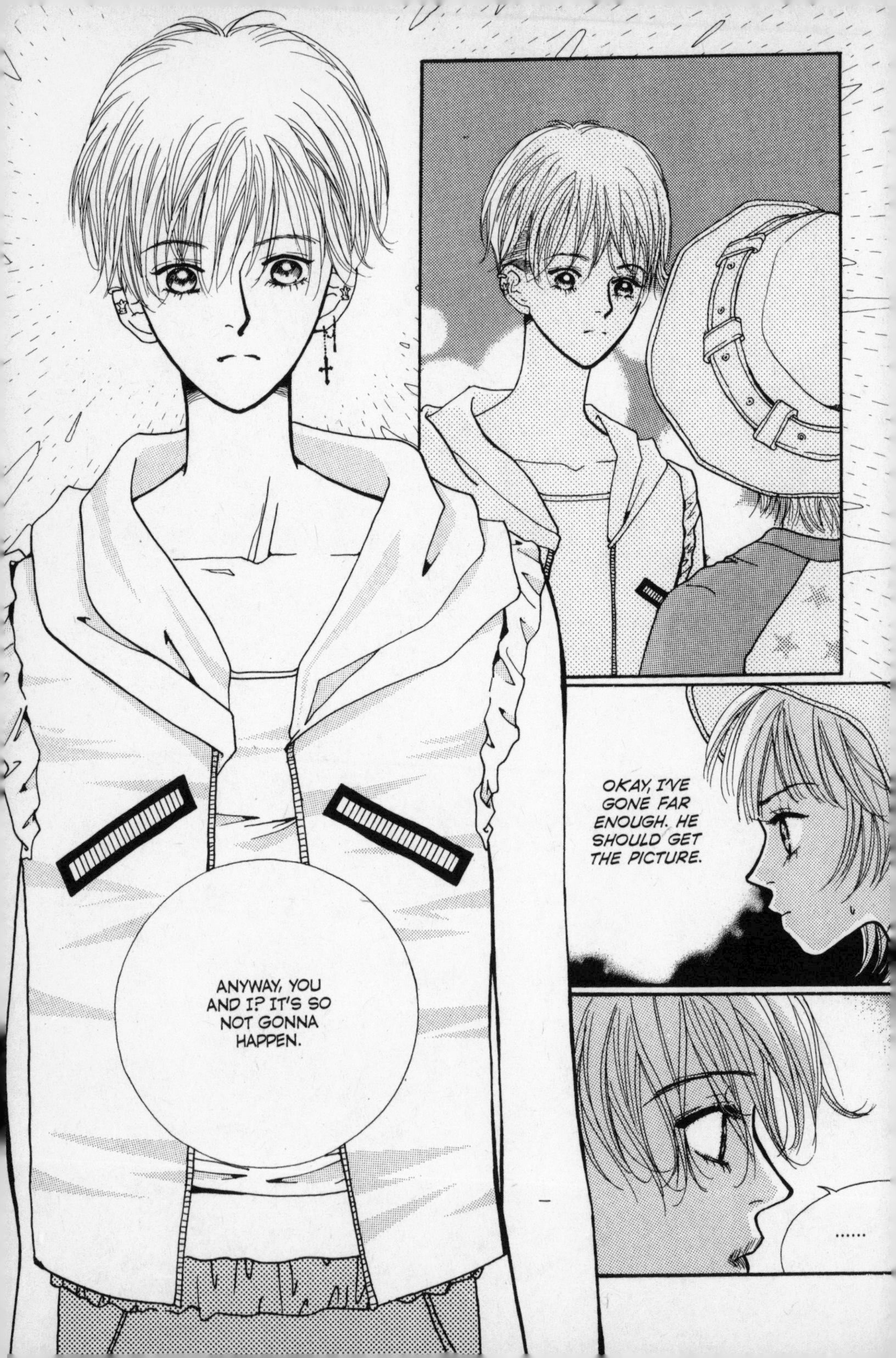
ANYWAY, YOU AND I? IT'S SO NOT GONNA HAPPEN.
OKAY, I'VE GONE FAR ENOUGH. HE SHOULD GET THE PICTURE.
......

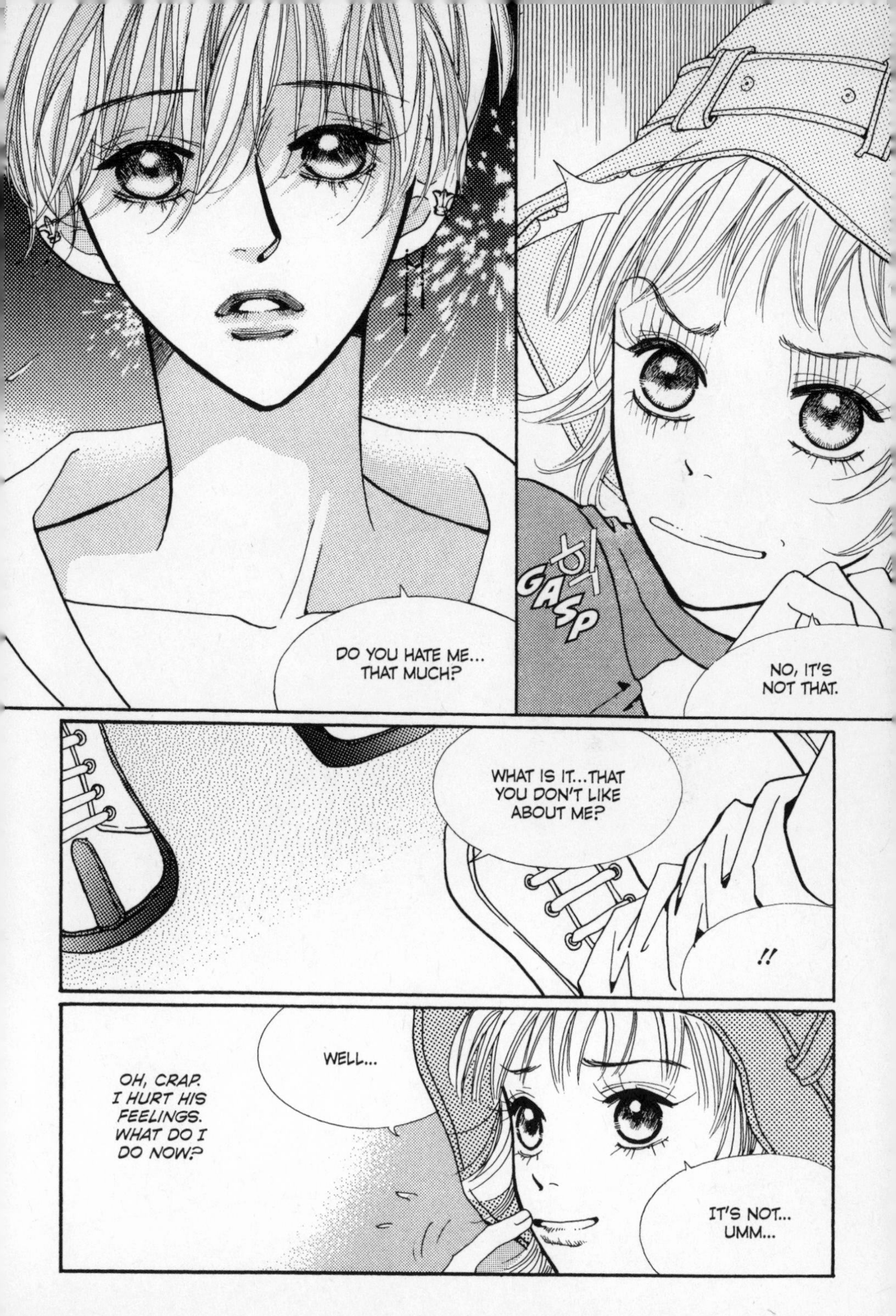
DO YOU HATE ME... THAT MUCH?
GASP
NO, IT'S NOT THAT.
WHAT IS IT...THAT YOU DON'T LIKE ABOUT ME?
!!
WELL...
OH, CRAP. I HURT HIS FEELINGS. WHAT DO I DO NOW?
IT'S NOT... UMM...

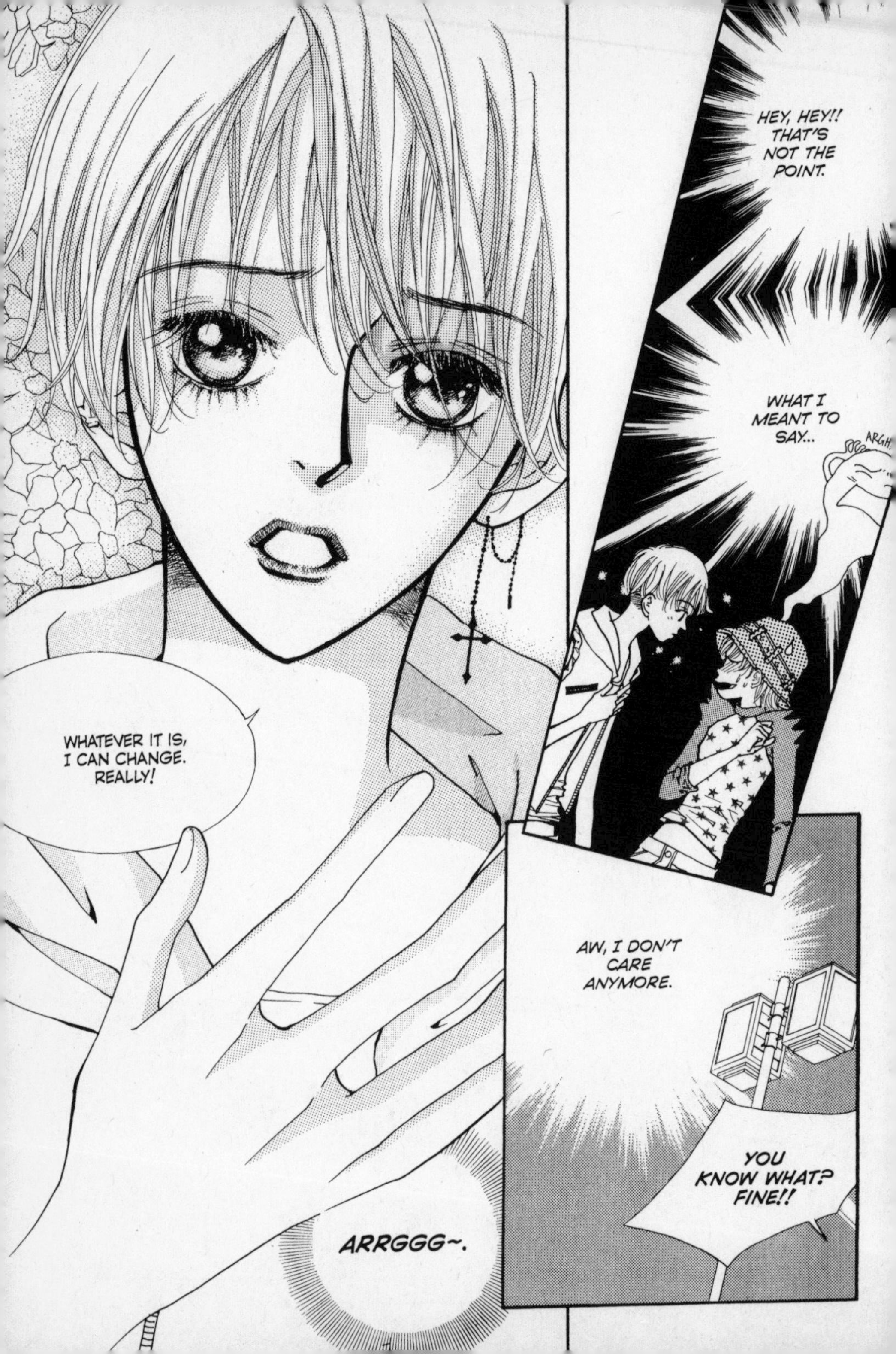
WHATEVER IT IS, I CAN CHANGE. REALLY!
ARRGGG~.
HEY, HEY!! THAT'S NOT THE POINT.
WHAT I MEANT TO SAY...
ARGH.
AW, I DON'T CARE ANYMORE.
YOU KNOW WHAT? FINE!!

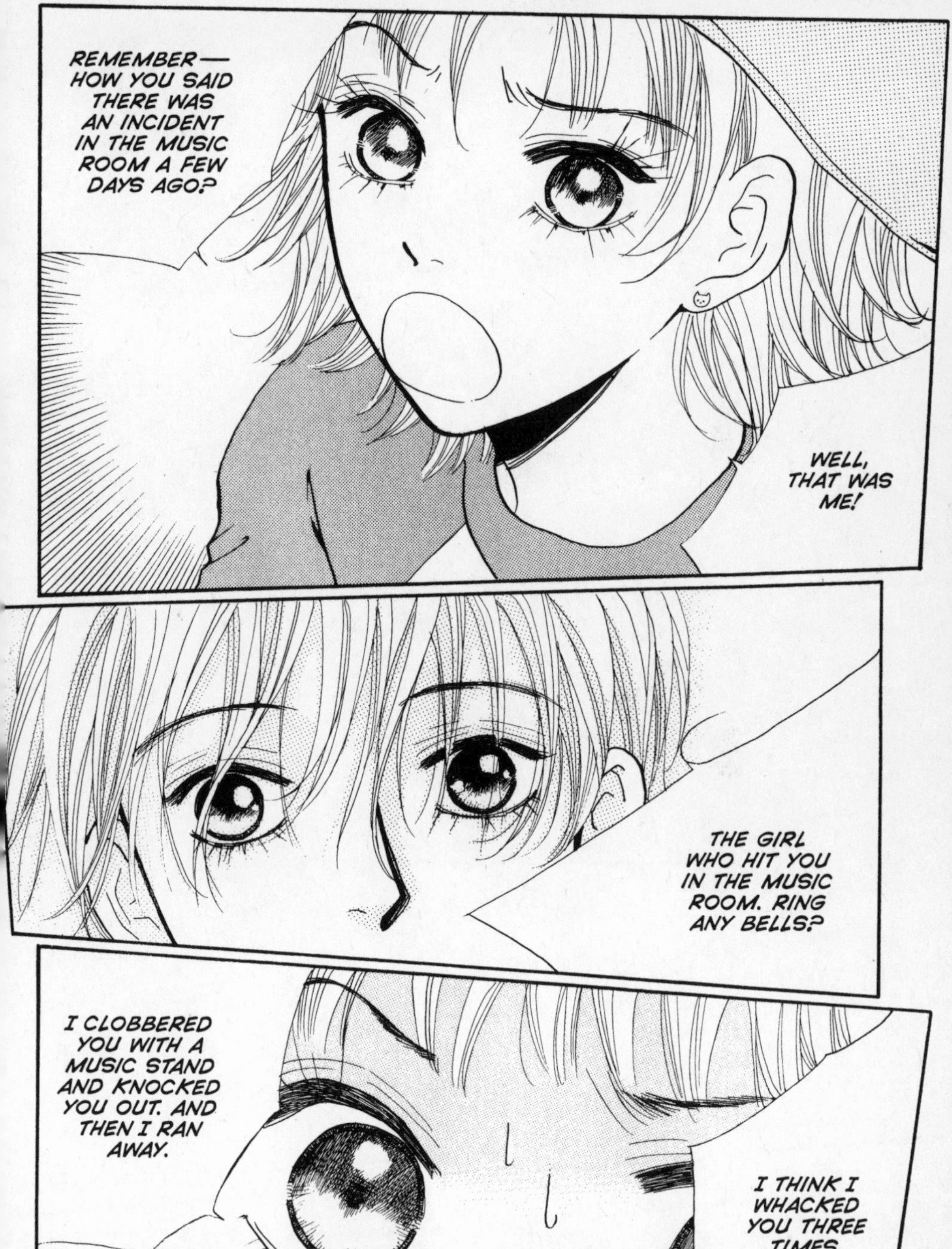
REMEMBER— HOW YOU SAID THERE WAS AN INCIDENT IN THE MUSIC ROOM A FEW DAYS AGO?
WELL, THAT WAS ME!
THE GIRL WHO HIT YOU IN THE MUSIC ROOM. RING ANY BELLS?
I CLOBBERED YOU WITH A MUSIC STAND AND KNOCKED YOU OUT. AND THEN I RAN AWAY.
I THINK I WHACKED YOU THREE TIMES.

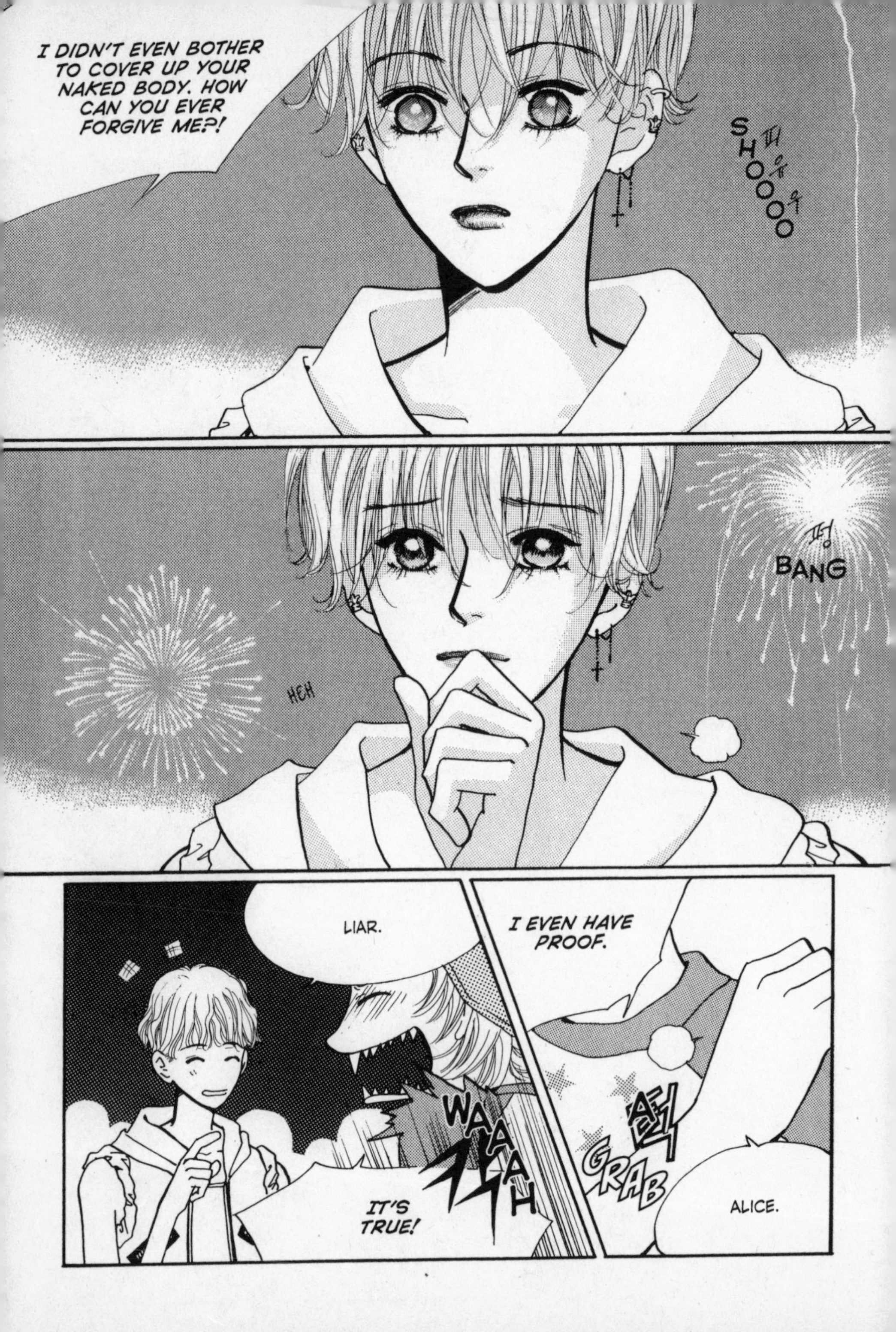
I DIDN'T EVEN BOTHER TO COVER UP YOUR NAKED BODY. HOW CAN YOU EVER FORGIVE ME?!
SHOOOOO
펑
BANG
HEH
LIAR.
WAAAAH
IT'S TRUE!
I EVEN HAVE PROOF.
덥석
GRAB
ALICE.

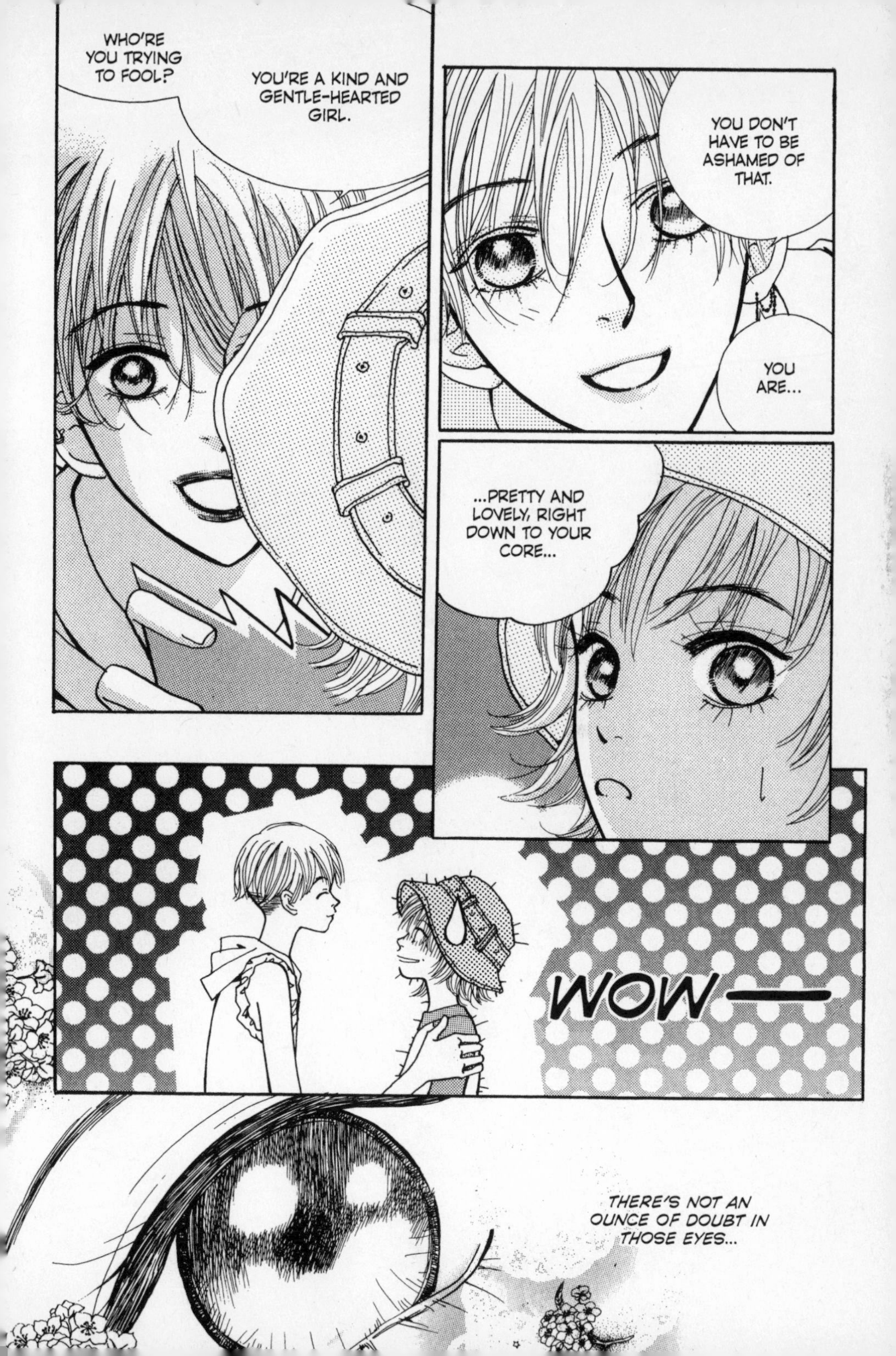

WHO'RE YOU TRYING TO FOOL?
YOU'RE A KIND AND GENTLE-HEARTED GIRL.
YOU DON'T HAVE TO BE ASHAMED OF THAT.
YOU ARE...
...PRETTY AND LOVELY, RIGHT DOWN TO YOUR CORE...
WOW—
THERE'S NOT AN OUNCE OF DOUBT IN THOSE EYES...

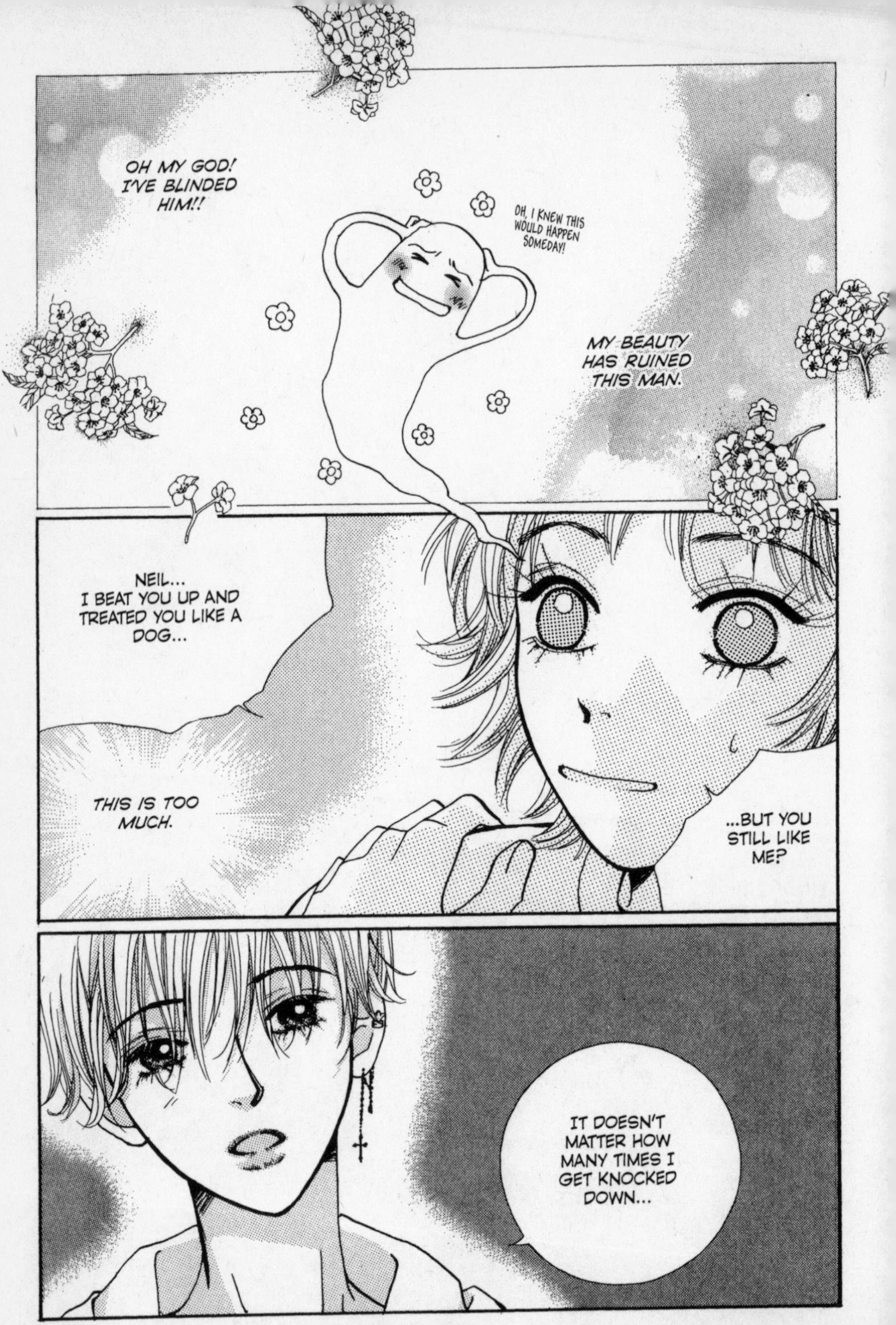
OH MY GOD! I'VE BLINDED HIM!!
OH, I KNEW THIS WOULD HAPPEN SOMEDAY!
MY BEAUTY HAS RUINED THIS MAN.
NEIL... I BEAT YOU UP AND TREATED YOU LIKE A DOG...
THIS IS TOO MUCH.
...BUT YOU STILL LIKE ME?
IT DOESN'T MATTER HOW MANY TIMES I GET KNOCKED DOWN...

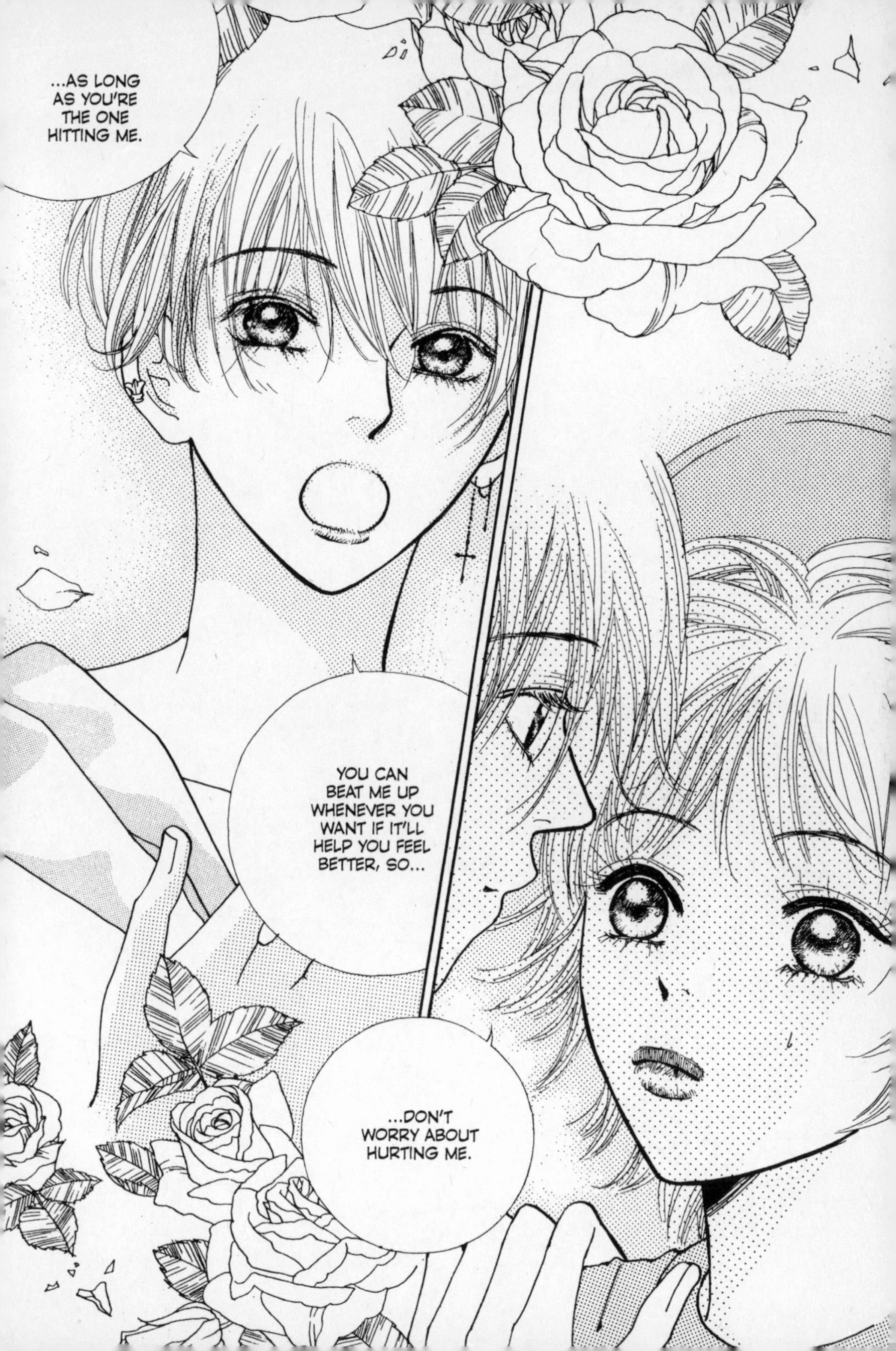
...AS LONG AS YOU'RE THE ONE HITTING ME.
YOU CAN BEAT ME UP WHENEVER YOU WANT IF IT'LL HELP YOU FEEL BETTER, SO...
...DON'T WORRY ABOUT HURTING ME.

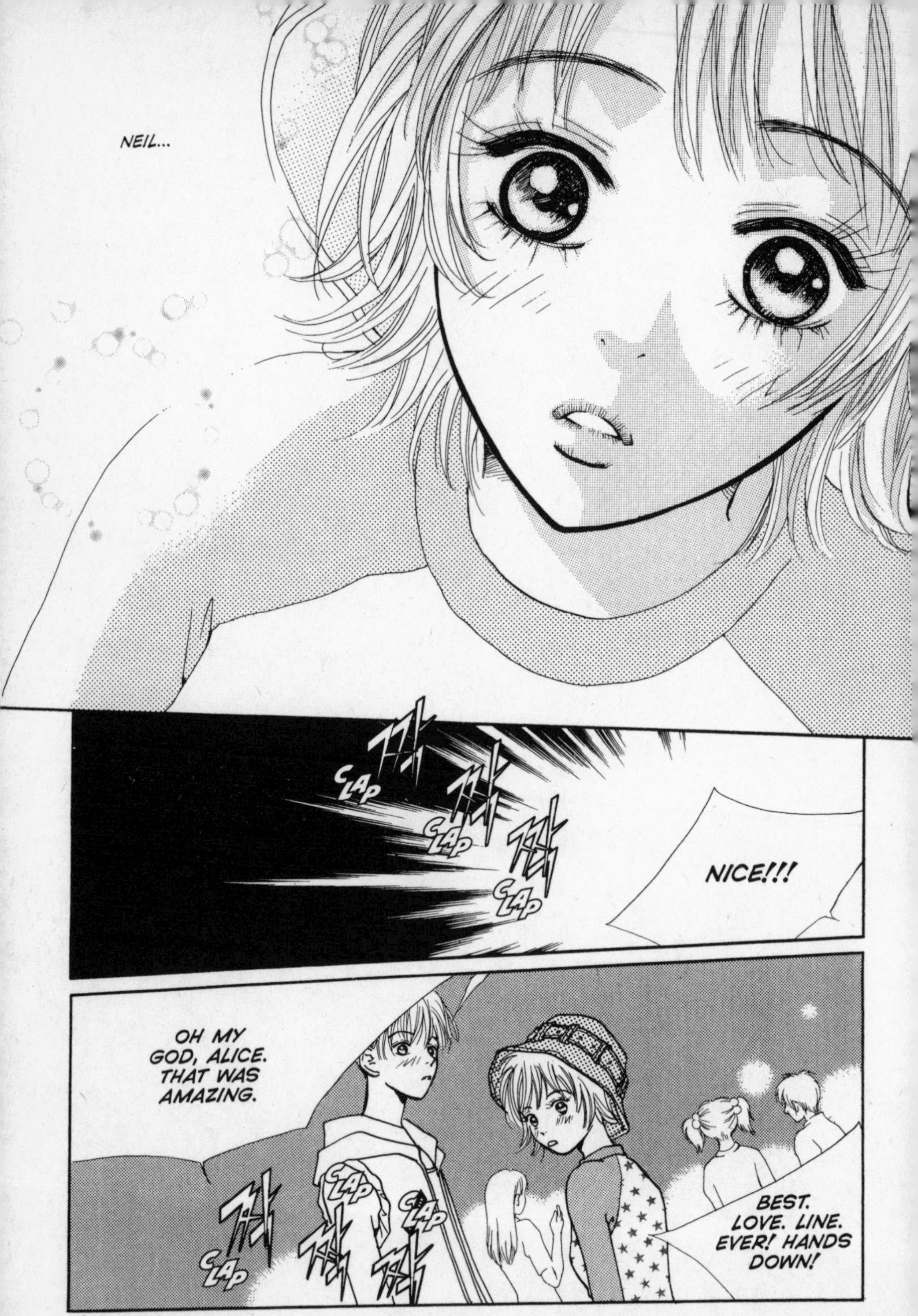
NEIL...
CLAP
CLAP
CLAP
NICE!!!
OH MY GOD, ALICE. THAT WAS AMAZING.
CLAP
CLAP
CLAP
BEST. LOVE. LINE. EVER! HANDS DOWN!

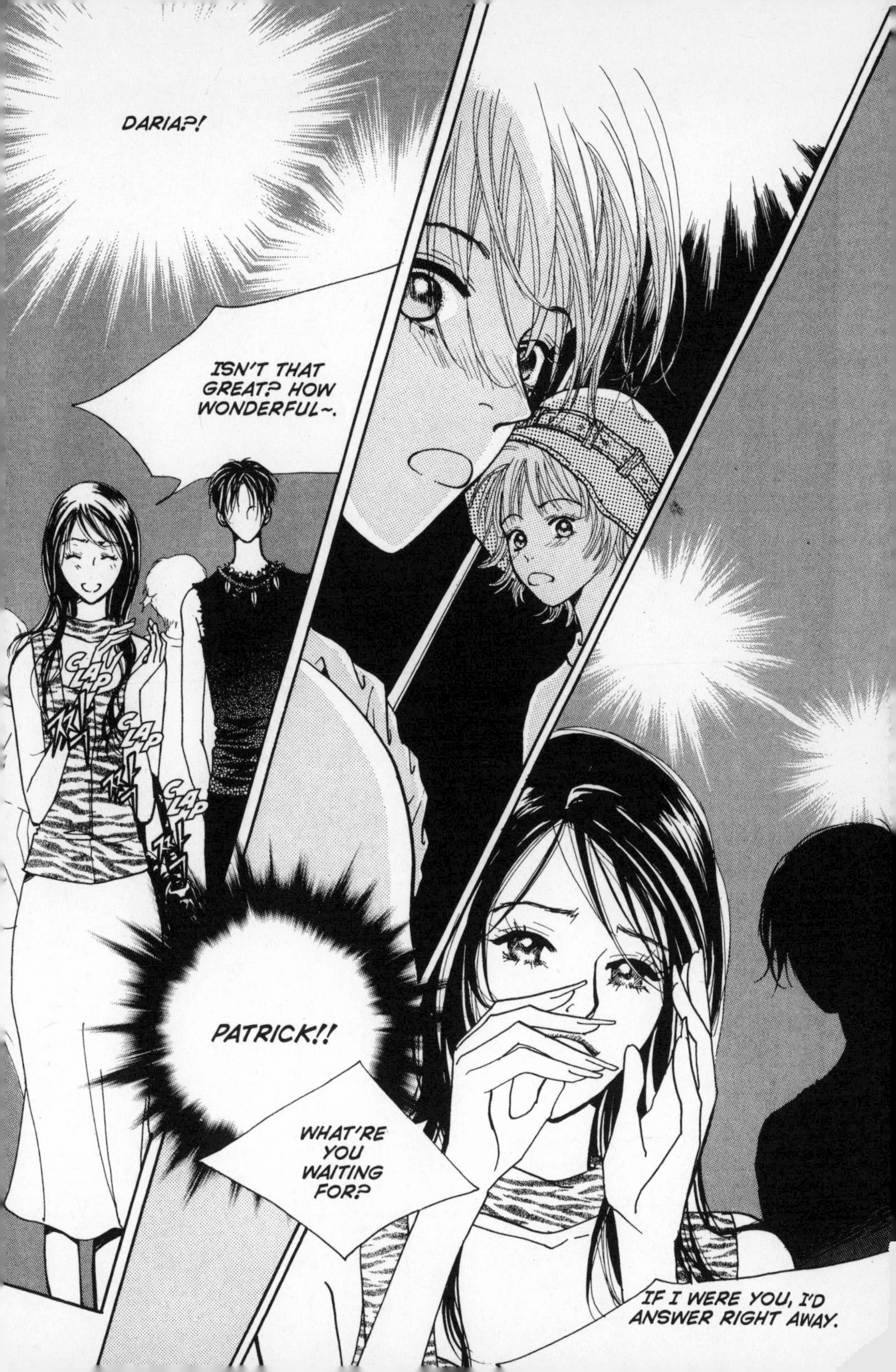
DARIA?!
ISN'T THAT GREAT? HOW WONDERFUL~.
CLAP
CLAP
CLAP
PATRICK!!
WHAT'RE YOU WAITING FOR?
IF I WERE YOU, I'D ANSWER RIGHT AWAY.

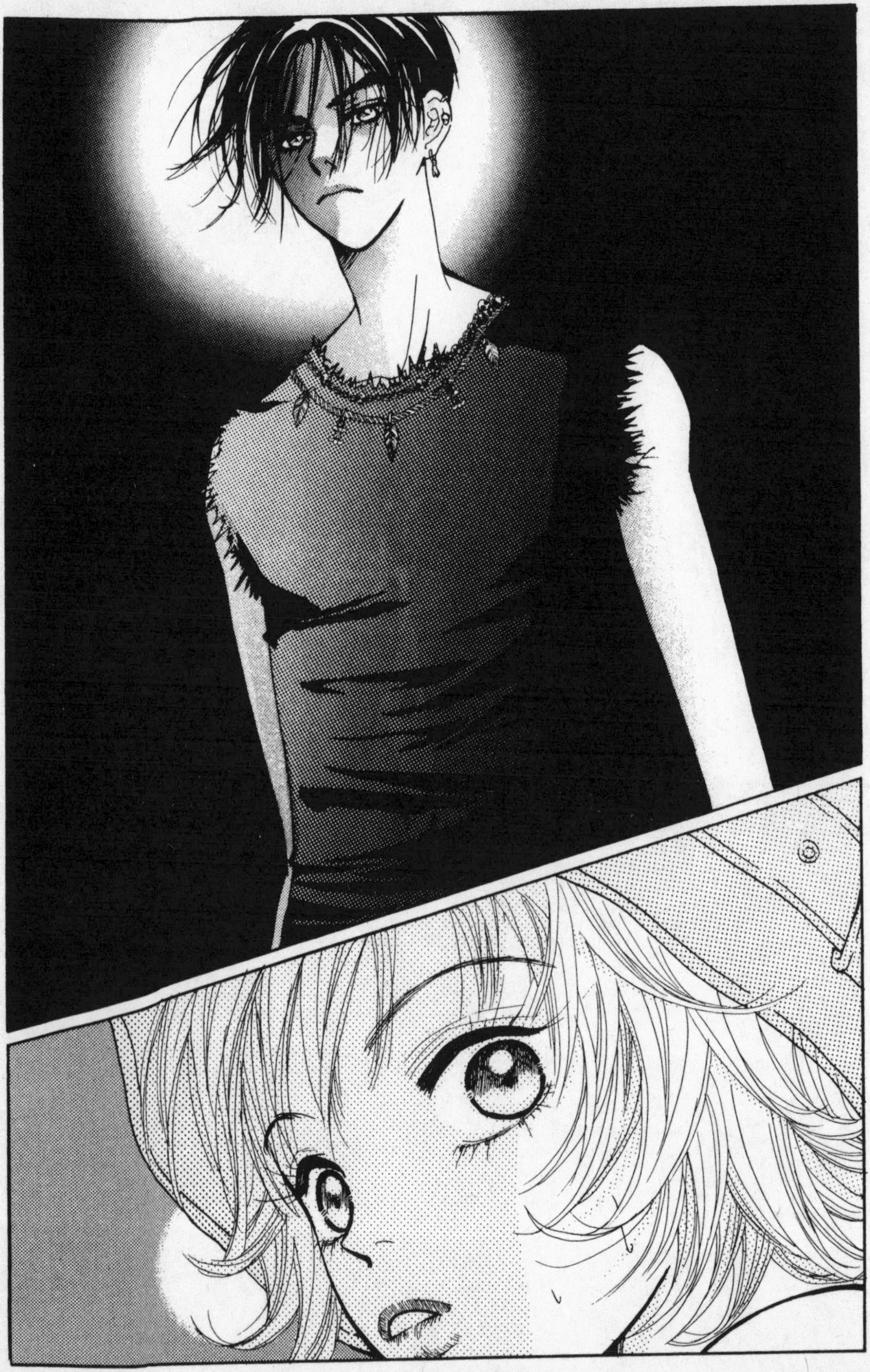

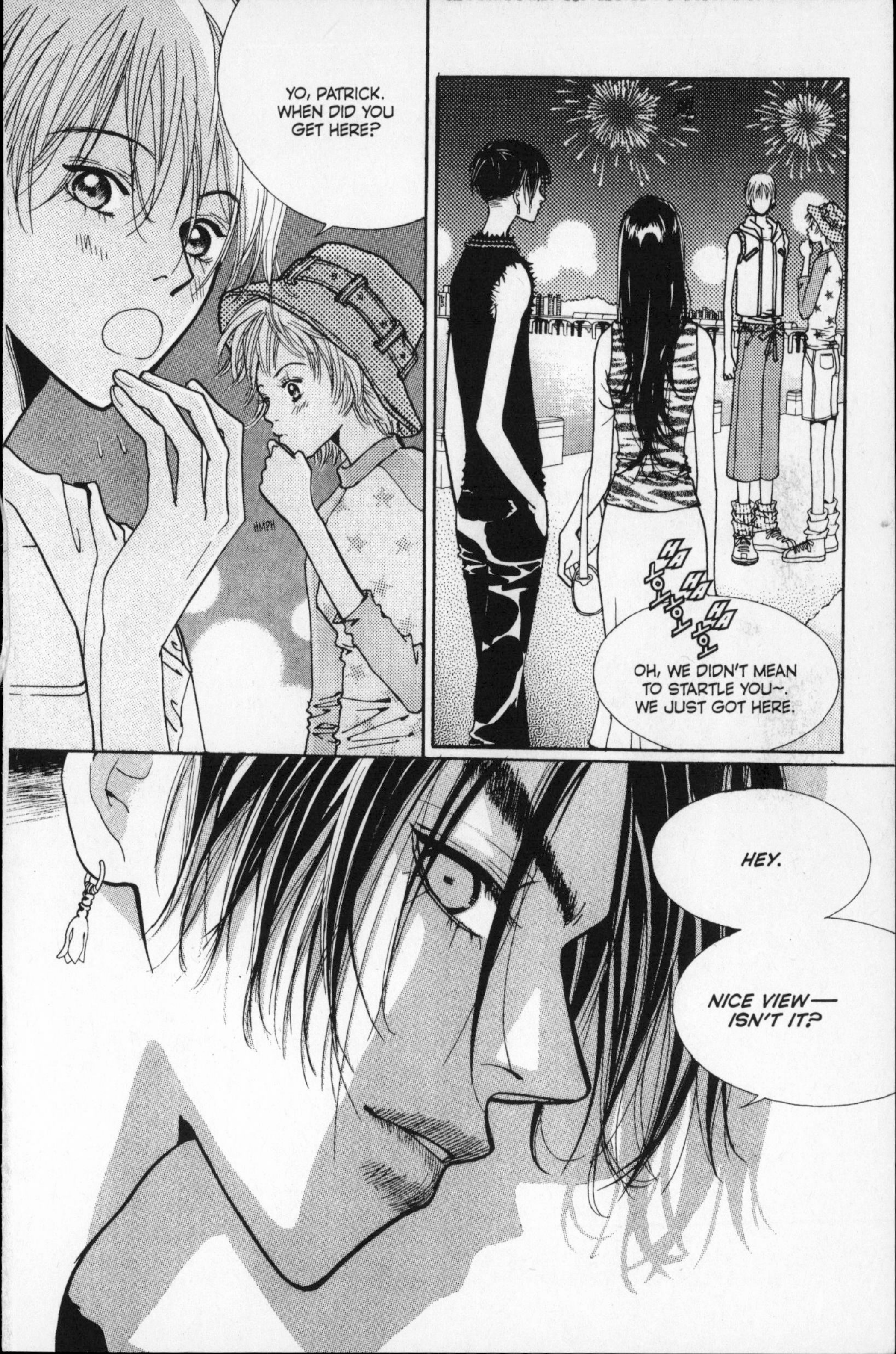
YO, PATRICK. WHEN DID YOU GET HERE?
HMPH
HA HA HA
OH, WE DIDN'T MEAN TO STARTLE YOU~. WE JUST GOT HERE.
HEY.
NICE VIEW— ISN'T IT?

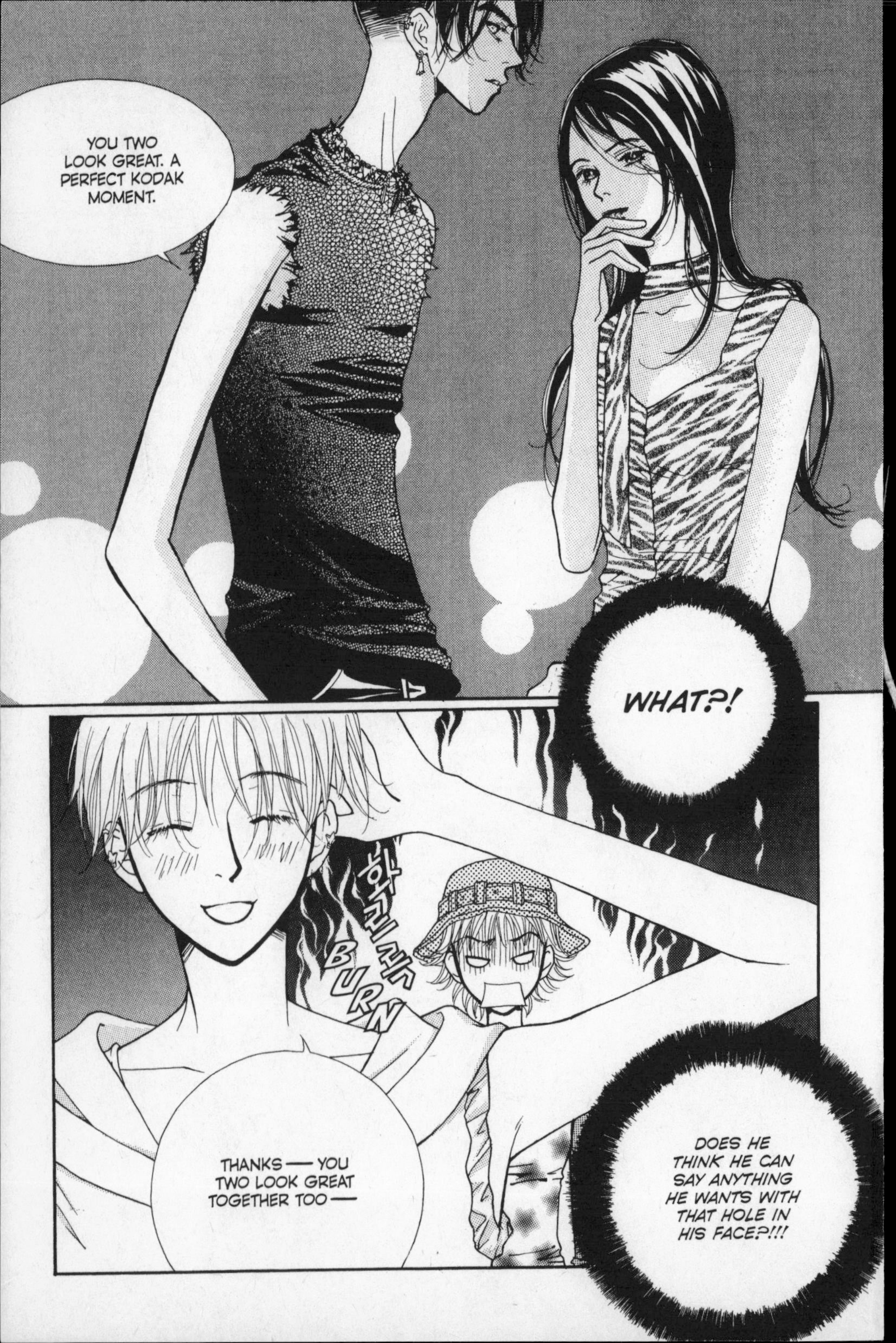
YOU TWO LOOK GREAT. A PERFECT KODAK MOMENT.
WHAT?!
BURN
THANKS — YOU TWO LOOK GREAT TOGETHER TOO —
DOES HE THINK HE CAN SAY ANYTHING HE WANTS WITH THAT HOLE IN HIS FACE?!!!

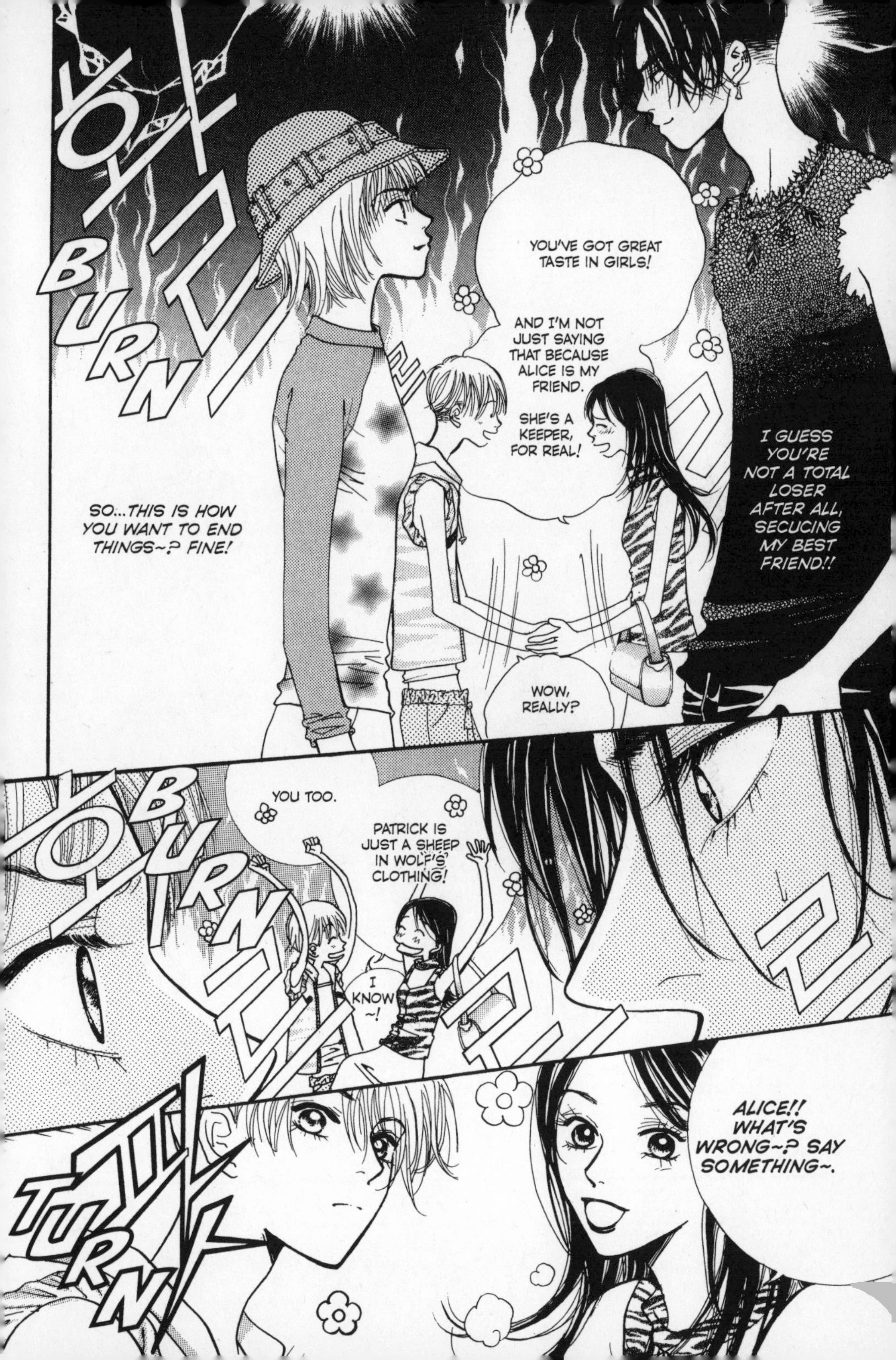

BURN
SO...THIS IS HOW YOU WANT TO END THINGS~? FINE!
YOU'VE GOT GREAT TASTE IN GIRLS!
AND I'M NOT JUST SAYING THAT BECAUSE ALICE IS MY FRIEND.
SHE'S A KEEPER, FOR REAL!
WOW, REALLY?
I GUESS YOU'RE NOT A TOTAL LOSER AFTER ALL, SECUCING MY BEST FRIEND!!
BURN
YOU TOO.
PATRICK IS JUST A SHEEP IN WOLF'S CLOTHING!
I KNOW~!
TURN
ALICE!! WHAT'S WRONG~? SAY SOMETHING~.

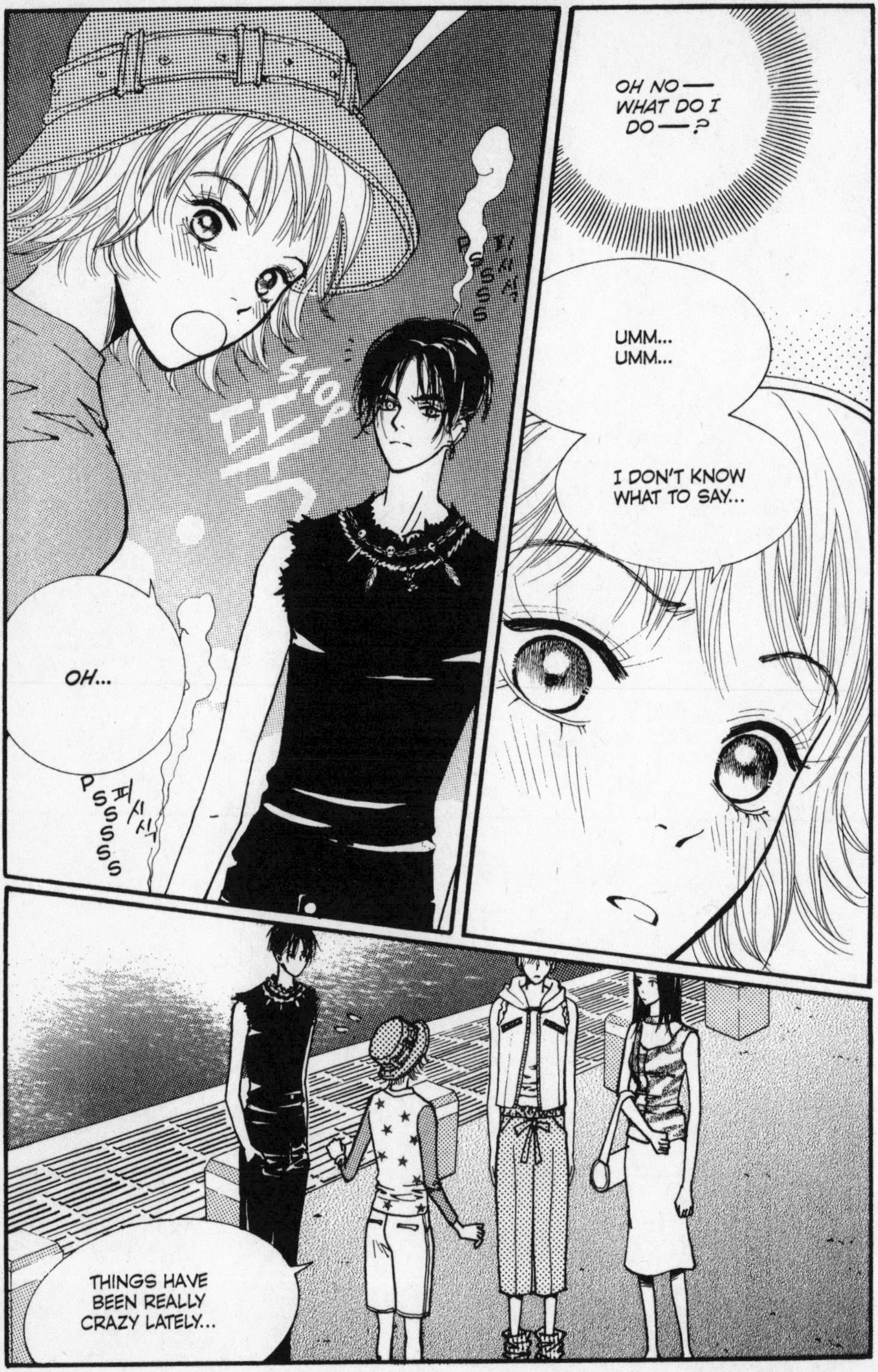
PSSSS
STOP
OH...
PSSSSS
OH NO— WHAT DO I DO—?
UMM... UMM...
I DON'T KNOW WHAT TO SAY...
THINGS HAVE BEEN REALLY CRAZY LATELY...

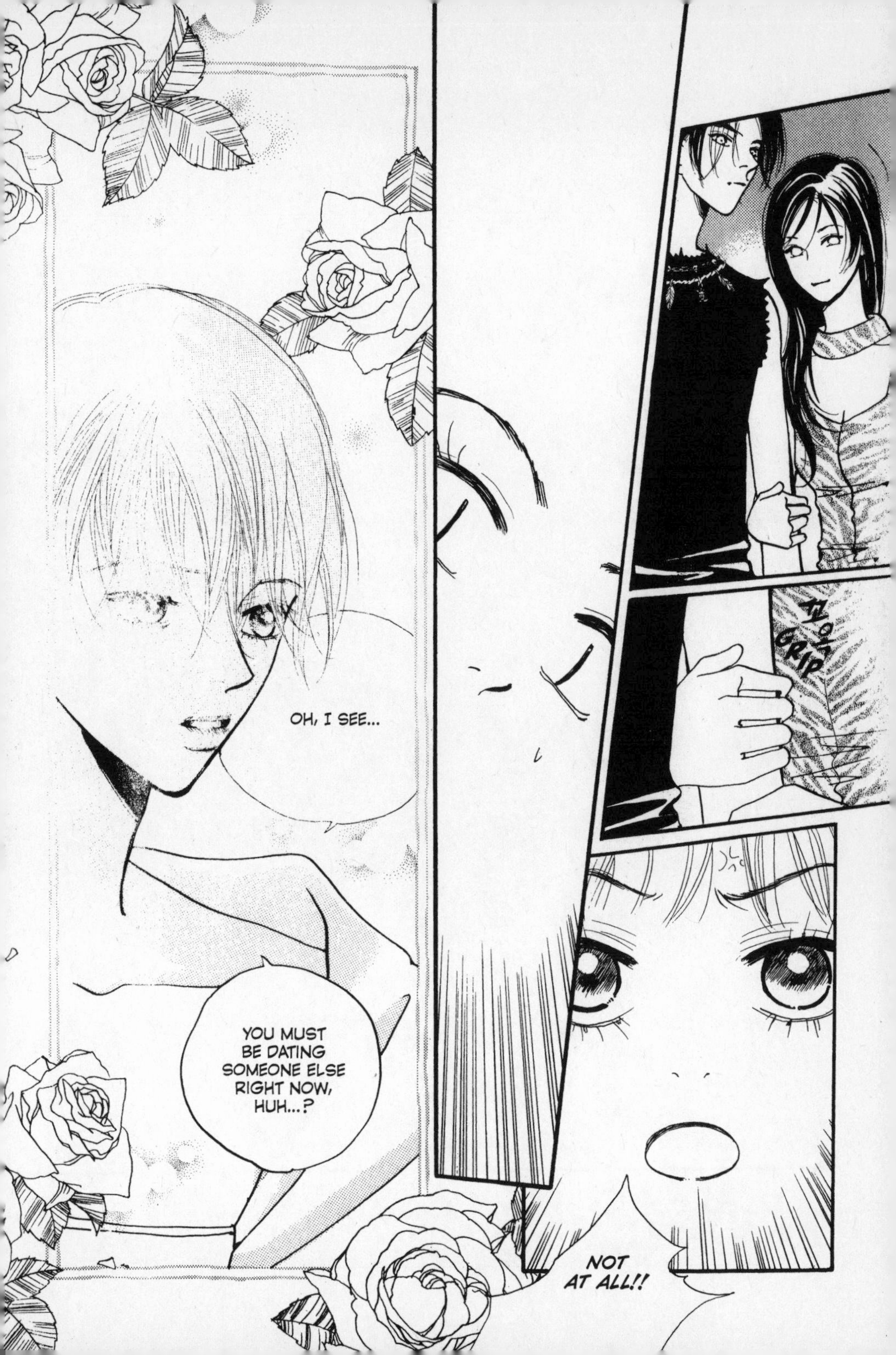
OH, I SEE...
YOU MUST BE DATING SOMEONE ELSE RIGHT NOW, HUH...?
GRIP
NOT AT ALL!!

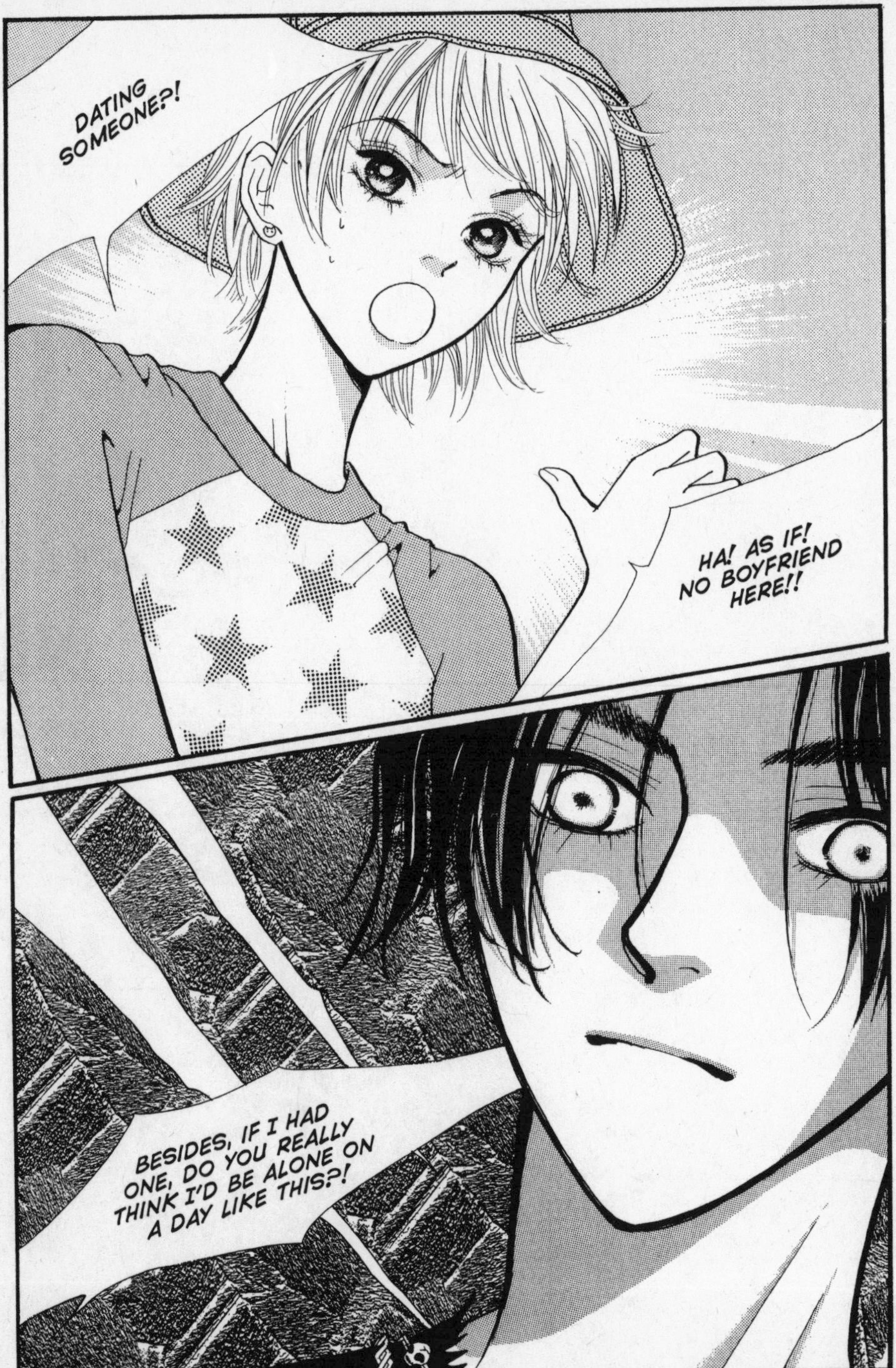
DATING SOMEONE?!
HA! AS IF! NO BOYFRIEND HERE!!
BESIDES, IF I HAD ONE, DO YOU REALLY THINK I'D BE ALONE ON A DAY LIKE THIS?!

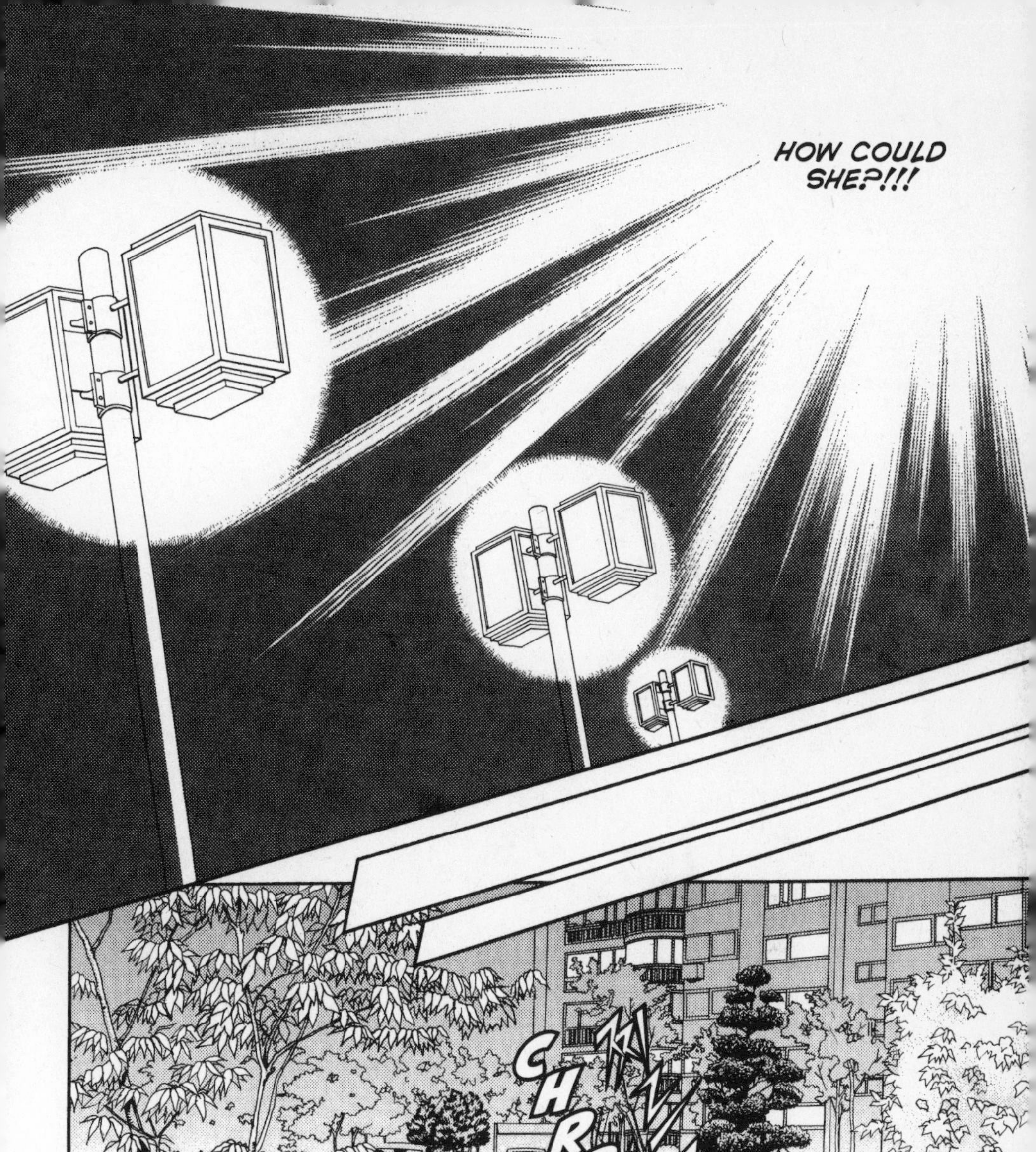
HOW COULD SHE?!!!
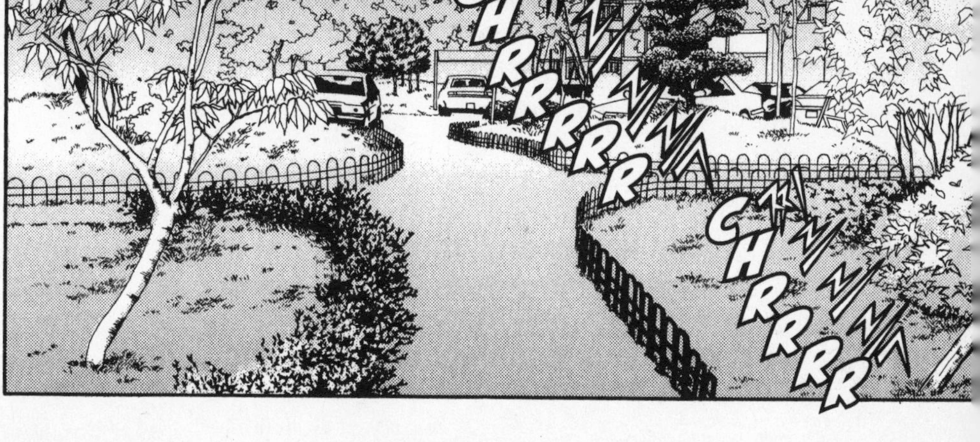
CHRRRRR
CHRRRR

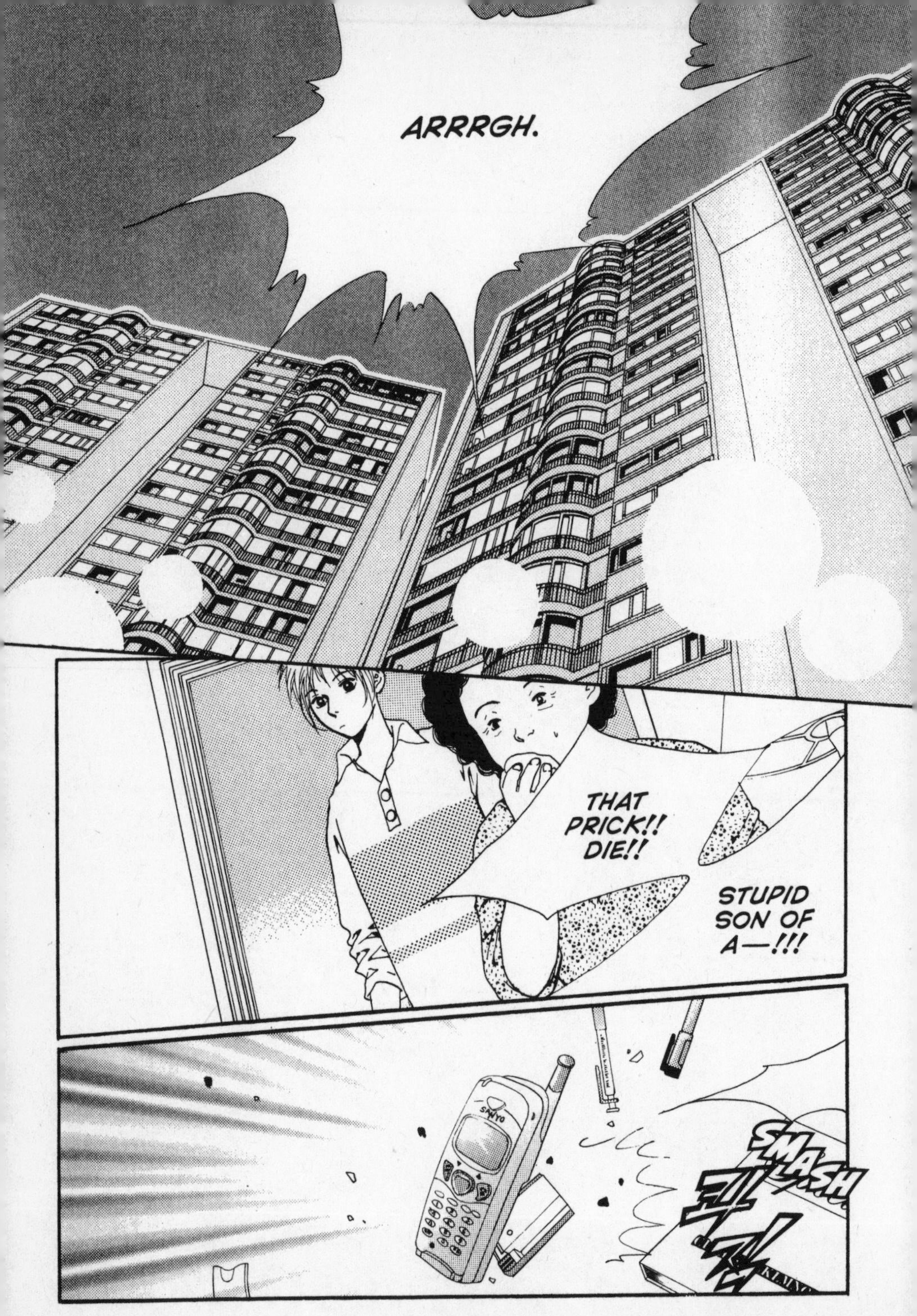
ARRRGH.
THAT PRICK!! DIE!!
STUPID SON OF A—!!!
SANYO
SMASH

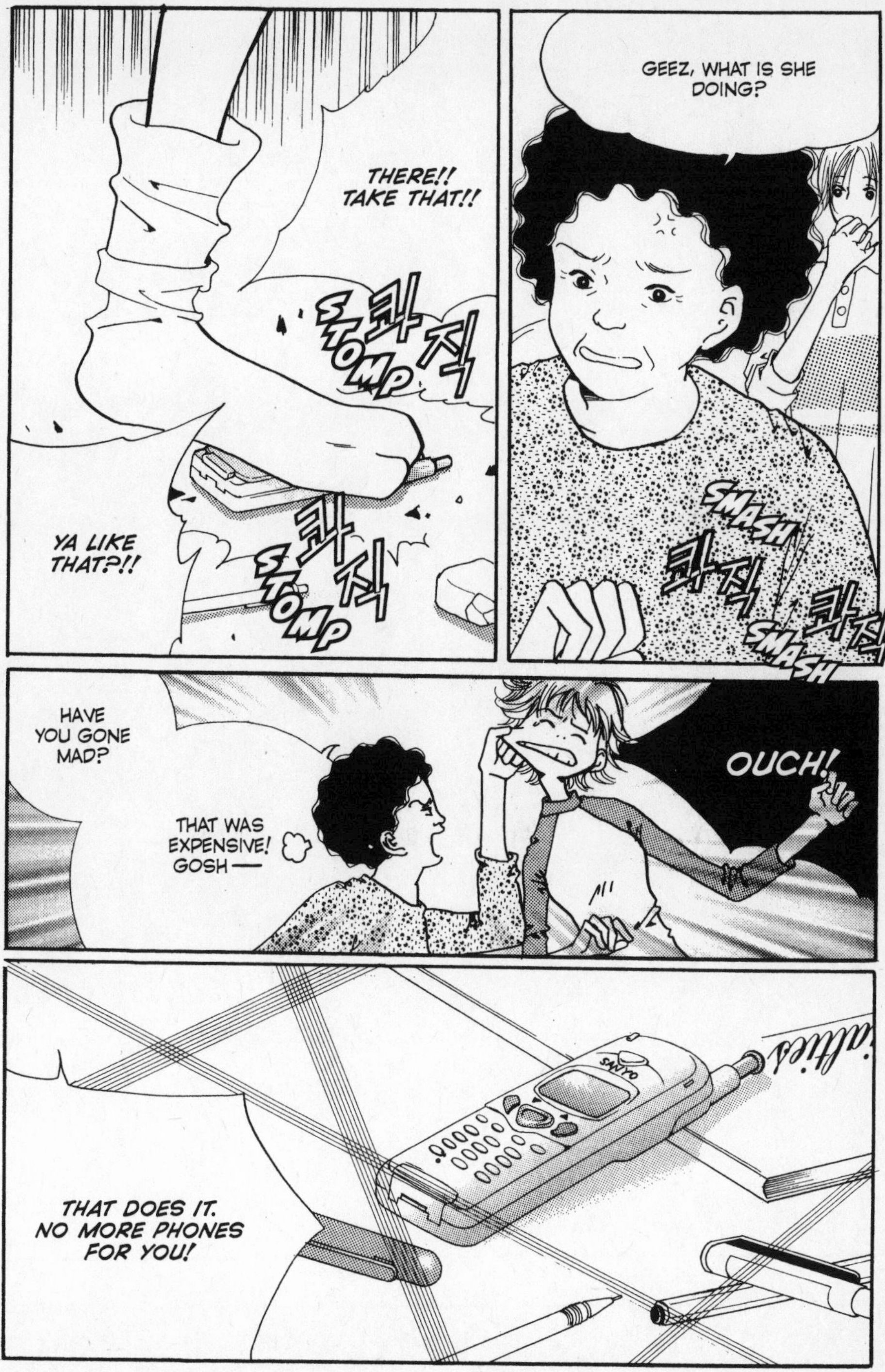
THERE!! TAKE THAT!!
콰직
STOMP
콰직
STOMP
YA LIKE THAT?!!
GEEZ, WHAT IS SHE DOING?
SMASH
콰직
SMASH
콰직
HAVE YOU GONE MAD?
THAT WAS EXPENSIVE! GOSH —
OUCH!
SANYO
THAT DOES IT. NO MORE PHONES FOR YOU!

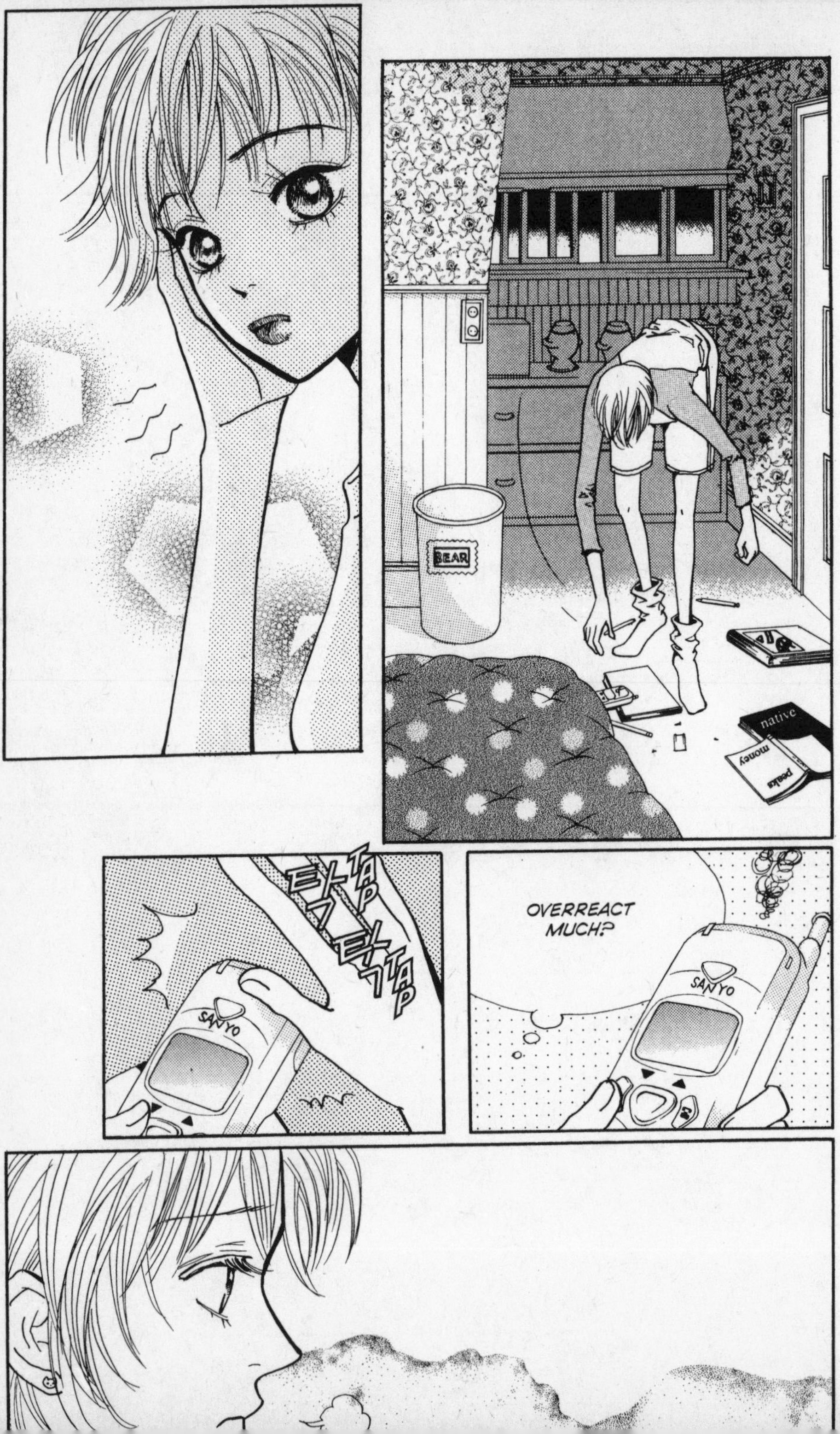
BEAR
native
money
peaks
TAP
TAP
SANYO
OVERREACT MUCH?
SANYO

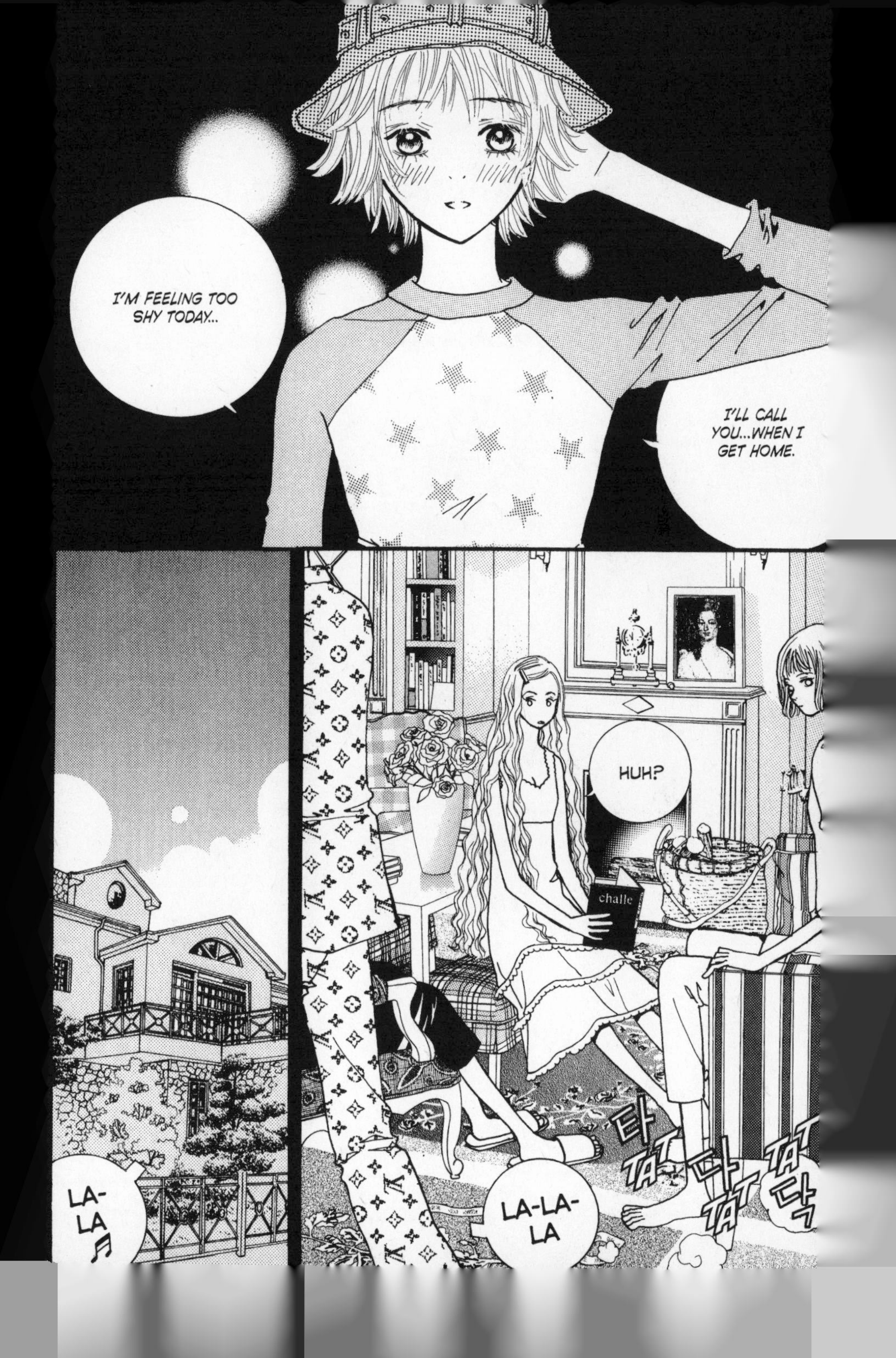
I'M FEELING TOO SHY TODAY...
I'LL CALL YOU...WHEN I GET HOME.
LA-LA♪
HUH?
LA-LA-LA
타 TA TAT
닥 TA TAT
TA TAT 닥

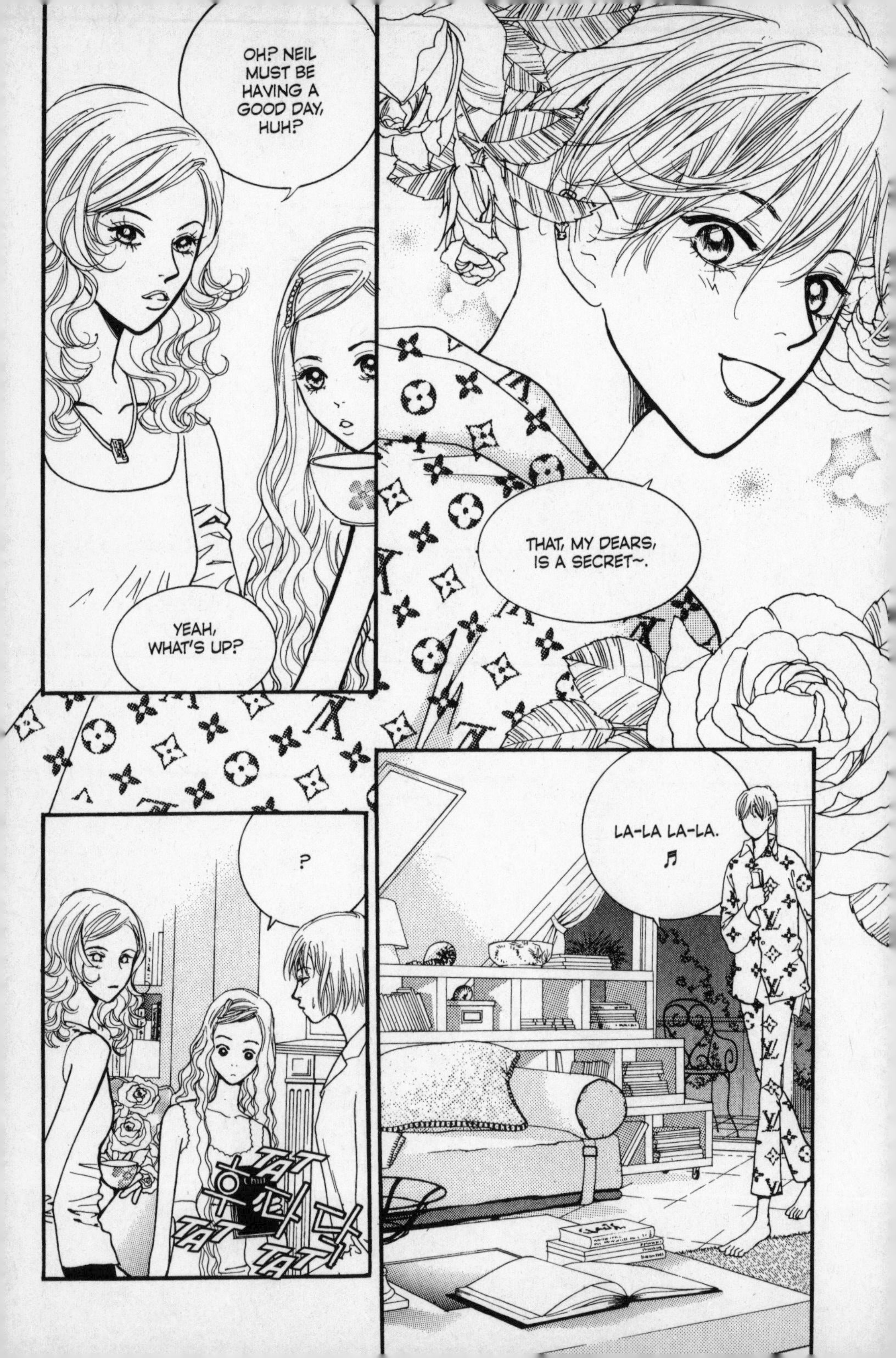
OH? NEIL MUST BE HAVING A GOOD DAY, HUH?
YEAH, WHAT'S UP?
THAT, MY DEARS, IS A SECRET~.
?
TAT TAT
TAT TAT
LA-LA LA-LA. ♬

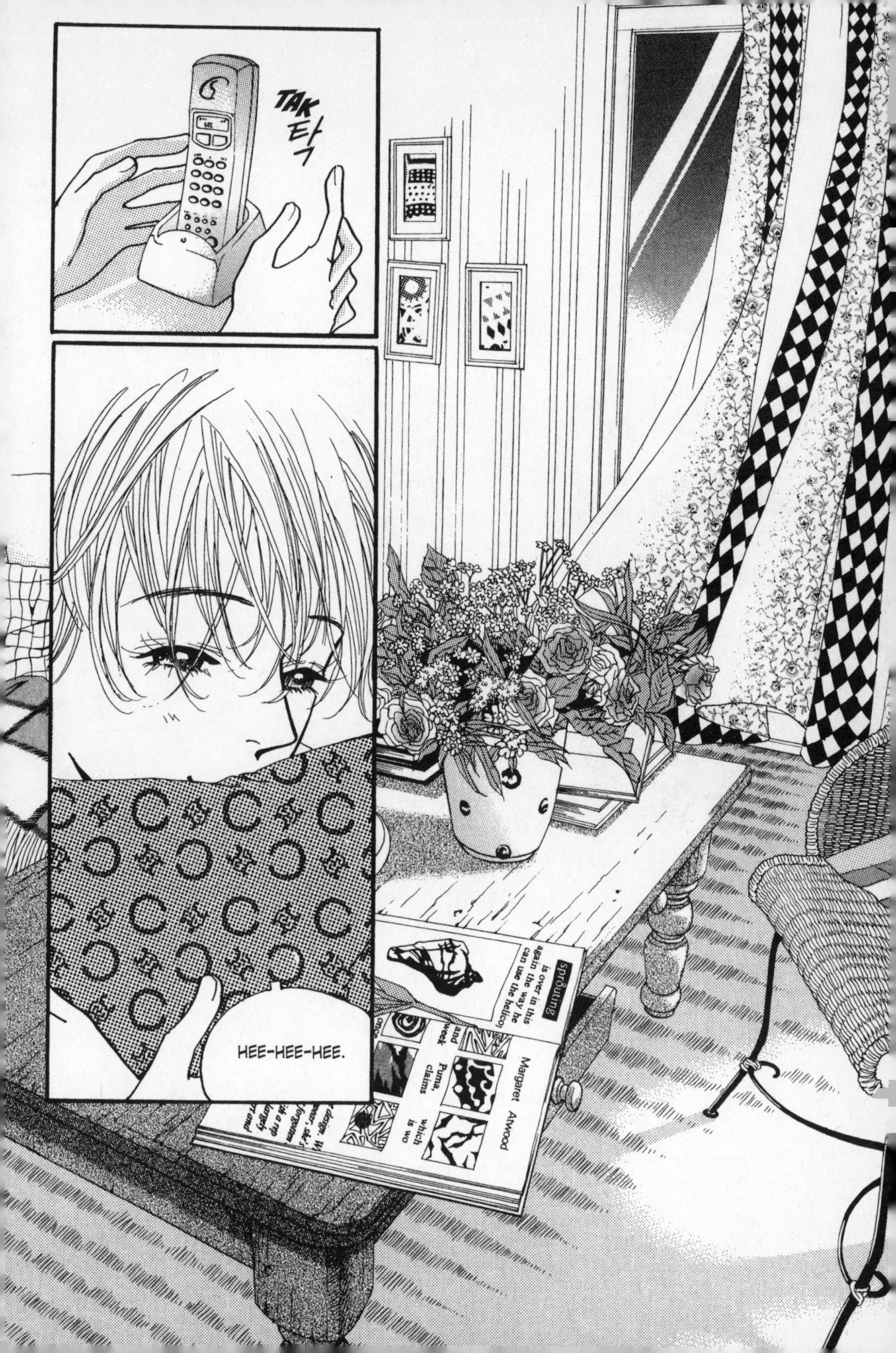
TAK
HEE-HEE-HEE.

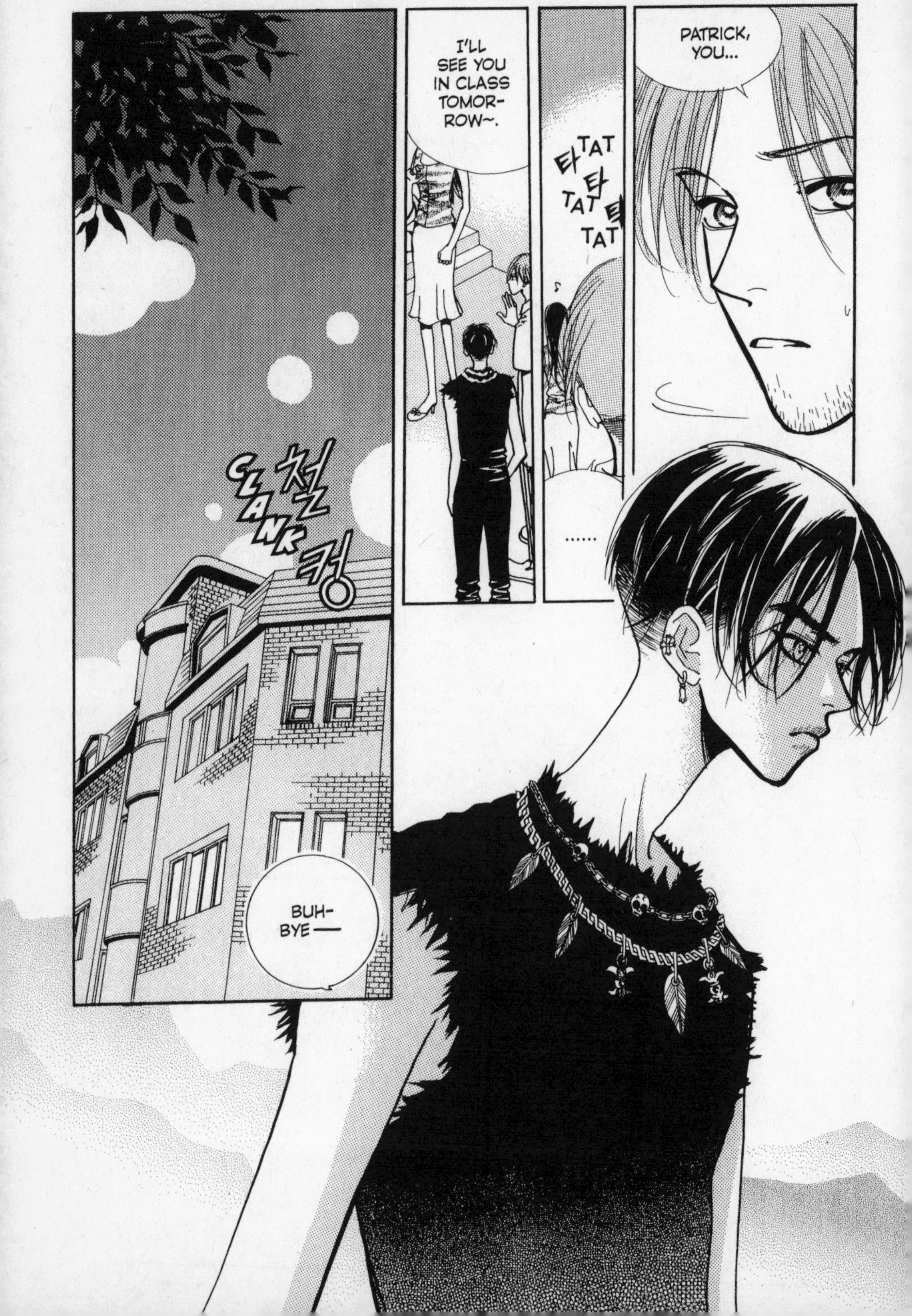

CLANK
철컹
BUH-BYE —
I'LL SEE YOU IN CLASS TOMOR-ROW~.
타 TAT 타 TAT 타 TAT
TAT
......
PATRICK, YOU...

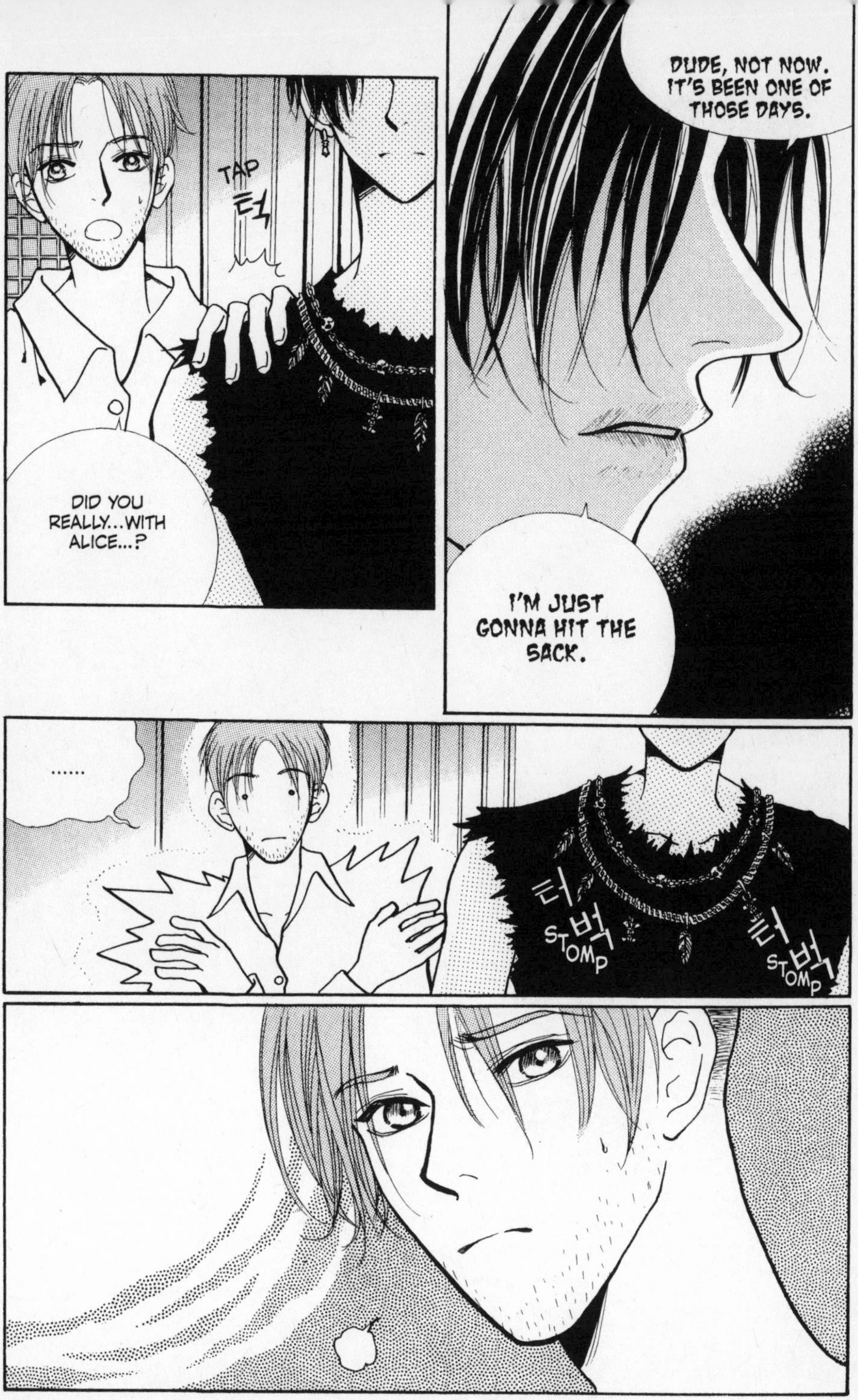
TAP
턱
DID YOU REALLY...WITH ALICE...?
DUDE, NOT NOW. IT'S BEEN ONE OF THOSE DAYS.
I'M JUST GONNA HIT THE SACK.
......
터벅
STOMP
터벅
STOMP

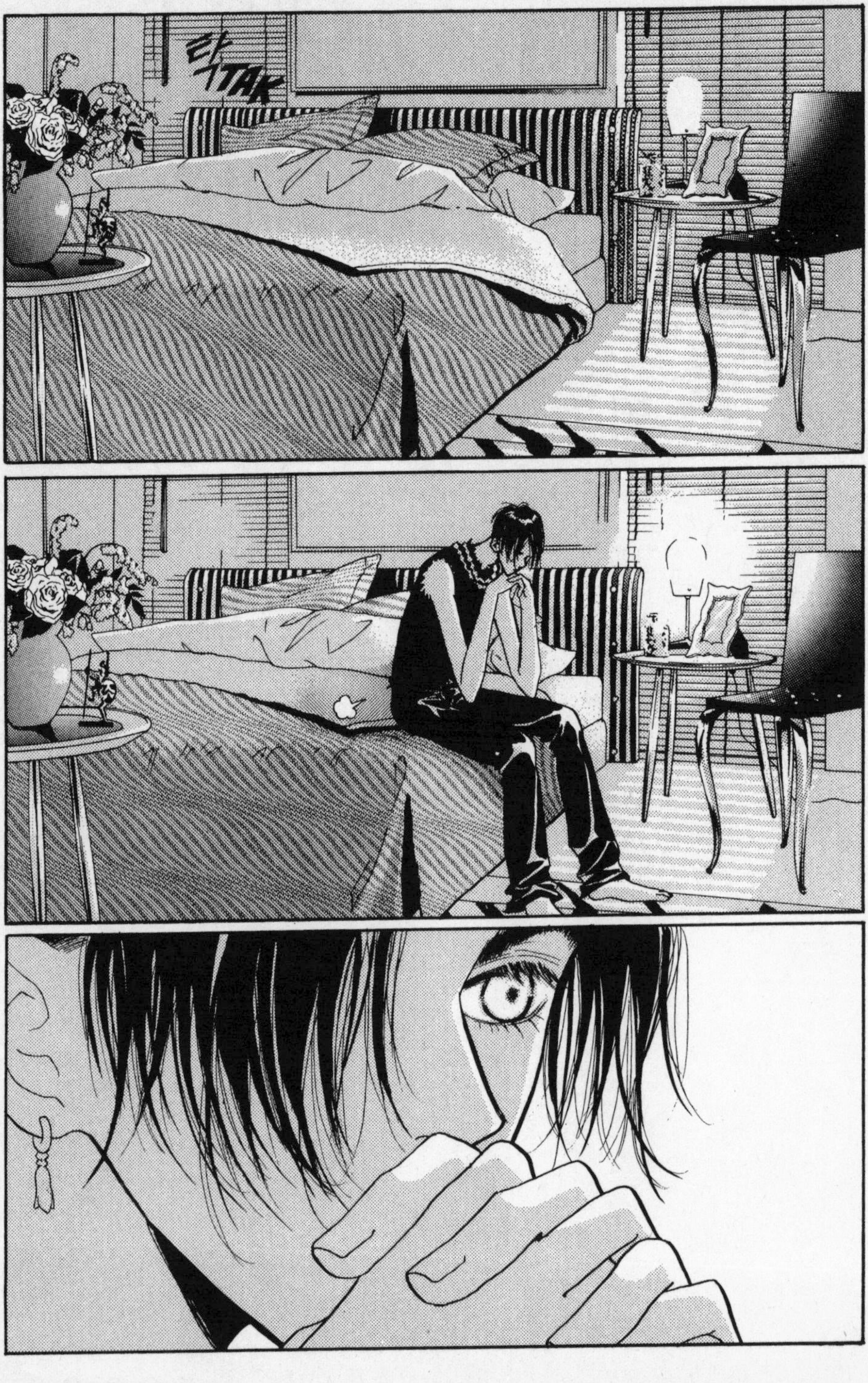
TAK

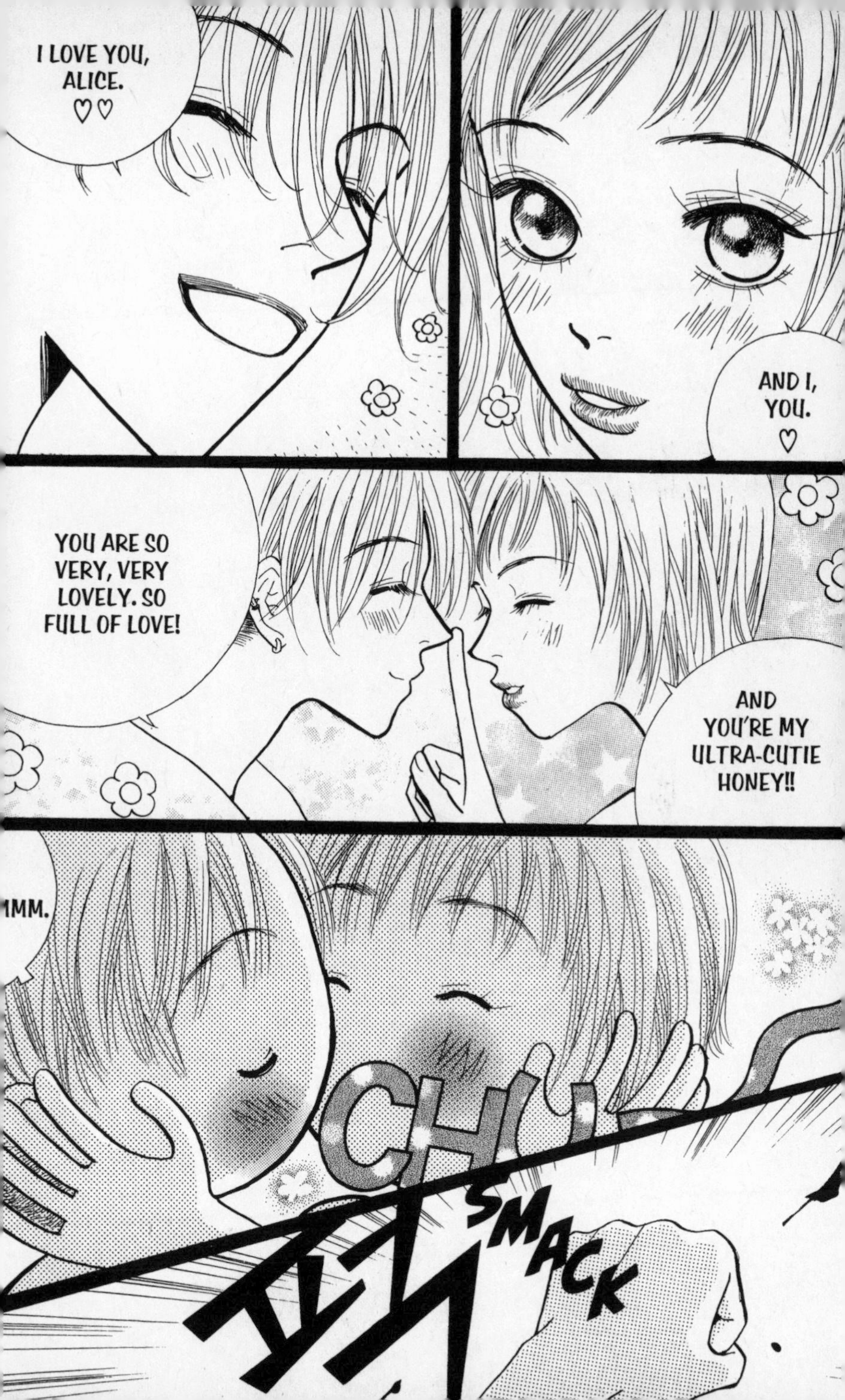
I LOVE YOU, ALICE. ♡♡
AND I, YOU. ♡
YOU ARE SO VERY, VERY LOVELY. SO FULL OF LOVE!
AND YOU'RE MY ULTRA-CUTIE HONEY!!
MM.
CHU
SMACK

WHO AM I REALLY JEALOUS OF?
NEIL...OR ALICE?

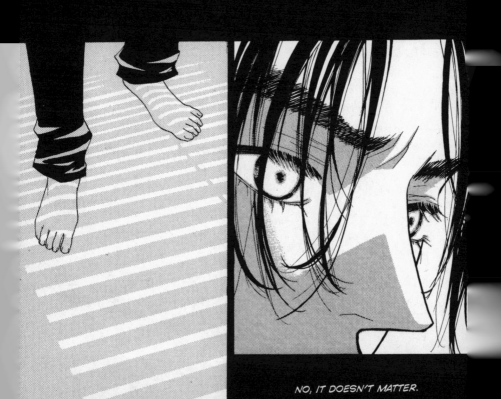

NO, IT DOESN'T MATTER.

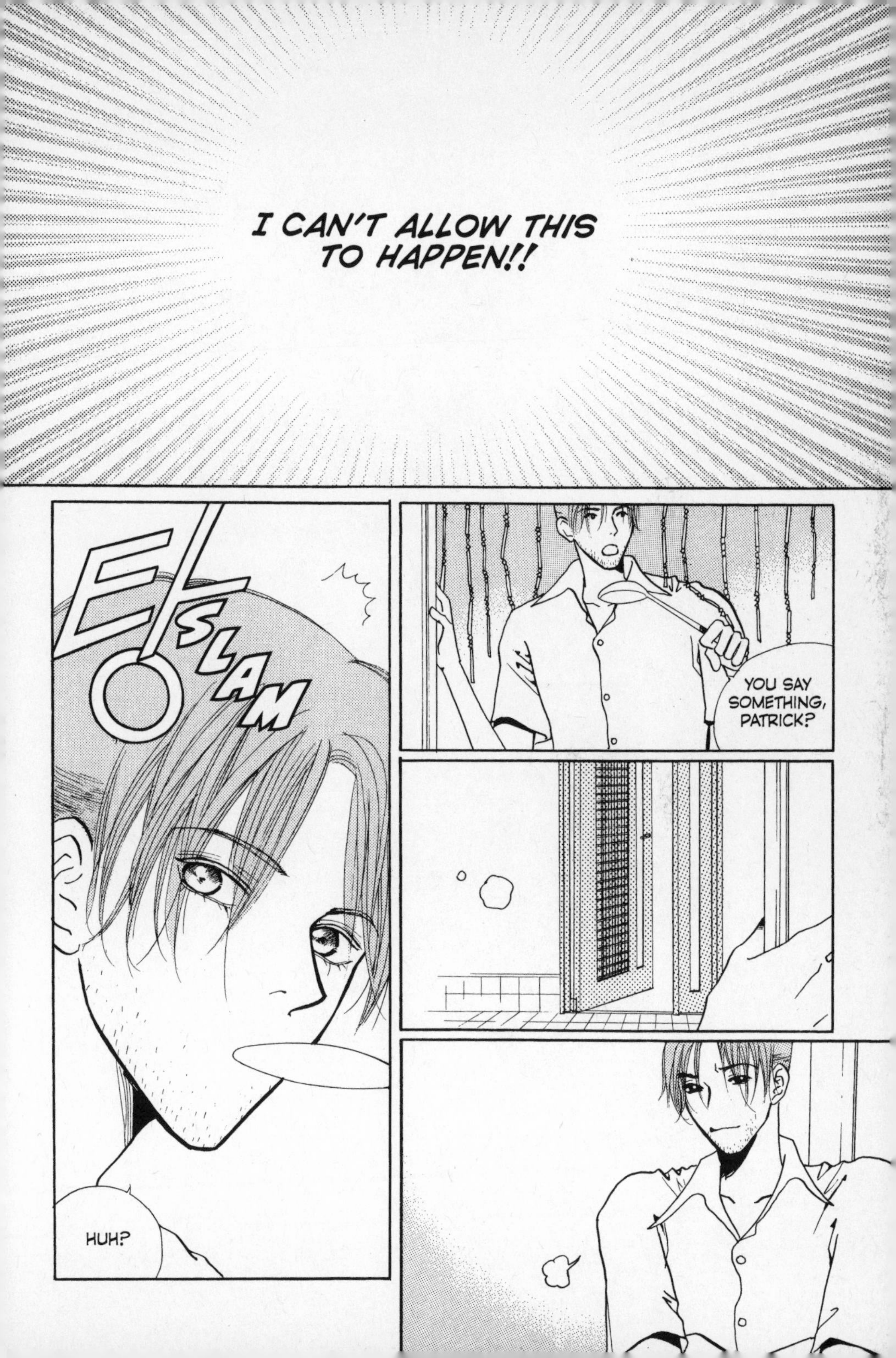
I CAN'T ALLOW THIS TO HAPPEN!!
SLAM
HUH?
YOU SAY SOMETHING, PATRICK?

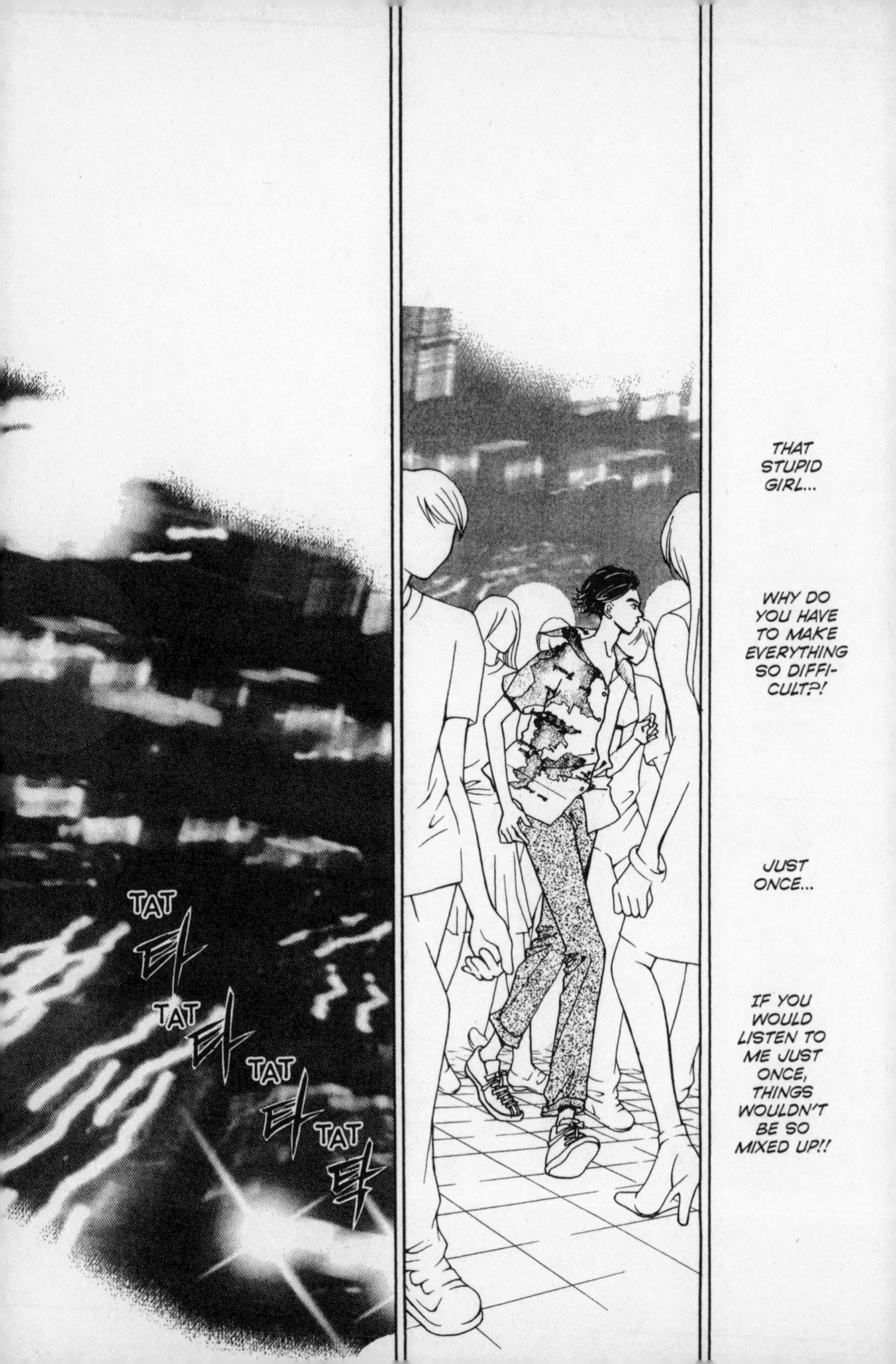

TAT 타
TAT 타
TAT 타
TAT 탁
THAT STUPID GIRL...
WHY DO YOU HAVE TO MAKE EVERYTHING SO DIFFI-CULT?!
JUST ONCE...
IF YOU WOULD LISTEN TO ME JUST ONCE, THINGS WOULDN'T BE SO MIXED UP!!

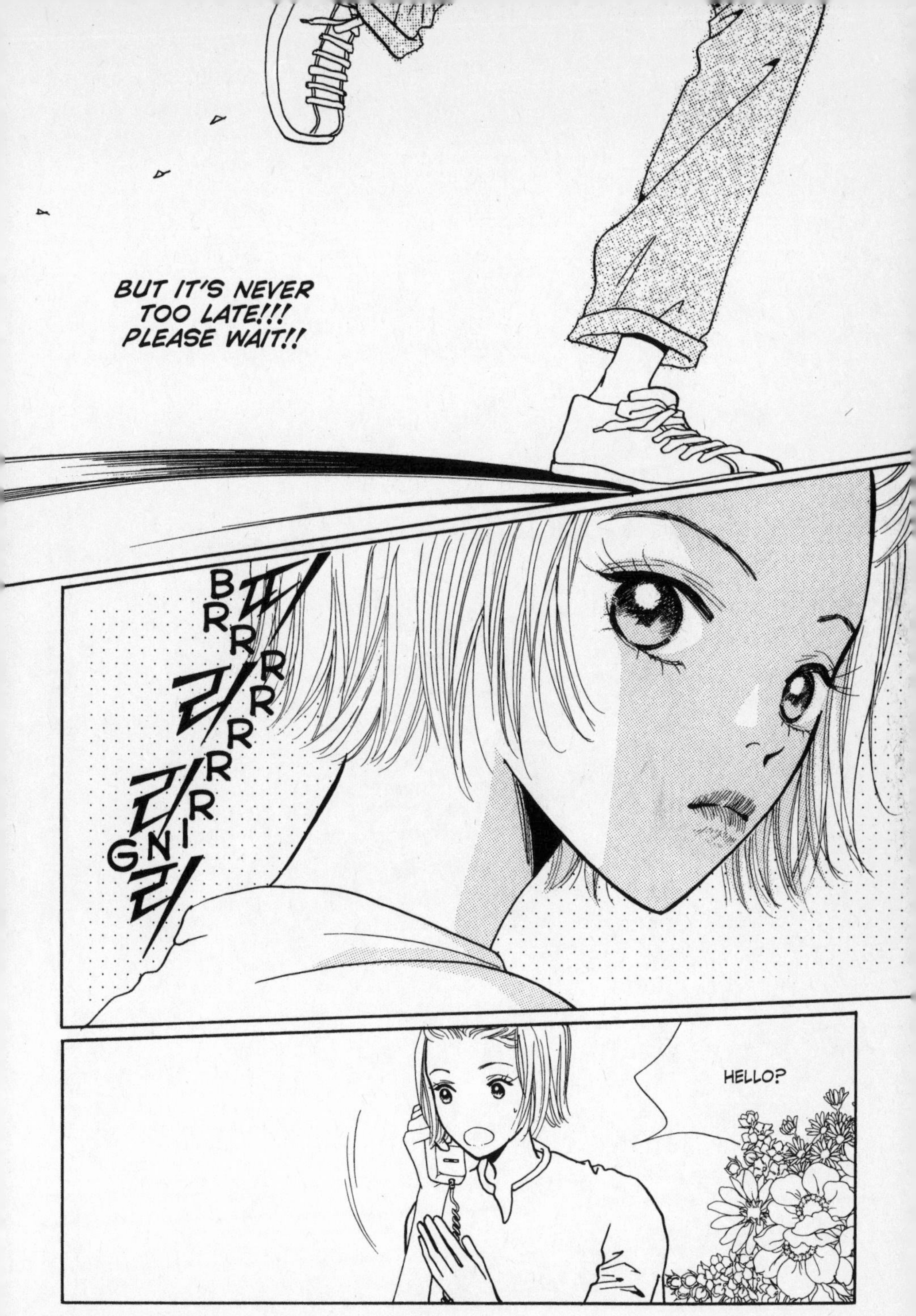
BUT IT'S NEVER TOO LATE!!! PLEASE WAIT!!
BRRRRRRRING
HELLO?

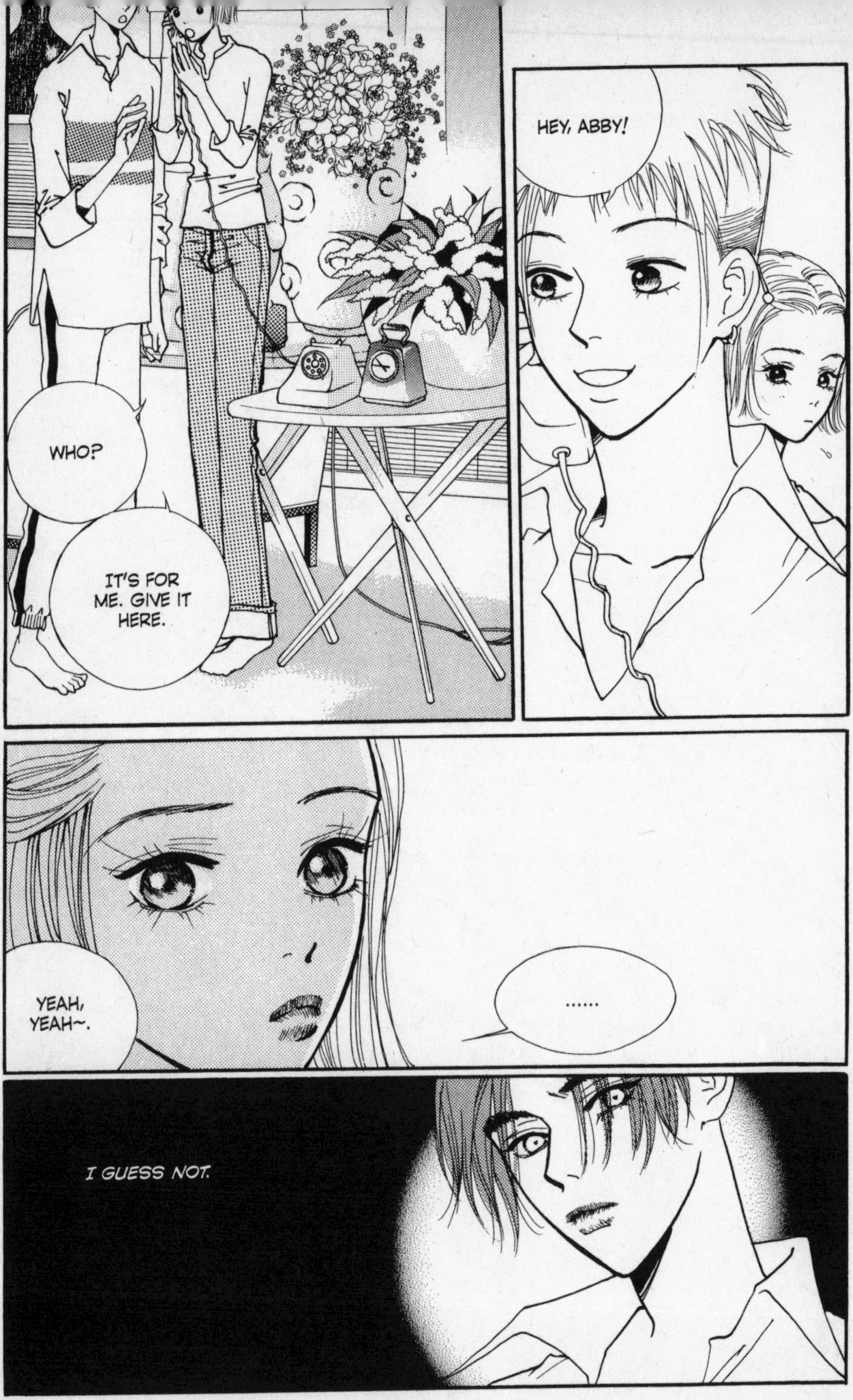
WHO?
IT'S FOR ME. GIVE IT HERE.
HEY, ABBY!
YEAH, YEAH~.
......
I GUESS NOT.

HOW COULD I FORGET~? PATRICK'S TOO HUNG UP ON HIMSELF. I BET HE'S ALREADY FORGOTTEN ALL ABOUT ME...
WE'RE FINALLY RID OF ALICE! YAY!
AWWW
OH NO. THIS CAN'T BE.

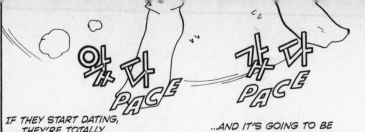

IF THEY START DATING, THEY'RE TOTALLY GOING TO BE ALL LOVEY-DOVEY...

...AND IT'S GOING TO BE RIGHT IN MY FACE EVERY DAY AT SCHOOL...

THIS IS SO NOT COOL.

GULP

TAK

HUH?

YOUNG LADY! JUST WHERE DO YOU THINK YOU'RE GOING AT THIS HOUR~?

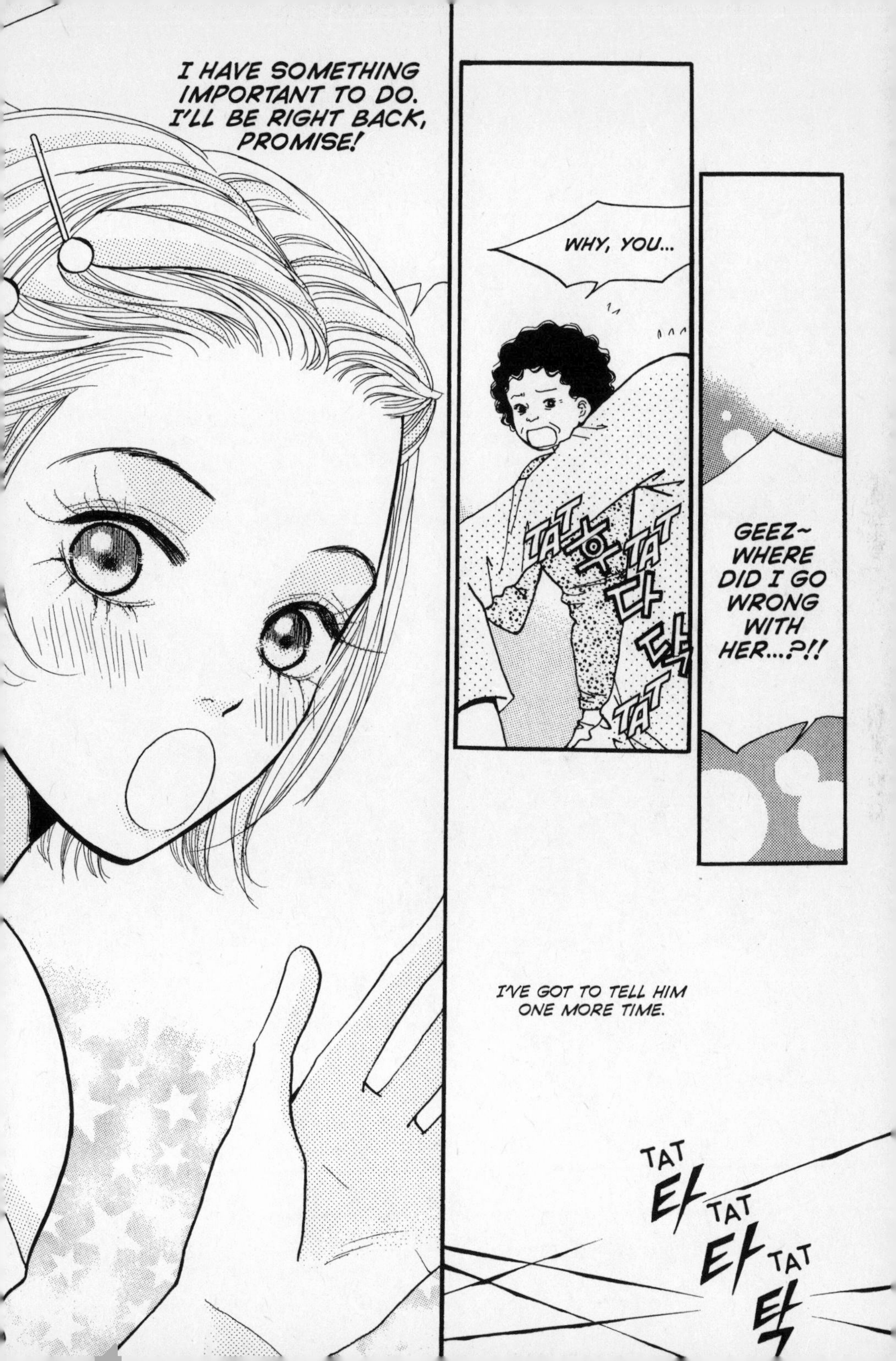
I HAVE SOMETHING IMPORTANT TO DO. I'LL BE RIGHT BACK, PROMISE!
WHY, YOU...
TAT 후 TAT 다 닥 TAT
GEEZ~ WHERE DID I GO WRONG WITH HER...?!!
I'VE GOT TO TELL HIM ONE MORE TIME.
TAT 타 TAT 타 TAT 탁

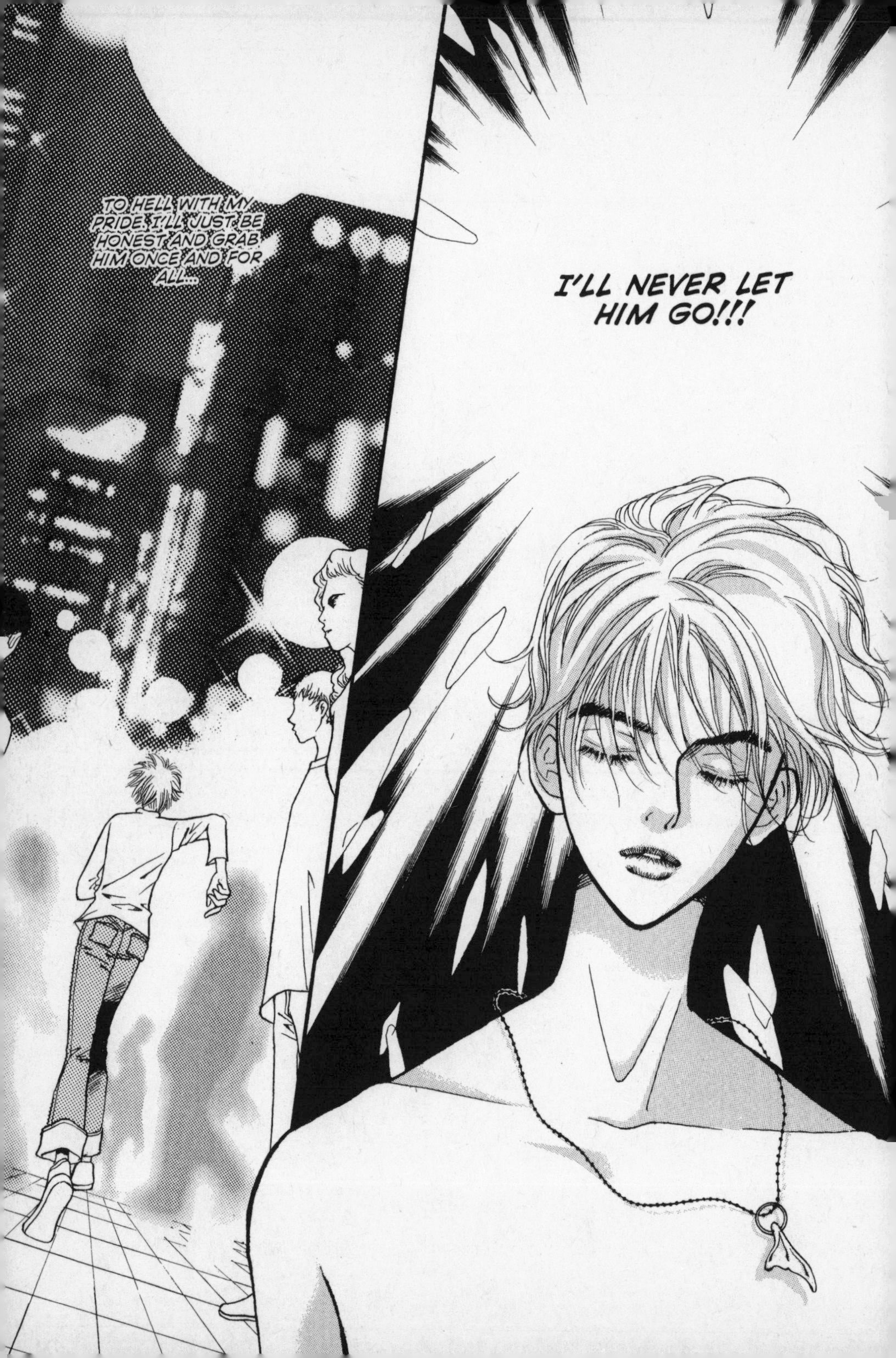
TO HELL WITH MY PRIDE. I'LL JUST BE HONEST AND GRAB HIM ONCE AND FOR ALL...
I'LL NEVER LET HIM GO!!!

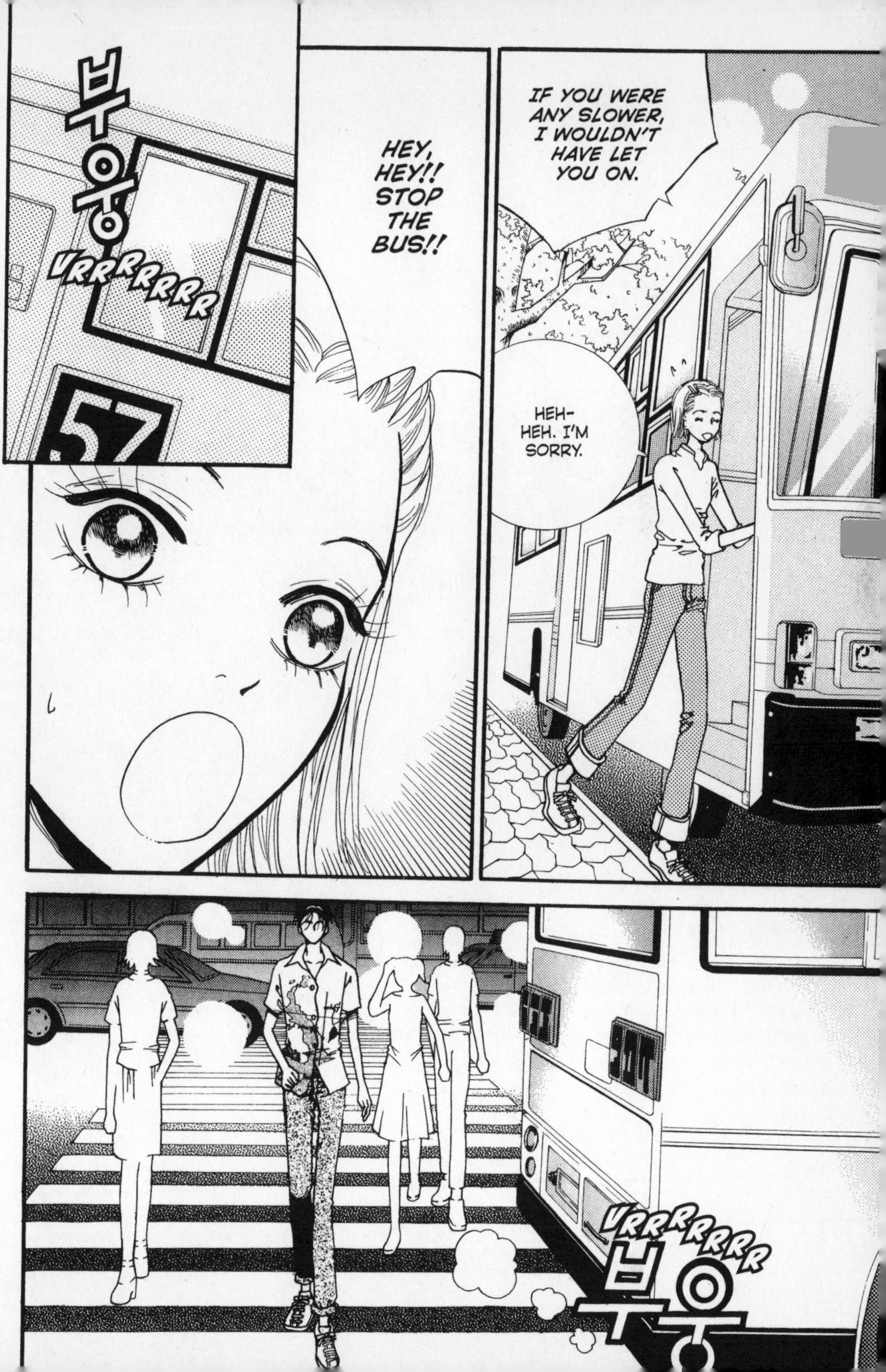
부웅
VRRRRRRR
HEY, HEY!! STOP THE BUS!!
IF YOU WERE ANY SLOWER, I WOULDN'T HAVE LET YOU ON.
HEH-HEH. I'M SORRY.
VRRRRRRR
부웅

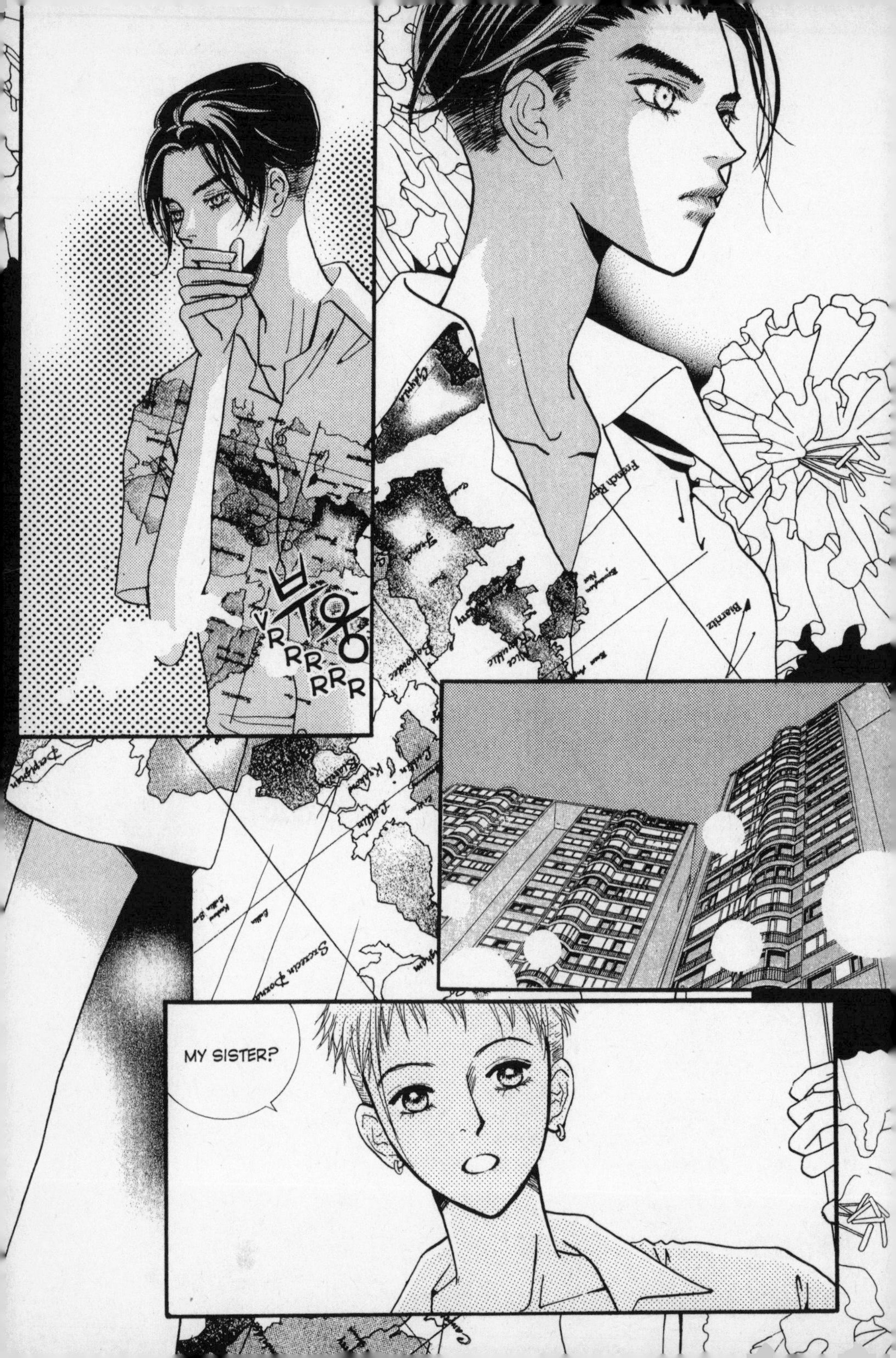
VRRRRRRR
MY SISTER?

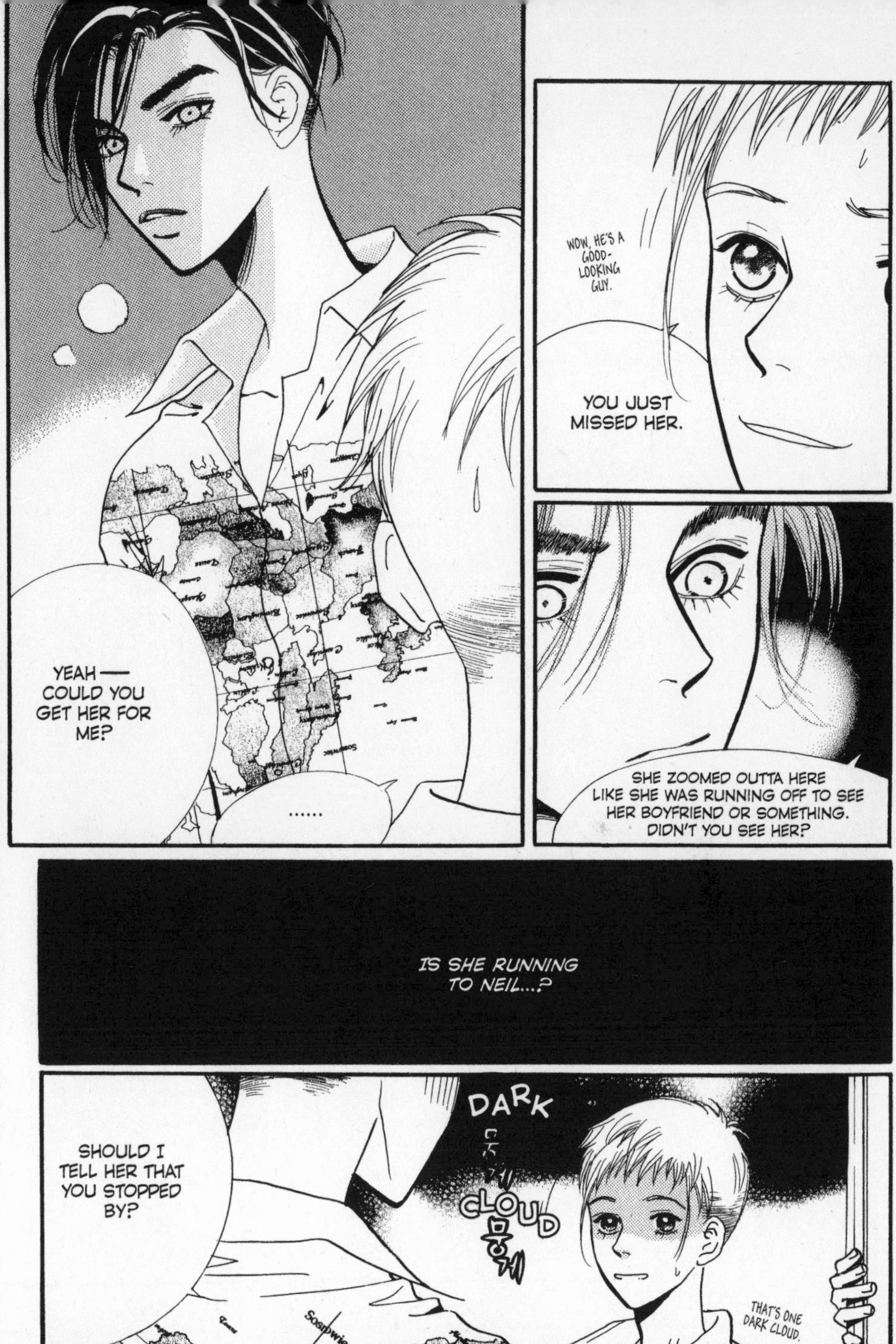
YEAH — COULD YOU GET HER FOR ME?
......
WOW, HE'S A GOOD-LOOKING GUY.
YOU JUST MISSED HER.
SHE ZOOMED OUTTA HERE LIKE SHE WAS RUNNING OFF TO SEE HER BOYFRIEND OR SOMETHING. DIDN'T YOU SEE HER?
IS SHE RUNNING TO NEIL...?
SHOULD I TELL HER THAT YOU STOPPED BY?
DARK
CLOUD
THAT'S ONE DARK CLOUD.

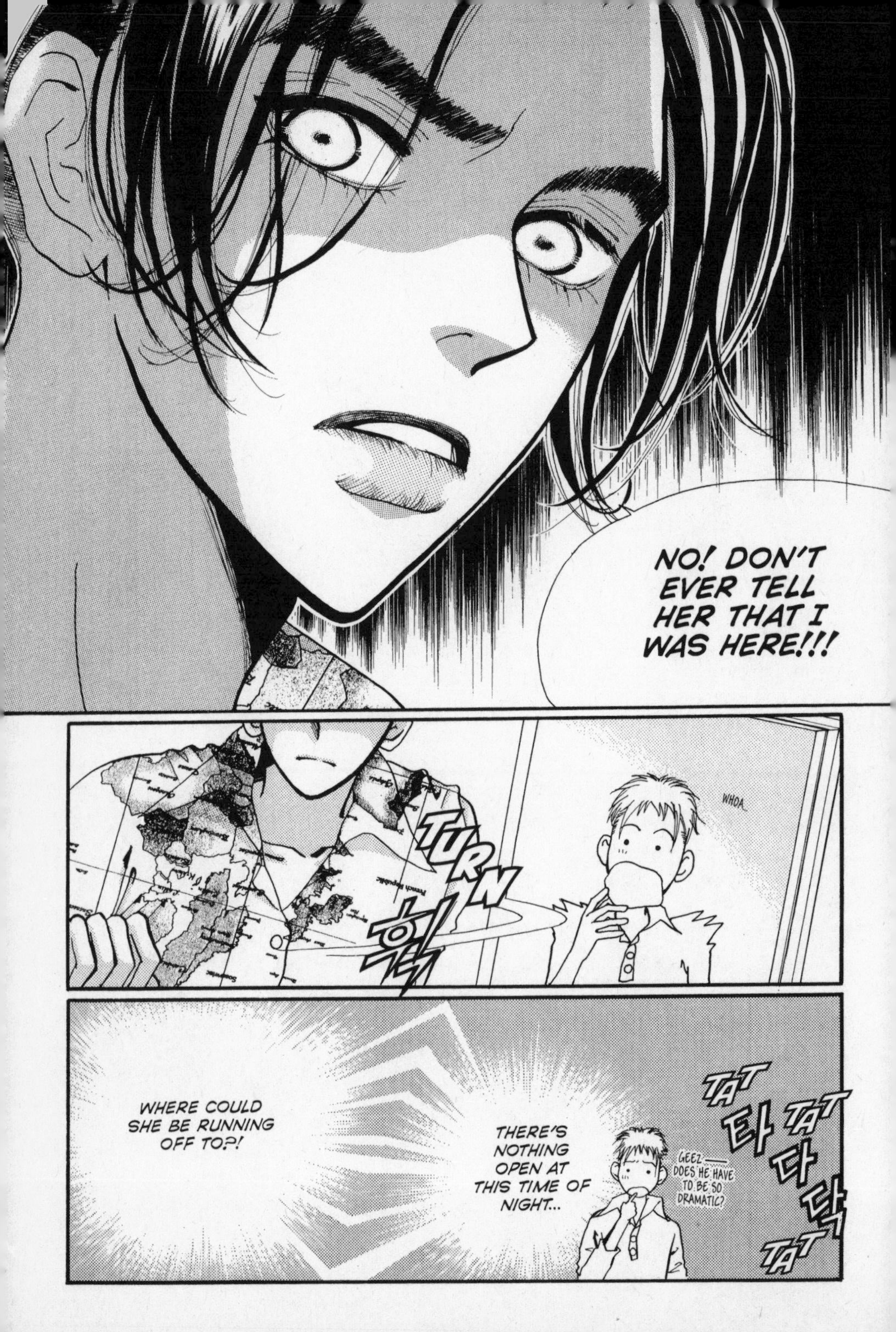
NO! DON'T EVER TELL HER THAT I WAS HERE!!!
TURN
휙
WHOA...
WHERE COULD SHE BE RUNNING OFF TO?!
THERE'S NOTHING OPEN AT THIS TIME OF NIGHT...
GEEZ— DOES HE HAVE TO BE SO DRAMATIC?
TAT
타
TAT
다
닥
TAT

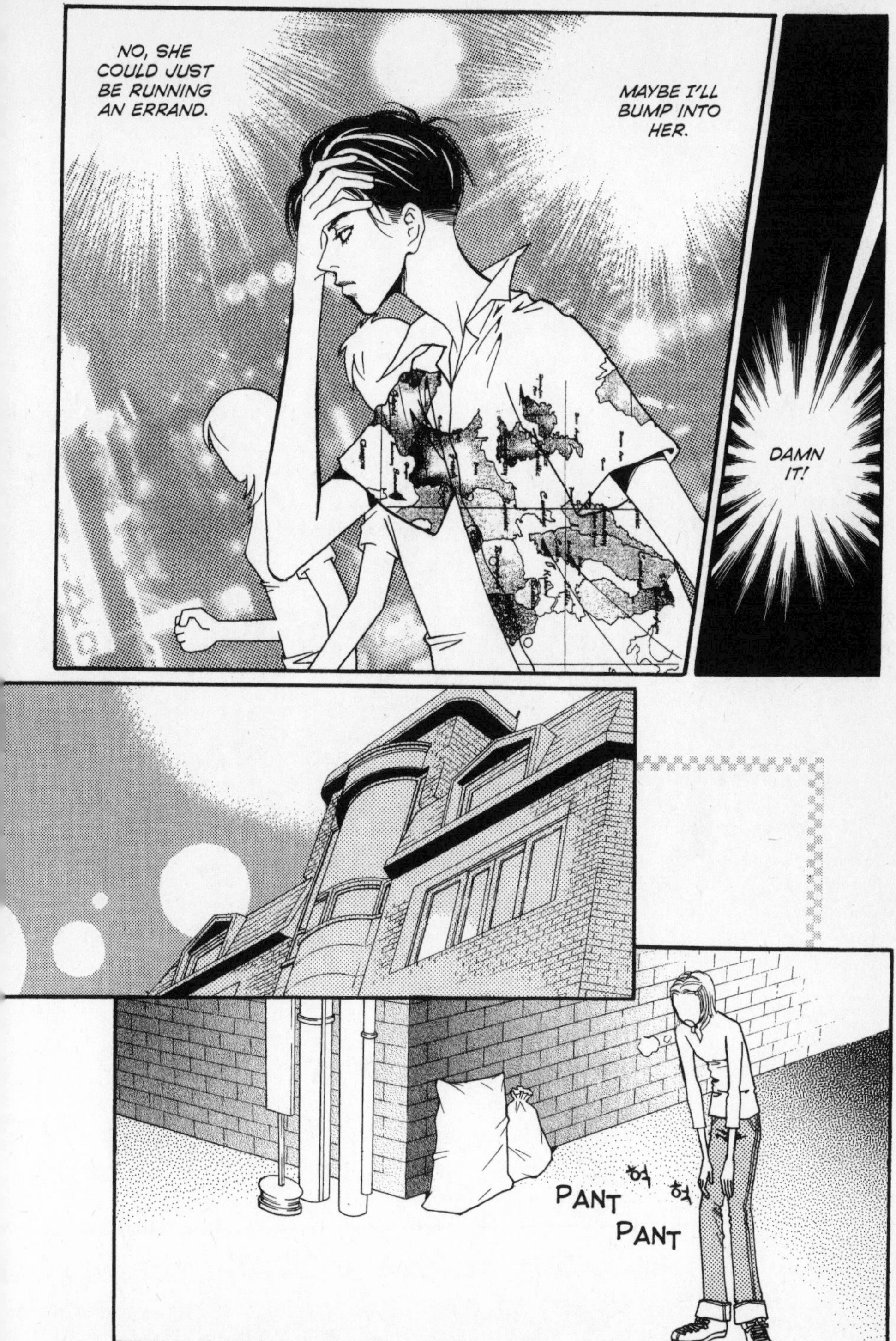
NO, SHE COULD JUST BE RUNNING AN ERRAND.
MAYBE I'LL BUMP INTO HER.
DAMN IT!
헉 헉
PANT PANT

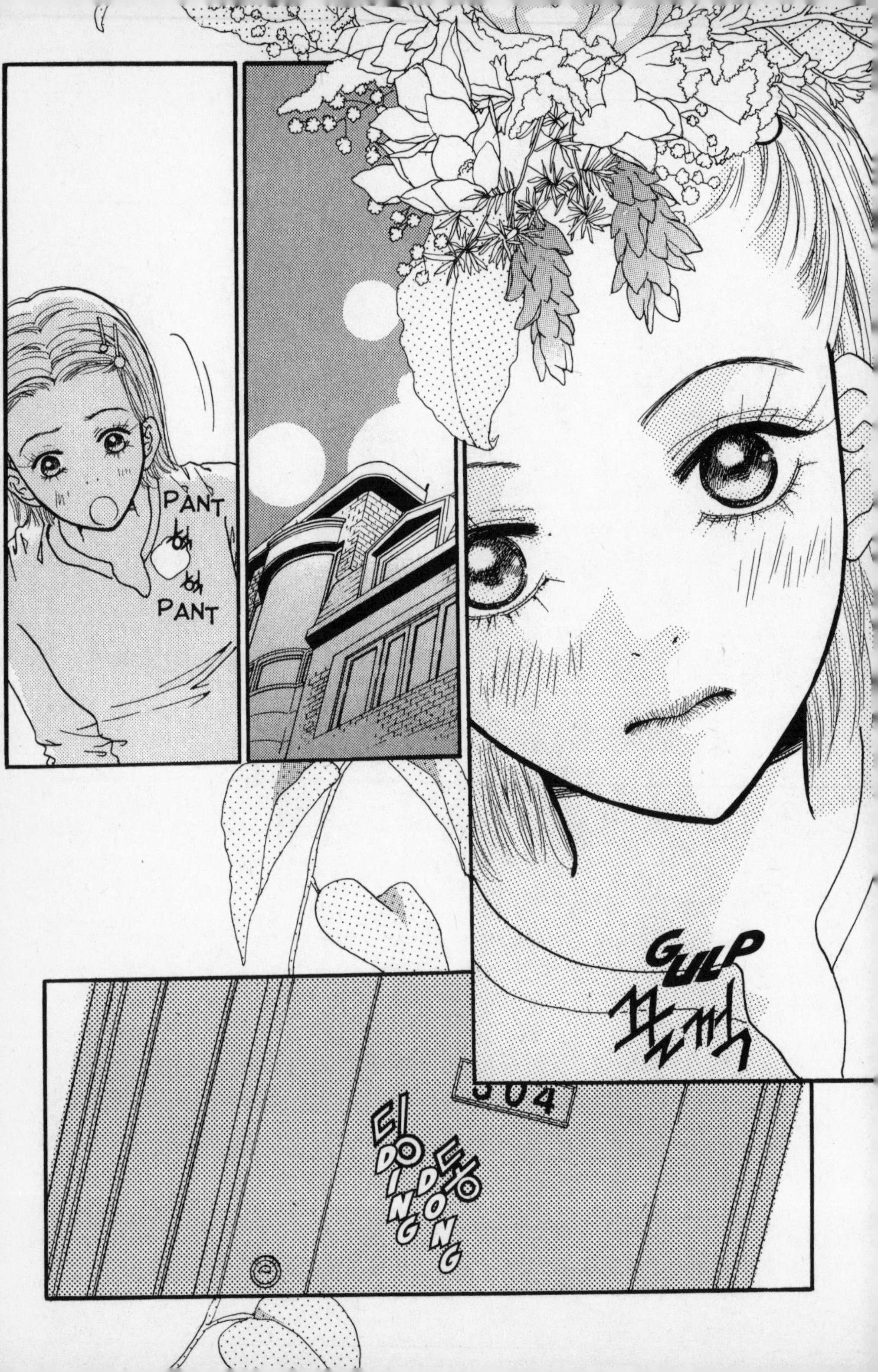
PANT
헉
헉
PANT
GULP
꿀꺽
딩 동
DING DONG

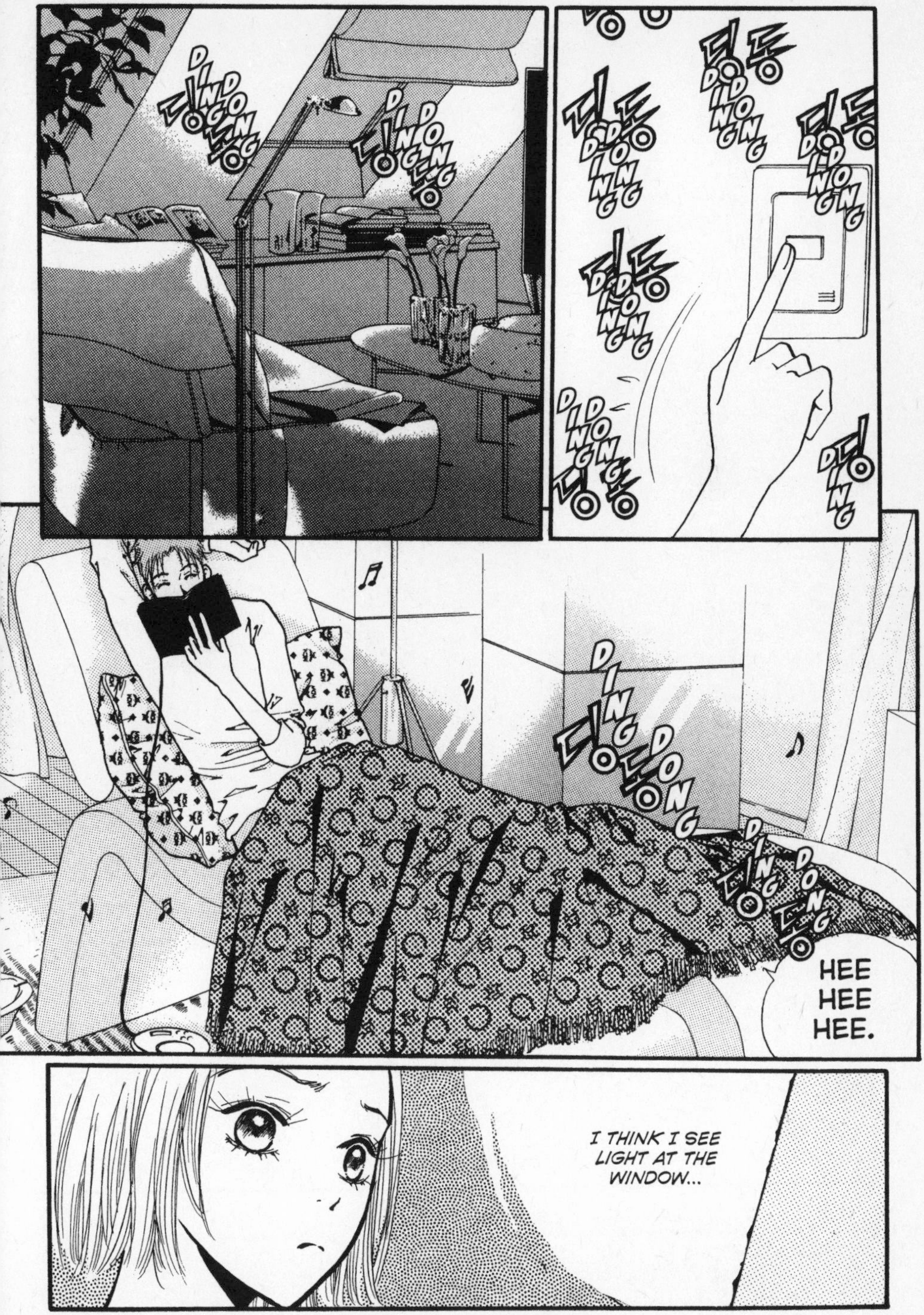
DING DONG
DING DONG
DING DONG
DING DONG
DING DONG
DING DONG
DING DONG
DING
DING DONG
DING DONG
HEE HEE HEE.
I THINK I SEE LIGHT AT THE WINDOW...

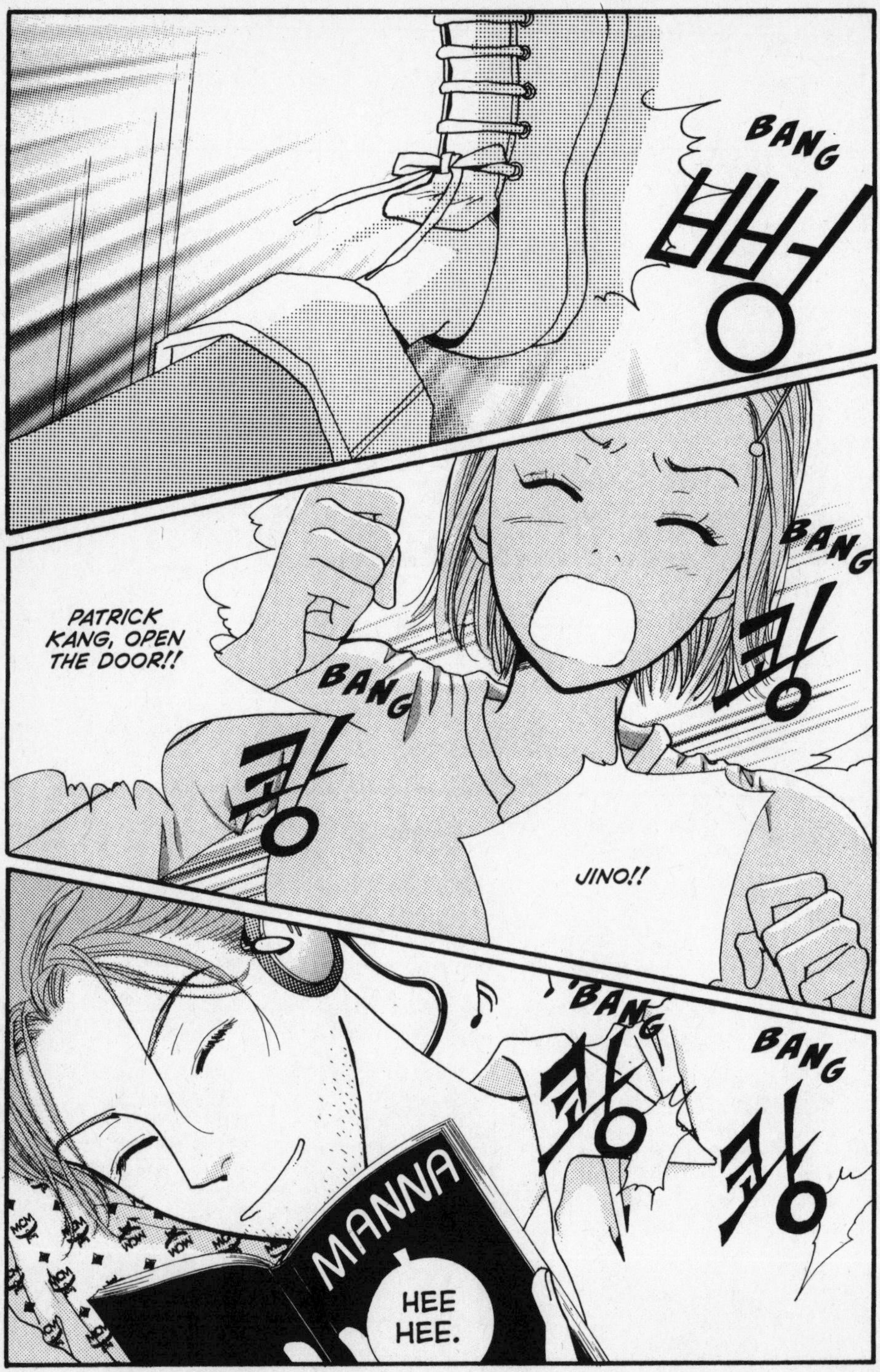
BANG
BANG
PATRICK KANG, OPEN THE DOOR!!
BANG
JINO!!
BANG
BANG
MANNA
HEE HEE.

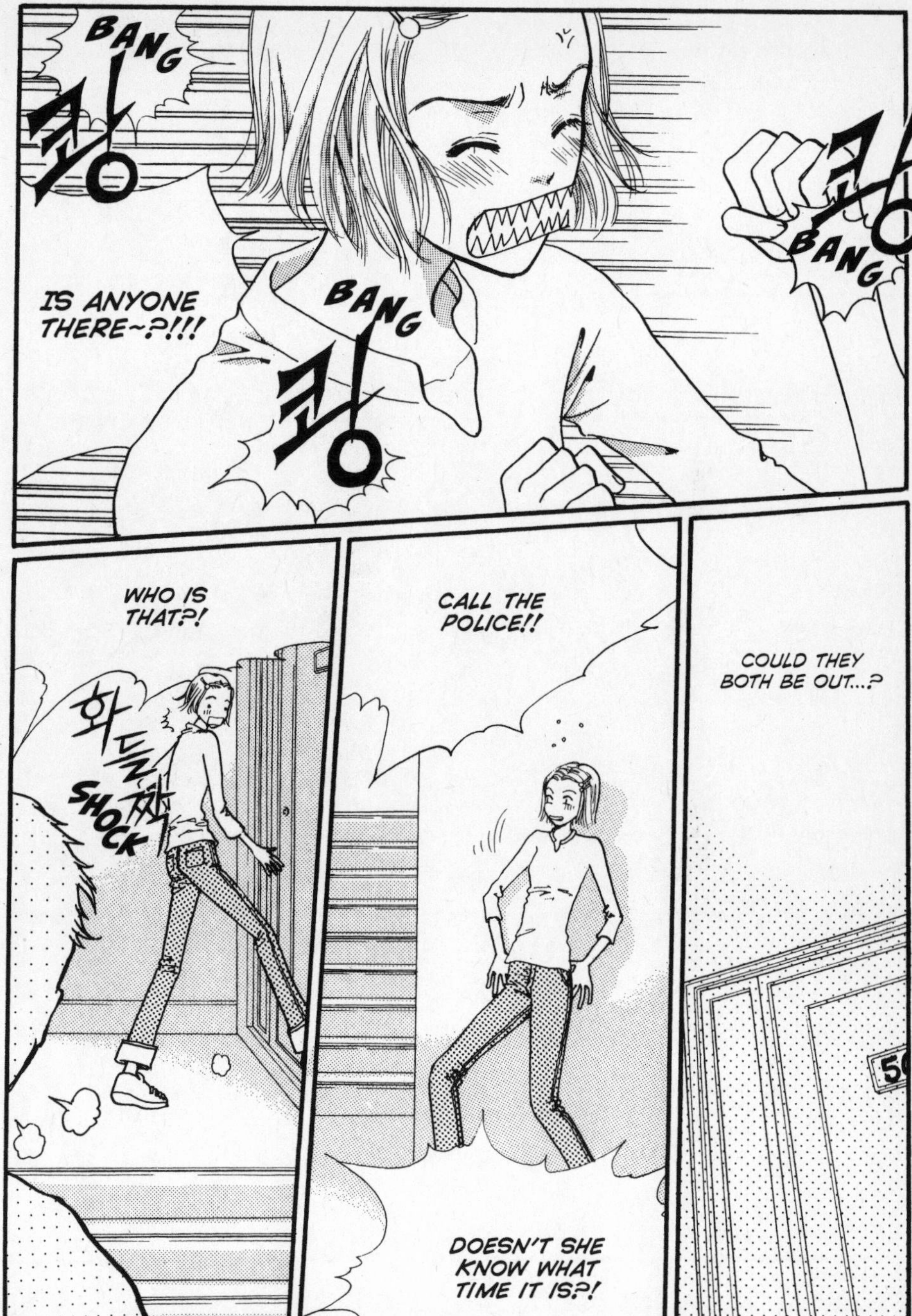
BANG
쾅
BANG
쾅
IS ANYONE THERE~?!!!
BANG
쾅
WHO IS THAT?!
화들짝
SHOCK
CALL THE POLICE!!
DOESN'T SHE KNOW WHAT TIME IT IS?!
COULD THEY BOTH BE OUT...?

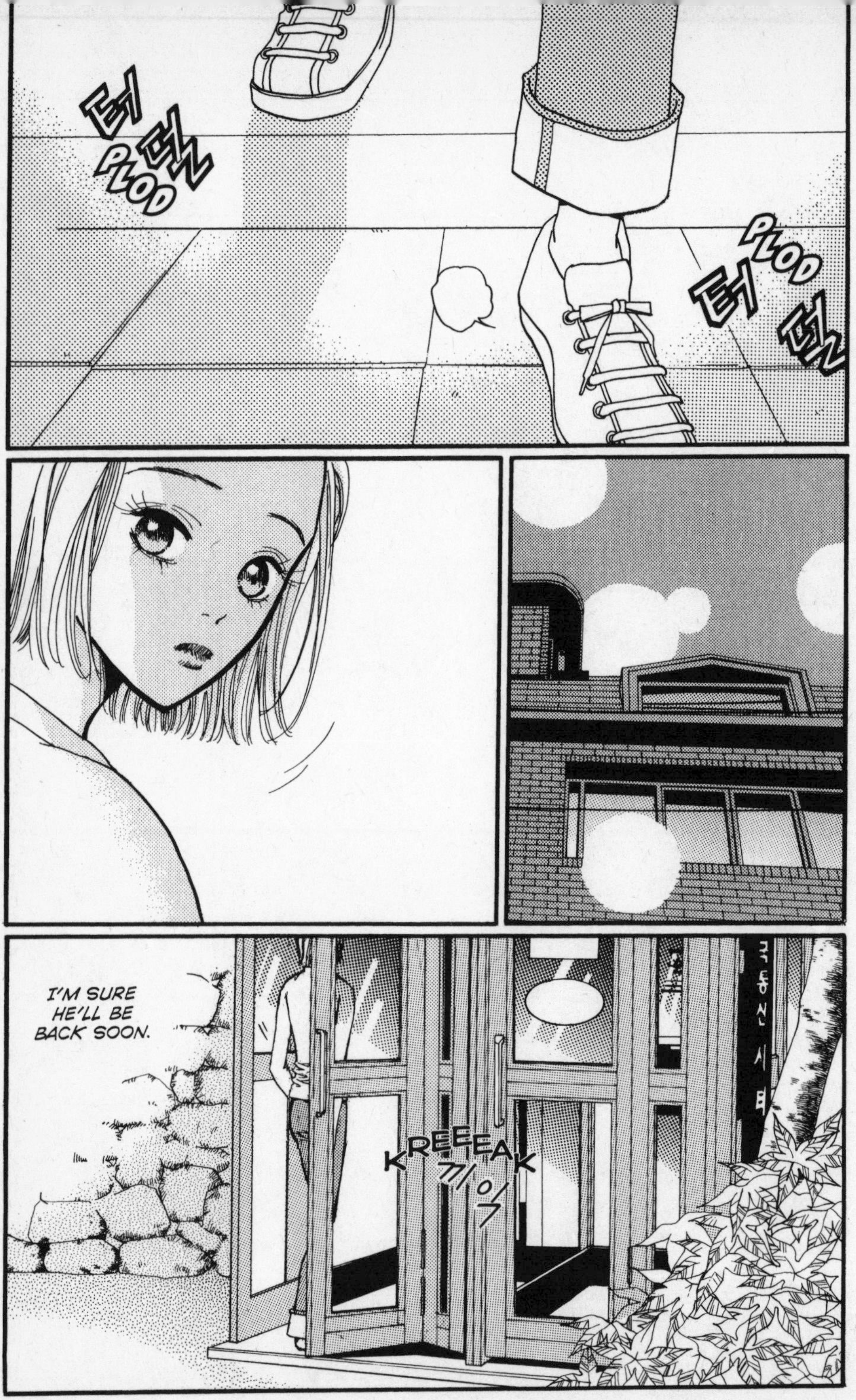
터덜
PLOD
PLOD
터덜
I'M SURE HE'LL BE BACK SOON.
KREEEAK
끼익

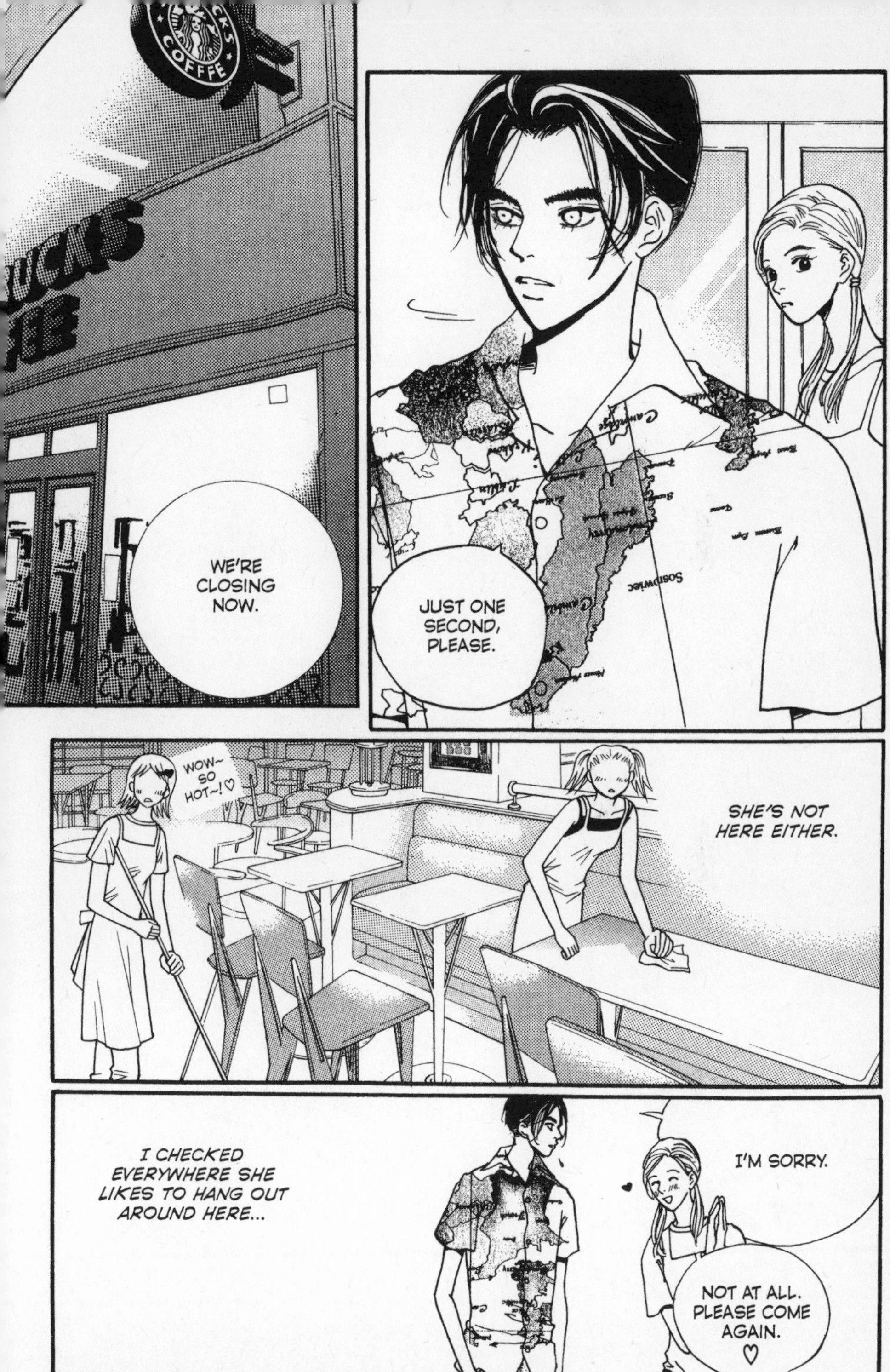
WE'RE CLOSING NOW.
JUST ONE SECOND, PLEASE.
WOW~ SO HOT~!♡
SHE'S NOT HERE EITHER.
I CHECKED EVERYWHERE SHE LIKES TO HANG OUT AROUND HERE...
I'M SORRY.
NOT AT ALL. PLEASE COME AGAIN. ♡

NO...THAT CAN'T BE.

SHE WOULDN'T GO TO NEIL'S PLACE THIS LATE AT NIGHT, WOULD SHE?

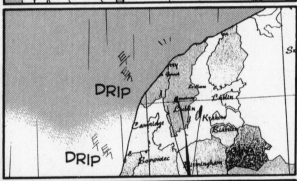

DRIP

DRIP

HMM?

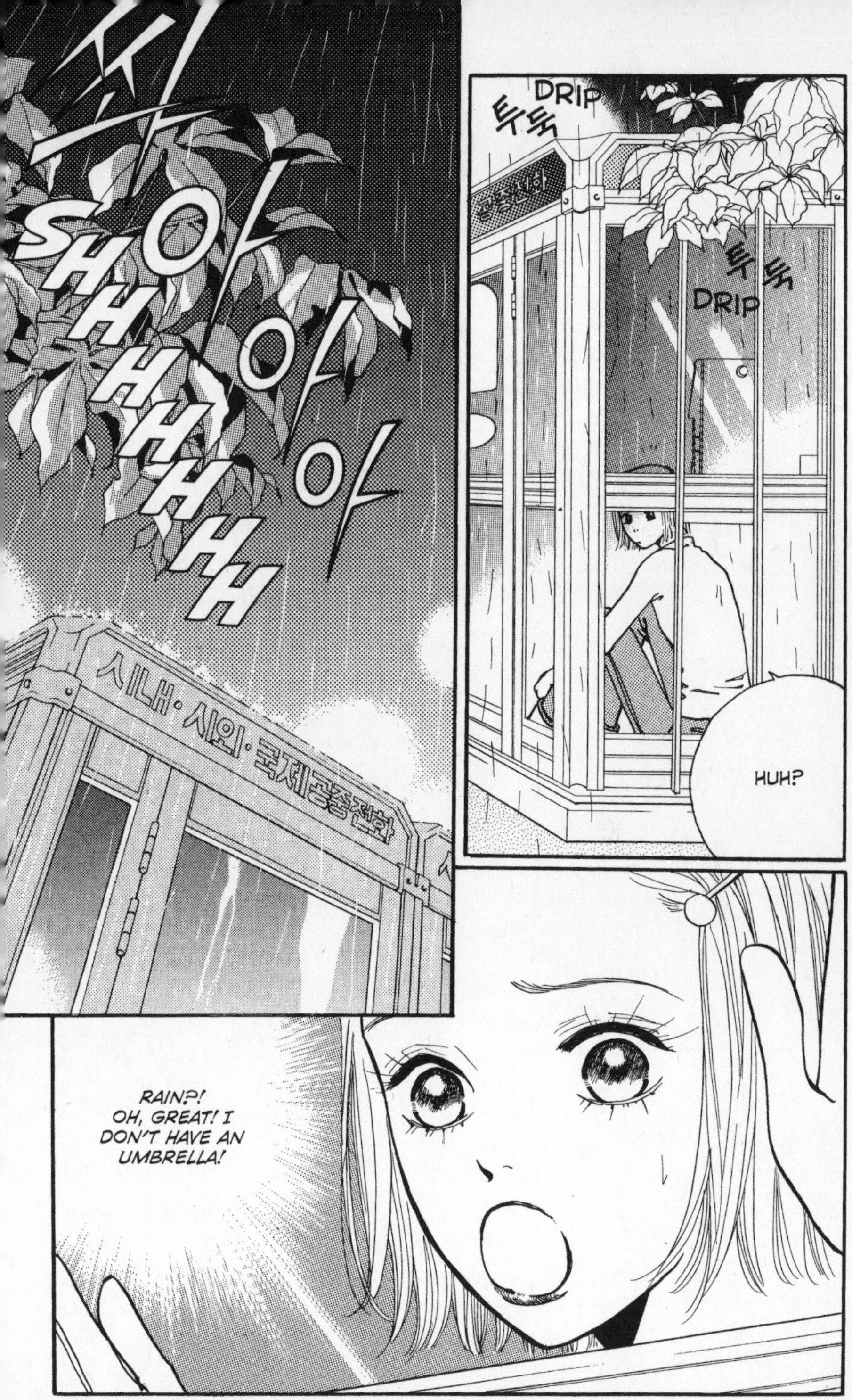

쏴아아아
SHHHHHHHH
시내·시외·국제공중전화
투둑
DRIP
공중전화
투둑
DRIP
HUH?
RAIN?! OH, GREAT! I DON'T HAVE AN UMBRELLA!

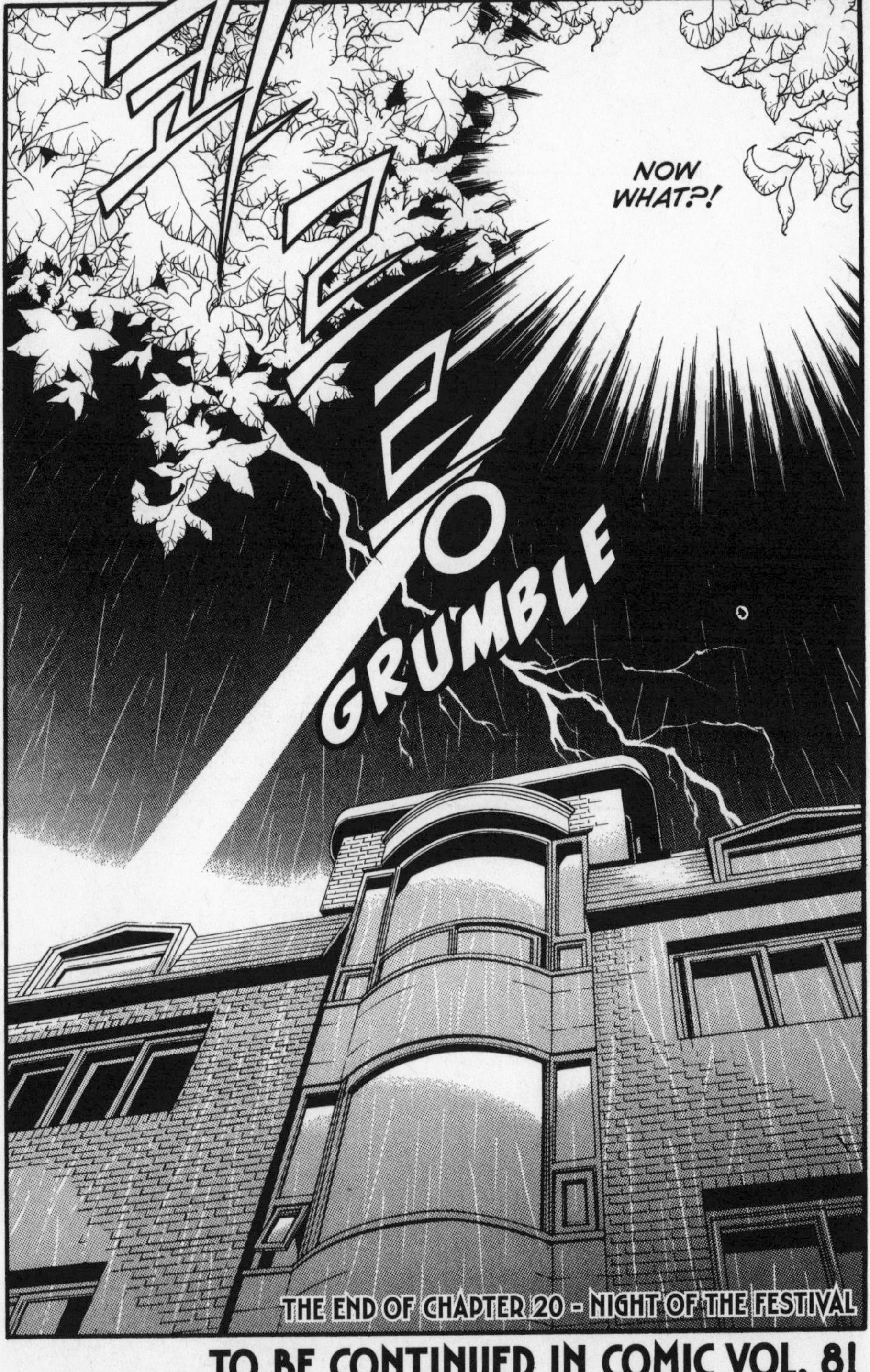
NOW WHAT?!
GRUMBLE
THE END OF CHAPTER 20 - NIGHT OF THE FESTIVAL

TO BE CONTINUED IN COMIC VOL. 8!

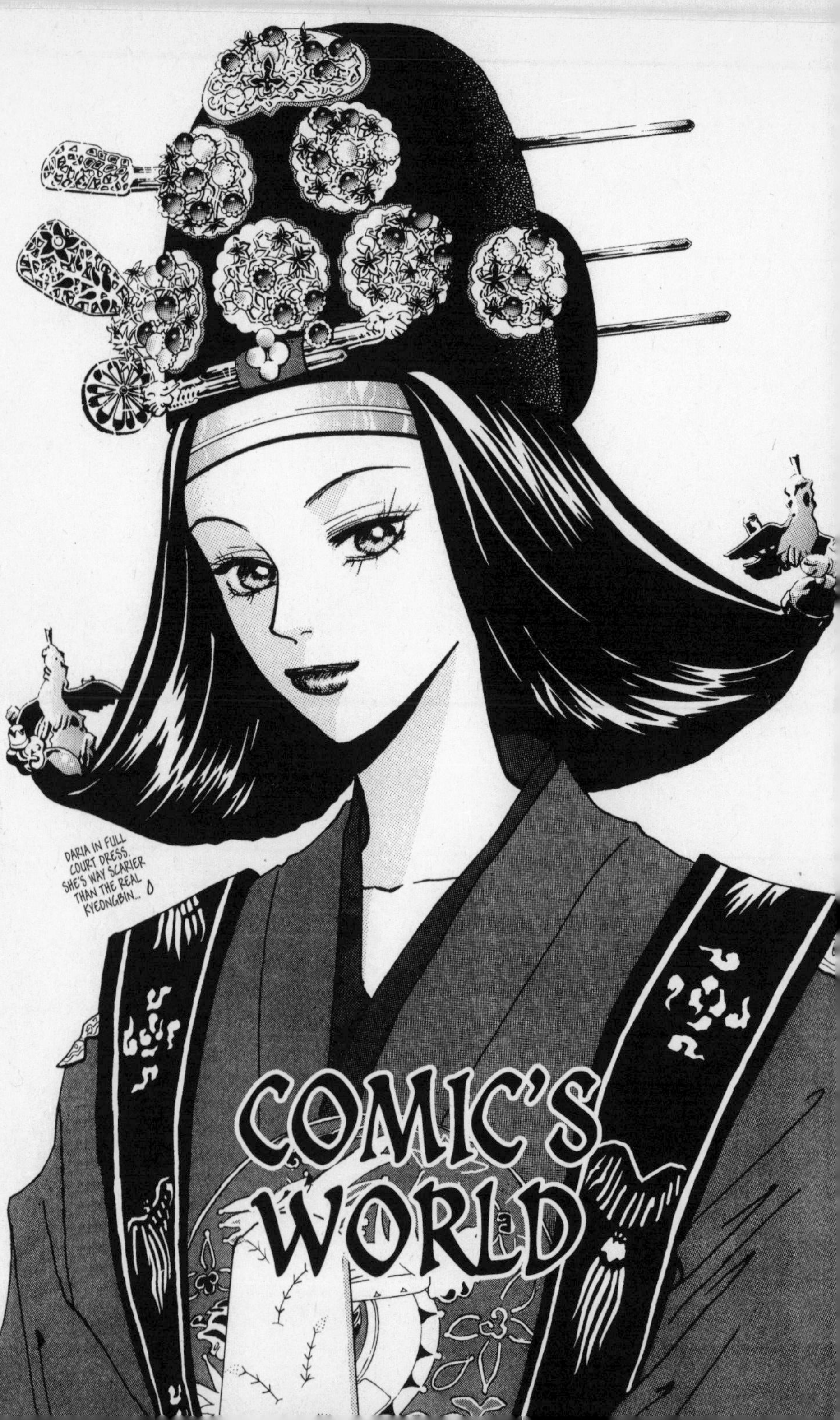
DARIA IN FULL COURT DRESS. SHE'S WAY SCARIER THAN THE REAL KYEONGBIN...
COMIC'S WORLD

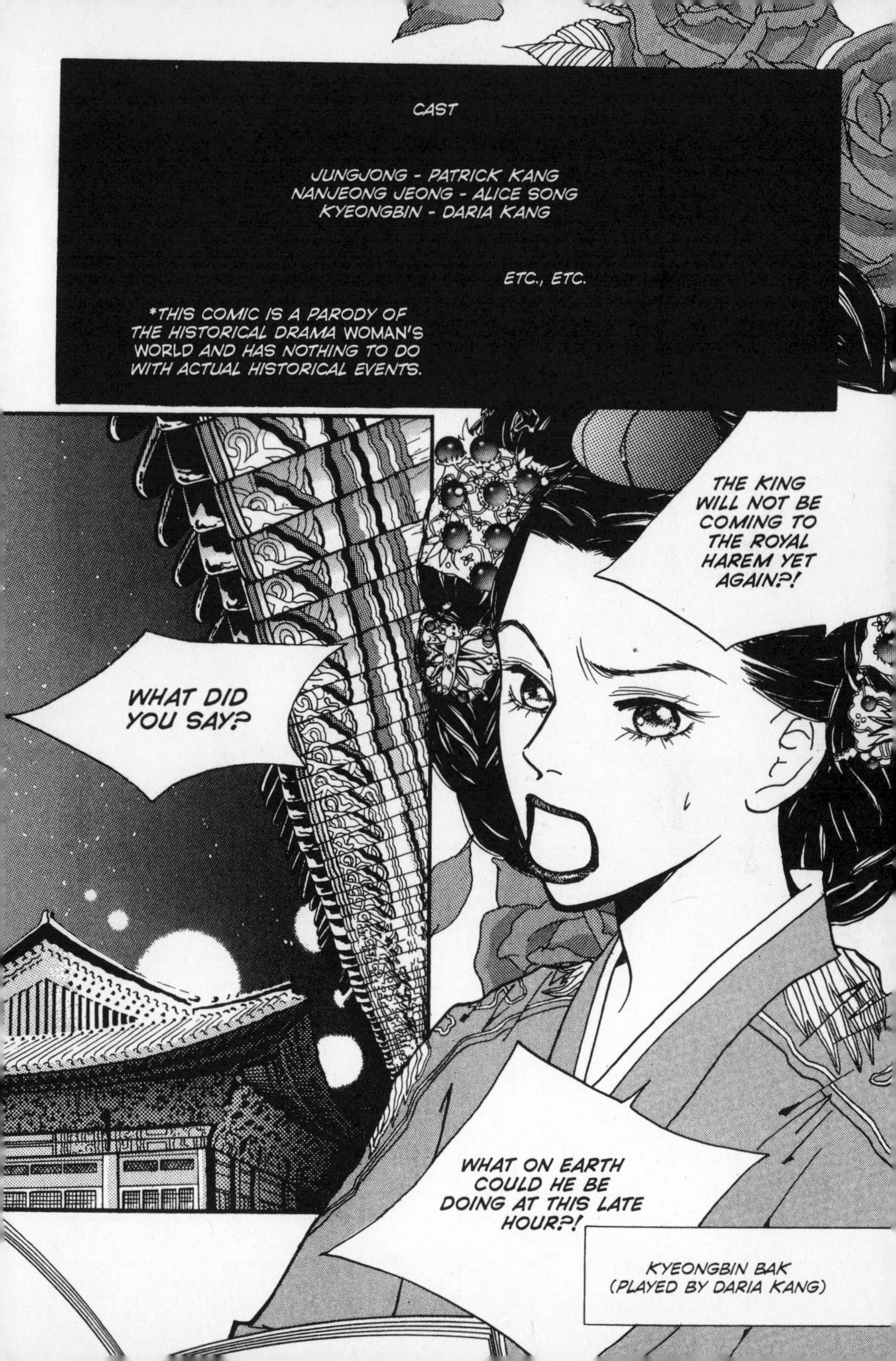
CAST
JUNGJONG - PATRICK KANG
NANJEONG JEONG - ALICE SONG
KYEONGBIN - DARIA KANG
ETC., ETC.
*THIS COMIC IS A PARODY OF THE HISTORICAL DRAMA WOMAN'S WORLD AND HAS NOTHING TO DO WITH ACTUAL HISTORICAL EVENTS.
WHAT DID YOU SAY?
THE KING WILL NOT BE COMING TO THE ROYAL HAREM YET AGAIN?!
WHAT ON EARTH COULD HE BE DOING AT THIS LATE HOUR?!
KYEONGBIN BAK (PLAYED BY DARIA KANG)

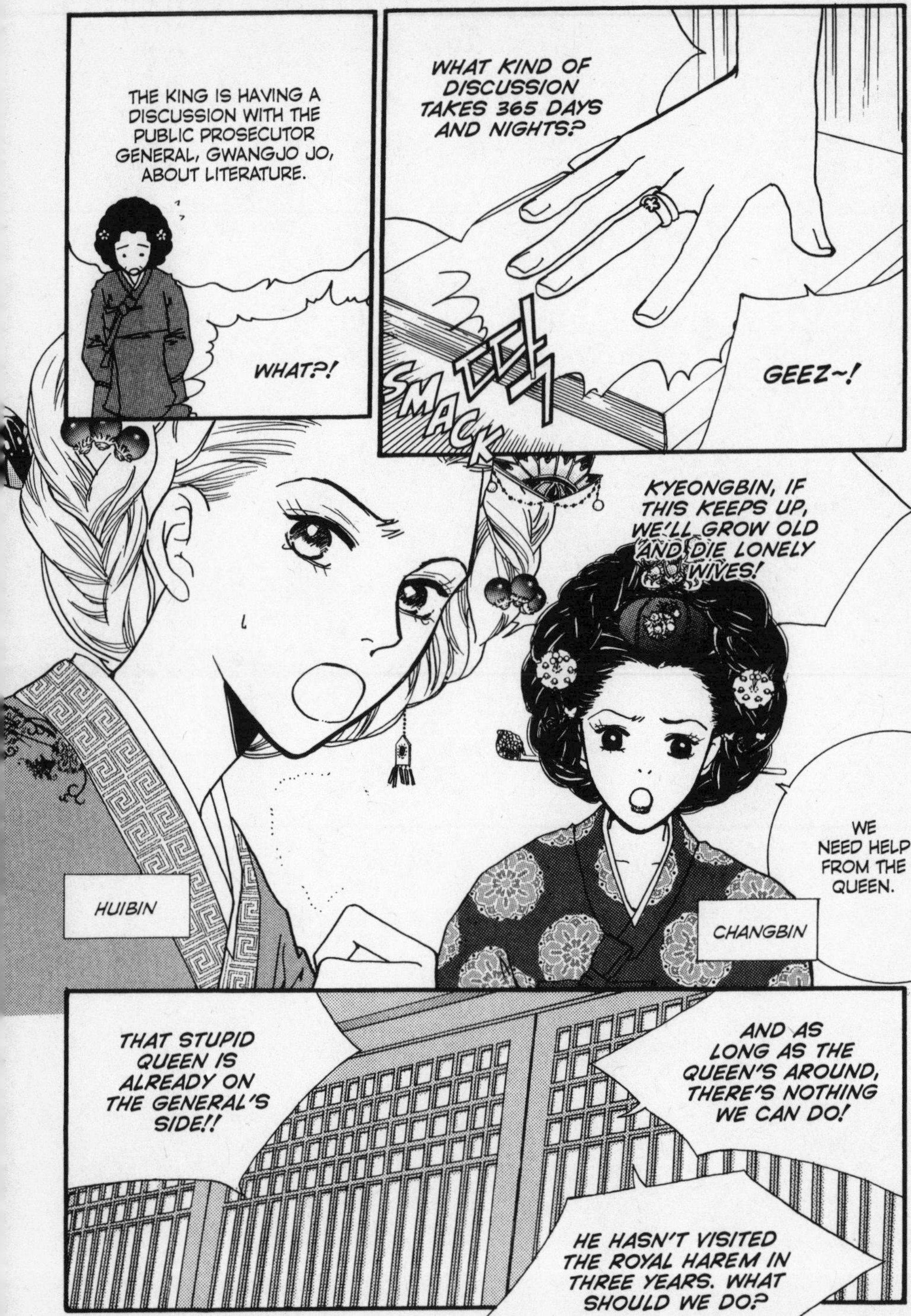
THE KING IS HAVING A DISCUSSION WITH THE PUBLIC PROSECUTOR GENERAL, GWANGJO JO, ABOUT LITERATURE.
WHAT?!
WHAT KIND OF DISCUSSION TAKES 365 DAYS AND NIGHTS?
SMACK
GEEZ~!
KYEONGBIN, IF THIS KEEPS UP, WE'LL GROW OLD AND DIE LONELY WIVES!
HUIBIN
CHANGBIN
WE NEED HELP FROM THE QUEEN.
THAT STUPID QUEEN IS ALREADY ON THE GENERAL'S SIDE!!
AND AS LONG AS THE QUEEN'S AROUND, THERE'S NOTHING WE CAN DO!
HE HASN'T VISITED THE ROYAL HAREM IN THREE YEARS. WHAT SHOULD WE DO?

GWANGJO... JO...

GWANGJO JO...

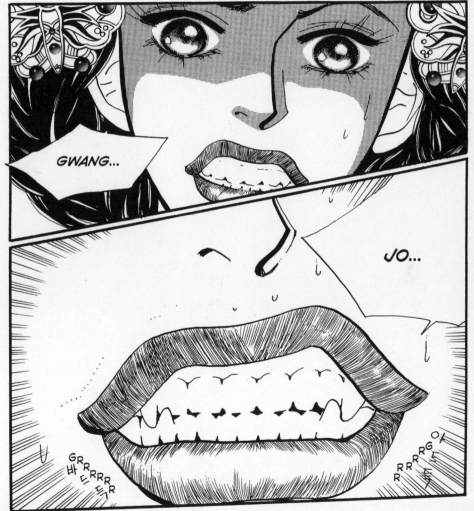

GWANG...

JO...

GRRRRRRR

RRRRRGE

OF

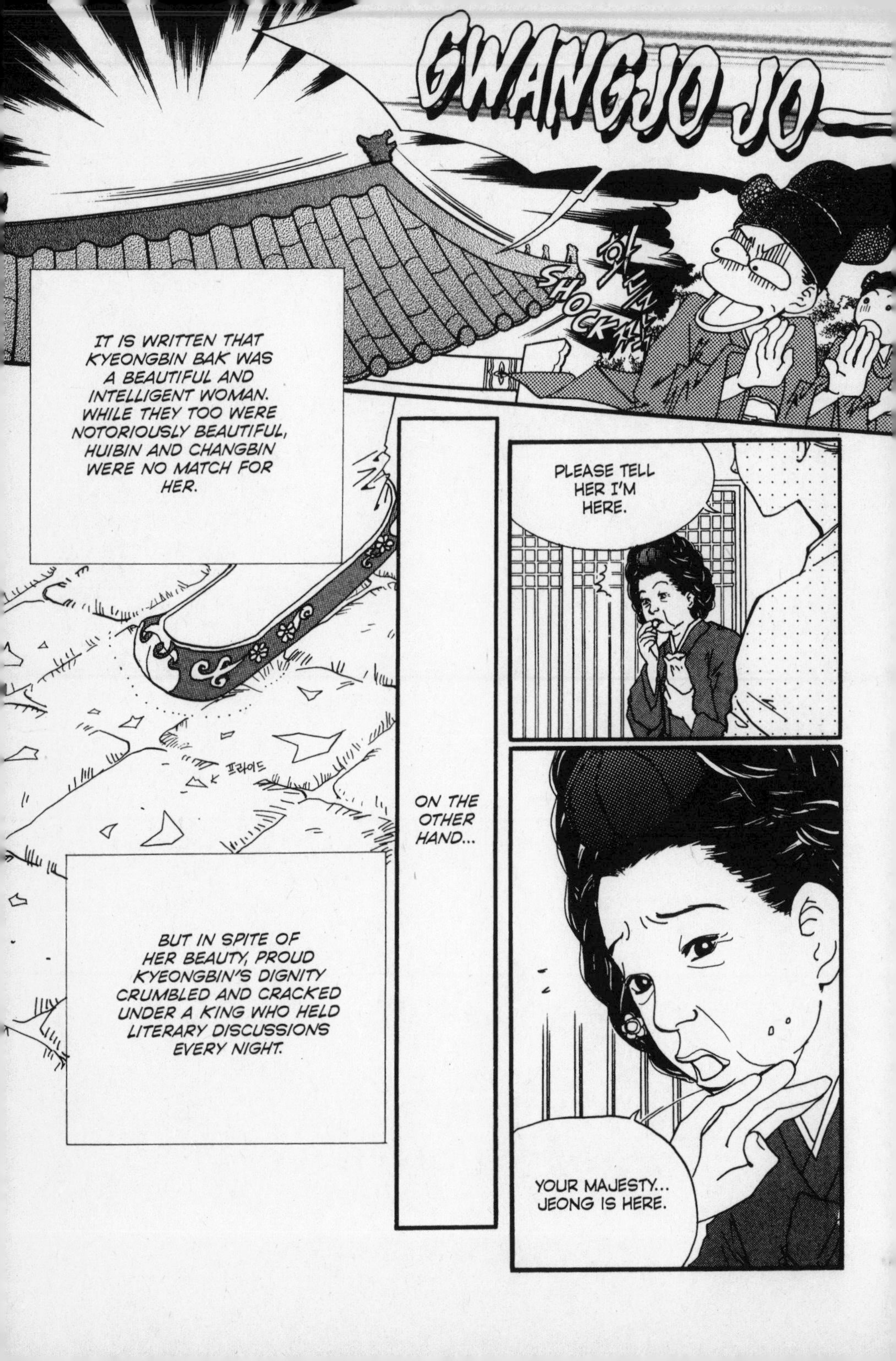
GWANGJO JO
SHOCK
IT IS WRITTEN THAT KYEONGBIN BAK WAS A BEAUTIFUL AND INTELLIGENT WOMAN. WHILE THEY TOO WERE NOTORIOUSLY BEAUTIFUL, HUIBIN AND CHANGBIN WERE NO MATCH FOR HER.
프라이드
BUT IN SPITE OF HER BEAUTY, PROUD KYEONGBIN'S DIGNITY CRUMBLED AND CRACKED UNDER A KING WHO HELD LITERARY DISCUSSIONS EVERY NIGHT.
ON THE OTHER HAND...
PLEASE TELL HER I'M HERE.
YOUR MAJESTY... JEONG IS HERE.

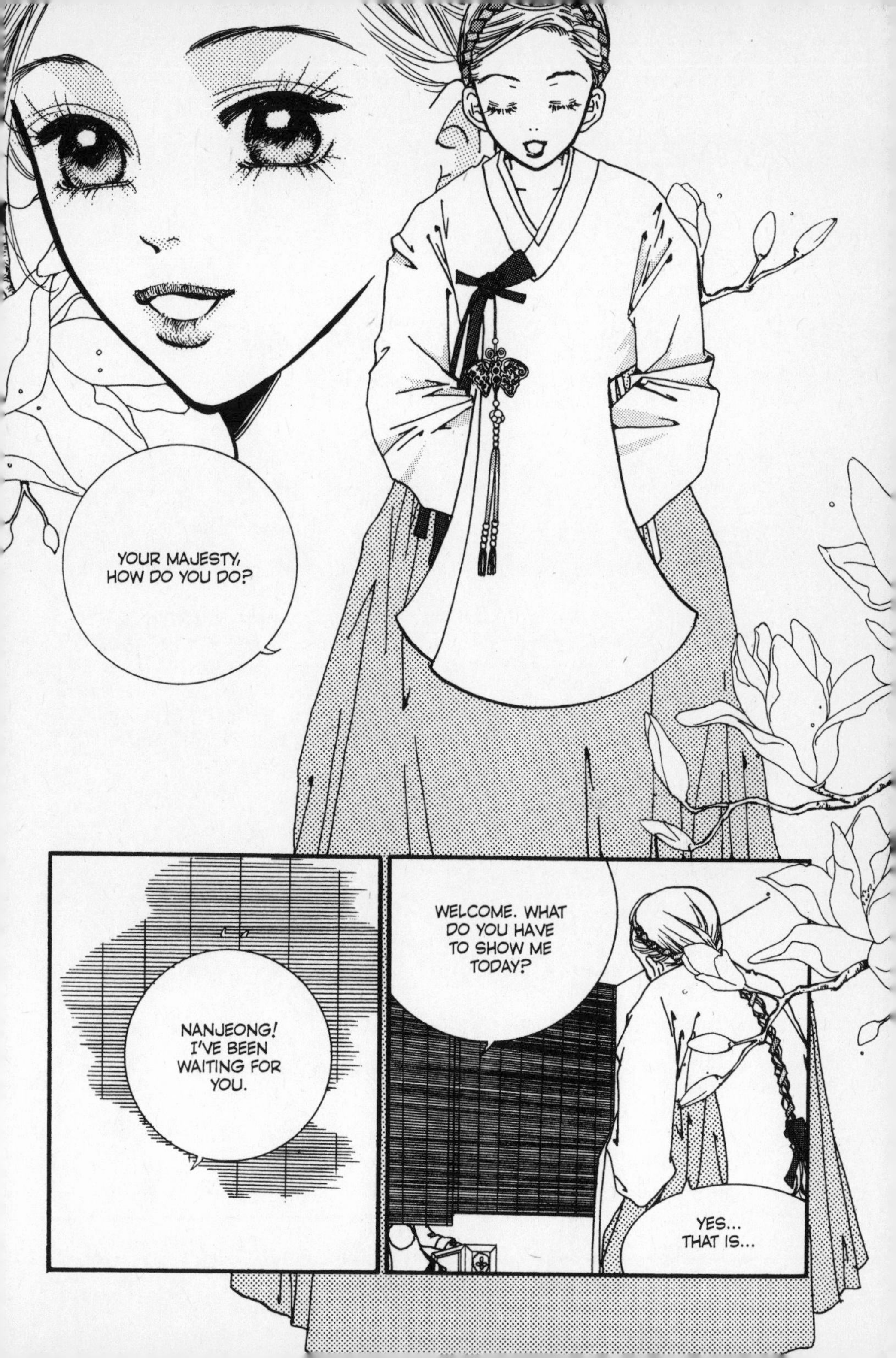
YOUR MAJESTY, HOW DO YOU DO?
NANJEONG! I'VE BEEN WAITING FOR YOU.
WELCOME. WHAT DO YOU HAVE TO SHOW ME TODAY?
YES... THAT IS...

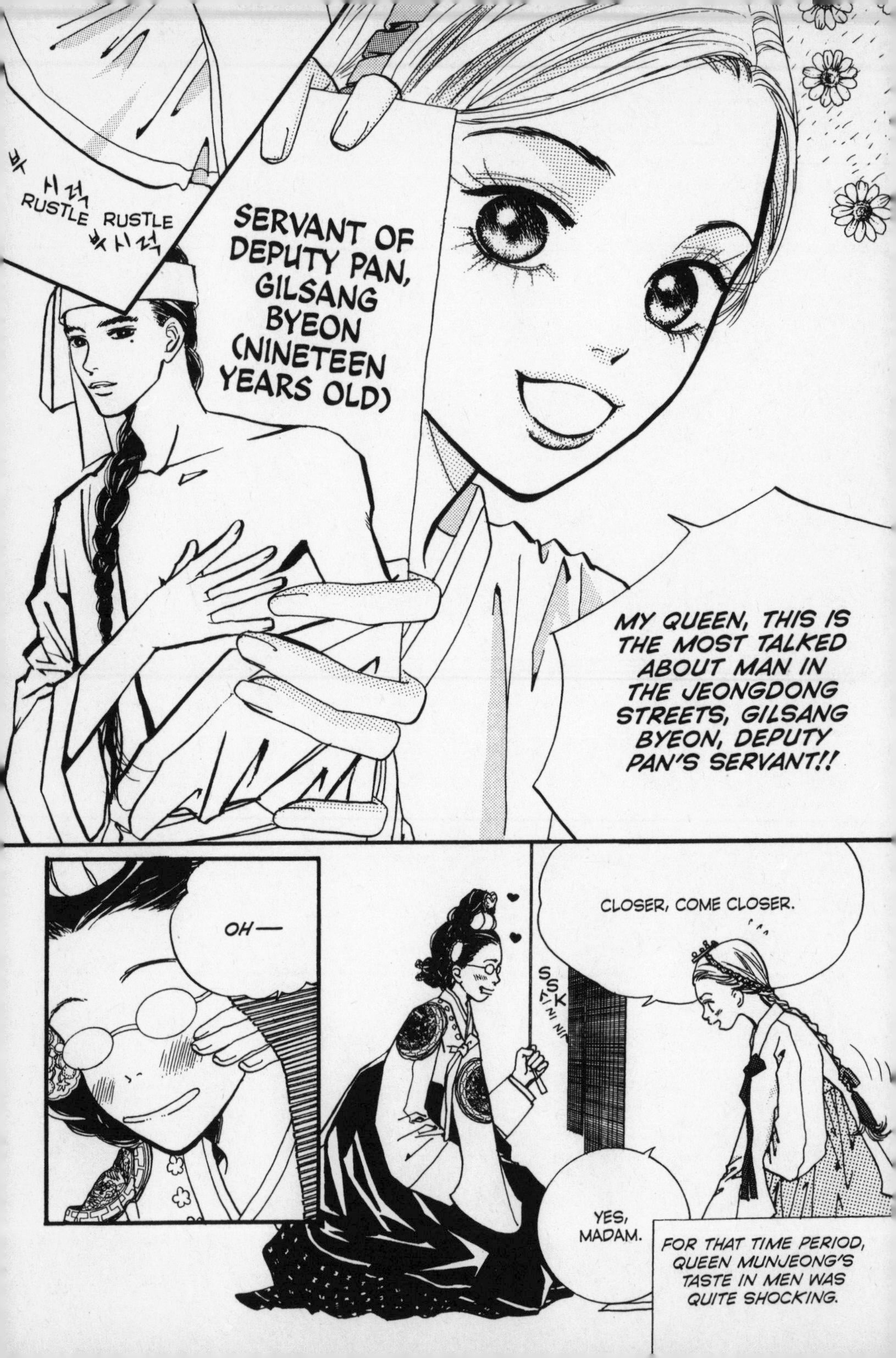
RUSTLE RUSTLE
SERVANT OF DEPUTY PAN, GILSANG BYEON (NINETEEN YEARS OLD)
MY QUEEN, THIS IS THE MOST TALKED ABOUT MAN IN THE JEONGDONG STREETS, GILSANG BYEON, DEPUTY PAN'S SERVANT!!
OH—
CLOSER, COME CLOSER.
SSK
YES, MADAM.
FOR THAT TIME PERIOD, QUEEN MUNJEONG'S TASTE IN MEN WAS QUITE SHOCKING.

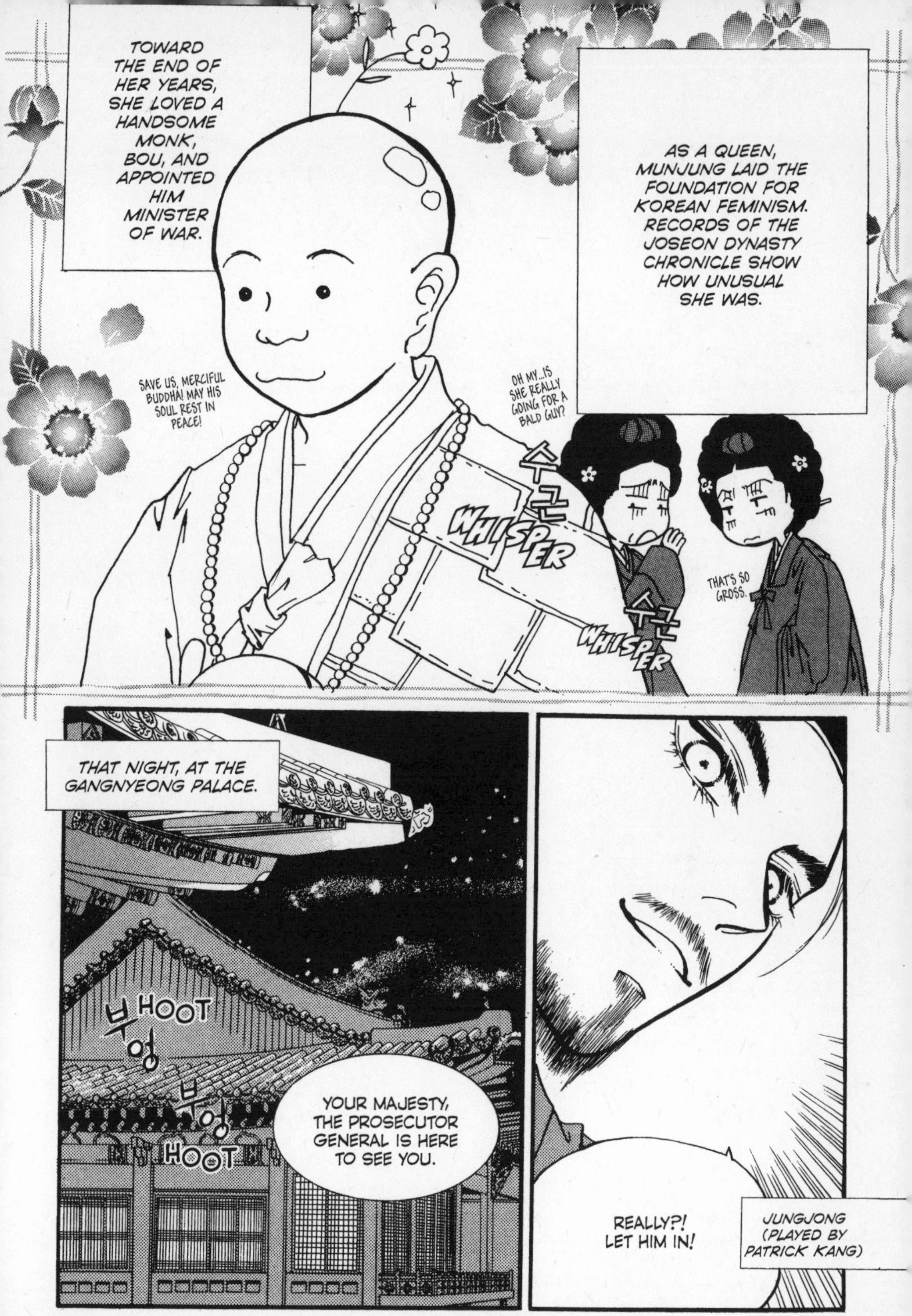
TOWARD THE END OF HER YEARS, SHE LOVED A HANDSOME MONK, BOU, AND APPOINTED HIM MINISTER OF WAR.
AS A QUEEN, MUNJUNG LAID THE FOUNDATION FOR KOREAN FEMINISM. RECORDS OF THE JOSEON DYNASTY CHRONICLE SHOW HOW UNUSUAL SHE WAS.
SAVE US, MERCIFUL BUDDHA! MAY HIS SOUL REST IN PEACE!
OH MY...IS SHE REALLY GOING FOR A BALD GUY?
수군
WHISPER
수군
WHISPER
THAT'S SO GROSS.
THAT NIGHT, AT THE GANGNYEONG PALACE.
부엉
HOOT
부엉
HOOT
YOUR MAJESTY, THE PROSECUTOR GENERAL IS HERE TO SEE YOU.
REALLY?! LET HIM IN!
JUNGJONG (PLAYED BY PATRICK KANG)

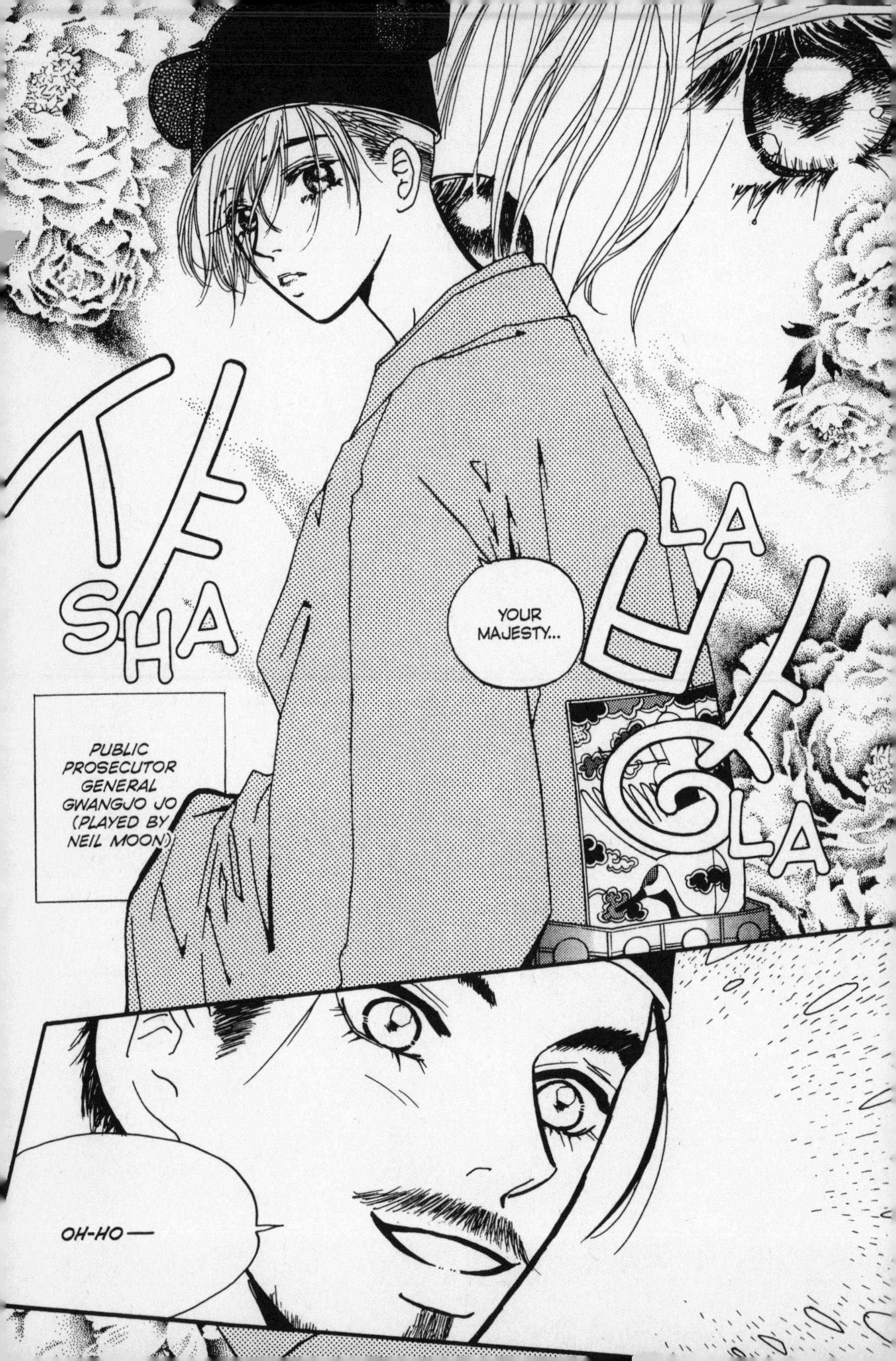
SHA
LA
YOUR MAJESTY...
PUBLIC PROSECUTOR GENERAL GWANGJO JO (PLAYED BY NEIL MOON)
GLA
LA
OH-HO—

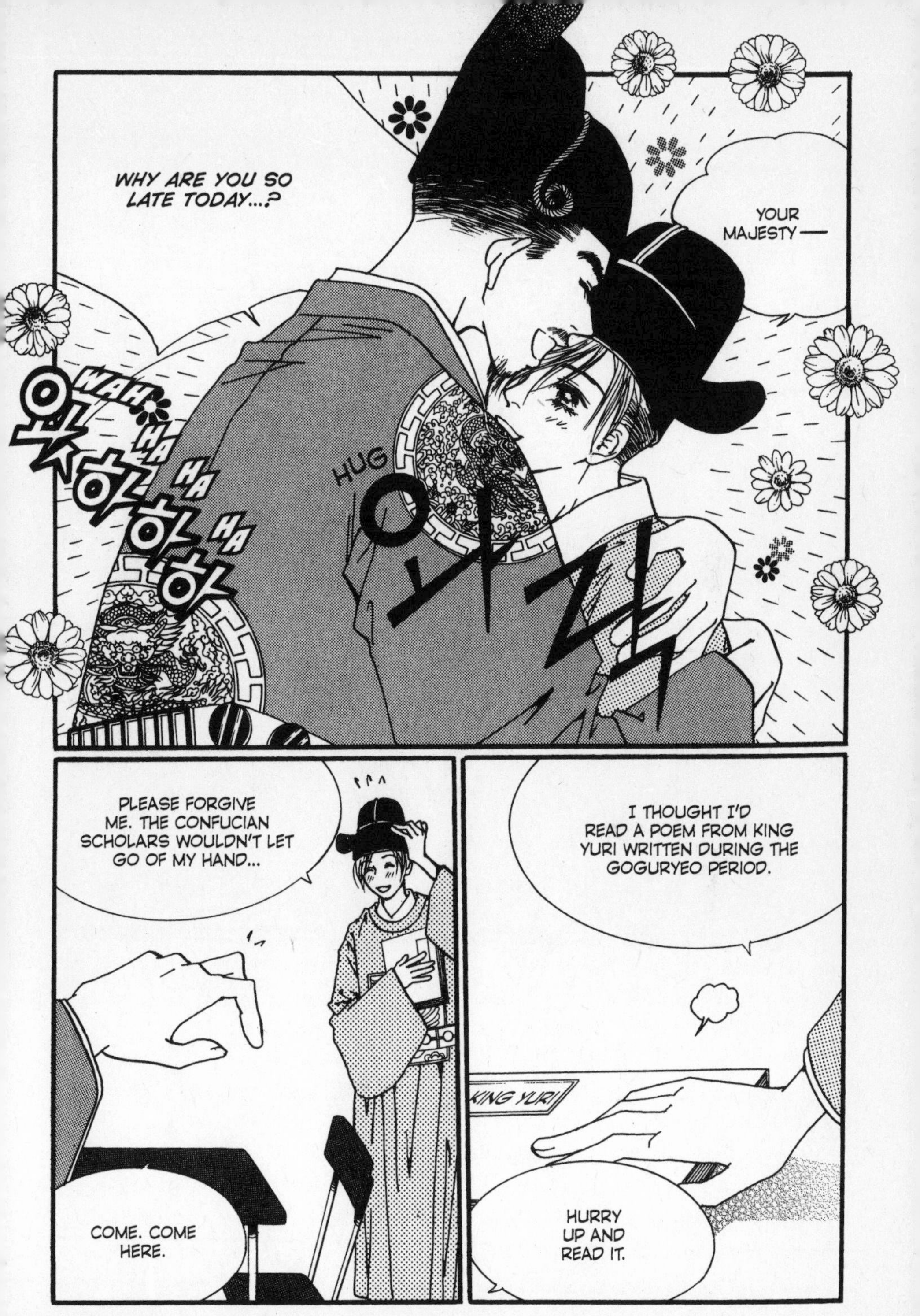
WHY ARE YOU SO LATE TODAY...?
YOUR MAJESTY—
와하하하
WAH HA HA HA
HUG
PLEASE FORGIVE ME. THE CONFUCIAN SCHOLARS WOULDN'T LET GO OF MY HAND...
COME. COME HERE.
I THOUGHT I'D READ A POEM FROM KING YURI WRITTEN DURING THE GOGURYEO PERIOD.
KING YURI
HURRY UP AND READ IT.

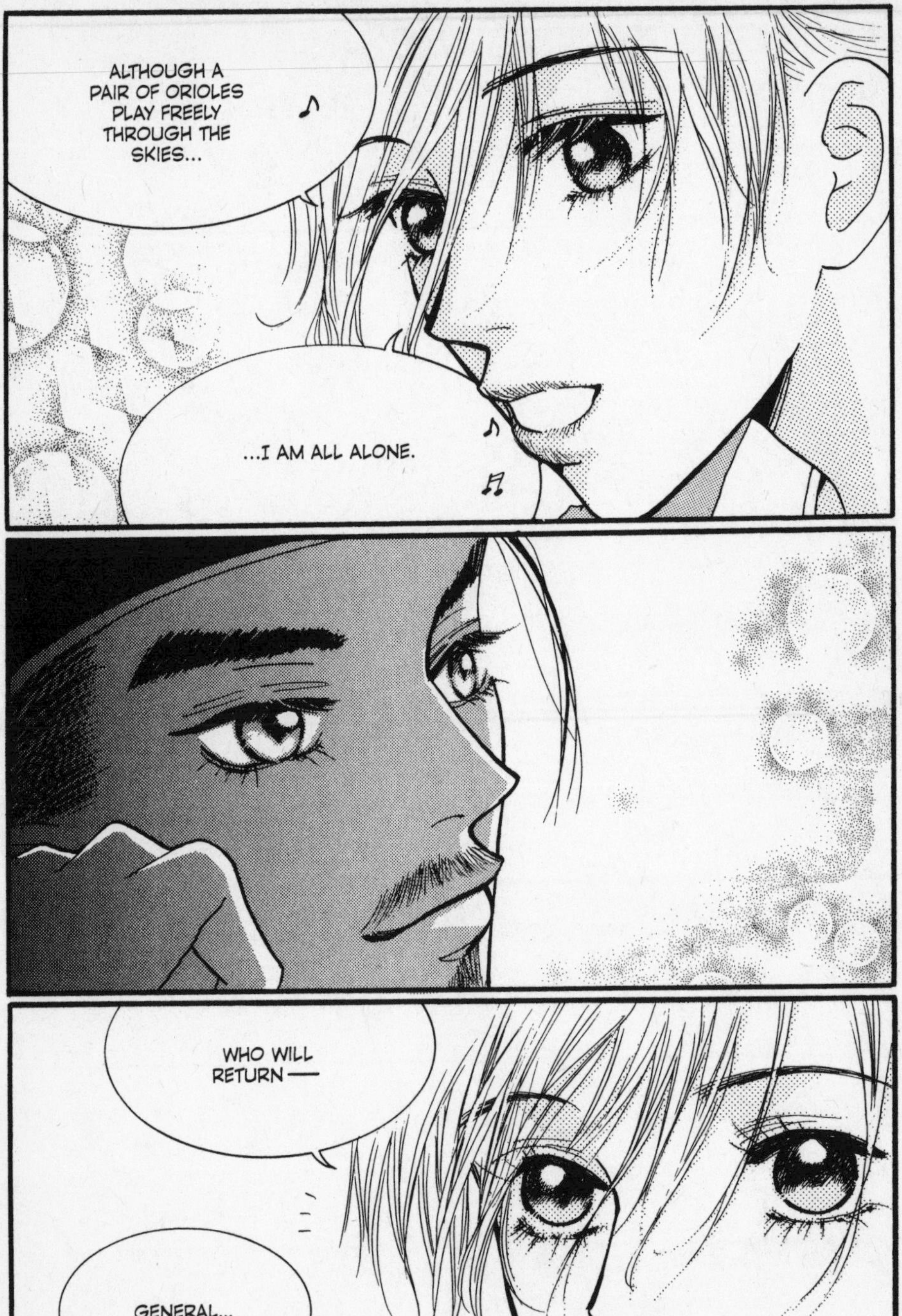
ALTHOUGH A PAIR OF ORIOLES PLAY FREELY THROUGH THE SKIES...
...I AM ALL ALONE.
WHO WILL RETURN—
GENERAL...

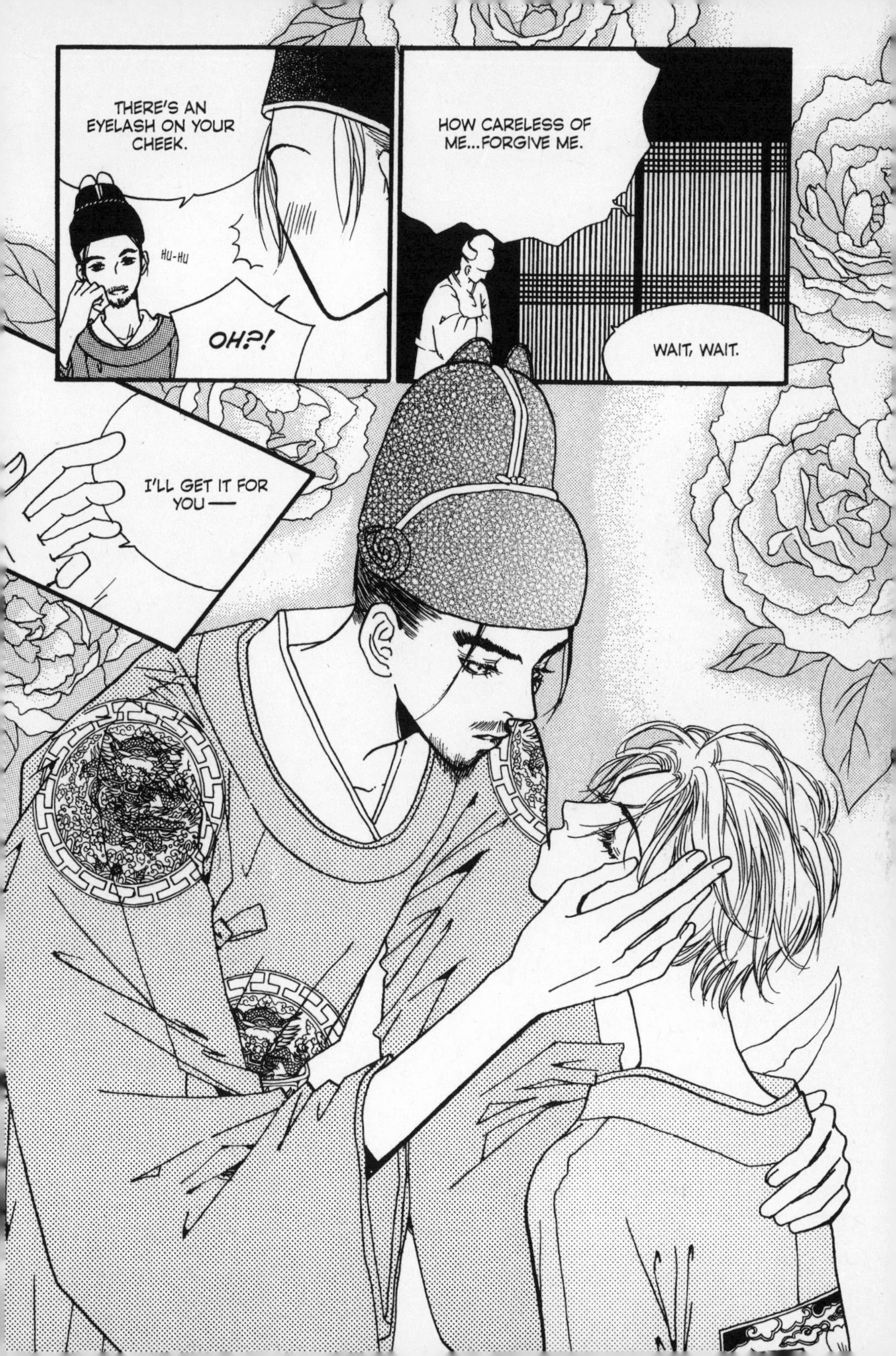

THERE'S AN EYELASH ON YOUR CHEEK.
HU-HU
OH?!
HOW CARELESS OF ME...FORGIVE ME.
WAIT, WAIT.
I'LL GET IT FOR YOU—

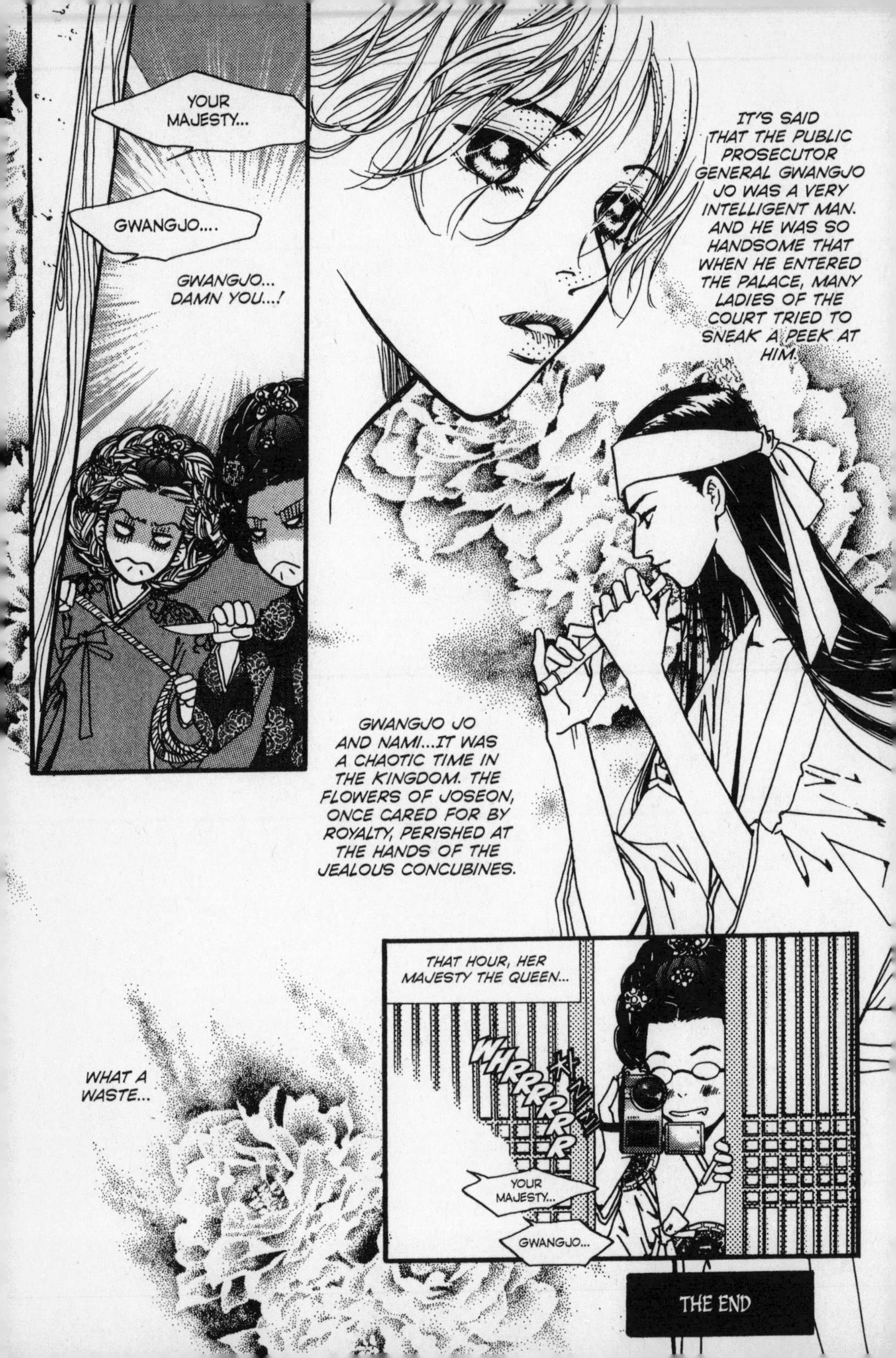
YOUR MAJESTY...
GWANGJO....
GWANGJO... DAMN YOU...!
IT'S SAID THAT THE PUBLIC PROSECUTOR GENERAL GWANGJO JO WAS A VERY INTELLIGENT MAN. AND HE WAS SO HANDSOME THAT WHEN HE ENTERED THE PALACE, MANY LADIES OF THE COURT TRIED TO SNEAK A PEEK AT HIM.
GWANGJO JO AND NAMI...IT WAS A CHAOTIC TIME IN THE KINGDOM. THE FLOWERS OF JOSEON, ONCE CARED FOR BY ROYALTY, PERISHED AT THE HANDS OF THE JEALOUS CONCUBINES.
WHAT A WASTE...
THAT HOUR, HER MAJESTY THE QUEEN...
WHRRRRRRR
KNIN
YOUR MAJESTY...
GWANGJO...
THE END

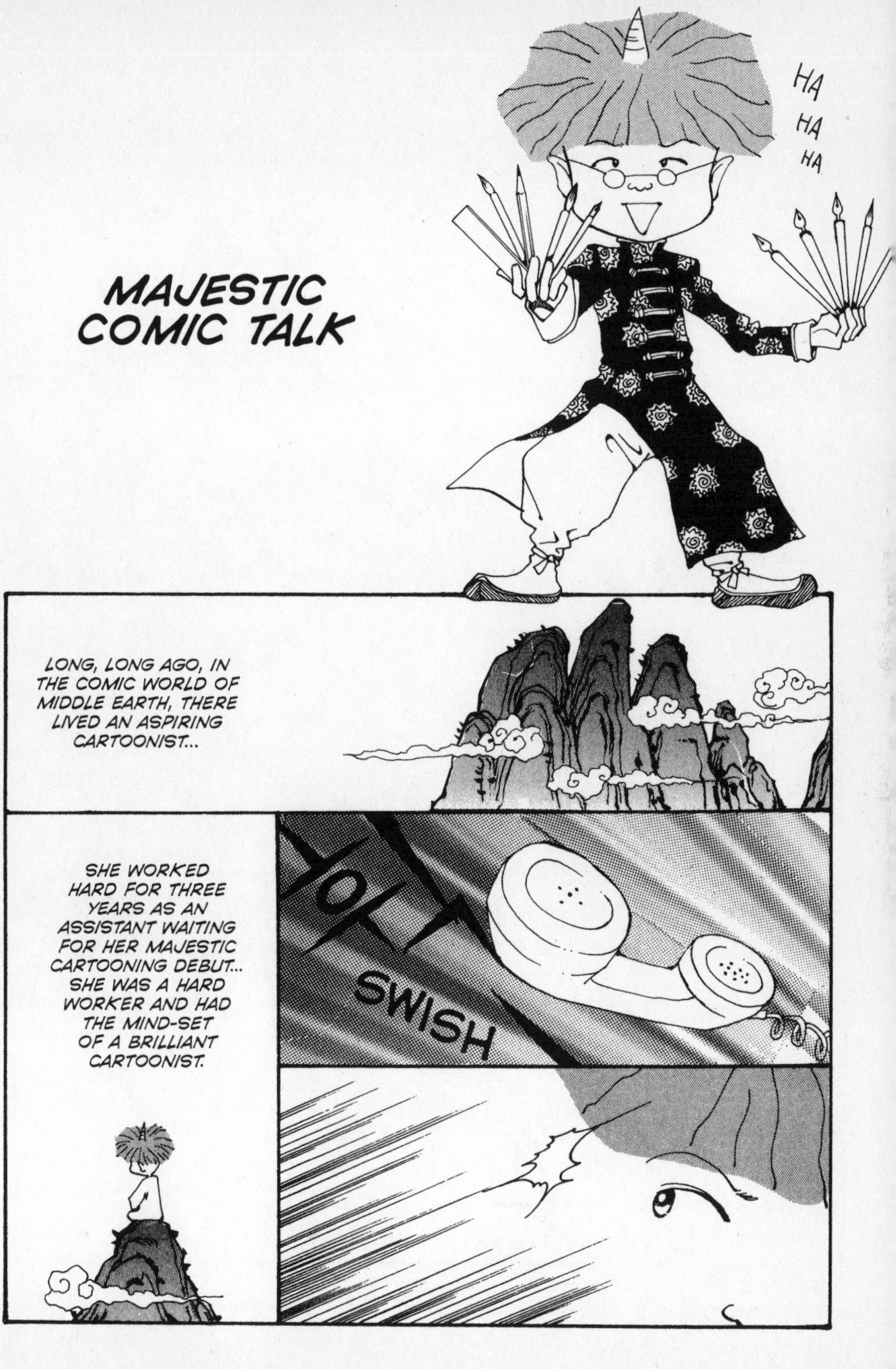
MAJESTIC COMIC TALK
HA HA HA
LONG, LONG AGO, IN THE COMIC WORLD OF MIDDLE EARTH, THERE LIVED AN ASPIRING CARTOONIST...
SHE WORKED HARD FOR THREE YEARS AS AN ASSISTANT WAITING FOR HER MAJESTIC CARTOONING DEBUT... SHE WAS A HARD WORKER AND HAD THE MIND-SET OF A BRILLIANT CARTOONIST.
SWISH

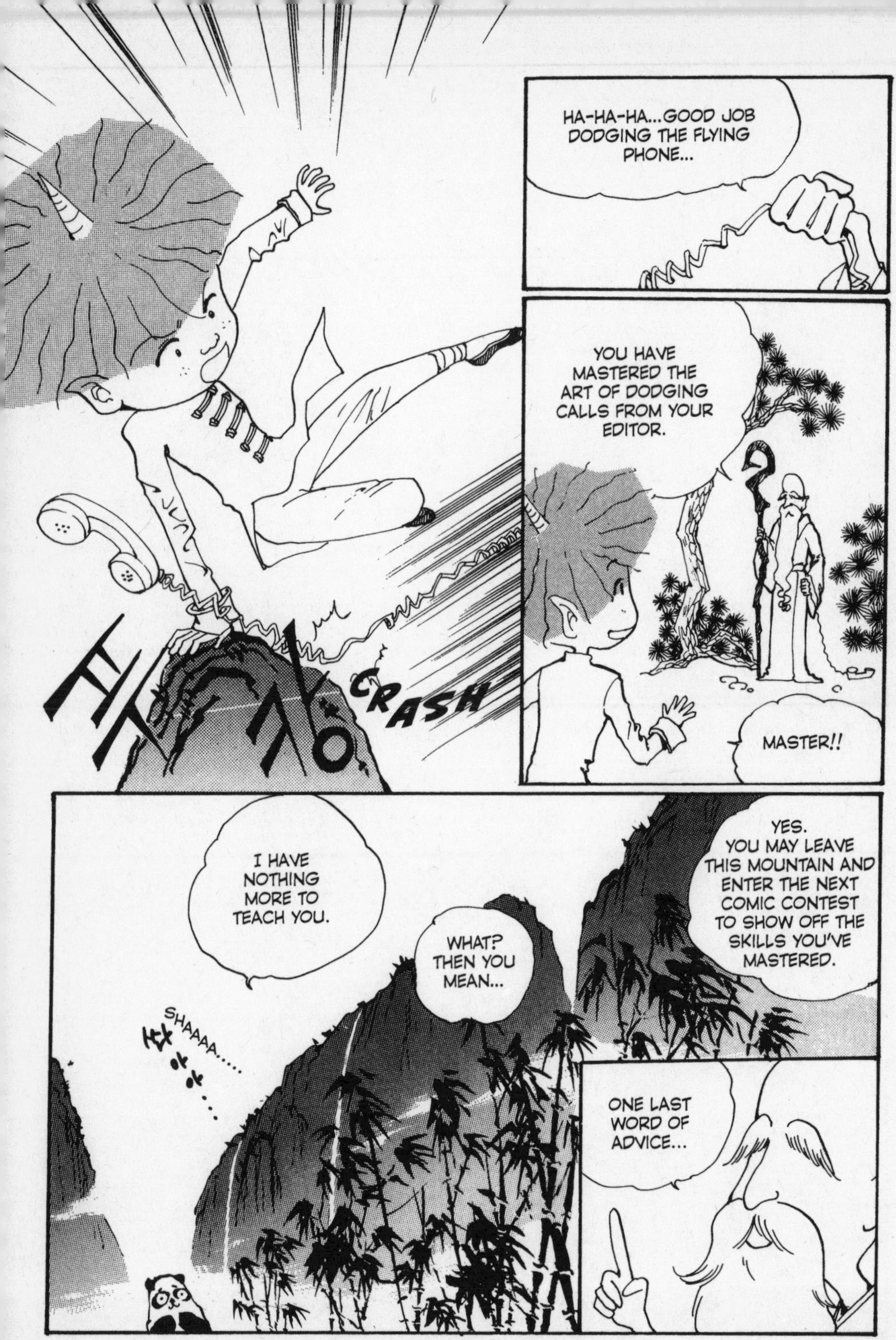
CRASH
HA-HA-HA...GOOD JOB DODGING THE FLYING PHONE...
YOU HAVE MASTERED THE ART OF DODGING CALLS FROM YOUR EDITOR.
MASTER!!
I HAVE NOTHING MORE TO TEACH YOU.
WHAT? THEN YOU MEAN...
YES. YOU MAY LEAVE THIS MOUNTAIN AND ENTER THE NEXT COMIC CONTEST TO SHOW OFF THE SKILLS YOU'VE MASTERED.
SHAAAA.....
ONE LAST WORD OF ADVICE...

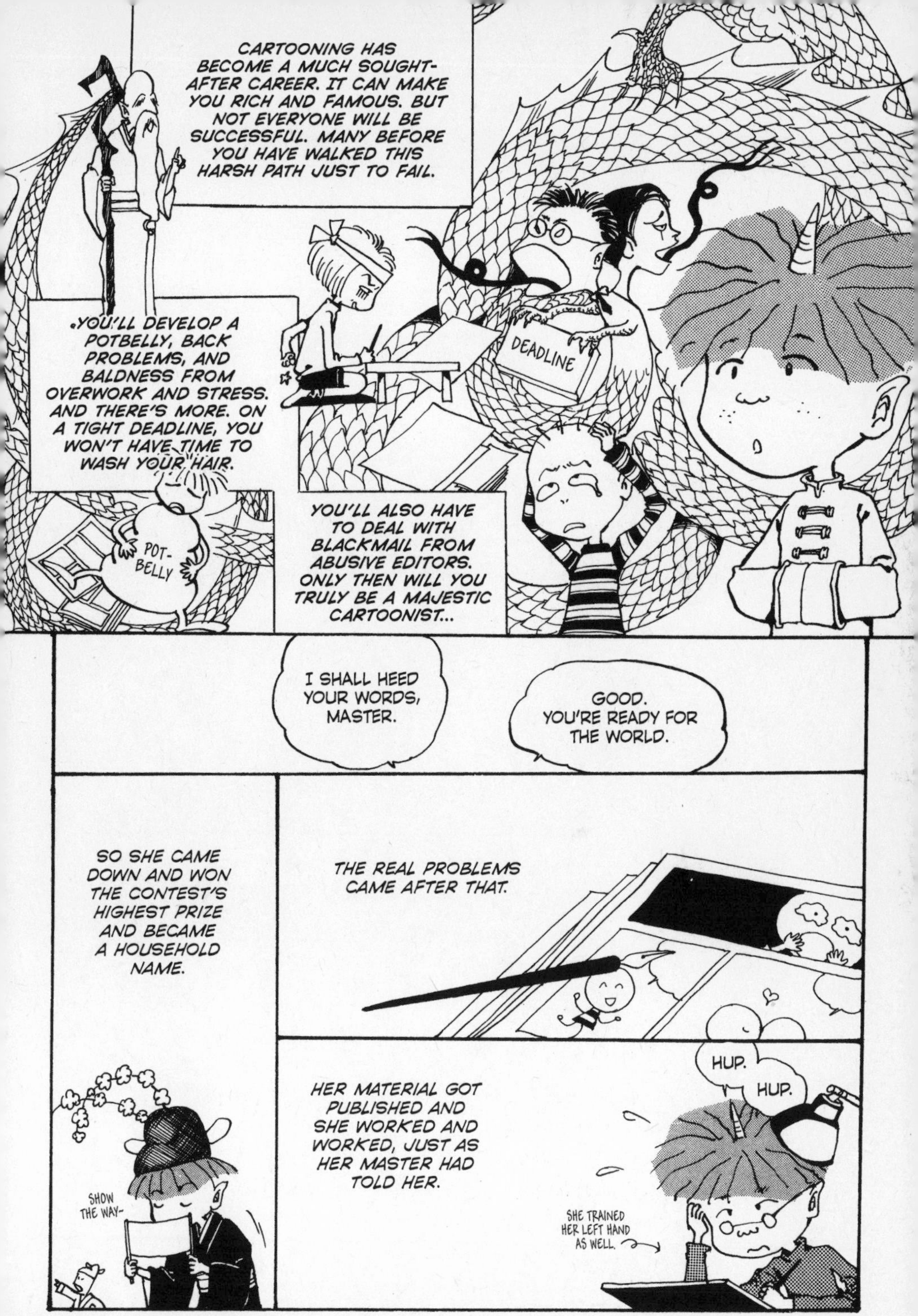
CARTOONING HAS BECOME A MUCH SOUGHT-AFTER CAREER. IT CAN MAKE YOU RICH AND FAMOUS. BUT NOT EVERYONE WILL BE SUCCESSFUL. MANY BEFORE YOU HAVE WALKED THIS HARSH PATH JUST TO FAIL.
YOU'LL DEVELOP A POTBELLY, BACK PROBLEMS, AND BALDNESS FROM OVERWORK AND STRESS. AND THERE'S MORE. ON A TIGHT DEADLINE, YOU WON'T HAVE TIME TO WASH YOUR HAIR.
DEADLINE
POT-BELLY
YOU'LL ALSO HAVE TO DEAL WITH BLACKMAIL FROM ABUSIVE EDITORS. ONLY THEN WILL YOU TRULY BE A MAJESTIC CARTOONIST...
I SHALL HEED YOUR WORDS, MASTER.
GOOD. YOU'RE READY FOR THE WORLD.
SO SHE CAME DOWN AND WON THE CONTEST'S HIGHEST PRIZE AND BECAME A HOUSEHOLD NAME.
SHOW THE WAY-
THE REAL PROBLEMS CAME AFTER THAT.
HER MATERIAL GOT PUBLISHED AND SHE WORKED AND WORKED, JUST AS HER MASTER HAD TOLD HER.
HUP.
HUP.
SHE TRAINED HER LEFT HAND AS WELL.

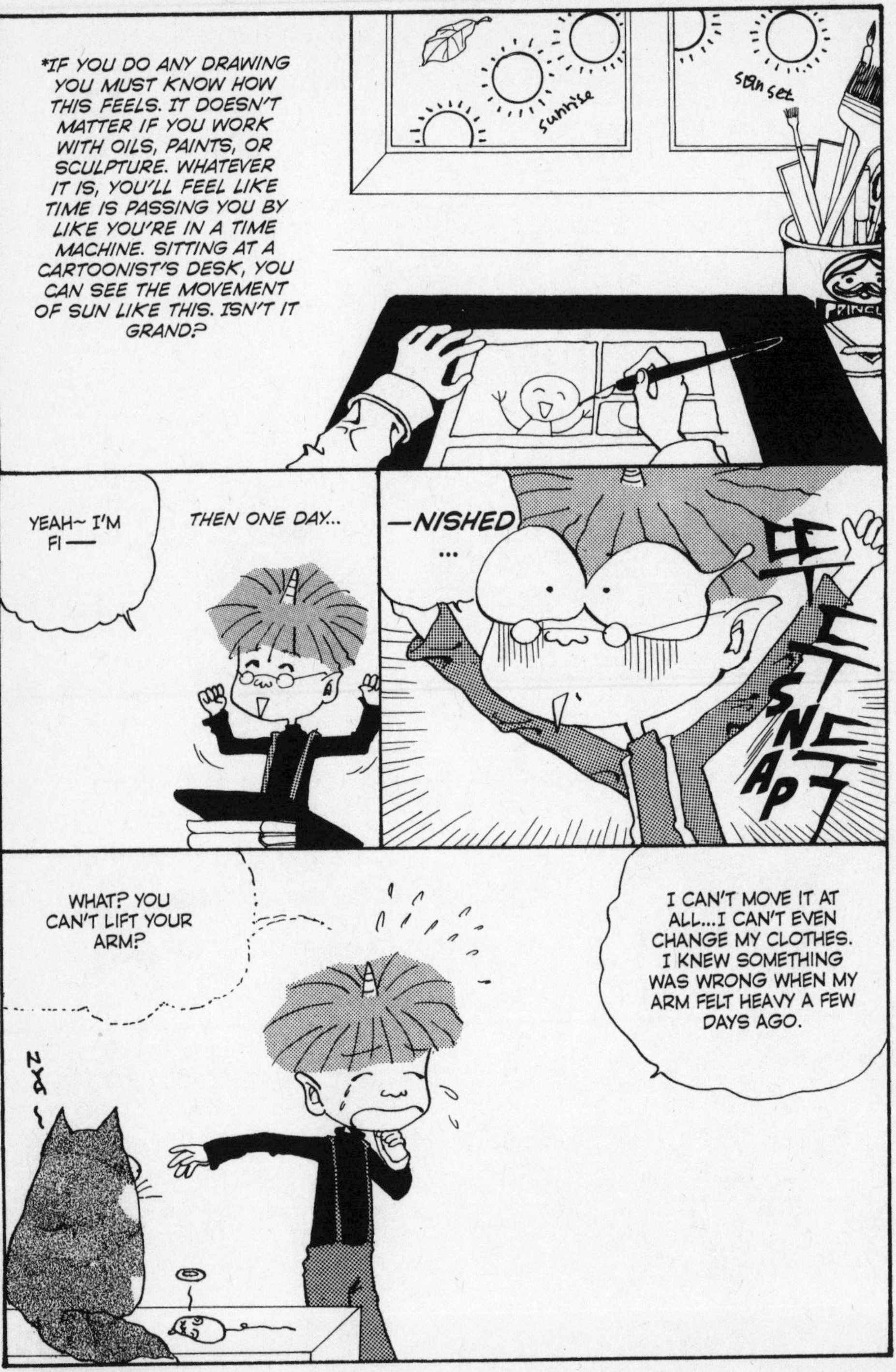

*IF YOU DO ANY DRAWING YOU MUST KNOW HOW THIS FEELS. IT DOESN'T MATTER IF YOU WORK WITH OILS, PAINTS, OR SCULPTURE. WHATEVER IT IS, YOU'LL FEEL LIKE TIME IS PASSING YOU BY LIKE YOU'RE IN A TIME MACHINE. SITTING AT A CARTOONIST'S DESK, YOU CAN SEE THE MOVEMENT OF SUN LIKE THIS. ISN'T IT GRAND?
sunrise
sunset
YEAH~ I'M FI—
THEN ONE DAY...
—NISHED ...
SNAP
WHAT? YOU CAN'T LIFT YOUR ARM?
I CAN'T MOVE IT AT ALL...I CAN'T EVEN CHANGE MY CLOTHES. I KNEW SOMETHING WAS WRONG WHEN MY ARM FELT HEAVY A FEW DAYS AGO.
NYA~

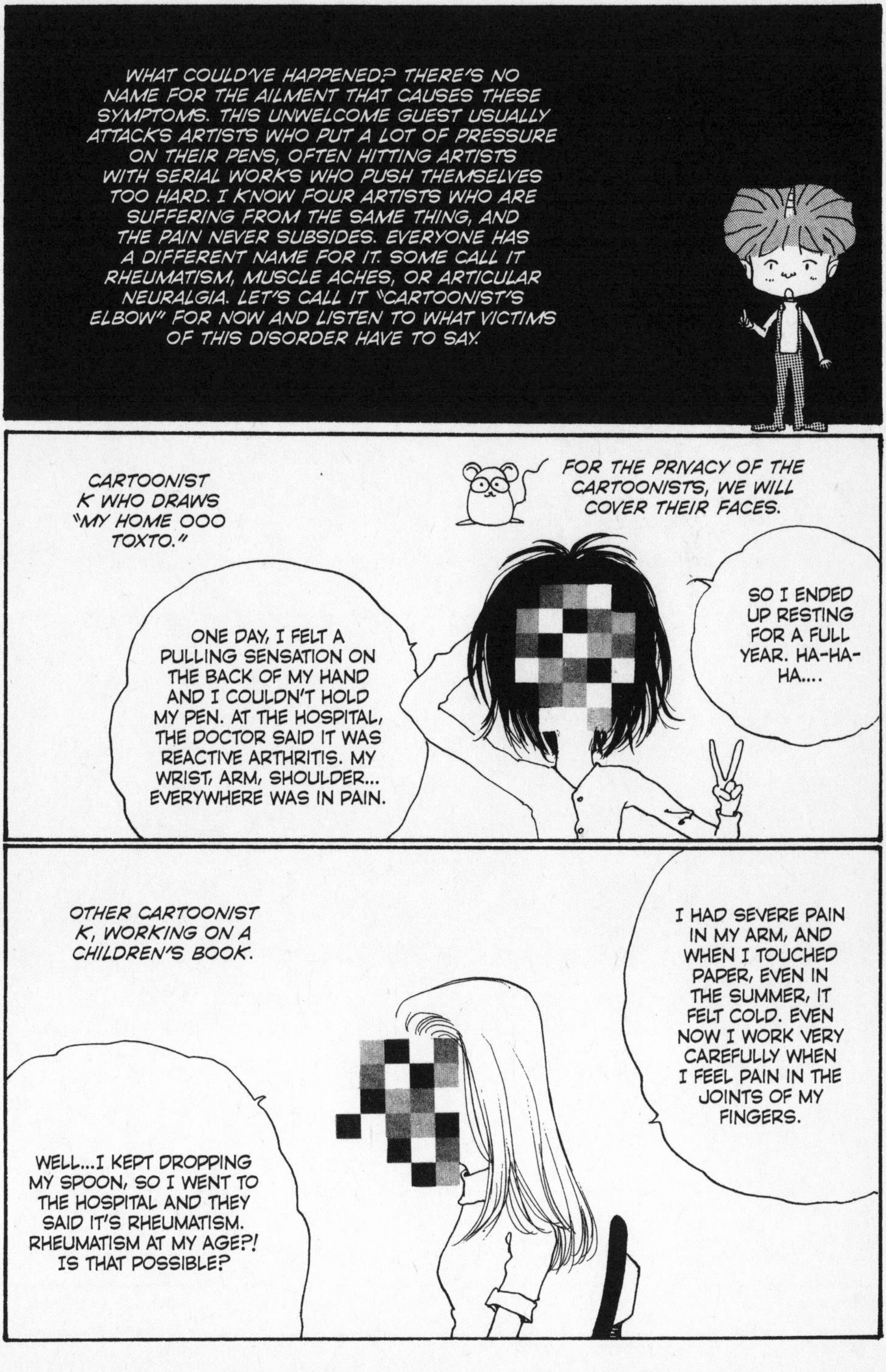
WHAT COULD'VE HAPPENED? THERE'S NO NAME FOR THE AILMENT THAT CAUSES THESE SYMPTOMS. THIS UNWELCOME GUEST USUALLY ATTACKS ARTISTS WHO PUT A LOT OF PRESSURE ON THEIR PENS, OFTEN HITTING ARTISTS WITH SERIAL WORKS WHO PUSH THEMSELVES TOO HARD. I KNOW FOUR ARTISTS WHO ARE SUFFERING FROM THE SAME THING, AND THE PAIN NEVER SUBSIDES. EVERYONE HAS A DIFFERENT NAME FOR IT. SOME CALL IT RHEUMATISM, MUSCLE ACHES, OR ARTICULAR NEURALGIA. LET'S CALL IT "CARTOONIST'S ELBOW" FOR NOW AND LISTEN TO WHAT VICTIMS OF THIS DISORDER HAVE TO SAY.
CARTOONIST K WHO DRAWS "MY HOME OOO TOXTO."
FOR THE PRIVACY OF THE CARTOONISTS, WE WILL COVER THEIR FACES.
ONE DAY, I FELT A PULLING SENSATION ON THE BACK OF MY HAND AND I COULDN'T HOLD MY PEN. AT THE HOSPITAL, THE DOCTOR SAID IT WAS REACTIVE ARTHRITIS. MY WRIST, ARM, SHOULDER... EVERYWHERE WAS IN PAIN.
SO I ENDED UP RESTING FOR A FULL YEAR. HA-HA-HA....
OTHER CARTOONIST K, WORKING ON A CHILDREN'S BOOK.
WELL...I KEPT DROPPING MY SPOON, SO I WENT TO THE HOSPITAL AND THEY SAID IT'S RHEUMATISM. RHEUMATISM AT MY AGE?! IS THAT POSSIBLE?
I HAD SEVERE PAIN IN MY ARM, AND WHEN I TOUCHED PAPER, EVEN IN THE SUMMER, IT FELT COLD. EVEN NOW I WORK VERY CAREFULLY WHEN I FEEL PAIN IN THE JOINTS OF MY FINGERS.

STILL, A CARTOONIST MUSTN'T LOSE HOPE. I'LL KEEP MY DEADLINE EVEN IF IT KILLS ME...

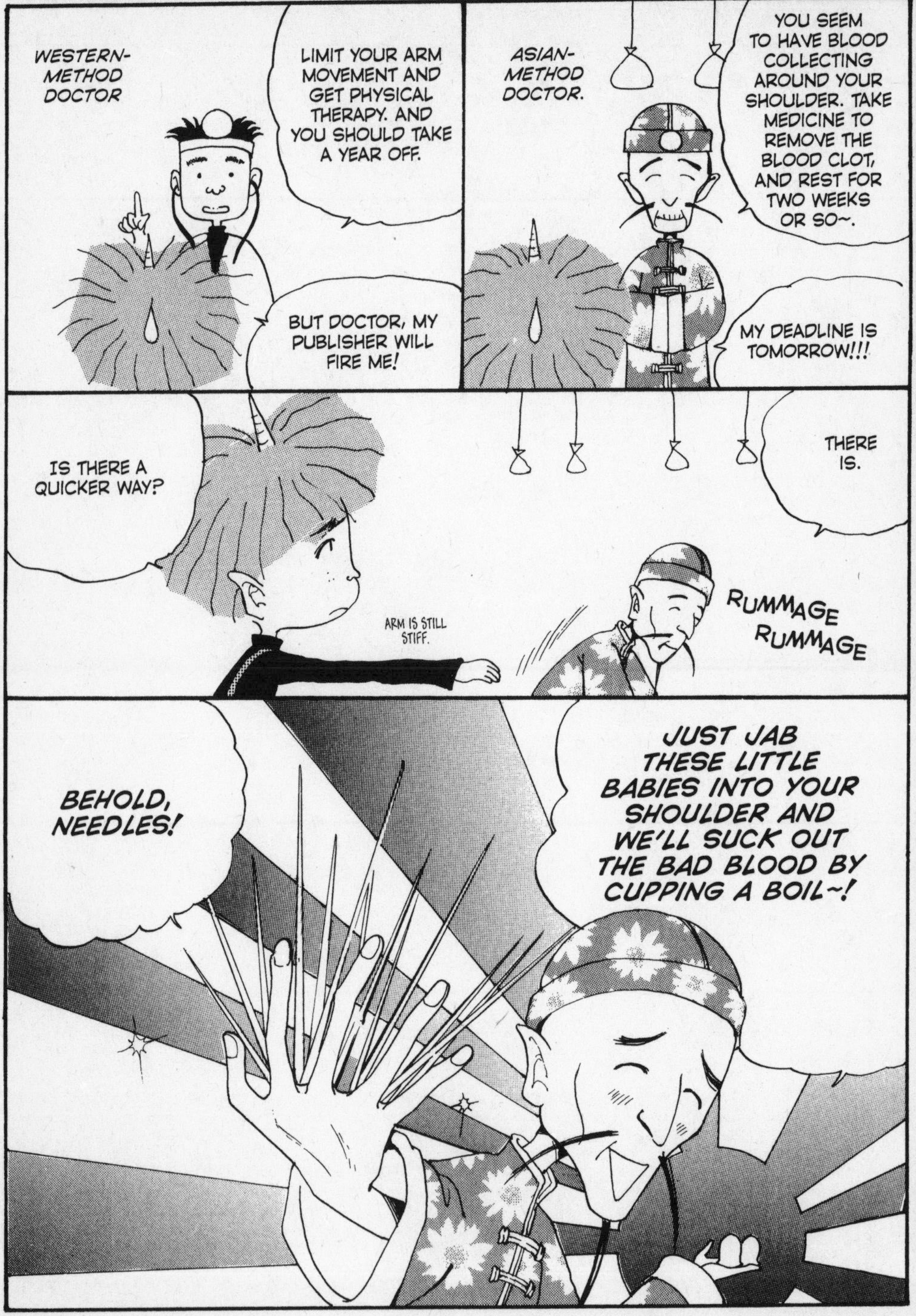
WESTERN-METHOD DOCTOR
LIMIT YOUR ARM MOVEMENT AND GET PHYSICAL THERAPY. AND YOU SHOULD TAKE A YEAR OFF.
BUT DOCTOR, MY PUBLISHER WILL FIRE ME!
ASIAN-METHOD DOCTOR.
YOU SEEM TO HAVE BLOOD COLLECTING AROUND YOUR SHOULDER. TAKE MEDICINE TO REMOVE THE BLOOD CLOT, AND REST FOR TWO WEEKS OR SO~.
MY DEADLINE IS TOMORROW!!!
IS THERE A QUICKER WAY?
ARM IS STILL STIFF.
THERE IS.
RUMMAGE RUMMAGE
BEHOLD, NEEDLES!
JUST JAB THESE LITTLE BABIES INTO YOUR SHOULDER AND WE'LL SUCK OUT THE BAD BLOOD BY CUPPING A BOIL~!

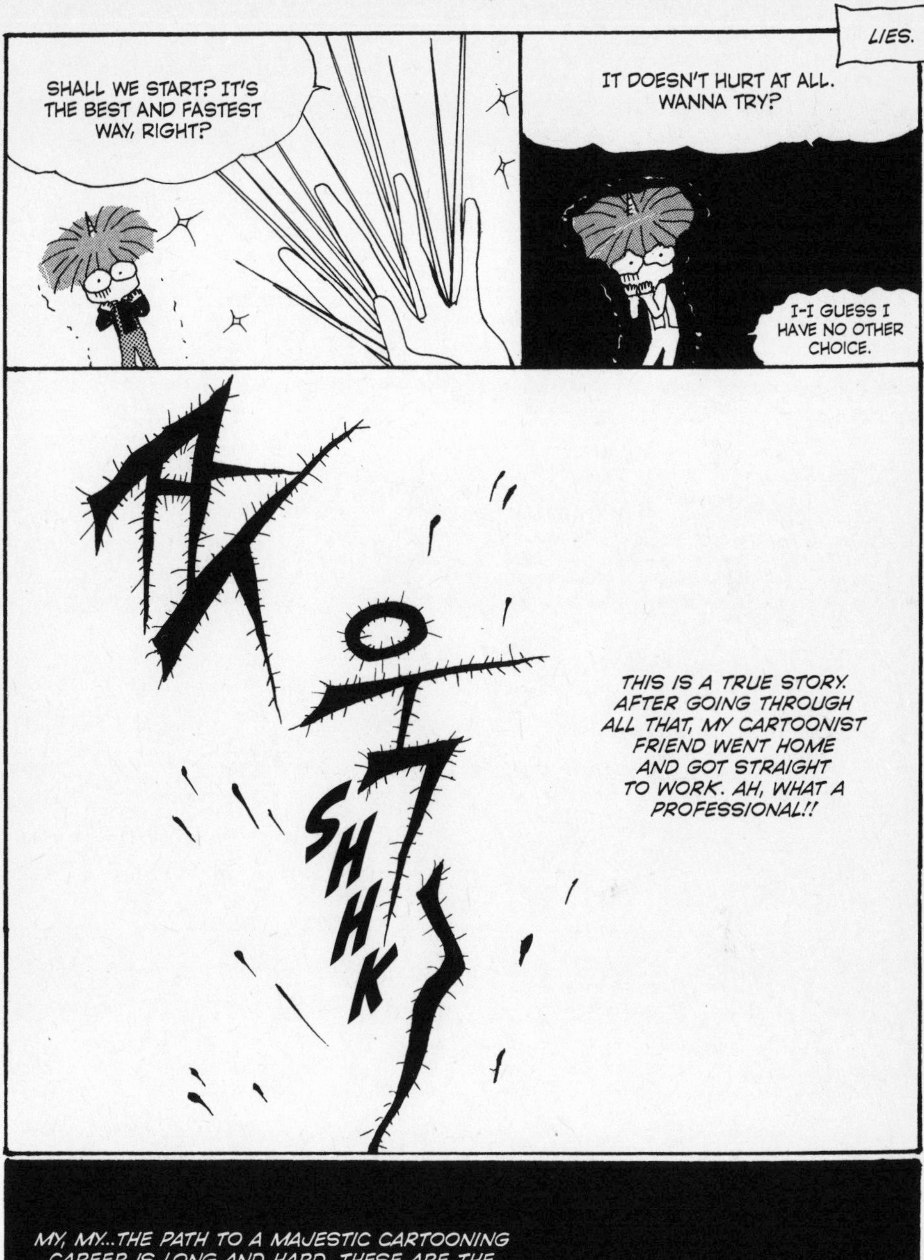
SHALL WE START? IT'S THE BEST AND FASTEST WAY, RIGHT?
LIES.
IT DOESN'T HURT AT ALL. WANNA TRY?
I-I GUESS I HAVE NO OTHER CHOICE.
SHHK
THIS IS A TRUE STORY. AFTER GOING THROUGH ALL THAT, MY CARTOONIST FRIEND WENT HOME AND GOT STRAIGHT TO WORK. AH, WHAT A PROFESSIONAL!!
MY, MY...THE PATH TO A MAJESTIC CARTOONING CAREER IS LONG AND HARD. THESE ARE THE STORIES OF CARTOONISTS WHO WERE JUST STARTING OUT. SO HOW DO EXPERIENCED CARTOONISTS DEAL WITH THESE PROBLEMS? LET'S HEAR IT STRAIGHT FROM A BIG-TIME CARTOONIST!

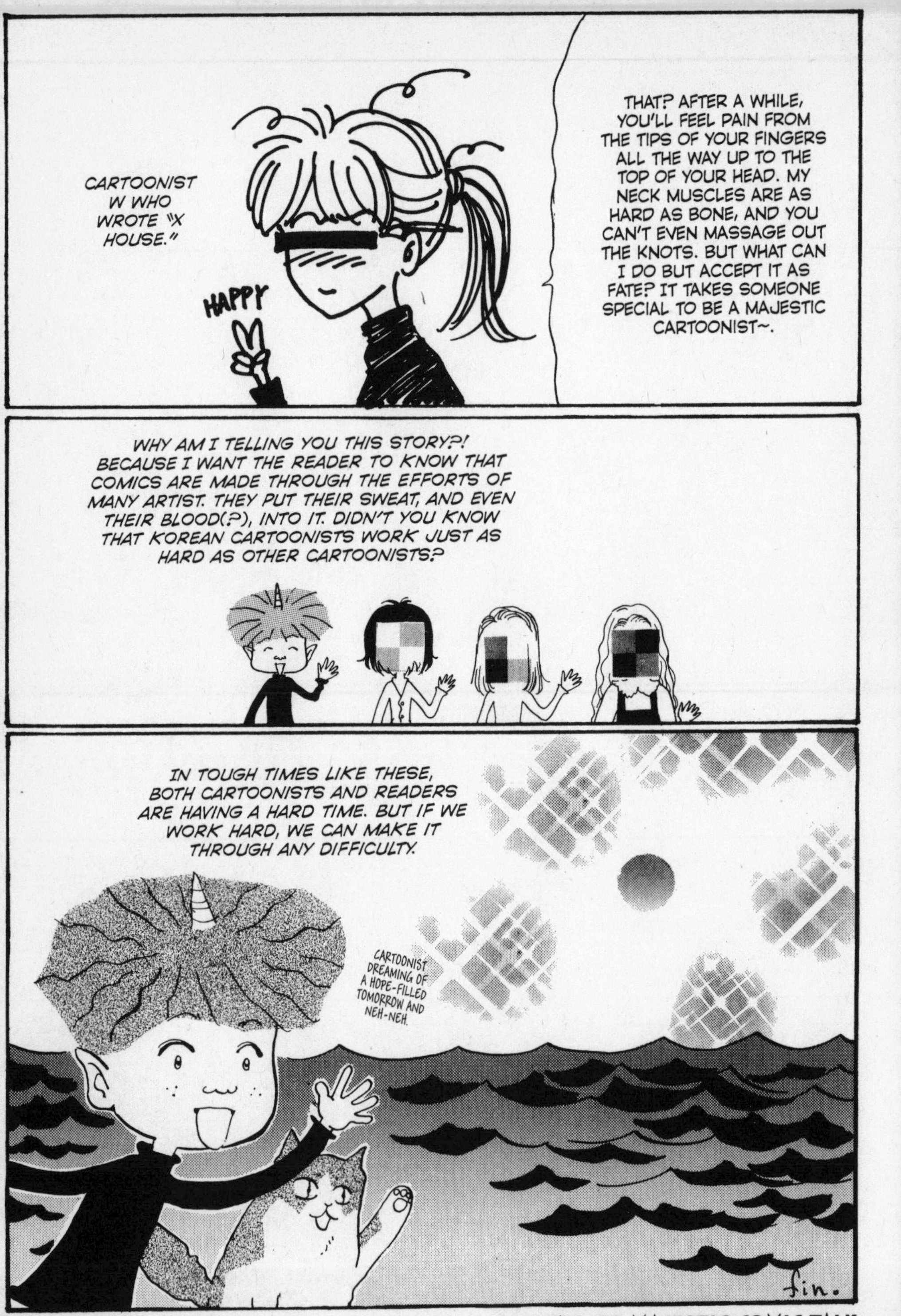
CARTOONIST W WHO WROTE "X HOUSE."
HAPPY
THAT? AFTER A WHILE, YOU'LL FEEL PAIN FROM THE TIPS OF YOUR FINGERS ALL THE WAY UP TO THE TOP OF YOUR HEAD. MY NECK MUSCLES ARE AS HARD AS BONE, AND YOU CAN'T EVEN MASSAGE OUT THE KNOTS. BUT WHAT CAN I DO BUT ACCEPT IT AS FATE? IT TAKES SOMEONE SPECIAL TO BE A MAJESTIC CARTOONIST~.
WHY AM I TELLING YOU THIS STORY?! BECAUSE I WANT THE READER TO KNOW THAT COMICS ARE MADE THROUGH THE EFFORTS OF MANY ARTIST. THEY PUT THEIR SWEAT, AND EVEN THEIR BLOOD(?), INTO IT. DIDN'T YOU KNOW THAT KOREAN CARTOONISTS WORK JUST AS HARD AS OTHER CARTOONISTS?
IN TOUGH TIMES LIKE THESE, BOTH CARTOONISTS AND READERS ARE HAVING A HARD TIME. BUT IF WE WORK HARD, WE CAN MAKE IT THROUGH ANY DIFFICULTY.
CARTOONIST DREAMING OF A HOPE-FILLED TOMORROW AND NEH-NEH.
fin.

THE END OF MAJESTIC COMIC TALK

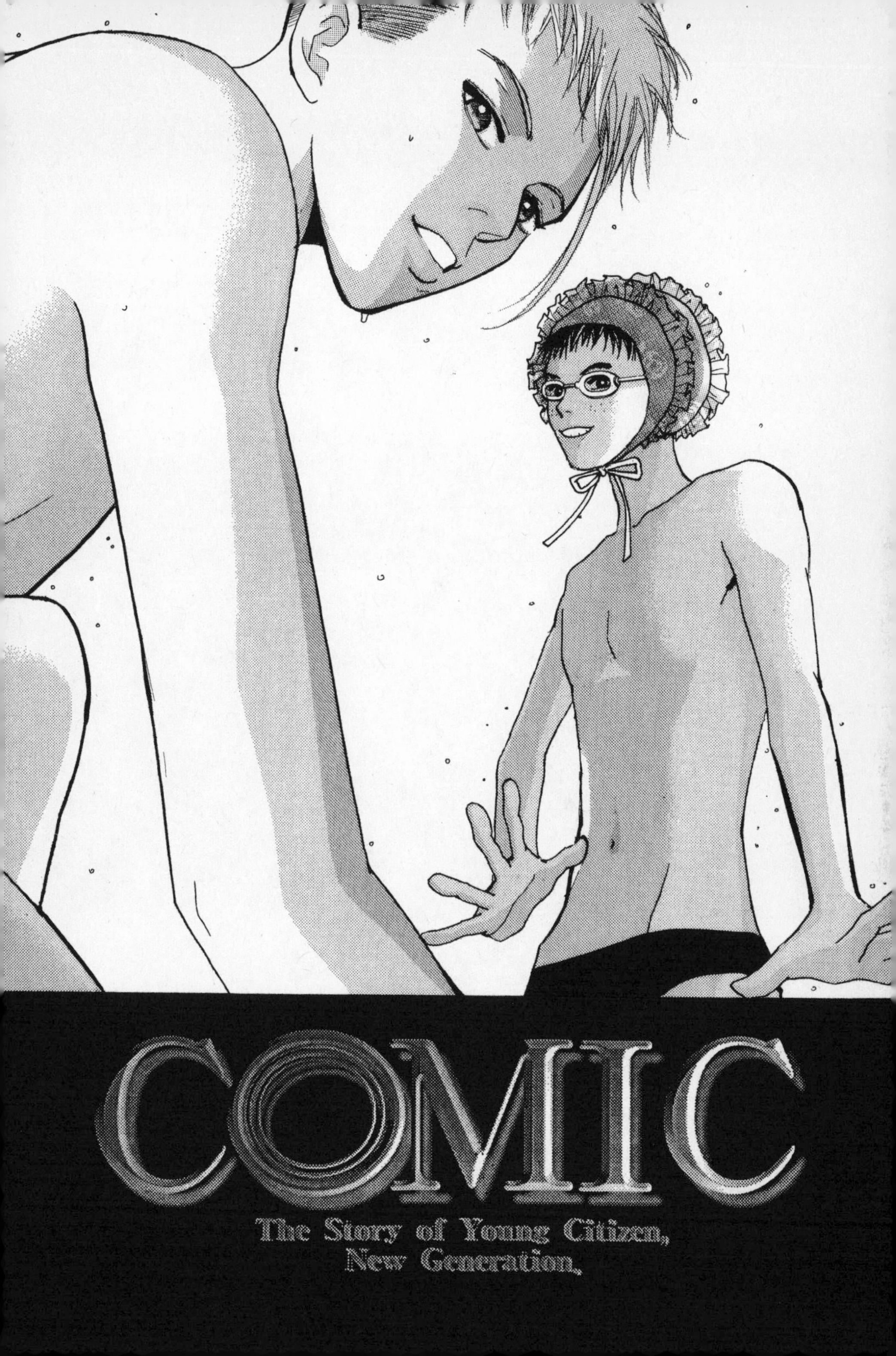

COMIC

The Story of Young Citizen,
New Generation,

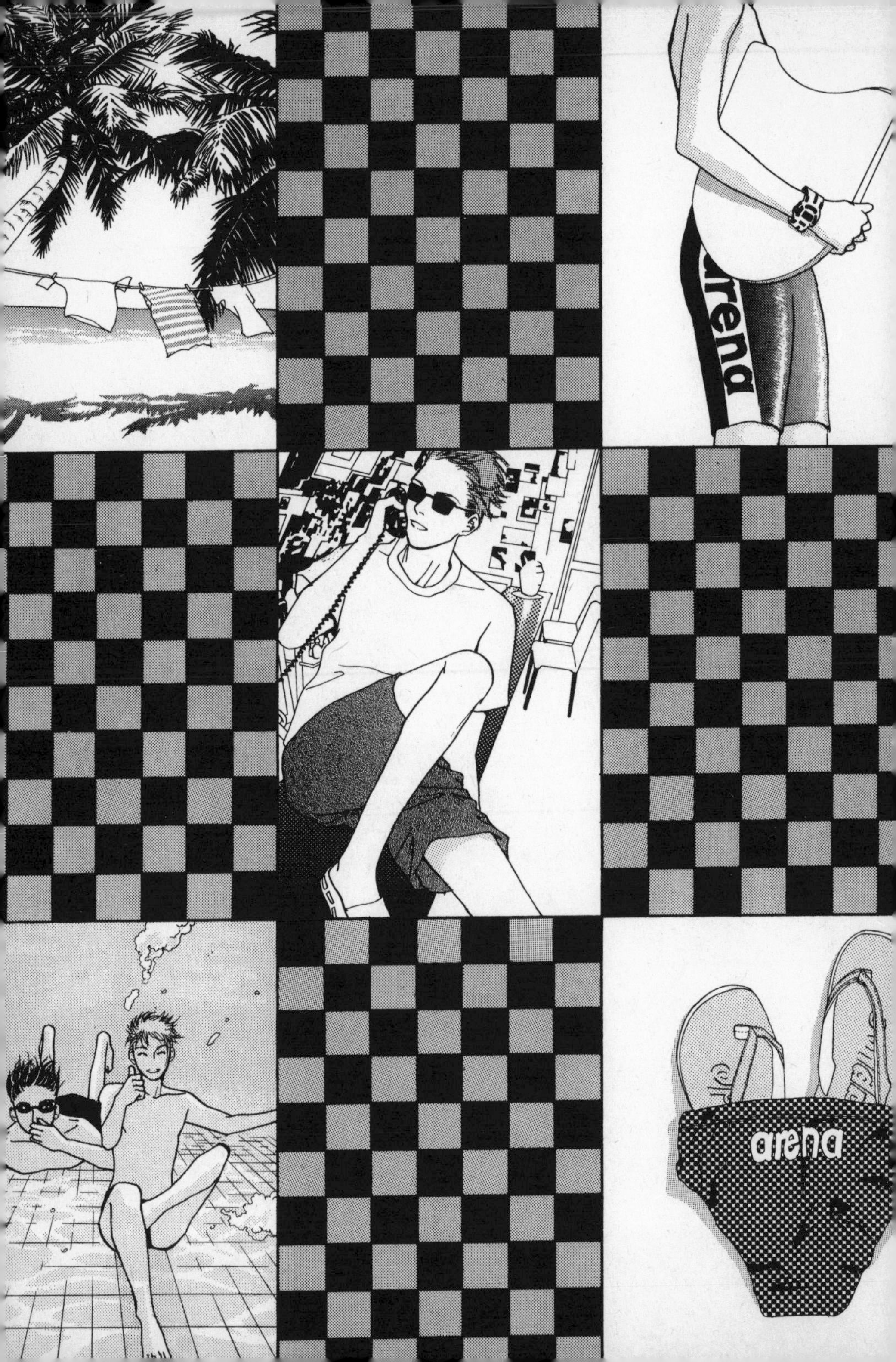
arena
arena

MINI INTERVIEW!

NAME: BRIAN CHAE

HEIGHT: 186 CM

WEIGHT: 80 KG

BLOOD TYPE: A

BIRTHDAY: DECEMBER 25TH, CAPRICORN

NICKNAME: MANATEE

SPECIALTY: HE CAN SWIM 2KM WITH BUTTERFLY STROKE.

FUTURE PLANS: TO DIE COMFORTABLY HOLDING MY GRANDSON AND -DAUGHTER'S HANDS.

WHEN I GROW OLD, I'M SURE THERE WILL BE A BEAUTIFUL GRANDMA BESIDE ME.
AFTER IT'S SNOWED A LOT, I WANT TO HOLD HER WRINKLED HAND AS WE WALK TOGETHER THROUGH THE NIGHT.
IF EVANGELINE ENDS UP BEING THAT GRANDMA, I COULDN'T BE HAPPIER.
ISN'T THAT WHAT A HAPPY LIFE IS ALL ABOUT?
ARRGG — ERIC'S SO ANNOYING, TEASING ME AGAIN, CALLING ME "OLD MAN."

SOME THOUGHTS ABOUT CAPRICORN FROM THE CREATOR:

CAPRICORNS TEND TO BE SERIOUS AND DOWN-TO-EARTH, AND ARE KNOWN AS DILIGENT, AMBITIOUS PEOPLE.
THEY'RE LATE BLOOMERS, SO THEY SHOW THEIR TALENT IN THEIR LATER YEARS. THEY DON'T SHOW THEIR EMOTIONS OUTRIGHT, BUT ONCE THEY OPEN THEIR HEARTS, THEY REMAIN LOYAL FRIENDS UNTIL DEATH.

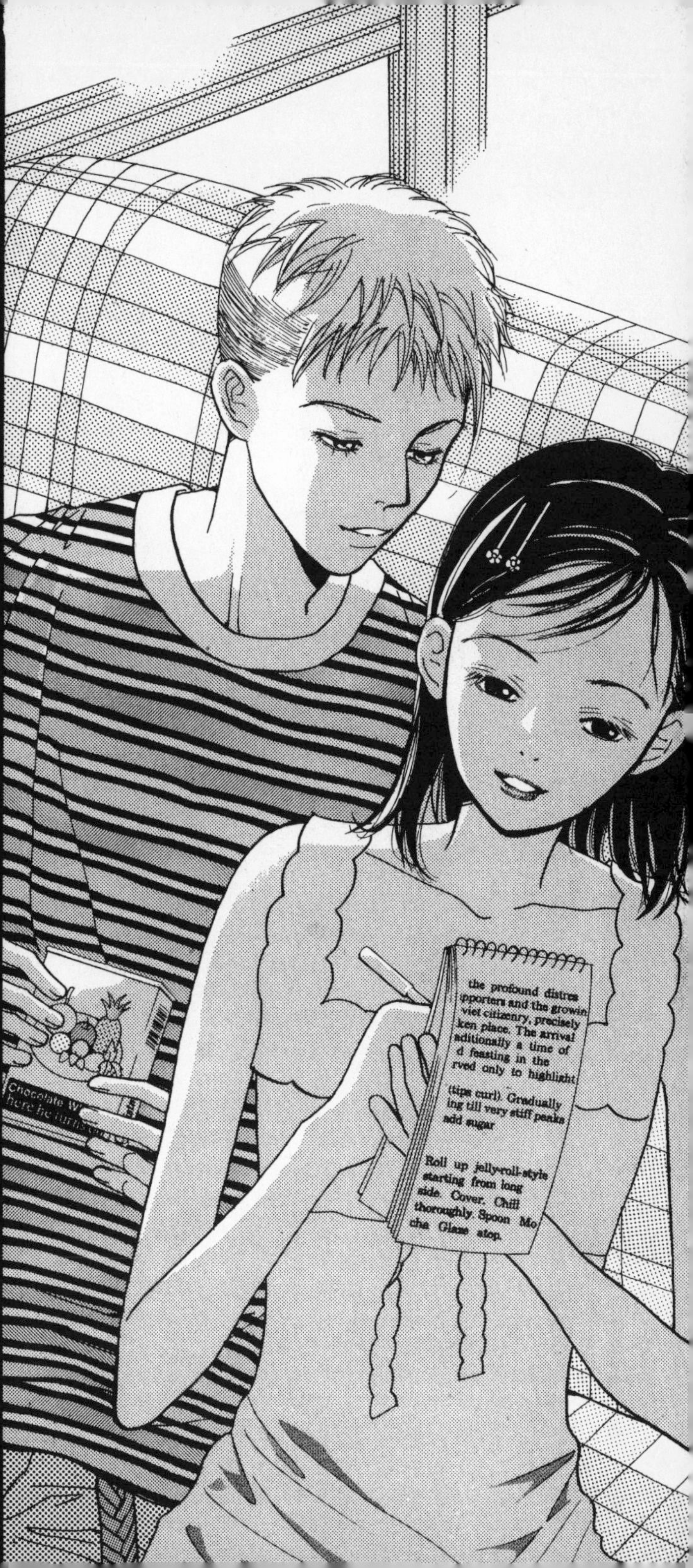
the profound distres
pporters and the growin
viet citizenry, precisely
ken place. The arrival
ditionally a time of
d feasting in the
rved only to highlight
(tips curl). Gradually
ing till very stiff peaks
add sugar
Roll up jelly-roll-style
starting from long
side. Cover. Chill
thoroughly. Spoon Mo
cha Glaze atop.

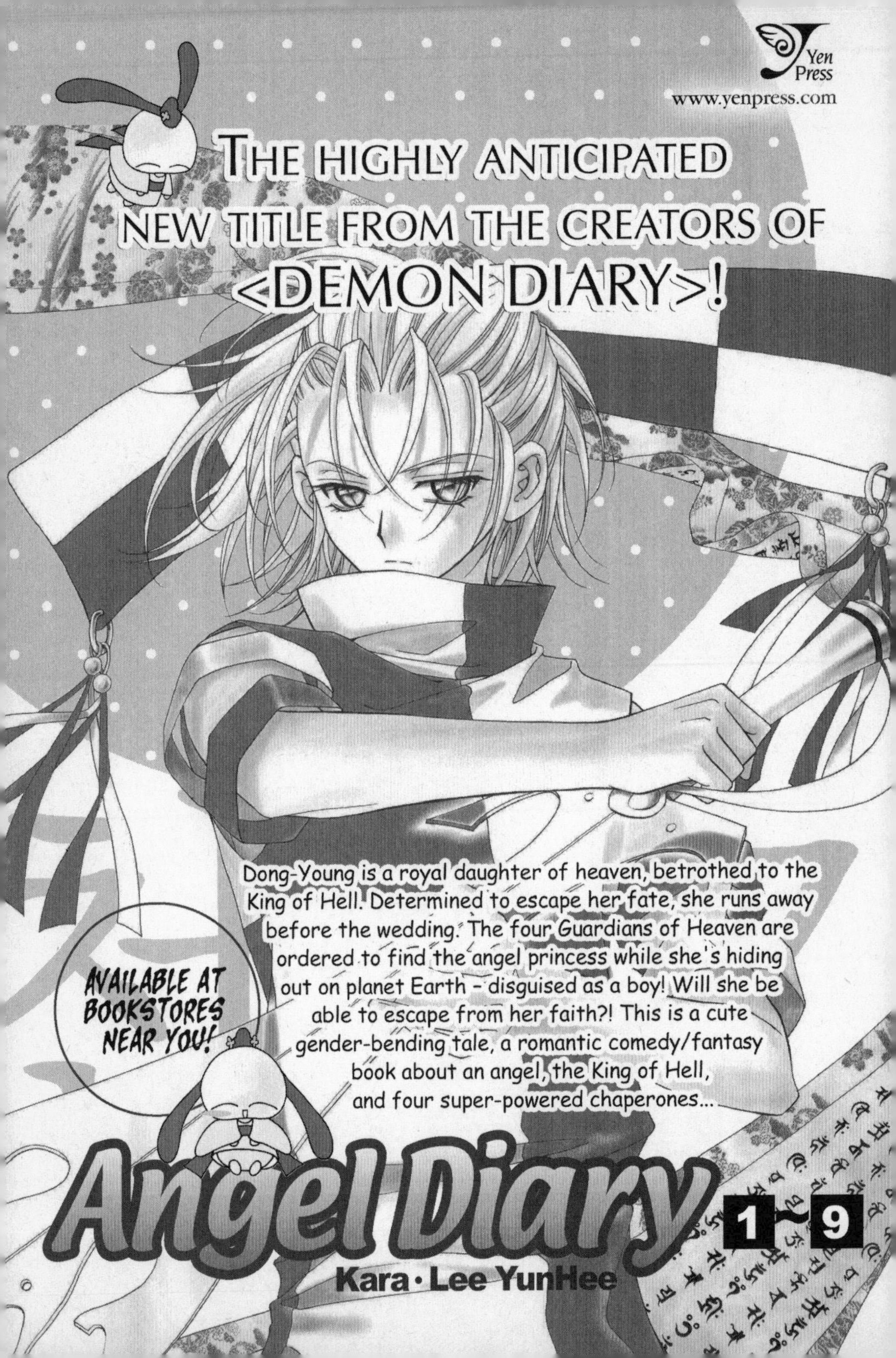
Yen Press
www.yenpress.com
THE HIGHLY ANTICIPATED
NEW TITLE FROM THE CREATORS OF
<DEMON DIARY>!
Dong-Young is a royal daughter of heaven, betrothed to the King of Hell. Determined to escape her fate, she runs away before the wedding. The four Guardians of Heaven are ordered to find the angel princess while she's hiding out on planet Earth – disguised as a boy! Will she be able to escape from her faith?! This is a cute gender-bending tale, a romantic comedy/fantasy book about an angel, the King of Hell, and four super-powered chaperones...
AVAILABLE AT BOOKSTORES NEAR YOU!
Angel Diary
1~9
Kara · Lee YunHee

Becoming the princess… Isn't that every girl's dream?!

Monarchy rule ended long ago in Korea, but there are still other countries with kings, queens, princes and princesses. What if Korea had continued monarchism? What if all the beautiful palaces, which are now only historical relics, were actually filled with people? What if the glamorous royal family still maintained the palace customs? Welcome to a world where Korea still has the royal family living in their everyday lives! Only for this one high school girl, Chae-Kyung, is this a tragedy, since she has to marry the prince — who apparently is a total bastard!

THE ROYAL PALACE

Goong

vol. 1 ~ 5

Park SoHee

Yen Press
www.yenpress.com

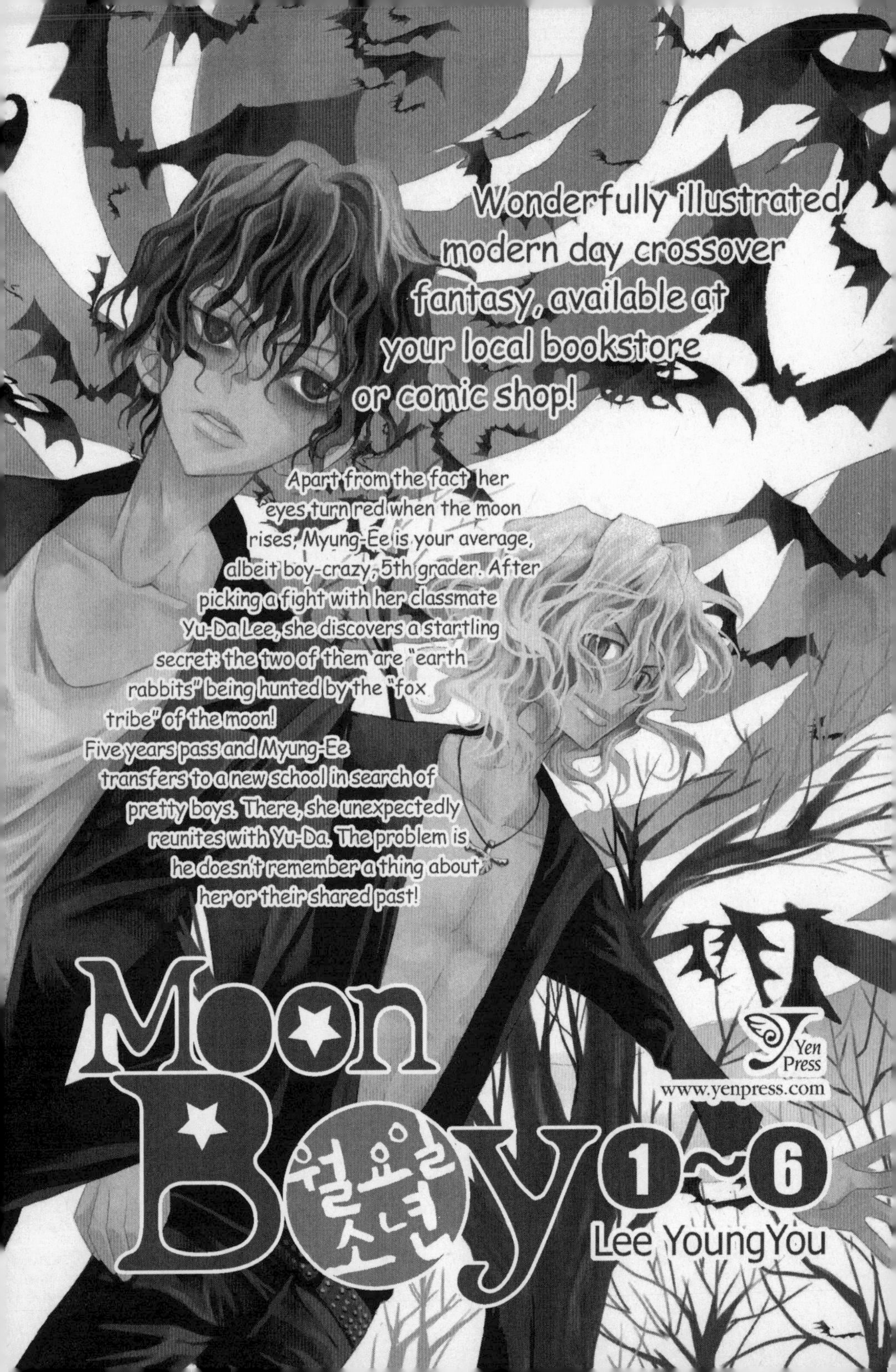
Wonderfully illustrated modern day crossover fantasy, available at your local bookstore or comic shop!
Apart from the fact her eyes turn red when the moon rises, Myung-Ee is your average, albeit boy-crazy, 5th grader. After picking a fight with her classmate Yu-Da Lee, she discovers a startling secret: the two of them are "earth rabbits" being hunted by the "fox tribe" of the moon!
Five years pass and Myung-Ee transfers to a new school in search of pretty boys. There, she unexpectedly reunites with Yu-Da. The problem is he doesn't remember a thing about her or their shared past!
Moon Boy
월요일 소년
1~6
Lee YoungYou
Yen Press
www.yenpress.com

Yen Press

www.yenpress.com

The newest title from the creators of <Demon Diary> and <Angel Diary>!

Once upon a time, a selfish king summoned the monstrous Bulkirin into the real world. The monster killed half of all human beings, leaving the rest helpless as to what to do. That is, until one day when a hero appeared and defeated the Bulkirin with the legendary "Seven Blade Sword." But···what does all this have to do with 8th grader Eun-Gyo Sung?! First, she gets suspended from school for fighting. Then, she runs away from home. The last thing she needed was to be kidnapped—and whisked into the past by a mysterious stranger named No-Ah!

Available at bookstores near you!

Legend

1-5

K a r a · W o o S o o J u n g

Totally new Arabian nights, where Shahrazad is a guy!

Everyone knows the story of Shahrazad and her wonderful tales from the Arabian Nights. For one thousand and one nights, the stories that she created entertained the mad Sultan and eventually saved her life. In this version, Shahrazad is a guy who wanted to save his sister from the mad Sultan by disguising himself as a woman. When he puts his life on the line, what kind of strange and unique stories would he tell? This new twist on one of the greatest classical tales might just keep you awake for another ONE THOUSAND AND ONE NIGHTS.

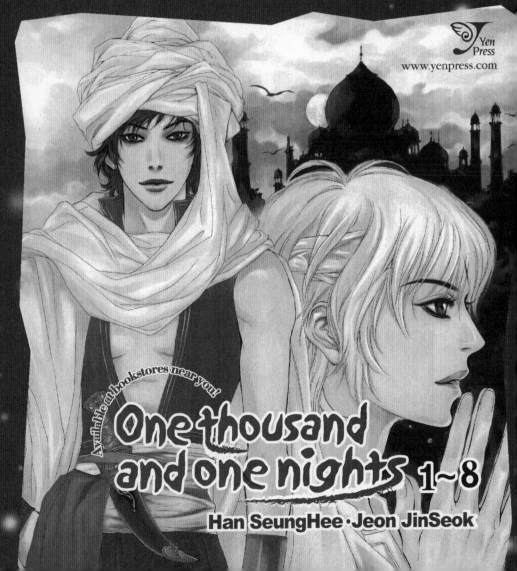

Yen Press
www.yenpress.com

Available at bookstores near you!

One thousand and one nights 1~8

Han SeungHee · Jeon JinSeok